Comparative Education

By The Same Author and Publisher:

- *Educational Philosophies in India*
- *Foundations of Education (2nd ed.)*
- *School Organisation (2nd ed.)*
- *Education in Ancient and Medieval India*

COMPARATIVE EDUCATION

S P CHAUBE

and

A CHAUBE

SECOND REVISED & ENLARGED EDITION

VIKAS® PUBLISHING HOUSE PVT LTD

VIKAS® PUBLISHING HOUSE PRIVATE LIMITED
E-28, Sector-8, Noida-201301 (UP), India
Phone: +91-120-4078900 • Fax: +91-120-4078999
Registered Office: Vikas Publishing House Private Limited, A-27, 2nd Floor, Mohan Co-operative Industrial Estate, New Delhi-110044
E-mail: helpline@vikaspublishing.com • Website: www.vikaspublishing.com

SALES AND BRANCH OFFICES OF VIKAS® AND S CHAND AND COMPANY LIMITED

Chennai : Ph: 044-2363 2120, chennai@schandpublishing.com
Guwahati : Ph: 0361-2738 811, 2735 640, guwahati@schandpublishing.com
Hyderabad : Ph: 040-4018 6018, hyderabad@schandpublishing.com
Jalandhar : Ph: 0181-4645 630, jalandhar@schandpublishing.com
Kolkata : Ph: 033-2335 7458, 2335 3914, kolkata@schandpublishing.com
Lucknow : Ph: 0522-4003 633, lucknow@schandpublishing.com
Mumbai : Ph: 022-2500 0297, mumbai@schandpublishing.com
Patna : Ph: 0612-2260 011, patna@schandpublishing.com

Comparative Education
ISBN: 978-81259-1130-2 Product Code: V7COE69TEDU10ENAB98O

Second Revised and Enlarged Edition 1998
Reprinted severtal times between 1998 and 2021, 2023
Reprint 2025

PRINTED IN INDIA
By Vikas Publishing House Private Limited, Plot 20/4, Site-IV, Industrial Area Sahibabad, Ghaziabad-201010 and Published by Vikas Publishing House Private Limited, E-28, Sector-8, Noida-201301

Preface to the Second Edition

In this edition of the book we have included a new section entitled Part VI—General Trends in Comparative Education towards the close of the book. Besides, we have also incorporated in it the latest data upto 1997 and other necessary corrections throughout the book. It is hoped that the book in its present shape will be more helpful to the students of the subject concerned.

Authors

Preface to the First Edition

Along with an analysis of the principles of Comparative Education, this book presents an objective account of the educational systems of U.S.A., Great Britain, India and Russia (after the disintegration of the former U.S.S.R.) from the pre-primary to the university stage. Such allied topics as adult education, teacher education, vocational education and youth welfare services have also been discussed.

While dealing with the educational systems of India, the major emphasis has been also on focussing the attention of the readers on those issues which, particularly, ail our education. In this attempt, we have sorted out such problems as those of compulsory education, student unrest, public schools, moral and religious education, national integration and Indianisation of education amongst many others and we have endeavoured to hint at some possible solutions of the same in a manner acceptable to all concerned.

In the choice of countries herein taken for discussion and selection and organisation of materials for the same we have been, principally, guided by the curricular demands of the subjects as taught to the graduate and post-graduate classes in various universities.

In the treatment of data, facts and figures upto 1992, we have tried to be as objective as humanly possible. In a work of this nature no originality and all-inclusiveness can be claimed. However, at some relevant places we have given our own evaluations of certain systems and issues. It is hoped that the same will arrest the attention of the readers.

We do not know to what extent we have succeeded in our professed objectives, but if this humble endeavour, stimulates any reader to make a more advanced study of the subject, we shall feel amply rewarded.

In the completion of this self-imposed stupendous task, we have freely derived help from numerous relevant standard works, research papers, journals and government publications. All these have been duly listed in the bibliography appended at the end. We express our gratitude to the writers and publishers of all these.

S.P. CHAUBE
&
A. CHAUBE

Contents

Part III
British Education

Part IV
Problems of Indian Education

Part V
Russian Education

Part VI
General Trends in Comparative Education

PART I

Principles of Comparative Education

1. Factors of Comparative Education.
2. Methods of Study of Comparative Education.
3. Development and Aims of Comparative Education.
4. Factors of National System of Education.

Chapter 1

Factors of Comparative Education

There are certain factors which influence the nature of development of education in a country. These factors are already present in a country and they are independent of the social situation of the place concerned. These factors are geographical, economic, racial, philosophical, linguistic, moral and religious. Besides, there are also some other factors which are based on the prevailing scientific tendency. These factors begin their influence on education from the beginning of the modern period of history. These are those of socialism, humanism, emotionalism and democracy. In this chapter we shall understand the nature of all these various factors.

The Geographical Factor

The geographical position has its inevitable impact on the culture, civilisation and education of a nation. The various countries of the world have different geographical positions. Therefore, their modes of living, civilization, culture, social institutions and educational systems are also different. The climate of a cold country is different from that of a tropical one. Therefore, ways of living and social organisation of the two types of countries are not the same. Social systems influence the educational organisation. An agricultural country emphasises agricultural education in its educational system, and an industrial country pays special attention to technological and industrial subjects in the organisation of its curriculum. In a cold country there is a long winter vacation and in a hot country a long summer vacation. Evidently, the educational structure of a country is conditioned by its geographical situation.

The Economic Factor

The educational system of a country is closely related with its economic condition. The aims and curriculum of education are framed according to the economic condition of the land. The belief about the economic system as adhered to by a country is inculcated in the citizens. For example, under the socialistic economic system, the State is the owner of all property. Therefore at the very primary stage of education children are given the impression that all property belongs to the State and each individual has to protect it. In the democracies like U.S.A. and India the situation is quite different. In these two countries the individual property is recognised. Therefore in the development of their educational systems full attention is paid to the rights of the individual. That is why in these countries "Public Schools" for the children of a few rich and higher class people are allowed to exist. Evidently, the economic factor is a very effective element and in the study of comparative education it occupies a special place.

The Racial Factor

In each country a number of races exist. These races influence its educational system. The race which considers itself superior to others tries to rule over them. If it succeeds in this attempt, then it tries to strengthen its control on them by developing a particular educational system. For example, the French and the British people established their colonies in Africa. Because they were 'white', these people thought that they were superior to the natives of Africa. So they developed a special kind of educational system to strenghthen their control over the black natives.

Thus, in South Africa, the racial factor has been an effective element in the educational system of that country. Similarly, during the British rule in India, the English people introduced a type of educational system in order to produce a special type of workers to man their administrative machinery. They did this to strengthen their imperialistic control over the country. Accordingly, English was made the medium of instruction and a particular type of curriculum was introduced. Their actions were prompted by the feeling that their culture and civilisation were superion to those of the Indian people. Needless to emphasise once again the importance of the racial factor in the study of comparative education.

The Linguistic Factors

The individual has to learn the language of the group in which he is born. The culture and civilisation of a country are expressed through its language although there are other features as well which unmistakably point to its culture and civilisation. However, the importance of the language cannot be denied. In the educational system of a country its language occupies a special place. We know that if the mother tongue is the medium of instruction, the people are generally of strong national character and if the medium is a foreign language the national character becomes weak. It is true that there are many other factors that are responsible for moulding the national character, but the medium of instruction has its own special importance, in the educational system. Those educational problems of a country which are related with its cultural elements can be understood on the basis of linguistic factors stated above.

Now we shall understand some other factors that may be grouped under the spiritual category. These are philosophical, moral and religious factors.

The Philosophical Factor

The education system of a country is influenced by the philosophy of the land. Philosophy influences life, therefore, its influence on education is quite natural. For example, in ancient Greece, Socrates, Plato and Aristotle based the educational system of the country on a particular philosophy of life and entrusted the administration of the country to philosophers. In China to-day, the educational system is based on communist philosophy. In ancient India the Gurukul system of education was based on Vedic philosophy of life. The educational system in the Buddhist period as obtained in Vihars and monasteries based on Buddhist philosophy. The Dayanand Anglo Vedic Colleges of modern India are based on the philosophy of life propounded by Swami Dayanand Saraswati. Similarly, there are some institutions based on Sri Aurobindo's philosophy. In modern India, some people are advocating a special system of education based on the Sarovodaya philosophy of Gandhiji and Vinoba Bhave. Thus the philosophical factor is a very important factor in the study of comparative education.

The Moral Factor

Some countries emphasise moral principles and some religious. In a democratic country moral behaviour of each citizen is specially emphasized, because moral behaviour is the soul of democracy. Thus in countries with a democratic setup, development of moral behaviour is specially emphasized as an aim of education as in Japan, Switzerland, Great Britain, India and U.S.A. Thus the moral factor is a very important element in the study of comparative education.

The Religious Factor

Religion occupies a very important place in an individual's life. History is testimony of the fact that thousands of persons have sacrificed their lives for the sake of religion. The history of Europe is full of such examples. In a religious country, the public is generally conservative and resents any change in its old traditions. Therefore in the organisation of an educational system we have to be careful about the religious sentiments of the people. In an industrialised country, due to scientific developments, old traditions usually begin to break-down and the society is re-constructed according to the needs of the time. Education has to pay a special role in this reconstruction. But opposite to this, in an agricultural country, the public is conservative and views any change with suspicion and it wants to preserve its religious traditions intact. Accordingly the educational system has to be organised. Needless to remark that the religious sentiments of the people have to be honoured in any educational system. Therefore, the religious factor cannot be ignored in the study of comparative education. Indeed, a comparative discussion of how different religious loyalties have given birth to various educational systems in different countries of the world will be very interesting.

Now we shall understand some such factors which may be regarded as results of scientific developments in the world. These factors are those of socialism, humanism, nationalism and democracy. The influence of these factors on education came to surface from the beginning of the modern age.

The Factors of Socialism

The impact of socialism may be sensed in the various aspects of our life to-day. Plato's ideas had the seeds of socialism. He advocated the state control of rearing and bringing up the children. Accordingly, he stood for complete state control over the development of education of children. This ideology influenced education in Greece for sometime in due course. Sir Thomas More of England in his book "Utopia" advocated socialistic principles in accordance with Plato's ideas. He held that the state must arrange for public education in order that the citizen may fulfil his duties to the state.

Rousseau, too, had advocated a socialistic pattern of society. He stood for universal education under the control of the State. Coudorcet may also be mentioned in this connection. Coudorcet stood for equal opportunity of education for all citizen. Rousseau and Coudorcet were supported by such writers as Saint Simon (1760-1825), Robert Owen (1771-1858), Charles Fouries (1772-1837), Etienne Cabet (1778-1856) and Louis Blanc (1811-1882).

Modern socialism has its origin in Marxism. Marx (1818-83) made Hegel's materialism as the base of his philosophy. Marx contended that the economic condition of a country is at the base of its social, political and spiritual process. According to socialism, the purpose of education is to develop the means of production for the welfare of the State. We find an example of this type of socialism in China and North Korea. Religion has no place in this type of education. Thus the factor of socialism has an important place in the development of education— therefore the importance of this factor in the study of comparative education cannot be overlooked.

The Factor of Humanism

Towards the close of the middle ages humanistic ideas were spread in Europe with the view to make man free of blind superstitions and to base his life on scientific ways. This spirit ultimately wanted to give full scope for the development of an individual. Humanism keeps human welfare as its prime aim. Man is considered to be the measure of everything. This idea in Europe took root from the beginning of the Renaissance. It penetrated the human mind so deeply that it ultimately resulted in the separation of the Church and State. During the sixteenth and seventeenth centuries some humanists advocated the introduction of some such ideas in education that the impact of humanism on the educational systems of their lands can be very well understood. Comenius in his emphasis on sense-training expressed only the influence of humanism. The effect of humanism on education was seen in France during the seventeenth century when education was separated from the Church and the State was made responsible for education of its citizens. New methods of teaching were devised in Germany because of the influence of humanism. England felt its impact, in the form of changes in the curriculum. In various countries such subjects as geography, mathematics and science began to be taught in such a way as to make them useful in practical affairs of life. Now attention began to be paid to the co-relationship between philosophy and science. In U.S.A., Thomas Jefferson and Thomas Panie supported the introduction of humanistic elements in the educational system. During the third decade of the present century, John Dewey of U.S.A. supported the incorporation of humanistic elements in education. In the present age, the impact of humanism may be clearly sensed in education. Today we consider only that curriculum and method of teaching good which promotes the growth of the individual. Thus we find that the humanistic factor influences education and we cannot ignore it in the study of comparative education.

The Factor of Nationalism

For strengthening the sense of unity the spirit of nationalism is created in a country. This is evident in India particularly after 1947. Here there are various castes, religions and languages. Regionalism erodes the very foundation of our national life. Inspite of these differences, our attention is drawn to the social, cultural and political unity inherent in our country in order to strengthen the national spirit. Accordingly, in our aims regarding education and the curriculum, special attention is given to the development of this sense of unity in the children. However, we have to note that the spirit of nationalism in a country may be helpful only when the international outlook is not forgotten, because then, one may become blind to the inadequacies of one's own country. This tendency can ultimately make the nation weak. The examples of Hitler of Germany and Tojo of Japan are eloquent testimonies to this. Evidently, the factor of nationalism influences the system of education and its study is important in comparative education.

The Democratic Factor

In democracy we find two forms, in one form political equality is emphasized and in another social unity. Within the first form come, U.S.A., Great Britain, France, India, Japan, etc. and in the other form China and North Korea may be mentioned. Because of its particular kind of democratic ideologies, each country has nurtured a special type of education. The differences found in their educational patterns are because of their different democratic faiths which are quite evident in their different aims, organisations and contents of education. In the study of comparative education we have to note these differences in order to understand the underlying elements correctly.

Summary

The Geographical Factor: The geographical factor influences the culture and civilization of a country. Education is closely related with culture and civilization.

The Economic Factor: Aims and curriculum determined accordingly. The people are urged to have faith in the prevailing economic system. Education is considered to be the chief means for developing this faith.

The Racial Factor: The races that consider them-selves superior introduced a system of education for maintaining their superiority.

The Linguistic Factor: The mother tongue is made the medium of instruction for developing a national character. The educational problems related with cultural aspects can be understood on the basis of language alone.

The Philosophical Factor: This philosophy of life influences education. The examples are of ancient Greece and India.

The Moral Factor: The moral aims are emphasized in a democratic set-up. Hence moral factor is important.

The Religious Factor: Close relationship between life and religion. Hence religious loyalties cannot be ignored in education.

The Factor of Socialism: Many countries have become socialistic. Hence their education is influenced by socialism.

The Factor of Humanism: In humanism man is the measure of everything. In modern educational systems human welfare is placed at the top.

The Factor of Nationalism: Nationalism is promoted through the aims and contents of education.

The Factor of Democracy: Democratic tendencies in many countries. Hence democracy has its impact on education.

Exercises

1. How does the geographical factor influence the development of education in a country?
2. What is the importance of philosophical factor in the development of education in a country?
3. Discuss the impact of democracy and socialism on modern education.
4. How does nationalism influence the aims and contents of education in a country?
5. Write short notes on the following:
   (a) Racial Factor in education.
   (b) Linguistic Factor in education .
   (c) The Factor of Humanism in education.
   (d) Democracy in education.

Chapter 2

Methods of Study of Comparative Education

In the various methods of the study of comparative education the following are noteworthy— Quantitative, Descriptive, Sociological, Historical, Analytical and Synthetic.

The Quantitative of Statistical Method

We have noted in the previous chapter that in the study of comparative education we analyse the similarities and factors inherent in the education systems of various countries. Hence, it is necessary to use the statistical method for finding out the progress or decline of education in a country. In this method various type of educational data are collected about a country. For example, the data about the number of students at a certain stage of education, expenditure on them, the percentages of passes and failures at various stages of education, expenses on teachers' salaries, school buildings and other items are collected, and the same are compared with the identical data of another country. Thus the progress or decline of education in any country is statistically analysed.

But the greatest difficulty of the statistical method is to procure reliable data. Generally, due care is not taken in the collection of data. Consequently, many of them are false. Another difficulty in this connection is that the various educational terms used in different countries do not connote the same sense. Therefore, their statistical analysis is falsified. Moreover, through the statistical method we cannot understand the educational characteristics that are the result of social, cultural, economic, political and religious situations of a country. Evidently the use of the statistical method is very limited.

The Descriptive Method

This method was used in the nineteenth century because the main purpose of comparative education then was to incorporate the good points of another country. For this, a detailed description of educational affairs of another country was necessary. So many educationists presented detailed descriptive accounts of educational systems of other lands. John Griscom of U.S.A. is worthy of mention in this connection. In 1918-19 he visited Great Britain, France, Holland, Switzerland and Italy and wrote a book entitled "A Year in Europe" describing their educational systems. An actempt was made in U.S.A. to incorporate some of the special characteristics of the educational systems as described in this book. In 1831, Victor Cousin of France published a Report on the educational system of France. Some of the educational characteristics of Prussia as described in this Report were imitated in Great Britain and France. Victor Cousin did not make a comparative study of educational systems of other lands in his Report. Therefore, his Report could be evaluated by only those persons who had a good knowledge of educational systems of other countries. Thus, in the nineteenth century only those person were able to understand comparative education who had a good knowledge of educational system of their own country.

Matthew Arnold of Great Britain and Horace Man of U.S.A. did some work in the area of descriptive method. Mathew Arnold studied the educational systems of France and Germany and published a report about France in 1859 and about Germany in 1865. Mathew Arnold in his description drew our attention also to those factors which distinguish the educational system of one land from that of another. Sir Michael Sadler and Paul Monroe followed Arnold's method. Thus, the study of comparative education became better organised.

Horace Man visited Germany, Ireland, Great Britain, France and Holland and in 1843 published a Report on the educational systems of these countries. Horace Man in this Report pointed out the special characteristics of the educational systems he had studied and also mentioned the specific element that should be imitated by others. Thus in his descriptive method Horace Man paid attention to the evaluation of the characteristics and their utilities. As a result, the later educationists also paid attention to the evaluation and utilities of characteristics of educational systems of other countries.

Henry Bernard, between 1856 and 1881, published thirty one volumes of "The American Journal of Education". In these volumes he described the educational systems of the various states of U.S.A. and of many foreign countries. And so he placed before us standard data. In this process he also interpreted the historical background of each educational system he described.

In his study of comparative education, Michael Sadler emphasized the point that we should study all those national factors that influence the educational system of a land and are responsible for its development and decline. He considered the study of comparative education as useful for one's national system of education.

The above account indicates that the descriptive method of comparative education was advocated by those educationists who wanted to promote and popularise the study of comparative education.

The Sociological Method

In the sociological method the educational problems are studied in a social context. This is done with the belief that the educational system of a country is conditioned by its social, cultural, economic, political and religious situations. Hence the educational problems of a country have their origin in some social problems and they do not exist by themselves as there is a close relationship between education and society. The sociological method of the study of comparative education does not emphasise only the past causative factors, but also those social and cultural aspects which may be responsible for the problem. It may be mentioned that the educational system of a country becomes useless when it does not run parallel to the social situation of the country and the aspirations of the people. The education in India as obtained during the British rule may be cited as a case in point, because the same did not satisfy the social needs in the country or the aspirations of the people. Hence the establishment of Kashi Vidyapith (Varanasi), Jamia Milia, Delhi and Visva-Bharti, Bolpur (West Bengal), in the country.

The sociological method suffers from the limitation that it ignores the contributions of individuals towards the growth of education. We know that in each country there are some individuals who have contributed immensely towards the growth of education in their countries.

The Historical Method

In the historical method we study the modern educational problems. This method reveals the basis on which the modern educational system is based. Needless to say that this knowledge may help us in eliminating undesirable elements in the system and further strengthening the desirable ones.

It will be wrong to think that we employ the historical method only to know the past in order that we may understand the present better. In fact, our purpose is also to improve the future by hinting at those factors which may be more useful. In the historical method we try to understand all those geographical, social, racial, political, religious and linguistic factors which influence the educational system of a country. Nicholas Hans, Schneider and Kandel have emphasized this method. But one of the great limitations of the historical method is that the data on which we base our study may not be reliable because in the collection of the same, due care is not observed. Therefore, conclusions derived cannot be very useful. We have to keep in mind that the historical materials about educational systems of various countries are generally not very reliable. This limits the utility of the historical data. Hence more research is needed for making them reliable.

Another difficulty with the historical method is that historians generally are not impartial in their accounts. They want to conceal undersirable elements about the history of their own country and look on facts relating to other countries with prejudice. Thus, the truth is not known. Consequently, by the historical method we cannot reach the right conclusions. The third difficulty of the historical method is that the past is unduly emphasized. Consequently, the study of comparative education becomes unbalanced

The Analytical Method

In the foregoing pages we have remarked several times that the educational system of a country has a close relationship with its social, political and economical conditions. It is because of this relationship that a comparative study has become necessary. In any comparative study we have to use analysis. Because through analysis we can separate the various elements and understand the importance of each independently. Analytical method can be useful only when the social and educational organisations are compared. For this comparison the following four factors are necessary—

1. *To Collect Educational Data*: To collect all the educational information through descriptive and statistical methods is necessary for analytical method.

2. *Interpretation of Social, Political, Economic and Historical Data*: This is necessary in order to understand similarities and differences found in the educational systems of various countries.

3. *Determination of Standard for Comparison*: After finding out the similarities and differences of the various educational systems, we have to compare the same according to certain standards. It is the business of the analytical method

to formulate these standards. Political philosophy, aims of education and the method of control of education may be cited as some standards for comparison. In the context of these standards, we shall understand the similarities and differences of educational systems of various countries. For example, we can say that since there is a difference between the political philosophies of India and China, therefore, we find differences in their educational systems.

4. *Interpretation and Conclusion*: On the basis of the above three aspects we interpret the collected data and reach certain conclusions on the basis of comparison.

Limitations of the Analytical Method : The above account indicates the utility of the analytical method but this method suffers from the difficulty that in the process of analysis no adequate attention is paid to the totality of the educational systems. We have to keep in mind, as we have already referred to in the previous chapter, that inspite of differences in the educational systems of various countries, there is an inherent similarity. The analytical method is prone to close our eyes to this inherent similarity. Therefore, in the study of comparative education the necessity of synthetical method has been conceived. We shall study this method below.

The Methods of Synthesis

We have already noted that in the study of comparative education, international point of view is now considered important. The method of synthesis emphasises this point of view. In this method the problems of education are studied on an international plane. Edmund King in his book "World Perspective in Education" has advocated this method. When we study the problems of education of various countries, we find some universal truths in their inherent differences, because there is much similarity in the needs and aspirations of the people of the world. The United Nations Organisation has contributed much towards the consciousness of this similarity. The method of synthesis is still in its infancy and needs further development.

SUMMARY

Statistical Method: Collection and comparison of educational data. Difficult to find reliable data. Educational terms used in various countries do not connote the same meanings. Hence limited utility.

Descriptive Method: The purpose of incorporating the good points. Accounts by travellers. Evaluation and utility of characteristics. Attention on national characteristics. Interpretation of historical background.

Sociological Method: The study of educational problems in social context. An educational problem is a social problem.

Historical Method: To study the causative factors of modern educational problems. The aim of building the future. In collection of data the necessary care is not observed. Hence the utility of historical method limited.

Analytical Method: To analyse the various educational elements. To collect educational data and to interpret social, political, economic and historical elements, determination of standards of comparison.

The Method of Synthesis: International view point. Search of universal truths in differences.

EXERCISES

1. Discuss any two methods of the study of comparative education.
2. Why has the historical method of the study of comparative education limited utility? Give reasons with illustrations.
3. What is the analytical method of the study of comparative education? Which other method can overcome its limitations? Discuss.
4. What are the special postulates of the sociological method of the study of comparative education? How have the same promoted the study of comparative education?

Chapter 3

Development and Aims of Comparative Education

Commonness and Differences of Factors Involved

To-day the various countries of the world are interdependent. An event in one part of the world has its natural and inevitable impact in the other areas of the globe. This is true not only of epidemics, earthquakes, wars, famines, floods, etc., but also of educational systems. In other words, the educational system of one country positively or negatively influences the educational organisations and systems of others. It is because of this that we have been stimulated to make a comparative study of the different systems of education as obtained in various countries. From this study, we have come to realise that the various educational systems prevailing in the different parts of the world have certain common factors and certain differences.

Comparative Study in Early Stages

Marc-Antoine Jullién de Paris began the study of comparative education in 1817. In this study, he emphasized the analysis of the common and different factors found in the various educational systems of the world. He wanted to give a scientific approach to education. So he detested the idea that education should be limited to narrow ideas of the ruler of a country. Therefore, he analysed the principles and conclusions of the various educational systems in a tabular form. He believed that by tabulation he would be able to elucidate some principles and rules regarding the educational systems concerned. Thus he emphasized the study of comparative education. However, few were aware of his views regarding this method before the twentieth century.

We have to note that comparative education did not begin with this kind of analysis. In the beginning of the twentieth century, many travellers in their accounts have included descriptions of educational systems of the lands they visited. These travellers also hinted at the social progress and economic prosperity of countries of their visits, and in this connection they emphasized the importance of the educational systems of the lands concerned. They contended that educational systems were responsible for the social progress and economic prosperity of the people concerned. Thus travellers' accounts of educational systems have occupied an important place in the study of comparative education.

Development of Comparative Education

We find three stages in the development of comparative education.

The First Stage:

The first stage in the development of comparative education begins with the ideas propounded by Antoine Jullien. This stage continued upto the beginning of the twentieth century. During the nineteenth century, the belief had gained ground that the characteristics prevailing in one country may be absorbed in the educational system of another. This belief resulted into the collection of data on education of other countries. These data were arranged in tables and an attempt was made to deduce some general principles from the same. Consequently, people began to believe that the educational system in a country may be organised according to these principles. But in the collection of the above data no attention was paid to social, political, economic and religious conditions of the country studied, although they have a direct influence on its educational system. Therefore, it was not considered necessary whether the country whose educational pattern was to be copied has the same cultural, social, political, economic and religious traditions as the other country had. In this first stage of development of comparative education, the names of Victor Cousion of France, Matthew Arnold of England, Horace Man and Henry Bernard of U.S.A., Tolstoy and Ushinsky of Russia and Domingo Sarminto of Argentina may be specially mentioned. These persons and their followers have opined that in the development of education of a country, it is necessary to study the educational systems of other countries. Thus the study of comparative education began in order to enrich the educational system of one's own country.

The Second Stage:

In the second stage, social, economic and other circumstances which influence education in a country were studied. Thus the influence of these factors in the context of educational development was specially noted and to what extent these factors were suitable for another country. So the tendency of blind imitation was discarded. Sir Michael Sadler of England was the father of this second stage. In 1907 he published an essay in which he emphasized the point that educational system of a country was related to the social environment of the land. Sadler's point of view was accepted by Issac Kandal and Robert Ulich of U.S.A., Friedrich Schneider of Germany, Joseph Lauwerys and Nicholas Hans of England.

The Third Stage:

The third stage starts in 1950. Bereday, George Z.F. regards this stage as a period of analysis. In this method, economic political, social and religious factors were analysed. Then it was inferred up to what extent that educational system was suitable or insuitable for another country. Thus the related factors of education were specially studied. Therefore, in the third stage, an attempt was made to reach a conclusion on the basis of various factors, whereas in the second stage this tendency was absent.

Robert Ulich, Friedrich Schneider and Issac Kandel have contributed significantly to the development of the third stage of the study of comparative education.

The Meaning and Aim of Comparative Education

We have seen that Antoine Jullien started the study of comparative education. But now the scope of comparative education has been further enlarged. Within comparative education, we now make an analysis of educational systems of various countries in order to understand their educational problems with a view to find out solutions of one's own educational problems. In this attempt, we also try to understand the philosophical background of the country concerned, as the same influences the educational system. There are certain foundations of education which are universal. When we talk of the philosophical background, it implies that we have to make a study of the same impartially. We have already noted that political, cultural, social, religious and economic conditions influence the educational system of a country. Therefore, the purpose of the study of comparative education is also to study the conditions and factors that influence education in a land for then alone we may succeed in finding out solutions of educational problems.

The purpose of the study of comparative education is also to study those differences that make the education of a country different from that of another. In studying these differences, we also study the causative factors of the same. We study the differences in the social, political, economic and religious situations which make various systems of education different from each other. However, let us not infer that the purpose of comparative education is to study the inherent differences in various educational systems. The purpose is to study those general principles on which development of education in any country is based. Thus comparative education highlights the universality of general principles in the existing differences. Needless to say that comparative education aims at strengthening international unity by drawing our attention to the universal general principles.

The purpose of comparative education is also to understand why the educational systems of some countries are progressive and of others, backward. The administrative system of the land influences the state of the educational system. For example, the administrative machineries of Switzerland, Canada, U.S.A. and Japan are combined with local autonomy and decentralised control. Consequently, in the educational systems of these countries, we find a reflection of their political philosophy. Thus political philosophy and the administrative systems of various countries determine the administration and control of education. The purpose of comparative eduction is also to study these elements in their proper perspectives.

We have to keep in mind that besides an analytical approach, synthesis is also emphasized in the study of comparative education. In this synthesis an attempt is made to understand how a social structure and political philosophy have influenced education. Thus, in comparative education we try to include the study of all these factors. Herein we study the impact of both formal and informal education. Consequently, we have included sociological basis of education as well; i.e., we study the place of social process, social control, social organisation and social change in the development of education of a country. Evidently, the scope of comparative education has become very comprehensive now.

Summary

The similarities and differences of factors in the study of comparative education.

The Beginning of Comparative Education: By Antoine Jullien the analysis of similar and dis-similar factors. Traveller's accounts. Attention on social and economic tendencies.

The Development of the Study of Comparative Education:

Stage I: Antoine Jullien's ideas, Imitation.

Stage II: Study of the social, political and economic conditions.

StageIII: The period of analysis of social, political, religious and other factors. The universal principles, aiming at international unity.

The Meaning and Purpose of Comparative Education: To bring in reform in one's own educational system. To study educational problems and their solutions. The study of philosophical, social, economic, political and religious conditions. The study of differences. The study of general principles. The idea of international unity. The study of causes of progressiveness and backwardness of education. The study of sociological foundations of education.

Exercises

1. Trace the various stages of development of the study of comparative education.
2. Discuss the meaning scope and purpose of comparative education.

Chapter 4

Factors of National System of Education

National factors of a country are closely related with nationalism and national system of education. Hence in the study of comparative education we should study those factors which make the education of a country national. In this chapter we shall study some such factors.

Cultural Consciousness

The educational system of a country may be called national only when through education an attempt is made to help the inhabitants to imbibe the culture developed by its ancestors. We can refer to three principal aims of education in the context of culture:

1. To preserve the ancient culture,
2. To acquaint the coming generations with one's own culture, and
3. To contribute towards the growth of one's own culture.

Needless to remark that the aim of education in a country should be to develop cultural consciousness.

Some Permanent Values of Culture

In each culture, there are certain values which are not affected by time and place. Some religious and cultural faiths may be included in these values. For example, faith in God, love for truth and non-violence and the ideal of universal brotherhood and justice are the permanent values of many cultures of the world. These values have come down to us through the ages and they have remained uninfluenced by time and place. Whereas against this, the culture of each country has certain values which are subject to time and place. In India, some such cultural values may be cited which bear the impact of history. It is a matter of living memory of the present generation that after the second World War (1939-1945) great changes have occurred in many of our life values (in fact this is true of any country). For example, joint-family system is breaking down, undersirable changes have occurred in the attitude of the youngers towards their elders, students do not show due respect to their teachers as students did twentyfive years ago, and the teachers also now care more for the increments in their salaries and other allowances than for teaching. In any meeting of teachers, there is more talk of groupism, backbiting and salaries than of students' welfare. Guardians do not respect teachers as they did before. Similarly, the relations between parents and children, sisters and brothers, husband and wife, masters and servants and between many other units of society have undergone great changes. Now we have begun to discard many old mores and modes and adopt more liberal attitudes. Thus, time and place have been changing many elements of culture.

It is to be noted that like the cultures of many countries of the world, some of the elements of Indian culture too, are age old and seemingly eternal. During the foreign rules in the country these eternal cultural values were always ignored in the educational system. Educational systems as obtained during the Muslim and British periods are an eloquent testimony to this. Many British documents clearly specify that their purpose was to ignore the Indian culture in the educational system with the view to inculcate in the Indians the values of the Western culture. For this, they introduced a particular system of education in the country. As a result, Indians began to lose faith and love for their own culture.

Necessity to Develop Love for one's own Culture

It is necessary to develop love for one's own culture through the educational system because it strengthens nationalism. In order to make the country strong and prosperous, the spirit of nationalism must be nurtured. However, this spirit should not make one blind towards the inadequacies in one's own country. In each country there are various types of communities, classes, castes and interests. Due to the lack of national feelings many people ignore national interests. Minorities in any country are suspicious about the majority. In certain contexts this may be true of the majority as well. Some of the activities of Hindus and Muslims in India may be quoted as examples. Sometimes Muslims raise a slogan of "Islamic culture and religion in danger" and sometimes Hindus protest that "Hinduism is in danger". The Indian Constitution guarantees protection to all religions and communities. But this is not enough for the preservation of the culture of the country. It is necessary to inculcate love for the country's culture. This is possible through the adoption of a national system of education.

In the context of Indian culture, the current educational system in India appears to be inadequate. Through our educational system, we have not yet been able to educate our citizens in national pride so that the Hindus may consider themselves Indians first and Hindus afterwards, and Muslims and Christians, Indians first and Muslims and Christians afterwards.

The history of education of U.S.A., U.K., Japan and France indicate that the people of these countries believe in certain traditions. So in their educational system, adequate attention has been paid to the preservation of these traditions. Consequently, in their systems of national education, we find a basis of cultural consciousness. By giving due place to religious faiths, ideals, social values and human values in the curriculum an attempt may be made to create a sense of unity in diversity. In this attempt the educational system of the country will get a cultural base. In the absence of this base, no educational system can be called national. For the preservation of the country's culture, it is necessary to give due place to the sub-cultures, of the land, as these are only the organic branches of the same 'one' tree-culture. By doing so the followers of these sub-cultures are united together for the preservation of the country's culture, of which their own is an essential part. Towards the realisation of this objective, education can be very helpful. Only when education is directed towards the fulfilment of this goal, the educational system of a country becomes national.

Economic Security

The economic security of the country becomes a determining factor of the type of education that it can afford to have. If the economic condition is poor, education becomes backward in many aspects. The history of any undeveloped country testifies this. In economically strong countries the educational aims and the curriculum are given a special direction for making the country prosperous. For example, in U.S.A. and Japan education is so patterned as to make the individual strong and capable enough to stand on his own feet after having received education. In India it is quite the opposite. Here college or university graduates do not know where to go after completing their education. So they continue to stay on in the university as long as they can and thus try to postpone for a few years the problem of their un-employment. This situation has resulted in over-crowding of our colleges and universities and fall of educational standard. In truth, the educational system is worse than worthless for instead of solving the un-employment problems, increases it. In the development of educational system, we have to keep in view the economic needs of the country, because through education, we have to prepare for various fields. It is true that for economic prosperity, other factors are also necessary, but importance of education in this context cannot be minimised.

The Growth of the Capacities of Citizens and National Development: The system of education should be such as to provide opportunities for the maximum development of each citizen. It is by developing individuals that the overall growth of the nation can be guaranteed. This does not imply loss of freedom of the individual. In fact, we only want that the wealth of the nation should not be concentrated in the hands of a few capitalists. This is possible only by ensuring the right growth of the capacities of all citizens.

No Class-Distinction: No class-distinction in the planning of education should be permitted, because this results in neglect of the education of other more capable citizens. This will result in social disparities and weaken the nation.

Proper National Character Necessary: In the absence of proper national character, the necessary leadership and cooperation of the people will be lacking. Because of this shortcoming the national system of education will not realise its objectives. With good leadership and people's cooperation, much can be achieved, even when the adequate economic resources are wanting. Evidently, there is a close relationship between economic security and national system of education.

Consciousness of National Unity

Only that system of education can be called national which strengthens a feeling of national unity. In each country there are various communities, religions, classes and languages. Therefore, the feeling of national unity is necessary to bring these varying units together. The people in U.S.A., and India are of varying races and languages. Hence it was necessary in these countries to bring the people into one fold by disregarding their provincial and regional differences. In the achievement of these objectives, education has played a very important role. In each country there are many political parties with a narrow outlook. The case of India may be cited. Because of the narrow outlook of certain political parties, India was partitioned in 1947. The British rulers wanted to weaken the feeling of national unity in the country, therefore they introduced an alien system of education which helped in strengthening the British empire but weakened the national feeling which was strengthened once again only after the achievement of Independence in 1947. In Great Britain the Education Act of 1944 was passed to strengthen the national feeling of unity. In U.S.A. education is considered as the chief means for developing the feeling of national unity. This was necessary because the people who had come from Europe to settle, had varying traditions, loyalties, beliefs and languages. The efforts of W.T. Harris, Henry Bernard and Horace Man in developing this national feeling are worth a mention.

We may easily understand how Herr Hitler in his Nazi Germany through a particular system of education strengthened the feeling of national unity. In Japan, too, its particular system of education has played a prominent role in strengthening national unity both before and after the Second World War.

Many countries in South East Asia and Africa have become independent after the Second World War. In strengthening their national feelings, they had to encounter opposition from many political parties. Therefore, in these countries an attempt has been made to include some such factors in the aims and contents of education which may foster nationalism in the citizens. Evidently, education has to play a special role in the development of nationalism in a country. So education is an important basis of national unity.

National Language as a Basis

Many languages may be spoken in a country, but only one enjoys the status of a national language. Everywhere the national language occupies a special place. The scientific, technological and other subjects are taught through the medium of the national language. The Government tries that every one acquires the capacity to express himself through the national language. Without one's own national language, no country can be strong. That is why in U.S.A. it was considered necessary to adopt a national language, as there were many languages spoken by the immigrants. Thus the place of the national language in the development of a national feeling cannot be over-emphasized. Therefore, in a national system of education special emphasis is placed on the study of the national language.

The Political Basis

The political philosophy which controls the government of a country has its inevitable impact on education. The examples of U.S.A., Japan and India may be cited. In U.S.A. and Japan the democratic influence can be easily perceived in their educational systems. In India democratic leanings are clearly perceptible in its educational plannings and organisations. Thus the political system of a country is closely related with its educational programme.

National System of Education and National Character

There is a close relationship between the national character and national system of education. For example, the national character of U.S.A. is democratic, so its educational system is democratic in most of its aspects. In China the national character is communistic. So its educational system, too, is governed by communism. The philosophy of life as followed in a country formulates its pattern of education. This philosophy of life, also shapes the national character. Hence there is a close relationship between national character and national system of education. So national character has been accepted as an important basis of national system of education. The various chapters of this book at relevant places will indicate how the national character of a country has moulded its national system of education.

Internationalism and National System of Education

This world is now knit into one unit due to the various scientific inventions. Any grave event in any part of the world affects the life of the people in another. The events in the Middle East, South East Asian and the Pacific countries bear an eloquent testimony to this. Now, people the whole world over are more easily governed by a single feeling than ever before because of the easy means of communications prevalent everywhere. Now the prosperous nations want to help the less prosperous ones. The prosperous nations, too, have to bank on other countries at times. The establishment and continuance of the United Nations Organisations is a clean expression of this inter dependence. Thus to-day. the feeling of internationalism or international co-operation is generated in individuals through the national system of education in each country. In text-books on various subjects we find much emphasis laid on the necessity of international co-operation in life. Attempts are being made to develop the national system of education in many countries through the help of UNESCO. Needless to say that the feeling of inter-nationalism now occupies an important place in the national system of education in a country.

SUMMARY

Cultural Consciousness: Through education to imbibe the culture developed by our ancestors. The temporary and eternal cultural values. To develop love for one's own culture, as it strengthens the national feeling. Blind nationalism is fatal. Nationalism through a national system of education. This basis of cultural consciousness necessary.

The Economic Security: Education according to the economic basis of the country. Economic condition may be bettered through education. Necessary to develop the capacity of the citizens.

The Consciousness of National Unity: National unity may be strengthened through a national system of education. For this reconstruction of curriculum is necessary.

The Basis of National Language: The study of national language for developing national unity. The national language the medium of instruction.

The Political Basis: Education influenced by the political system established in the country.

National Character and National System of Education: Education and philosophy of life. Close relationship between national character and national system of education.

***Internationalism and National System of Education*:** International inter-dependence. Exchange of teachers and students in countries of the world.

Exercises

1. Discuss the place of cultural consciousness in the national system of education in a country.
2. How is national unity related with national system of education?
3. What is the place of economic security in the development of a national system of education?
4. How does the political system influence the national system of education?
5. Discuss the place of national language in the national system of education.
6. Why is internationalism emphasized in any national system of education?

PART II

American Education

5. The General Nature and Aims of American Education.
6. Nature of Education Administration.
7. State Educational Administration.
8. Administration and Organisation of Local Schools.
9. Pre-primary Education.
10. Primary Education.
11. High School Education.
12. Adult Education.
13. Teacher Education.
14. Universitv and College Education.

Chapter 5

The General Nature and Aims of American Education

The General Background

The nature and aims of education of a country are conditioned by its social needs, ideals and aspirations. The case of U.S.A. is no exception to this. Therefore, in order to understand nature and aims of education in U.S.A. we have to understand its culture, civilisation and changes that have taken place in its social, political and vocational traditions.

U.S.A. is a new country of the New World. But it is the oldest democratic form of government. Most of the people of this land have migrated from European countries. Hence, its general public represents a mixture of the old American settlers and Europeans. The impact of European civilisation is clearly manifested here.

When the Europeans colonised this land permanently, they tried to spread primary education with a view to spread literacy. Primary education, though available to all, was however very expensive. Higher education was based on European classical method and this was available only to children of upper class and administrative group. The children of the people settled in the Southern part of the country would go to their parental lands i.e., European countries for receiving primary education. Before the advent of the eighteenth century, such was the state of affairs.

Some middle and high schools were established in U.S.A. during the seventeenth century. But children of only a special class of people could receive education in such schools. These schools, thus, were not much useful from universal point of view. The famous William and Mary College was established during this time. The State of Massachussets was the pioneer in the expansion of education. In 1647, in Massachussets a law was promulgated requiring all the boys and girls to be given education according to their social needs. It was laid down that in cities with less than hundred families, primary schools should be established and in cities with greater number of families Latin Grammar Schools should also be established. Due to this law education got a universal turn and the local public began to participate in educational activities.

The geographical conditions of a country mould its social values and needs. This is true for U.S.A. as well. Hence, the geographical circumstances and environment necessarily changed the imported European system of education. Consequently, a common school system was evolved. The special feature of this system was that it made no distinction between rich and poor, high and low and boy and girl. The boys and girls usually started schooling at four or five years of age and continued their education till they attained marriageable age or a sense of personal responsibility. Thus a system of education from nursery class to college level was developed.

The Europeans in their colonies had generally adopted the European system of education at first. But the people in U.S.A., evolved their own system of education on the European pattern according to the needs in their various localities. On the basis of the rules of Puritan theocracy and enacted laws, the local public established schools. Thus education spread in many areas but the older communities residing in densely populated areas could not control schools established in distant areas. Therefore, school districts were established according to the educational needs of the new areas.

In America, the second struggle for freedom, due to public

awakening in the nineteenth century, is specially important. During this period along with political, social and industrial development, significant reformative changes for educational expansion were brought about. The State Governments began a scrutiny of the available educational facilities with a view to foster cultural development. Some State Governments tried to centralise the educational facilities but such efforts failed. Others established State Boards of Education having honourable citizens and members of State legislatures as members on them. Under these Boards of Education, significant reforms and changes in educational administration were made. Most of the progress in education in the state of Massachussets was possible only due to the activities of these State Boards. Indiana, Ohio, Michigan, North Carolina and Rhode Island were some other states which made notable progress. One important step in the educational facilities and reforms was that the State Governments gave financial help for the construction and renovation of school buildings. The salary scales of teachers were revised to enhance their financial status. Normal schools were opened for their training. Encouragement for establishing both private and public schools was given and the number of such institutions soon increased sufficiently.

The Necessity of Various Types of Education

The early education in the United State of America was purely classical. Western civilization, culture, literature, history, geography and philosophy were mainly studied. There was no place for scientific and vocational education. At that time, it seemed difficult to spend much on educational facilities due to the poor financial condition of the country, and compared to the financial resources, the educational expenditure was excessive. Common man was unable to bear the educational expenses of his children. This condition continued upto the middle of the nineteenth century. Now, due to public awakening, need fcr scientific and vocational education began to be felt. At that time, the country needed such graduates who were trained from the scientific and vocational point of view. Therefore, the Government took reformative steps in that direction. Keeping in view the poverty of the masses, free primary schools were established, necessary changes in the prevailing subjects were made and the curriculum was made scientific, vocational and technical according to the need. Denominational schools were made public. Thus changes in traditional, aristocratic and classified education were brought about.

Although, most of the people in America had migrated from Europe, yet many of them, belonging to different communities and groups, wanted to maintain their religious and political identities. Consequently, they did not co-operate fully in the centralisation of educational facilities. By and by, this attitude changed towards nationalism and led to the centralisation of education. Thus prevailing education system began to change. The industrial and political revolutions in France and England also affected the American atmosphere. Because of the industrial and political influence, an industrial plan was prepared in America. In order that the students may contribute to the growing national progress, a plan for imparting different types of scientific, vocational and technical education along with general education, was presented. As a result, provision for training in different occupational and engineering subjects was made in the curriculum.

The freedom of a country may be stable only when there is no shortage of educated, vocationally strong and noble citizens. So, the general education of a free country must inculcate qualities of good citizenship. This is one of the prime needs of a free nation. Vocational, industrial, technical and scientific education along with general education makes the citizens strong and capable. Such citizens can contribute significantly through their active co-operation to the progress and economic independence of the nation. Thus, educationists in America, rightly understood the need of making education all-round, multi-dimensional and multi-purpose in order to create responsible citizens in the country and society at large. Accordingly, subjects connected with allied training were included in the curriculum. So, the aims of modern education in America seem to emerge in different forms.

The General Aims of Education

1. *To Develop a Sense of World Citizenship*

Mutual contacts are developing fast in this scientific age. The citizens of a country are coming into contact with others in one respect or other. In such a situation national citizenship alone will not help, therefore, as in other countries, one of the main aims of American education is to arouse an interest and curiosity in the wide and varied knowledge of the world with an open mind, shunning a narrow outlook. The American citizen can establish relations with the citizens of other countries only if he possesses a many-sided knowledge about them. By doing so, on the one hand he will gain maturity of mind through the knowledge of the world, and on the other he will develop international understanding to become an able world citizen.

2. *To Develop a Sense of Co-operation*

In thc public sphere, there are people of different talents. They require human virtues for closer co-operation amongst each other. These human qualities are love, sympathy and co operation. The citizens of today must have faith in humanity, equality and co-operation in order to lead a happy life. So the other aim of American education is to develop qualities of humanity and co-operation so that a person may strive for collective, social progress by co-ordinating old and modern knowledge wisely.

3. *To Introduce Vocational Point of View in Education*

The purpose of American education is to prepare a citizen for life. In the modern age, the vocational point of view is considered very important, so provision has been made for vocational and technical education along with general education. A number of multi-purpose technical schools have been established in U.S.A. Guidance centres have been established for providing vocational guidance to students. Through these schools and centres the students are given vocational guidance according to their interest, aptitude, need and ability, and they are trained accordingly. Thus the trained student not only improves his economic status, but also contributes significantly to the economic development of the country.

4. *To Develop the Qualities of Citizenship*

America is a democratic country. The success of democracy depends on ideal citizens. Efforts are made in U.S.A. to develop qualities of ideal citizenship from the beginning. Qualities like tolerance, knowledge of one's rights and duties, respect for the views, and rights and duties of others and the spirit of selfless social service are developed in the people there. The citizens are educated to behave according to the accepted social ideals.

5. *Provision for All Types of Education*

For success of democracy the citizens should be fairly well educated. Just as freedom is the birth right, so is education. There are three main characteristics of American educational system - (1) Universal (2) Compulsory (3) Free. Most of the schools in America fulfil the needs of the common people and they are managed by specific communities. Education is compulsory for the boys and girls from 7 years to 16 years of age. At some place, this limit has been raised to 17 and 18 years while at some other places, the lower age limit has been reduced to 4 or 5 years. Thus in America, education is compulsory from 4-5 years of age to 17-18 years for both boys and girls.

The purpose of compulsory education was the spread of literacy along with expansion of education and to bring maximum number of boys and girls under compulsory attendance. This law is called as the 'Law of Compulsory Attendance'. Earlier people strongly opposed this law and claimed that the law was against 'Parental Rights'. But that opposition died when better sense prevailed and the people accepted the Law of Compulsory Attendance. And so education became universal.

According to census reports, around the middle of the present century, the student community was 1/5 of the total population. Education is not only compulsory in America but it has been made free also by extending educational facilities. All the elementary schools in the country offer free education. Free education had begun in America in the nineteenth century. Apart from free education, free transport service from home to school, free mid-day meals and free medical care are available to students. The old one-roomed schools have been converted into multi-roomed, modern, well-ventilated schools. For organising games and sports, central halls have been constructed along with gymnastic departments.

In America, there is a provision for education from the nursery to the university stage. Generally all the boys and girls receive education upto 16 years of age. Seventyfive per cent of the students continue their education upto the Higher Secondary stage and 16 percent go upto the college level. Vocational and technical schools impart training to 50 percent of the student community. Besides public schools, private and denomination schools also exist. Twenty percent of the total student population receive education in privately managed primary schools. Private secondary schools are less attractive than primary schools but private colleges and universities have made much progress. The number of students studying in these institutions is equal to that in public schools. We also find private vocational schools, experimental schools and training colleges contributing to the education system of America. Denomination schools are quite sufficient in number but they are not very attractive. Therefore the number of students in those schools is less than the number in private schools.

Another reason for universal education in America is the availability of transport facilities along with all other educational facilities. Free transport brings about ten million boys and girls from home to school every day. According to the statistics in 1953 about 40 million students and in 1992, 90 million students were receiving free educational facilities. At present 90 per cent boys and girls are receiving education whereas in the beginning of this century the percentage was 55. Full-time and night schools are in sufficient number in America.

Universal education in United State of America, is mainly due to the public schools. Education is universal in the sense that it is imparted without any consideration of poor or rich, black or white, private or government. The child of every strata of life receives education conveniently according to his interest, aptitude and need. These public schools bear the responsibility of educating the boys and girls of the country efficiently and devotedly.

SUMMARY

Background: U.S.A. was first colonized by Europeans who started schools on the basis of European traditions, culture and literature. Although, the language was English, yet customs and traditions of different countries of Europe influenced the education of America. Education was expensive in the beginning and was available mainly to high class and specific groups but later on it became universal. Schools began to be established by the common people. At that time the aim of education was the study of Western civilization, culture and literature and subjects like geography, history and philosophy.

Various Types of Education: In the middle of the nineteenth century, political and industrial revolutions in France and England affected U.S.A. Scientific, vocational and industrial education began to be included in the curriculum. Education was made free. It was made compulsory for boys and girls upto 16 years of age. Isolated schools were centrally administered. Public schools were established for providing free primary education. Laws of compulsory attendance were made.

Aim of Education: The aim of American education is to develop able citizens in order to make democracy strong and also to teach them lessons in world citizenship. This education inculcates curiosity for knowledge, a sense of civic rights and duties, vocational and industrial capability, capacity for national progress and a feeling of selfless service for social welfare. Education there is free, compulsory and universal for boys and girls from 7 to 16 years of age. Transport facilities, medical facilities and free mid-day meals are easily available to students. Most popular and efficient are public schools. But private and denominational schools also provide education. Guidance centres in schools give vocational guidance to students. We can find schools which provide education and training in different occupations and industries in U.S.A. The student is trained with all possible facilities according to his interest, aptitude, ability and need.

Exercises

1. What are the aims of education in U.S.A.?
2. Critically examine the educational philosophy of the United States of America.
3. What was the general form of education in U.S.A. before 1850?

Chapter 6

Nature of Educational Administration

It has already been stated in the previous chapter that the population of U.S.A. consisted of immigrants from Europe. This population had inherited different religious and economic ideals from their European communities. Their religious belief made them conservative and they had become staunch devotees of their religious and economic beliefs. Materialism had made them individualistic. Therefore, whenever there was a demand for centralisation of administration, they opposed it. Ultimately in 1789 the supporters and opponents of centralisation entered into an agreement and they framed the United States Constitution of 1789. According to this constitution Federal and State Governments were constituted and the powers of the Federal Government were clearly defined.

Americans had adopted the European system of education in the beginning. It was greatly influenced by the British system of education. Although now it has been sufficiently changed and reformed according to the new needs and American atmosphere, yet it can still be said to be partly influenced by British system of Education. Most of the people consider the American system of Education as a national system of education, but in the absence of central organisation it is different from other national educational systems. Just as in England, educational organisation is considered to be an individual affair so also in America, education is not free from individual responsibility. In the absence of a clear cut distribution of educational powers and responsibilities between the centre and the States, education has become mainly a State subject. Educational system of about 50 States is based on their own independent systems. There is some difference or the other in the independent systems of the various States. We cannot consider it as a mistake of the educationists and leaders of America that they could not formulate those basic principles of a national system of education which could help in classifying the organisation of education and in assigning responsibilities. Contemporary conditions might not have permitted the inclusion of educational responsibility in the Constitution. Moreover, the educational problems could not be given any constitutional provision because much before the framing of the Constitution, colonies had their local public schools, Government schools, private schools and denominational schools which were fulfilling their obligations independently as one unit.

Even after the adoption of the Constitution and Amendments of the Constitution, there is no specification of the distribution of the educational responsibilities. The tenth Amendment of the Constitution simply indicates that the State Governments are free to use those powers which have not been reserved for the Federal Government or for the use of which the States Governments have not been debarred. Thus the State Governments accepted the entire responsibility of educational organisation. We do not mean to say that the Federal Government is entirely apathetic to educational problems. On the contrary, the Federal Government influences education indirectly, if not directly.

The States could not utilise the educational powers conferred on them through occasional Amendments of the Constitution. This may be due to the adherence of the public to their traditional rights and their conservatism. While supporting the Constitution, the public considered educational responsibility as their own, although the need for a uniform system of education and equipping it with all possible facilities and modern researches and scientific inventions was being stressed on them again and again. It is perhaps because of this reason that schools in America are being managed by about 20,000 local educational councils. It is only in Labrador State that the State Government manages and organises the administration of the schools and the financial responsibility also is that of the Sate Government.

Cooperation of the Federal Government in Education

It has already been made clear that the Federal Government influences and controls educational organisation indirectly, although the State Governments are free to conduct their own independent systems of education. The Federal Government has given them Land Grants from time to time and have also helped them financially for training in Technical, Industrial and Agricultural subjects. In the eighteenth century, the land which was not owned by the public was under Federal Government. That land was given to the States for establishing educational institutions on the condition that the State Governments would preserve it and use its income for the expansion of free education. The Federal Government continued to give Land Grants to the State Governments for opening new institutions from time to time. In 1830, the United State Congress extended Land Grants and help still further. By the end of the nineteenth century, State Governments were given financial assistance under the Smith Hughes Act for training in Technical, Industrial and Agricultural subjects at the secondary level. During the last years of the nineteenth century when the civil war started, the Federal Government gave sufficient Land Grants to the State Governments for Technical and Agricultural schools under the Morril Act. During the Second World War the Federal Government handed the Land Grant system and its patronage to the State Governments.

The Federal Government conducts its educational programme through its education office. Education office has been established to control and implement the educational programmes. In 1939, the Department of Education Office, hitherto independent, was attached to the Federal Security Agency. Other departments of the Federal Government also continued to give financial help and grants for the provision of education in allied subjects. For example in 1897, the Department of Agriculture, under the Morril and Hatch Act, gave Land Grants and financial help for improvements in agricultural education. In 1917, the Federal Government by establishing Federal Board of Vocational Education also provided financial assistance. In 1920, the assistance given by this Board was transferred to the State Governments and the provision of education for abnormal people was also included in this arrangement. In 1912, the Department of Commerce and Labour established Childrens' Bureau of Education. The main aim of the Bureau was to study the problems of civilian conservation corps and to formulate child welfare plans. Thus the different departments of the Federal Government gave grants and financial help to State Governments for specialised education in allied subjects.

The Federal Government not only gave Land Grants and financial assistance to the State Governments for special programmes and educational plans but it also encouraged and assisted Private Agencies and Community Agencies. During the depression period of the third decade of the current century, the Private Agencies and Community Agencies started certain educational programmes and later on, these agencies became educational institutions. In 1933, the Government established Civilian Conservation Corps to provide employment and vocational training to the unemployed persons. Similarly, another institution namely the National Youth Administration was established in 1935. This institution helped in the absence of any vocation and provided part-time jobs to students during education. After 8 or 9 years, this institution had to be closed for want of popular support. Seriousness of the Second World War led the Federal Government to establish two more institutions— Public Works Administration and Civil

Aeronautic Authority. These institutions were affiliated to the Federal Government in order to compensate for devaluation and National Defence. National Defence Organisation helped in the training of the defence personnel and thus fulfilled its obligations successfully.

After the War, the Government was faced with the problem of employing the persons returning from the army. Therefore, in 1944, the Servicemen's Re-adjustment Act was passed in order to overcome unemployment and for providing vocational training. For this purpose, curriculum was re-adjusted to include vocational training and provision of financial help and also of scholarships was made for the successful execution of the Act. The arrangement was made to help the ex-servicemen and other persons returning from the army to a great extent in earning a living. In 1948, the Federal Government further extended their help to the institution in order that it may not face any deficit and may carry on its work successfully.

Educational Programme of the Federal Government for giving Encouragement

The Federal Government of U.S.A has been giving sufficient financial help and Land Grants to the State Governments. The educational programmes of the Federal Government may be classified under the following groups:—

1. *Help to the State Governments*: The Federal Governments gave help to the State Government in various forms, e.g., Loans, Percentage, Grant for educational expenditure, Grant-in-aid, Vocational Rehabilitation Grant, Forest Reserve and Mineral Royalty Grant. Similarly, Land Grants also take different forms, e.g. Agricultural and Technical Land Grants, Satine Grant, Section Grant and Swarup Land Grant. State Governments gave grant-in-aid to the schools according to their needs.

2. *Help to the Areas administered by the Federal Government*: The Federal Government helps in the expansion of education in the areas under its direct control by providing finances for its employees, State Governments and private educational institutions.

3. *Partial Help by the Federal Government*: The places within the boundaries of the U.S.A. and those which are under the control of the Federal Government receive partial or full help from the Federal Government.

4. *Help for Education of Red-Indians*: The Federal Government holds the entire responsibility of education of the Red-Indians.

5. *Responsibility for Training of its Employees*: The Federal Government holds the responsibility of training all those persons who are in the service of the Federal Government.

6. *Co-operation in Educational Programmes Abroad*: Federal Government encourages all those educational programmes which are sponsored by the joint efforts of the other countries of the World.

7. *Publication of the Educational Information of the States*: The Federal Government publishes and diffuses information regarding educational progress and activities in the States.

8. *Bringing Uniformity in the Education of Different States*: The Federal Government tries to bring uniformity in the education of all the States, but does not pressurize the States for it.

The Federal Government provides most of the financial help and grants to the States without any control and pre-conditions but for some grants it tries to see that the prescribed rules and conditions are fulfilled.

Education Office

The Federal Government was keen for the execution of its plans for educational organisation since the middle of the nineteenth century. It established the Central Department of Education in 1867. This Department of Education was named as Education Office in 1930. Henry Bernard was appointed as its first Education Commissioner. In the beginning the Education Office was meant to conduct the educational programmes of the Federal Government but during the Second World War, it was attached to the Federal Security Agency.

The President appoints the Chief of the Education Office,

known as Education Commissioner. The Education Commissioner is appointed for an indefinite period. The following were the functions of the Education Office in the beginning:—

(a) Functions pertaining to plans for educational reforms.

(b) Provision for the education of Negroes and Non-European communities.

(c) Provision of Education in Columbia city, Hawaii island, Alaska and other such places.

(d) Efforts for seeking inter-state co-operation and co-operation of the various departments of the Federal Government for providing educational facilities in different states.

Later on with the vocational and industrial progress, the Education Office also began to undertake vocational and industrial development programmes. Besides, its efforts for education development at the inter-state level, collection of the statistics of the educational progress in the states, its publication and propagation, necessary reforms in the educational system, additional training subjects, proper school organisation and the control of the Federal Government on them became the additional functions of the Education Office.

During the Second World War the Education Office had been attached to the Federal Security Agency. Consequently, it was assigned the task of Federal-Security education. The Education Office did a pioneer and praise-worthy work in that direction. Thus the office increased its importance in the War-time security efforts. The Federal Security education included the direction and control of all types of educational plans related to war, development and progress of industrial education, organisation of civil security force, conducting of National Youth Administration and provision of work for the unemployed and their vocational training. However, inspite of its sincerity of purpose, the Education Office could not achieve complete success in its efforts, because of the apathy and distrust of the State Governments. The State Governments were suspicious and afraid lest the Federal Government should gain complete control over them and thus they lose their independence. It was because of this suspicion that the Constitution of America and the various Amendments of the Constitution did not make any specific mention of the educational responsibilities. The public feeling that the Constitution has neither delegated educational powers to the Federal Government, nor with-held them from the State Governments led the public to think that those powers had been reserved for the State Governments and the public. As a result the State Governments began to establish direct contact with the various departments of the Federal Government without any information to the Federal Government. Thus the importance of the Education Office was minimised. Today the functions of the Education Office are very limited. The Education Commissioner supervises his office, prepares reports on the basis of statistics collected from the schools of different States and gives it wide publicity.

State Education Board

State Education Boards have been organised for educational planning and control. State Education Commissioner is the Chairman of the Board. State Education Department advises and helps the State Education Commissioner. There are County Boards under the State Department. These County Boards function at the District level. The Chairman of the County Board is known as Superintendent of Schools. The County Board supervises the work of Education Township, School Board and Local Board. In the beginning, the Constitution accorded the responsibility of organising education to the State Governments but for their convenience they delegated these powers to the Local Board. But the American people believe that the Local Boards are unable to fulfil the responsibility of educational reforms and development successfully. They also believe that the resources of the local boards are limited due to which educational plans cannot be completed successfully. Local influences make the schools individualistic. Consequently, State Education Boards frame general rules for schools, prepare educational programmes and control the institutions. State Boards, like the Central Governments of other countries, prescribe qualifications and lays down minimum standard of efficiency in the school activities without much interference.

Local School Board

Most of the immigrants from Europe were Catholics. They were very orthodox as far as their religious and social feelings were concerned. Therefore they established schools in their colonies according to their religious and social beliefs. These schools were controlled and managed by their religious leaders, priests and missionaries. School expenditure was also borne by them. With the passage of time and changing circumstances, the administration of these schools came under the control of the local boards. Even today these local boards administer the schools.

The members of the Local Boards are elected by the people. These members elect the administrative officer of the local school board. The administrative officer is known as the Superintendent of Local School. The term of the members and Superintendent is indefinite. But the Board does not consist of more than 9 members. Most of the administrative work is conducted by these Local School Boards. The number of these Boards in the whole country is about 201,000. These School Boards frame the school curriculum according to their social traditions and inclinations. State control on these schools is only with regard to standard of education and training in vocational subjects, otherwise they are entirely free in the selection of optional subjects, extra-curricular studies and religious subjects. In some schools the study of the Bible is compulsory, while in others its study is not permitted. Most of the schools in U.S.A. are in the hands of the Local School Boards. Only the centrally administered areas have schools controlled by the Federal Government. In Delavair State, the educational organisation is in the hands of the State Government. Due to strong patriotic feelings in U.S.A., the subjects related to patriotism and nationalism occupy an important place in the curriculum.

Democratic American System of Education

According to the leader of American freedom, late President Abraham Lincon, Democracy meant 'A Government of the people, for the people and by the people'. Democracy in U.S.A. has been established on this basis. They believe that the individual is not for the state, but the state is for the safety and welfare of the individual. There will be no dearth of able citizens in a democracy if people are mentally and culturally developed. It is, therefore, the duty of the state that it provide all possible educational and other facilities to its people in order to make them capable and worthy citizens. Every individual should get an opportunity of development according to his need, interest and aptitude without any distinctions of caste, colour or creed. This work can be done by the Government alone. All the social units in U.S.A. are free to develop this national feeling and for this there is no provision of any political or social system. National Education in America follows the following three traditions:—

i) English should be the medium of instruction.
ii) Educational literature should be universal.
iii) Education should conform to the national ideals.

Education in U.S.A. has been classified into different stages. The following are the four main stages of American education:-

a) Primary stage
b) Secondary stage
c) College or Higher Education
d) Vocational stage.

Institutions from Primary to College stage are administered by the Local School Boards on State responsibility. Vocational education is given after secondary and college stage. The public schools do not give vocational training. Vocational training institutions are quite separate from public schools and are conducted by the Federal and State Government. Besides general courses, facilities exist for industrial courses, vocational courses and professional specialization.

Public Schools administered by the Local School Boards are the pillars of American Educational system. These schools fulfilled the need of scientific and vocational education much more efficiently and successfully than the schools administered by the Federal Government. These schools have gained importance also because of their structural changes with the change in needs and ideals. This is the reason that these schools could provide necessary facilities and training as soon as a new system of education was introduced or the need for some new educational change was felt. These schools provide all possible facilities of training in commercial and professional subjects as well as in specialization.

The Fundamental Tendencies of American Education

Although, almost all states in U.S.A. have their own independent systems of education, yet there are certain similarities in their diverse systems. These similarities are considered as the Fundamental Tendencies of American Education. They are as follows:

(a) *Universal and Free Education*: Education in U.S.A. is classless, secular and free. Every child gets compulsory and free education without any distinction of religion, caste, colour or creed. Education is imbued with the feeling of nationalism and patriotism which makes the American citizen capable and patriotic.

(b) *Democratic Ideal Based Education*: American schools are governed by the Boards constituted by the elected members of the people. These schools are established by the people and for the people. Thus education there is democratic and presents the democratic ideal. People get equal opportunities. Education is the responsibility of the State Governments but the local units fulfil their obligations freely.

(c) *Single Ladder System*: All the states have similar stages of education. All the states have primary, secondary, and higher and vocational stages of education. Technical and vocational education is given after the secondary stage. Lower stages prepare students for higher stages.

(d) *Similar Financial Resources*: Most of the educational expenditure is borne by the people. State Governments and the Federal Government give grants-in-aid.

(e) *Dynamic Trends and Experimental Facilities*: Educationists base the educational system of a country on the ideals adored by the country. This is true of American educational system also. The facilities for various scientific inventions exist because of the thought and guidance of educationists propagated from time to time. This has made American education new and most modern. American education not only prepares the citizen for his own life but makes him capable of contributing to society as well.

SUMMARY

The people of U.S.A. are very sensitive about their individual beliefs and rights and so education could not be centralised. And there was no specification of educational powers for the States and the Federal Government. Till now education has been the responsibility of the State Governments which organise their educational systems through local units. The local units are given a free hand in their management.

Contribution of the Federal Government in Education: Although the Federal Government does not control education directly, but it influences the educational sphere by giving Land Grants and other financial aids through the various programmes of the Education Office. In 1920, the Federal Government transferred the Federal assistance to the patronage of the State Governments. They help the individual and collective institutions from time to time. During the depression period of the third decade of the current century they provided financial help to the States to overcome unemployment and also provided occupational facilities to the ex-servicemen of the army after World War II.

Encouragement Programmes of the Federal Government in Education: The Federal Government gives Land Grants and Grants-in-aid. It itself manages the education of Red Indians and the areas under Federal administration. Helps in the training of the Government servants and co-operates in educational projects abroad.

Education Office: Education office is the executive department for educational programmes. Its Chairman is the Education Commissioner. At present the work of the Education office is to prepare a report on the progress of the schools by collecting statistics from the States. Besides this, educational reforms, execution of national plans, vocational and technical education, organisation of education for non-European communities (Negroes and American Indians), provision of education in Columbia city, Alaska and other colonies and seeking co-operation of different departments for the States are the main functions of the Education Office.

Educational Administration of States: Excepting Delavair State, all the states have handed over educational organisation and administration to the local boards. States Governments look after the standards of education, curriculum and frame general rules of education, control on schools, fulfil educational plans and manage vocational and technical education. State Education Boards have been established for this purpose. The Chairman is known as State Education Commissioner. County Boards, Townships and Local Boards are under him.

Local Education Administration: Most of the schools in the States are organised by local Boards. They are independent and complete units from the administrative point of view. Central and State Governments have only a nominal control. The number of the local boards in America is about 201,000. Nine elected members constitute the Board. Its Chairman is Superintendent of Local Schools, elected by the members. He is the Chief administrative officer. These Boards are free to organise education according to the needs and in the interest of the people.

Democratic System of Education: The schools in America are responsible for providing equal opportunities of education to all without distinction of colour, caste or creed. The schools, as a complete unit, change with need of the time and place.

Fundamental Tendencies of American Education: The American system of education though different in different states is similar in some respects. These similarities are known as Fundamental Tendencies of American Education. They are: Universal and Free education, Democratic Ideal, Stage-wise system of education, Similarity of Financial Resources, Dynamic Trend and Experimental Facilities, etc.

Exercises

1. 'The Education in America is democratic.' How far do you agree with this view? Support your answer with examples.
2. 'The Federal Government of U.S.A without full control on educational organisation is not apathetic to its obligations'. Discuss.
3. 'Education Administration in U.S.A. is that of gradual development.' How? Explain.
4. Schools in U.S.A. prepare 'noble citizens', is it correct? If so, How?
5. 'American schools and educational organisations enjoy complete freedom. Government interference is limited.' Establish the truth of this statement.
6. Write short notes on the following in American Education
   (a) Education Office
   (b) State Education Board
   (c) Local Administration
   (d) Democratic tendency

Chapter 7

State Educational Administration

Educational freedom in U.S.A. is no less important than the political freedom. From the constitutional point of view the responsibility of education rests with the States. The States delegate their powers to the local administrative units. These administrative units conduct educational organisation according to the needs, interest and traditions of the people. The units enjoy complete freedom in their administration. The State exercises only as much control as is necessary and tries to maintain freedom of the people and the aims of educational programmes of the State, the responsibility of their execution always lies with the local administrative units. The States have their own independent systems of education. And naturally, different States have different systems of education.

The people in U.S.A. did not favour Federal control or education as well as uniform pattern of education. They were afraid that it might encroach upon their traditional rights and freedom. And in spite of all financial help and grants from the Federal Government, the responsibility of education remained with the State Governments. The State Governments feel satisfied by transferring educational administration and organisation to the local boards. Thus local boards, also known as Public Boards, are free to make educational provisions.

They establish institutions according to the needs, interest and traditions of the people. The State-governments however, exercise some control on their working, i.e. the State Board of Education has been established for the determination of educational policies, approval of budget, distribution of grants, and general supervision.

In U.S.A. schools were established in the colonies according to the needs and traditions of European immigrants. Changes in the organisation of schools and their curriculum were brought about according to American atmospheres, mutual contact of different European communities and with increase in population. Local Boards which organised education according to social needs, interests and traditions freely, were established for managing the schools. Federal Government and State Governments looked after these schools only under special circumstances. Connections with Federal Government were only on moral grounds as a member state of the federation. The Federal Government and the State Governments provided all possible help to the Local Boards for running independent schools freely. Thus the Local Boards got legal approval for the development of an independent spirit.

There could be no doubt that the local boards carried out educational development plans according to the changing social and political atmosphere but they had very limited resources which obstructed their plans of development. On request, the State Governments gave financial help on the condition that the Local Boards shall maintain a minimum standard of education prescribed by the Government.

When the Federal and State Governments began to give financial assistance to the Local Boards and other local institutions, they became active in fulfilling their financial obligations. The grants were given in proportion to the collections of the Local Boards and schools. This improved the situation making local institutions self-sufficient, but along with it, the control of State Governments on them increased.

During the third decade of the nineteenth century (1820 to 1830), there was an important educational change. At that time, the number of European immigrants was on the increase. As a result, the number of children seeking admission in schools went up so much that the schools with their limited resources were unable to meet the situation. Besides, the difficulty of transport facilities from home to school for the children, forced the public to demand educational facilities from the State Government. They considered it as their right and the responsibility of the State Governments. The State had begun to give help on the condition that the school should maintain a minimum standard of education. Thus, a good number of schools and institutions came under the control of State Governments. The control benefited the Local Boards to the extent that they got legal approval in the bargain.

The historical development of education in U.S.A. clearly proves that education is the responsibility of State Governments. State Government is the largest unit for education. For the first time in 1784, Rezents Board was established at State level for the purpose of presenting educational policy and framing rules. But it did not make significant contribution alone. In 1812 the first Superintendent of Education was appointed in New York. His work was to distribute the grant given by the State Government to the schools and local institutions. Afterwards, within some years, Superintendents of Education were appointed in the States of Massachussets and Connecticut. Secretary of Education Horrace Man and Henry Bernard did much work for the expansion of education in these States. They brought about public awakening in the field of education through the publication of articles and journals.

The good results of the above efforts led to the establishment of units of educational control and by 1850 Education Control Offices were established both in Northern and Southern States. Superintendents of Education were appointed in all the States. The constitutional struggle helped the State Governments in getting the right of control on schools and educational institutions. In 1890 for the first time, the Superintendent of Education in Indiana State was given the right of selecting good books for school curriculum. In 1897, the judgment of New York High Court confined the right of establishing schools on the Superintendent of Education also.

State Education Administration

Chief Education Administrative Officer— Education Commissioner:

State Boards of Education have been established to control educational institutions. The head of the Board is known as Chief State School Officer. He is also known as State Commissioner of Education or State Commissioner of Public Instruction. The procedure of appointing this officer is not the same in all the States. In eight States, he is nominated by the Governor. In eight other States, he is elected by the members of the State Board of Education and in the rest of the States he is elected by the people. Fifty per cent of the States have laid down minimum qualification for the post, one-third of the States have no minimum qualifications for him and in the rest of the States the qualification is determined by the Election Laws of the States. In 13 States, it is 2 years, 25 States have 4 years terms and in 5 States it is from 1 year to 6 years and rest of the States have no definite period. In most of the States the State School Officer functions as the executive officer.

State Department of Education

For the help and discharge of responsibilities of the State School Officer, there is a State Department of Education. Education experts and professional employees are included as members of the State Department. The number of these members is not the same in all the States. According to the statistics of 1948, their maximum number was 506 in New York and minimum 12 in the South Dakota. In addition, there are clerks whose number depends on the size of the Department. The members are mainly connected with their sub-divisions and, therefore, they are called Divisional Officers. Divisional Offices work under the Department of Education.

The number of sub-divisions is not definite. They are organised on the basis of need and structure of the State.

State Board of Education

State Board is the highest institution of Education in the State. It is found in every State except in Nebraska, Mann, Illinois, Ohio, Rhode Island, Iowa, Wisconsin and Southern Dakota. In addition to the State Board, there is a Board of vocational education for carrying out the vocational programmes of the Federal Government. In eight States, Board of vocational education also functions as State Board of Education. In New York, State Board of Education is known as Rezents Board. The number of members on the State Board of Education is not definite. In most of the States their number is 7 and in rest of the States, it is from 3 to 12. In New York, these members are elected by Legislative members. In about 35 States, they are nominated by the Governor, in 8 States they are ex-officio and in 4 States, they are elected by popular vote. In some States, people from the education profession are nominated as members of the Board. But most of the States have members elected by the people.

The Chief Education Officer is concerned with the State Board of Education. But this relationship is different in different States. In 27 States, he is the member of the State Board, in 30 States, he is the Administrative Officer, in 13 states he is the Secretary of the Board or Administrative Officer, and in 20 States he is member and Secretary and in 10 others he is the member and Chairman of the State Board of Education.

Duties of the Education Commissioner

The Chairman of the State Board of Education is called Education Commissioner. He is the Chief Officer for the development and expansion of education. His duties are as follows:

1. To distribute grants according to the need of the schools and institutions.

2. To collect educational statistics.
3. General supervision of the schools.
4. To prescribe minimum standard of education for schools.
5. To frame general rules for the local schools.
6. To prepare curriculum for the prescribed minimum standard.
7. To prescribe curriculum for the Teachers Training Schools and award Training Certificate.
8. To preserve the educational rights of the minorities by controlling and making the schools public.
9. In some States, he selects text-books for different levels.
10. To preside over the State Board and to prepare budget.
11. To supervise State Education Offices and look after the appointment and establishment of the supervision authorities.
12 To issue instructions to different administrative bodies, viz. Country Board, Township and School Districts and advise them for reforms of educational provisions.
13. To make efforts for uniformity and unity of the State educational institutions.
14. He contacts the Federal Education Commissioner for making education international. He also participates in the Education Conferences organised by the Federal and State Governments.

Appointment, Qualifications and Terms of the Education Commissioner

There are no prescribed rules for the appointment, qualifications and term of the Education Commissioner. States decide regarding the appointment, term and qualifications according to their traditions. Generally he is elected by the Hon'ble citizens of the State. In some States he is nominated by the State Board of Education or the Governor. In some States, the qualification is a graduate degree, some prefer a post-graduate (M.A.) degree and still others prefer an experienced person along with degree or post-graduate qualifications. As for the term, a period of 2 years, 4 years and 6 years is prevalent.

Appointment, Qualifications and Term of Members

Members are elected by the prominent persons of the State. But it is not a rule in every State. In some States, they are nominated by the Governor, in some they are both elected and nominated while in some others they are ex-officio-members. Ex-officio members are Governors, Ministers and Legislators. In some States, the number of representatives both nominated or elected is fixed for the political parties, geographical and social units and the members are appointed on the basis of that fixed number. There is no national law for qualifications. Their term is also akin to that of the Education Commissioner. Education Commissioner is the Chief Administrative Officer of the State Board of Education.

Educational Responsibility of the State

The State Government fulfils it educational responsibility through State Board of Education, Education Commissioner and Department of Education. The Department of Education makes provision of education from nursery to adult stage and provides educational facilities to the common man and the rich man alike. The Department of Education is authorised to seek the co-operation of the public for the development and expansion of education through private, Government and other allied agencies.

In U.S.A. there is no uniform pattern of education. Only the State is responsible for education. Some States exercise control on education and in some there is no interference in the work of local institutions and public board. Educational Constitution is clear in some States while in others it is not, so the schools in the States are influenced by the local social climate. In general, the educational policy of States is in accordance with the educational policy of public boards or feelings of the public representatives.

Similarities in Different Systems of Education

As a result of the independent system of education in the States, there is dis-similarity in the systems but certain provisions of the system are common. Freedom, affluency, abundance of vocational training, individual and collective development and progress are the commonly recognised feelings. All the States have the following common elements in education:—

1. *Universal, Free and Compulsory Education* : Schools run by Government and local boards give free and compulsory education. Education is compulsory for the children of a prescribed age-limit. Educational facilities are available to the people without any distinctions of colour, class or creed.

2. *Determination of an Ideal Standard of Education*: The State Governments have transferred their educational obligations to the local boards. But they force the Local Educational Boards to maintain a minimum standard of education. If there is a fall in the standard, their educational rights are withdrawn from them. One of the main conditions of granting financial help is that the schools should maintain the prescribed standard of education.

3. *Inter-State Uniformity*: Every State tries to bring uniformity in the organisation of educational institutions. For this uniformity, a minimum curriculum is prescribed.

4. *Compulsion of General Rules*: The State Governments have tried to bring uniformity in the schools of the State by prescribing some general rules. These rules are related to admissions, school-leaving, age-limit, provision of free education, age and qualifications of teachers and a minimum syllabus.

5. *Centralisation of Education*: The State allows the local institutions and board to utilise the educational rights but with-holds certain specific administrative rights. Local units included in the Department of Education exercise full control over County Boards, Townships, School Districts and other local educational institutions.

Summary

According to the American constitution, the responsibility of education is that of the States. The State delegate their powers to the local boards. These boards are free to conduct education according to the need and atmosphere of the society. But the State Governments have their control on these local boards for specific administrative purposes. The people get universal, compulsory and free education and higher education for internationalism. The educational activities of the State are directed by the State Board of Education, Department of Education and its Chairman, the Education Commissioner.

State Board of Education and Duties of the Education Commissioner: State Boards are established on the basis of various traditions. The number of its members, their qualifications and terms are not definite. Education Commissioner is the Chief Administrative Officer. His duties are to distribute Government grants, to prescribe and maintain standard of education, to collect educational statistics, to prepare a minimum syllabus, to prescribe qualifications of teachers, to provide for teacher training and award them certificates, to formulate general rules and educational policy, to safeguard the educational rights of minorities, to make education universal, free and compulsory, to establish Government schools, selection of text books and preparation of curriculum, to manage State Board and Department of Education, to prepare budget and to make efforts to bring uniformity in education. For these duties, he is advised by the State Board of Education. Country Boards, Townships and School Districts control schools.

The Appointment of Education Commissioner and State Board: In some States the members are elected by the people and in some, they are nominated by the Governor. The qualifications and term of the members and Education Commissioner are not definite and similar in all the States. The term is from 2 to 6 years. The Education Commissioner and State Boards have a close relationship. He is a member of the Board in some States; Chairman, Secretary or Chief Officer in some other States.

Assistant Commissioners, Directors, Inspectors and clerks help the Education Commissioner in controlling and distributing Government grants. The Department of Education enforces the general policy of education and conditions of grant-in-aid. It is divided into Divisions and Sub-divisions. The Chairman of Country Boards are Superintendents of Education.

EXERCISES

1. How did the State obtain educational rights in U.S.A.? How did the present administrative structure emerge? Classify with examples

2. Who is the Chief Education Officer in the State? What are the duties of State, the Commissioner of Education?
3. Although the Federal Government has not declared any National Policy of Education, yet the education systems in the States are similar in many respects. Explain this statement.
4. How is educational administration conducted in U.S.A.? What is the relationship between the education administrator, Department of Education and State Board of Education? Explain.
5. Explain the organisation and duties of :–
   (a) State Department of Education.
   (b) State Board of Education.

Chapter 8

Administration and Organisation of Local Schools

U.S.A. has a democratic system of education. Hence it has become customary for the people to fulfil their obligations freely. In U.S.A., in every sphere of life, the citizen thinks of doing his work freely and dutifully. This is also true of the educational sphere. The Federal Government and the State Governments have transferred their responsibility to the local boards and public institutions in order that they may perform their functions according to the interest, need, capacity and traditions of the people. Thus the democratic traditions encourage the local boards to function independently. And, therefore, education is organised by local boards for obtaining desired development in the field of education.

In every State in America, local administrative unit of one type or the other may be found. Except Delaware State where educational administration is in the hands of the State Government, all the States have local administrative units. Twelve Southern States have County Boards for the control and organisation of education. In 9 States, like New England, State Township or town people control public schools. School Districts are found in Western and Mid-West States. Some States have been divided into County Boards and Local Boards both. In rest of the States, education is organised and controlled by Local Boards. The nature of Local administration of education is wholly influenced by geographical conditions, culture, civilization and local atmosphere. And, therefore, the local administrative units are not similar in every state in U.S.A.

The administrative units of densely populated States are not bigger than the units of thinly populated States. So, these units in Southern States are big. In the beginning, population increased in towns and schools were established there. These schools were administered by town administrative units. These units organised education in the nearby areas also. But no sooner did the people begin to settle in rural areas, they established One-Room Schools which were complete and independent units in themselves. The number of students in these schools was only from 10 to 49—far less than the numbers in Town schools. Only one teacher taught all the subjects at different levels. But with the development of means of transport and communication, education expanded in rural areas. One room-schools were united to make bigger schools and the administrative units of the bigger schools were expanded. One room school in isolated areas were consolidated.

Local Education Board

Educational organisation in U.S.A. is in the hands of local Education Boards which manage the schools on the basis of social and group interests, traditions, needs and ideals of the people. They operate independently inspite of the control of the States on them. The local Education Board have different names in different states, i.e., Board of Trustee, The Education Board, The School Board, The School Committee, The County or County Board of Education, Town or Township Board of Education. These Boards are organised by electing the members in a very democratic manner. Inspite of different names, these administrative units are very much similar from the administrative point of view.

The number of local boards is more than 201,000. They are of four types—Basic, Intermediate, Coterminous and Non-

Coterminous. We cannot assign definite groups to these forms; the classification is based on their characteristic features. 'Basic' administrative units are influenced by the local people and even to-day they are working on the same lines. 'Intermediate' units have both local and Government influence. 'Coterminous' units have only the Government influence. 'Coterminous' unit have only the Government influence and 'Non-Coterminous' units are under neither local nor Governmental influence. They are entirely independent.

Functions of Local Education Board

Superintendent of Education is the administrative officer of the Local Board. The function of the Board is neither executive or administrative but it is simply Legilative. The Education Board formulates education policy, examines the progress of the students and evaluates their work. In fact, the main function of the Board is to coordinate the facilities and needs of teachers, local population, classes and groups according to the interest, needs and traditions of the place and at the same time to preserve its freedom while achieving national goals and following State directions. From time to time Local Boards organise conferences to which Educationists and honourable citizens are invited. Members of the School Boards are also invited and are consulted on educational projects proposed by the State and on State Educational Policy. Thus the views of the local people are also ascertained. The Local Boards execute those programmes that are accepted by the State Boards of Education after the consent of the members participating in the conferences. Members of the Local Boards thus formulate educational policies and programmes. The members are the recognized representatives of the people.

Seclection of Members, their Qualification and Term

Local Boards are constituted by member selected in various ways. In some States they are selected on the basis of popular votes and in other States, they are selected by local Administrative Boards, not connected with education. In States where the State Government conducts the educational affairs they are nominated by the Education Commissioner of the County Board. In some States the members of the Local Boards are nominated by the members of the Municipal Boards or the Executive Committees of Corporations or the Chairman of the Municipal Boards or the Mayor.

The number of members is determined according to the dimension of educational area but it is not definite in any State. However, the number does not exceed 9. Their term also is not definite. Mostly it is from five to seven years. While nominating or electing the members, care is taken to see that the representation of any particular political party or group or social institution is not overwhelming.

There is no prescribed qualification for the members of Local Education Boards. Any person who is a citizen of the State, lives within the jurisdiction of the State and has public support, may be elected as member of the Board. But from the point of view of an ideal selection, it is seen that only a person who is educated, interested in educational programmes, is one of the guardians of students, anxious for social and educational development, a man of good character, capable of participating in public welfare work, able to give original ideas on education development and pays tax to the Government, is elected to the Board as a member.

Local School Superintendent

Duties of the Superintendent:

The Administrative Officer of the Local Education Board is Local School Superintendent. It is a very important post. If the Superintendent is a public relations officer as well, he can perform his duties successfully because he has to keep contact with teachers, students, local administrators, local social and political groups, and other educational boards. The Superintendent sees to the implementation of educational programmes, education policies and rules directed by the State. His duties may be summarised as follows:

1. He contacts State Education Board, Department of Education, education officers, and public social associations, political parties, schools, administrators, teachers, students and citizens, for educational development.
2. He gets the prescribed educational policy, rules and education programmes, implemented.
3. He supervises the administration, buildings, needs and progress of the schools. He controls the entire educational activities of the school.
4. He informs the State regarding social tendencies, traditions, needs, interest and ideals of the local people.
5. He collects statistics of educational progress for his evaluation.
6. He secures full public co-operation and assures the people that educational system is being organised according to their needs.

Selection of the Superintendent, Qualifications and Term:

The schools are established by the local public to educate their children in order that they become able citizens of the country. Thus life pattern of future citizens depends on the dedication, capability and ability of the Superintendent. Therefore, a person of impressive personality, capable of fulfilling his obligations is selected as a Superintendent. Hence it is customary for the State to select to the post of Superintendent a person who is an educationist, studious, effieient, devoted, experienced in teaching and supervision, capable of establishing public relations, post graduate of a University, man of character, able administrator and a good orator.

Regarding the term, there is no fixed national or state policy. The term depends on the efficiency, temperament, devotedness and public contacts of the Superintendent.

The Other Units of Educational Administration

The educational responsibility of most of the States is

carried out by the Local Education Boards. But in some States there are other adminstrative units instead of Education Boards. These units adopt different forms according to the size, area, population, name and functions. Some of the main units are as under :—

County (Rural) Board System:

These Boards are mainly found in villages and are not connected with Town administration. They are wider and more developed than the Local Education Boards. Of all the educational organisations, they are the most successful, capable and systematic. Their number is more than three thousand and found in Georgia, Tennessee, Kentucky and Virginia States.

The administarator of the Country Board is known as County Superintendent of Education and is selected by the Board itself. These Boards try to conduct a more efficient, developing and useful system of education than the Town Educational System. The organisation and development of rural education depends on the efficiency and devotedness of the County Superintendent. The duties of the Superintendent are to control schools, to provide educational facilities to them, to construct an appropriate curriculum, selection of teachers, to prepare rural education programmes, development of rural education, implementation of educational projects, etc.

County Boards have emphasised the consolidation and centralisation of education in rural areas. One-room-schools have been united to make bigger schools. Changes have been brought about in the construction of one-room schools. County Boards have established small units called School Districts under their control. The County Board has one major drawback and that is, its members are elected by the people. Political parties participate in the elections and therefore, these Boards are generally dominated by political parties. As a result, many useful educational projects and programmes are not accepted. The public is well aware of this drawback and they are now trying to replace political people by educationists. It is hoped that this change will make the County Boards more successful and efficient administrative units.

Township or Town System:

Township is the administrative unit of small cities and towns. It is an independent, educational administrative unit. Its scope depends on the size of the town or city. In some places, Townships look after the administration of adjoining rural areas. New-Jersey, Pensilvania, Iowa, Michigan, Illinois and Indiana States haveTownship systems. In New England, there is a Town system. Township and Towns are quite progressive as the towns are densly populated and hence there is no shortage of students. The people of towns are more educated and progressive than the people of rural areas hence, Township or Town systems are able to get educated leaders. Educational atomosphere and large population make it convenient to implement modern educational projects and establish well-equipped schools.

Town Educational Boards, also known as Education Committees, are established for educational organisation of the town. The people elect the members of the Education Board and these members select Township School Superintendent or Township School Principal.

School District System:

School District is considered to be the oldest and smallest educational administrative unit. School Districts have those one-room-schools, where one teacher teaches all the subjects at different levels. In some places, these School-Districts are so small that the children of only a few families receive education in them—their number not exceeding 8 or 10. With the development of education, these School Districts have become a part of Education Boards or Local Education Boards. Even then their number is about 1,00,000. American people consider this system incomplete and unsatisfactory for these institutions suffer from communalism and isolation and therefore, only a few families take advantage of these schools.

Poor people do not get any advantage. Moreover, projects of educational development or general reformative schemes cannot be implemented in these schools. The American people are in favour of converting these small units into bigger units so that there are chances of desirable reforms in this direction.

School Districts have their schools managed by District Education Board which are quite independent. They hold supremacy in policy decisions, educational programmes, prescribing qualifications for teachers, their selection and pay scales, reforms in school buildings and all other financial matters concerning their schools.

When European Colonies were establised in America, the immigrants had to face a very complex and troublesome atmosphere. They established one-room schools in their small colonies in order that their children might not go very far for receiving education. These schools were established according to the need of the colony. So, these schools were multi-purpose and economical. This advantage led to the expansion of one-room schools. Later on, School Districts were established for managing them. The number of these institution is maximum in New England because this type of system first originated in this state.

City School Organisation:

In the field of education, a city is that area were 25 to 30 thousand people live. But the Federal Government has accepted all those areas as Urban where the population is more than 2,500. This system is quite separate from Township system. Except those States which have Township system, the big cities of other States have City School Organisation.

The City School Organisation is more developed than the educational system of rural areas, as the people in the cities are more educated. The result is that for conducting the educational system, educated citizens, educationists, leaders and workers with progressive ideas are easily available. Multi-roomed schools are established to give education to a sufficient number of students who were available as a result of the large population. In these schools new, scientific and modern educational projects can be easily implemented because of the availability of all educational facilities. Transport facilities also make this organisation more progressive.

Educational Administrative Unit:

City educational organisation is conducted by City Education Board. In some places, the Chairman of this Board is Superintendent of City Education. In some places, the Superintendent and the City Board work separately while they work jointly and as associates in still other places. There are different traditions in different places for the selection of Superintendent and the members of the City Education Board. In cities, where the population is more than 30 thousand, the members are elected by voting. In some cities, they are nominated by the Mayor of the City, City Council and Legislature members. The Superintendent of City Education is elected by members of the City Education Board.

Organisation of the City Schools:

City Board designs programmes for educational projects for all the schools within its jurisdiction. These programmes and projects are executed by the Education Superintendent and his associates and other educational officials of the city. Assistant Superintendent, Headmasters and teachers are the associates of the Superintendent.

City Education Board is entirely responsible for the teaching process. The experts of Health, Medicine and Physical Education and Psychology form the second category of officials who manage the teaching of these subjects under the supervision of the Education Superintendent. The Superintendent of City Education is the representative of the City Board. The number of officials under the Superintendent and the Board depends on the area and population of the city.

The Superintendent of City Education:

The Superintendent does not belong to any speical class. Any person belonging to any community, class, group and religion or place may be a candidate for the post but he should have completed a 4 years degree course from a university, or should have obtained a Master's Degree. In other places the qualifications are quite different. His term has been found to be from 1 year to 21 years depanding on his efficiency, capacity and dedication. The economic status of the Superintendent is sufficiently high in places where he undertakes important and responsible work. His annual salary may be from 3 thousand dollars to 14 thousand dollars.

The City Education Superintendent is wholly responsible for the educational organisation of the city. He appoints the officials and workers of his department of his associate officials appoint them on his behalf. He implements the educational policy, rules and projects prescribed by the Federal and State Government and contacts the members of the Board departmental officials and other workers for the execution of the policies and projects. He also formulates educational rules, educational policy and programmes for educational organisation. He gives his consent for curriculum and text-books. His duties include management and supervision of schools, improvement of school buildings, their sale and construction, provision for the health and medical care, gymnastics, games and sports and attendance. He is also authorised to transfer officials, servants and teachers, punish or dismiss staff and fix their salaries.

City Education Board:

In places where there is a provision for the City Education Superintendent and City Board both, the Superintendent and the Board act as a legislature. The Superintendent is the Chairman or Administrator of the Board. The Board is not obliged to accept the proposals or recommendations of the Superintendent. Generally, the City Education Board formulates education policy and the Superintendent implements it as in the case of the State Education Board. In places where only Education Boards exist, the duties of the Superintendent are performed by the Board.

The number of the members of the City Board depends on the size and area of the city. Their minimum number is 3 and maximum 21. In cities where the populaiton is about 1,00,000, the number of members is 7 or 8. The term of the members is usually 2 to 4 years, but their term is 7 years in cities where the population is large. There is no prescribed qualification for the members of the Board, however, people elect able and learned members.

Summary

In America, the educational organisation has been left to the eaucation Boards in order to give freedom to the people for doing their work on democratic basis. Except Delawair State, all the States have independent administrative units which, influenced by the local atmosphere, depend on local population. But their organisation is sufficiently similar.

Local Education Board: The people elect the members of the Board, some are nominated. These Boards are more than 150000. The members of the Board select the local school Superintendent. The term of the members is 5 to 7 years. No qualification is prescribed. Its functions are to design educational policy, programmes and projects, to implement the State or Federal educational policy, to know the local needs and traditions through the members of the Board, administration and control of education, to seek the co-operation of various departments for obtaining educational facilities and to establish public contact.

Local School Superintendent: The main duty of the Superintendent is to implement the rules, programmes and projects proposed by the Education Board. He is the Chief Administrative Officer of the Board. There is no prescribed minimum qualification for him. An able person is selected.

Other Educational Administrative Units:

County (Rural) Board System: It is one of the successful systems in the educational sphere. It is found in Georgia, Tennessee, Virginia and Kentucky States. The educational system and administration is in the hands of County Board and the Superintendent.

Township System: The system is prevalent in New Jersey, Pensylvenia, Iowa, Illinois and Indiana States.

It is one of the oldest and smallest systems. This system is for the organsiation and administration of education in rural areas. One room-schools are found in these areas. The system exists mostly in New England where it originated.

City Education System: This system is found in cities where the population is more than 25 to 30 thousand. It is one of the most successful and progressive educational systems.

Education Administrative Unit: City Education Boards and City Education Superintendent are the administrative units of the city educational organisation.

Organisation of City Schools: City Education Boards and City Education Superintendent and their officials are responsible for educational organisation and administration.

City Education Superintendent: His qualification is not prescribed but he should be a graduate or post-gratuate. His term is from 1 to 21 years. He is responsible for all educational organisation and administrative work.

City Education Board: Its work is legislative. It is the highest unit. Its organisation depends on the population and extent of the town. The term of the members is from 3 to 21 years. Qualifications are not prescribed. Its work is carried on with the co-opertion of the Education Superintendent.

Exercises

1. In U.S.A., the Educational Organisation of the States is based on independent systems which make them different but even then the inherent educational aims are quite similar. How?
2. How is the 'City Educational System' different from 'County Board System'? Explain the City Education System.
3. 'The American democrative educational system is expressed through Local Education System'. How? Give examples.
4. Explain the organisation of the following and explain how they contribute to the American Education System:—
   (a) Local Education Board
   (b) Township
   (c) School District
   (d) County Board.

Chapter 9

Pre-Primary Education

The first six or seven years of the child's life play a significant role in the development of his personality. Hence, primary education starts from a certain age in all the countries. In England the tradition is to start regular education at the age of 5, in U.S.A., France, Germany and Italy at the age of 6 and in Russia at the age of 8. The inclinations acquired during the first six or seven years develop and take a stable form to the extent that it becomes the nature of the child in due course.

The child begins to inherit traits as soon as he is conceived in the mother's womb and begins to learn something or the other from his environment soon after his birth. Though this learning process is informal, yet due to his traits, he begins to express that behaviour in the process of learning according to his aptitude. Hence there has been an attempt to educate the infant even before the age of 6 or 7 years. This educational system is called 'Infant Education' or 'Pre-Primary Education'. Froebel had stressed the importance of infant education. In the latter years of the eighteenth Century (1709), Jean Oberlin had established infant schools in France at first. Robert Owen of Scotland started an infant school at Lanark. Froebel's views on child education had a great influence on all the neighbouring countries of Europe and infant schools were established at several place in Europe. Different countries tried different experiments in this direction. Germany evolved a new method of infant education. School based on this method was called 'Kindergarten'. In England, too, such infant schools were established. Nursery schools were opened in London and Manchester. In U.S.A., the first kindergarten school was opened in 1856 in Wisconsin state.

In U.S.A. nursery education is supposed to have started in the early part of the twentieth Century. In 1919 it was in New York that the first nursery school was established. The people of U.S.A. did not encourage nursery education because some people were not in favour of putting the burden of education on the immature minds of children at such a young age. In 1920 some arrangement for infant education was made in Teachers College of Columbia University. But due to the depression in U.S.A. from 1920 to 1930, the Kindergarten school plan and the nursery school plan remained in abeyance. But soon after this crisis was over, the Federal Government gave sufficient financial assistance to these plans according to the New Deal Act. Consequently, from 1930 to 1940 the enrolment in nursery schools rose upto 3,00,000 and the enrolment in Kindergarten schools went upto 6,75,000. In this way, in the fourth decade of the current century infant education progressed much faster. The fast industrial development there also accounted for the quick growth of infant education. The establishment of these schools proved beneficial to those mothers who were employed in industries. They were much relieved to leave their children in these infant schools during work hours. A healthy attitude in the direction of their personality development could also be created along with child care. This was the reason why nursery schools were established in large numbers in prominent towns and industrial centres only.

Pre-Primary Education System

The educational system of pre-primary stage may be divided in three groups according to age of the child.

I. Group Education from conception to the age of two years.

II. Group Education from 2 years to 3 years of age.

III. Group Education from 3 years to 5 or 6 years of age.

Knowledge of Parents about Infant Education and Infant-home Education :—

Before the birth of the would-be child, parents create proper environment and conditions for his life. The fetal stage is a very important time for the development of traits of an infant. At this time ignorant parents upset the trait formation of the would be infant and thus good traits are not formed during fetal stage. Hence parents should be conscious of their responsibilites for the formation of good traits. By mere education, without the knowledge of psychology of the pre-natal period, it is not possible to fulfil this responsibility successfully. In order that the parents may be acquainted with the prenatal psychology and may get the necessary guidance for creating suitable environment, training schools and guidance centres for would-be parents are necessary. The first year after the birth of a child, is considered to be very important from the point of view of his nutrition. At this time parents should be conscious, right-minded, dutiful and acquainted with psychological principles concerning infant care. Though the number of centres for providing training and guidance to parents for creating proper environment for would be children is insufficient, even then there are many guidance centres, clinics and research centres under the Education and Health departments which are giving proper training and guidance to parents regarding their duty for creating proper environment for their would-be children. But only one particular section is taking advantage of these institutions and not the entire public. Some local institutions are providing proper guidance and psychological knowledge to local people, but this knowledge should be made available to the masses.

Nursery Education

People in America are generally very busy. Parents are not in a position to look after their children due to pressure of work and lack of time. Hence they feel the necessity of turning to some responsible person or institution under whose protection they may leave their children and thus devote themselves to their work whole-heartedly, without any worry regarding their children; and their children may also gain efficiency in fulfilling their daily needs. It is expected that the child should develop co-operative tendencies one year after his birth, when he begins to sit and walk. At this age the child wants to play, eat and live with children of his age. He also tries to fulfil his natural needs such as eating, going to toilet, bathing, cleaning of teeth and dressing. The small child cannot discharge these function efficiently. In the beginning he depends upon his parents to help him with these functions. So the people in U.S.A. want the establishment of some such institutions which may provide their children necessary practical training in the discharge of these functions. Consequently in U.S.A. nursery schools, child education centres and kindergarten schools have been established by State and public for the education and care of children. Leaving their wards in those institutions for the whole day, parents attend to their work without any worry. In their absence children learn practical things like eating, playing and fulfilling their natual needs at the proper time and get practical education through games and recreation.

There is no definite age for admission to nursery schools. In some schools it is two or three years and in others it is four years. There are schools which admit children with the intention of providing protection to children because their parents cannot go out to work if they keep their children at home. In this way, the age limit for admission to nursery schools and nursery centres is from 1 year to 4 years. There are about 4000 various types of nursery schools. These are still run by private agencies and have not come under the public sector. These schools could be established only in big cities and in industrial centres though every common family needs them.

In U.S.A. there are three types of nursery schools (i) Schools run by religious organisations (ii) Schools run by private agencies (iii) Schools run by local bodies or State Governments or Federal Government. But the number of all such nursery schools is insufficient. In order to remove this shortage, local public has established Infant Education Schools at different places. These schools are known as Cooperative nursery schools.

Cooperative Nursery Schools

Americans are so busy that they do not get time to look after their children properly. Hence some families co-operatively established such schools where their children could get a homely atmosphere. These schools, by trying to make children eager to learn thing and by arousing in them a desire for right conduct, attempt to develop their personality. These schools impart education through the medium of collective programmes, functions, games and recreation. The study of environment outside the school is done through tours and excursions. Children are given opportunities to visit local places of importance, playgrounds, museums, big buildings and big projects and organisations.

These schools are run by the co-operative efforts of families. Parents give financial assistance to these schools in the form of subscriptions. All the parents co-operate in the programmes of the schools in order to encourage their children and to know their interest and capabilities. The management of these schools, fixation of programmes, curriculum construction, selection of books, selection of teachers and such other duties are discharged by a Committee selected by the concerned public. Fathers of children utilize their leisure time in decorating the class rooms and maintaining the play grounds and school garden. Mothers co-operate with teachers in making arrangement for breakfast, in dressing up the children and in their education, games and recreation. Parents propose useful programmes for the schools from time to time. Every month parents visit the school in order to know the progress of their wards and to acquaint themselves with future programmes. Sometimes parents take part in functions and collective programmes organised by the schools. In this way parents get knowledge of infant education and feel satisfied. It is in this way that these schools, taking the help of Adult Education Department, contribute much to the development of adult education.

Kindergarten Education

In U.S.A. just as the nusery schools educate children, so also the Kindergarten schools impart education to children. But the difference is that the kindergarten education is considered to be post-nursery education. The period of kindergarten education is form three to six years of age. In some schools children below three years are also admitted. Kindergartens have two main objectives :—

(i) To follow the pattern of nursery education for developing natural abilities of children and to arouse the curiosity of children towards education.

(ii) To provide subject-wise education to children and to prepare them for primary education.

As the first objective, group feeling and spirit of co-operation are inculcated in these schools through games and recreation. The facilities for working, living and playing collectively make them capable of living co-operatively as well as improve their health and create a tendency for self-help. These activities also create self-dependence, interest and curiosity for knowledge. The second objective is to lay the foundation for primary education. Hence programmes are chalked out for the mental, physical, social and cultural development of children according to their needs. They are prepared for primary classes by imparting knowledge of common words and numbers. In U.S.A., kindergarten schools were established as a result of industrial development. Due to industrial and materialistic tendency the life of people became very busy. People became consicious of the future of their children and thus started these public institutions for the education and protection of their children. This system of education is very popular, though it is not compulsory.

The efforts to establish kindergarten schools started in the nineteenth century. But their sufficient development took place in the twentieth century. By the beginning of the current century hundreds of such voluntary associations had been formed which established private Kindergarten schools. Now, for the establishment of public Kindergartens, State Governments give sufficient grants in addition to financial assistance by the public. Generally, the educational level of Kindergarten schools has been accepted as the first primary unit. The State Governments issue necessary instructions to these public Kindergartens. Officers and experts of Education Department inspect these schools in order to maintain the educational level set for them and motivate the teachers to maintain proper standards. Sometimes a special teacher is appointed who in addition to doing supervision of these schools, gives approval to matters pertaining to the programmes of the schools. In 1997 there have been about 30,90,000 students getting education in these private Infant Schools. In the establishment of such schools, private efforts are quite praiseworthy.

American Infant Schools are financed by local funds. State Governments also give additional grants. Local Boards are authorised to make arrangement for pre-primary education and to work for its expansion according to local needs. Legislative facilities by the State Governments are also available for the establishment and protection of Kindergarten schools. Inspite of all this, there is still a great demand for their expansion and development.

Summary

In U.S.A., the development of pre-primary education is the result of the vocational tendency and busy life of people there. Parents are unable to keep their children with them during their hours of work. Hence there was a need for such schools which might give young childern protection and an educational enviroment. That is why the following types of schools were established for the education of pre-primary stage.

Knowledge of Parents about Infant Education and Infant-home Education: If parents are not familiar with child psychology, they are unable to bring up their children according to their needs. In order to meet this need research and guidance centres have been established under the health department of the States. Clinics also meet this need. Other private organisations also provide knowledge of child psychology to parents. Inspite of all this, there is a great need of their expansion.

Nursery Education: Among the childern of 1 to 3 years of age, the satisfaction of the gregarious instinct and the development of qualities like cooperative spirit are achieved through the medium of games and recreation. The atmosphere of these schools is homely where childern pass their time pleasantly even without the presence of their parents. These schools are run by local boards, city education boards, cooperative organizations and private agencies in vocational and industrial centres. Co-operative nursery schools are most important. They are administered and financed by the local public. State governments also give grants. Parents take interest in the programmes of these institutions and visit the schools every now and then to give co-operation to teachers.

Kindergarten Education: Generally childern in the age group of 3 to 6 are admitted in these schools. Kindergarten education is considered to be post-nursery education. Kindergartens prepare childern for primary education. They develop the personality of the child by inculcating desirable qualities in them. They are run by state governments, local boards, social organizations and private agencies. State governments and local boards give them directions and various programmes as well as financial assistance for the implementation of the programmes. At various places public Kindergartens have been established. Public is mainly responsible for their administration and development. The Government tries to maintain the educational level through departmental experts. A special teacher is appointed for the supervision of these schools as well as for approving their programmes. More than 25,00,000 children get education in private and public Kindergartens. There is still a great demand for their expansion.

Exercises

1. Explain the nature and development of Kindergarten Education in U.S.A.

2. What facilities have been included in the Nursery Education System in U.S.A. ? How do the parents help the Nursery Education System?

Chapter 10

Primary Education

Just as the strong foundation is very important in the construction of a building, in the same way primary education is very important in the education of the child and the progressive development of his personality. At this stage the nervous system of the child is very delicate but it is very receptive. All the important traits of character such as discipline, handwork, co-operative spirit, group feeling and self-dependence are developed during this period. The future citizens of the nation may become capable of having qualities of good citizenship only after successful completion of primary education. The foundation of socialization is laid at this stage.

In fact, primary stage arouses great curiosity in those students who have not attended any infant education school before. Primary education is a form of compulsory general education. It is also a stage leading to expansion of literacy.

Aims of Education at Primary Education Stage

In U.S.A., primary education is the post-kindergarten education. This education is a unit of the fundamental education. Primary schools cannot be separated from the kindergarten method. Generally, kindergarten school and nursery school systems are adopted in the primary educational system. Education is imparted in accordance with child's age and stage of development.

In U.S.A. primary education is arranged so that children may get preliminary education for citizenship and socialization according to their social needs and thus fulfil their basic educational needs. In the primary schools, this education is imparted with a view to inculcate democratic and social values. For socialization of the child, playing and studing together, making social contacts and following social ideals and ideal standards of conduct are emphasized. Through various programmes effort is made to cultivate desirable qualities among students, such as, proper use of time and occasion, knowledge of principles of good health, exchange of views and thoughts, patience to listen to the opposite views of others and sense of duty. Despite many dissimilarities in the methods of teaching adopted at this stage, there are many similarities in the aims of primary education of U.S.A., which are given below :-

(1) *Creation of Sociability and National spirit:* Man is a social being. Child is a part of the society. It is very necessary to develop in the child a tendency to work in accordance with society and to follow social ideals. Nation, state and associations, are social units. World is a big society. Hence a feeling of world citizenship should be developed in the child. Primary education should impart knowledge of social rights and duties. These are the ideals of American primary education.

(2) *Consciousness of Health:* Through the medium of games, sports and play-methods, primary education aims at making children healthy and creating in them an awareness for good health.

(3) *Development of Spirit of Freedom:* In American schools opportunities are provided to children to work freely and to understand the meaning of freedom through various special programmes. From the point of view of rights and duties exercise of freedom should be porper, desirable and unrestricted. It is impressed upon the children that co-operative spirit should be developed as a result of freedom.

(4) *Harmony between Individualistic and Socialistic Ideas:*

If only individualistic ideology is allowed to flourish then the child's personality cannot adjust to modern social environment. Hence where facilities and opportunities are provided to children, they are also directed to inculcate social feelings. Individuality can develop in social setting only.

(5) *Development of Self-reliance:* The primary education is so arranged that children try to fulfil their daily needs themselves and become self-dependent. Kindergarten system lays stress on self-help which is further developed at the primary stage. Education at this stage, aims at providing opportunities to children to solve their day to day individual, domestic and social problems themselves.

(6) *Development of Socialization:* Socialization is achieved by teaching social ideals. Hence, social ideals and social qualities should be developed in children in order to strengthen the idea of socialization. Children are directed to accept social ideals by imparting knowledge of reading, writing and elementary mathematics. Social feeling is easily developed by establishing relations with other members of society. It is developed in children by various programmes through the medium of co-operation and association.

(7) *Development of Creativity:* In America, with the advancement of scientific knowledge, many tools have been developed which serve as teaching aids. The use of these instruments such as audio-visual aids, by teachers or students not only entertains them but also develops creative tendencies in them. In these schools, creativity is generally developed through the medium of documentary films, news reels, magic lanterns, photographs, radio programmes and newspapers. Providing opportunities for acquisition and development of knowledge through lectures, debates and seminars is considered to be the main aim of education there.

Nature of Primary Education

In U.S.A. the entire curriculum below secondary stage is included within the primary education stage. Lower secondary classes also come under primary education as there is no junior high school stage. After completing primary stage, the child directly enters secondary stage. These schools are known as Grade Schools and Grammar schools. They are called Grade schools because the syllabus of study of the whole year is divided into grades and vaious classes are formed on the basis of one year' study. Others are known as Grammar Schools because facilities for reading, writing and arithmetic are provided in them.

The educational system of all the schools in America is greatly influenced by the public which accounts for differences in the nature of education. In different states the educational system, duration of education, curriculum and programmes are different according to the traditions of the people of respective states. In the educational system of some states, old traditions are followed and in others, new schemes and traditions are well-adapted. The differences existing in different aspects of education are as follows.

Duration of Education and Classification:

The American educational system was established on the basis of old traditions, but the educational systems are being renovated in the light of modern researches and in accordance with development of new projects. Though the new schemes also cater to the needs of local people, even then differences exist according to the levels of different social classes. In these schools, no national or state-wise system is prevalent regarding formulation of educational policy and curriculum construction. In U.S.A., generally children of 6 to 8 years of age continue primary education upto the age of 12 or 14 years. But this system has been changed in some states due to introduction of new schemes of primary education. Thus two types of schools exist. In one type of schools, children are admitted at the age of 6 and they are taught upto the age 14 years. At some places these eight years of study are considered as the graded classes of primary stage. At other places the first three classes are considered equivalent to kindergarten education. Classes IV, V & VI constitute the primary stage and classes VII & VIII are regarded as the classes of junior secondary standard. These schools are regarded as traditional schools. In the schools of the second type children of 6 to 8 years of age are admitted and they are taught for six years. In this way six classes of six years constitute the primary stage and classes VII & VIII are attached to secondary education stage. The first two or three classes of the six years of study are regarded as equivalent to kindergarten education and remaining form the primary education stage. These schools are based on new schemes.

Generally American schools have five working days in a week. The programme of a working day continues for 5 or 5 1/2 hours, i.e., from 9 a.m. to 12 o'clock and from 1 p.m. to 3 p.m. In lower classes, the duration of working hours is reduced to 4 or 4 1/2 hours. The number of working days in one year also differ not only in schools of different states but also in different schools of the same state. The number of working days ranges between 152 and 187 days. Upto 1950 the average number of working days throughout U.S.A. was 180. Later an attempt was made to create uniformity in all the states. Even in the duration of teaching periods there were wide differences. It was decided to have periods of 15 to 30 minutes duration and 25 or 30 teaching periods per week. It was also decided that there should be atleast 171 working days in a year. However, some differences do exist even now due to the influence of local environment. In village schools, the number of working days per year is less as compared to those in urban schools and periods in lower classes are shorter than periods in higher classes.

The Compulsory and Universal Aspect of Education:

In U.S.A. primary education is universal, compulsory and free. According to statistics collected in 1930, 63.3 per cent children of 6 years and 95.3 per cent children in the age group of 7 to 13 years were attending primary schools. But due to regular decrease in the birth rate, the number of students in primary schools declined significantly from 1930 to 1936. This decrease was noticed mainly in lower classes whereas upto

1934, there was progressive increase in the number of students in higher classes. But from 1934 to 1936, the decrease was noticed. In comparision to 4.2 per cent decrease within a period of six years, i.e., from 1930 to 1936, there was 1.8 per cent decrease in two years only, i.e., from 1934 to 1936. But as soon as the Second World War was over, there was sudden increase in the birth rate, which forced the local people and Govt. to work hard for the expansion of education. To meet this demand, single teacher schools were established and single-room-schools were fully converted into primary schools.

Seeing that the enrolment in schools was very low, the compulsory attendance act was enacted in 1918 and it was strictly observed. Various states and public organizations endeavoured to expand educational as well as transport facilities. As a result, education became compulsory and universal. In the eight classes of primary schools, attendance of children in the age group of 7 to 17 is compulsory in 33 states of U.S.A. According to the Supreme Court judgement delivered in 1954, no discrimination of class or colour can be observed in schools. However, in Western Virginia separate schools for whites and blacks exist even now due to discrimination between the two.

Curricula and Educational Programmes:

In U.S.A.. the general aim of primary education is to prepare worthy citizens. In democratic states the main aim of education is to develop the feeling of citizenship in students and the curriculum of schools is framed accordingly. By the nineteenth century, the only aim of education was to provide instruction in 3 Rs (Reading, Writing and Arithmetic). But since the beginning of the twentieth century, an effort was made for all-round development of children and thus a new programme of studies was framed. At that time spelling, grammar, literature, composition, music, history, geography, elementary science, psychology health education, etc., were the main subject taught along with instruction in 3 Rs. Now 5 Rs have replaced 3 Rs and Reading, Writing, Arithmetic,

Relationship and Recreation have been included in the curriculum. Now-a-days, special stress is laid on the training of social character. New criteria of determining the curriculum for the training of social character and development of citizenship has been adopted. Local public and State Governments both are active in the construction of curriculum and administration of schools. Local Boards in urban areas have more facilities than those in rural areas. In rural areas State Governments enforce the curriculum, so, there is naturally some interference by the government from administrative point of view. The curriculum of American primary schools is being revised and modified as a result of psychological developments and research.

American educationists base the curriculum on practice of subject, training and projects of educational developments. These developed curricula can not be enforced in each and every school. Even then, they have sufficiently contributed to subject matter organization and are being used to achieve the desired success.

Publishers of text books also give some help in the development of curriculum. They prepare text books according to modified and developed schemes. Their interest in education is clearly visible in their publications.

Americans have great faith in secularisim. They are not in favour of making religious education a part of curriculum. They believe in imparting religious and moral instructions for the sake of developing human qualities only.

Administration and Organization of Primary Schools

In U.S.A., we do not find uniformity in the administration and organization of primary schools. The organization of primary schools differs from state to state and from region to region due to absence of any national policy on the subject. On the basis of organization, we may present the following classification :

Departmental Organisation of Schools:

Under this system, those schools are included in which

there are different subject teachers. Every subject teacher is provided a separate room which is fully equipped with necessary material aids and other equipments. The subject teacher teaches his students in the class room especially prepared for the particular subject. This system was first introduced in New York in the twentieth century. Now this system is prevelant in all those schools which are under the education department. Generally, this system is found in VII, VIII and IX classes. The higher classes of primary schools are run according to this system.

Traditional System of School Organisation:

Some change has taken place in the old system of single-room schools as well in the light of modern developments. In single-room schools, only one teacher teaches all the subjects in one room. Such schools are found in rural areas and interior regions. Now according to changing traditions some change has taken place. In view of the number of students and the number of classes many teachers are appointed in place of one teacher and many rooms are provided in place of one room. In one room one teacher teaches two or three classes. At some places one teacher and one room are provided for one class. These teachers are appointed on the basis of number of classes and not on the basis of subjects and this system depends upon the number of students. These teachers teach all the subjects to the classes placed under their charge. In single-room schools the supervision is done by the teacher who is known as Teacher -Principal. In those schools where separate teachers are appointed for different classes one teacher is assigned supervisory duties and he is called Supervising - Principal. This system is found in those schools where the enrolment is high.

Platoon Type Organisation:

Though this system was considered suitable for both secondary and primary stages, now it is prevelant in primary schools only. First of all this system was enforced in Indiana

State, but it developed remarkably in Detroit. This system came in vogue in the first decade of the current century but by the third decade it had developed sufficiently. By then this system had been adopted by 1068 schools in 202 towns of 41 states. The special feature of this scheme is that it is economical, and it increases the efficiency and solves the problem of shortage of school buildings. Apart from being economical and more useful, it is also helpful in developing the personality of children and their individual interests and aptitudes.

Under this system all the children of the school are divided into 2 or 3 groups. When one groups studies in the class room, the other group keeps itself busy in games, exercises, tours, practical work and social services, and carries on activities in gymnasium hall, laboratory, auditorium and school shops. After finishing the work the first group takes the place of the second group and the second takes the place of the first.

Administrative and Financial Control:

From the point of view of administrative and financial control, there are two types of schools in U.S.A. In the first type fall schools which are run and financed by religious organizations. In these schools religious instruction is imparted and Bible, religious treatises, Church system and religious programme form part of the curriculum. The schools of second type are run by local bodies and local organizations. Their expenditure is met by public donations and tuition fees. These schools, unlike religious schools run by Catholics, are not much influenced by religion, though religious and moral instruction is imparted there. These schools which are run by religious organizations and local bodies are known as private schools and are few in number. Another type of schools which are different from private schools are the Public Schools. They are in large number and form the back-bone of American system of education. Their expenditure is met by public taxation and they are administered and controlled by public representatives. It is a special feature of schools of U.S.A. that guardians, teachers, officers and administrators co-operate in the administration of schools. Officers and principals provide such opportunities to parents, guardians and popular leaders as may acquaint them with the interests, aptitudes and the progress of students so that they may give their constructive suggestions. Thus parents, guardians, teachers, officers and public in general, all co-operate in making the school system more suitable, sound and modern.

The buildings and rooms of primary schools are fully equipped with modern facilities and equipment. Transport facilities are available to students. There is a provision for interesting subjects like painting, art, music and handicraft.

Summary

Aims of Education at the Primary Stage: The aims of American primary education are development of healthy citizenships, tendency of socialization, good nature and tendency of doing useful and creative work. Social ideals and social tendencies are developed through collective programmes, group living, games & sports, recreation and programmes of health and physical training.

Nature of Primary Education: Due to local social needs and diversities of environment, differences in outer form of primary education system do exist but there is internal similarity in all the systems.

Duration of Education and Classification: There are two types of schools in America. The schools of first type impart education from class I to class VIII. In the schools of the second type, the higher classes (VII & VIII) are attached to schools of secondary level; and only six year education is imparted there. In the first type of schools education is imparted from six years to 14 years of age where as in the second system education is imparted from six year to 12 years of age. Schools remain closed on Saturdays and Sundays. The teaching work continues for 5 to 5 1/2 hours. The number of working days in a year ranges from 152 to 187.

The Compulsory and Universal aspect of Education: Education is compulsory for all the children between seven to fourteen or sixteen years of age. Discrimination of class, colour, religion and creed is not observed. Education is univeral. Schools based on colour discrimination exist in Virginia only.

Curricula and Educational Programmes: Now 5 Rs have replace 3 Rs and Reading, Writing, Arithmetic, Relationship, and Recreation have been included in the curriculum. Religious educations is secondary. In addition to these literature, history, geography, health education, agriculture, music, art, handicraft and home science have also been included in the curriclum.

Administration and Organisation of Primary Schools: From the point of view of organization, there are single-room or multi-rooms schools, in which one or more teachers teach all the subjects to all or several classes in one or more rooms. Single-room schools are more common in rural areas. From the point of view of administration, at some places students are divided into two groups. One group studies the subjects of the curriculum in the class room and the other group is kept busy in out-door programmes at the same time. In the second shift, the order is reversed. Primary schools may be divided into private schools and local public schools. Private schools are run by religious or social organizations and religious education is also imparted in them. Local public schools are run by the public and religious teaching is secondary in these schools.

Exercises

1. Describe the nature of primary education in U.S.A.
2. In U.S.A. the curriculum and abundance of educational activities at the primary stage have contributed to the success of its educational system. How ?

Chapter 11

High School Education

The organisation of secondary education in U.S.A., has been a great struggle. By nature, Americans love freedom and have great faith in democracy. It is because of this tendency that primary education in U.S.A. became compulsory and universal. Secondary education was developed as a result of compulsory primary education and industrial revolution. Americans had to face the problem of getting jobs. It was difficult for the government to provide jobs to every literate persons. Hence it was decided to give further education to children. According to the policy of the government, employment of minors was prohibited. Hence it was considered necessary to make arrangement for the education of chidren till they became adults. From this point of view provision of secondary education was considered necessary.

Latin Grammer Schools

After their settlement in U.S.A., the migrant Europeans were concerned that their coming generation might be deprived of their old culture, civilization, literature and religion. Hence religious leaders and priests established Latin Grammar schools. The expenditure of these schools, was met by religious associations and religious minded people. Due to high fees and the policy of class discrimination in education, only children of rich section of society could get education in these schools. The Latin Grammar schools were started by the followers of the Puritan faith with a desire to provide education through the medium of religious curriculum. The first school of this type was established in Boston in 1635. Upto the nineteenth century the Latin Grammar school system was based on old traditions. But due to changes in environment, social awareness and educational aptitude these Latin Grammar Schools showed improvement. The public began to lose confidence in the leadership of priests and these schools were replaced by Academies.

Academies

Benjamin Franklin is considered to be the founder of American academy. Under the leadership of Benjamin Franklin, it was felt that seondary education should not only be conservative and traditional but it should also prepare students for future life by developing in them vocational efficiency. In this way it was planned to conduct education in such a way as to make it vocationally useful. Consequently in 1751 the first Academy was established in Philadelphia. These academies were very much liked because those students, who could not study further due to certain reasons, could get employment after getting vocational training in these academies. So by 1830 about 500 academies had been established in the country. The most important feature of this system of education was that it prepared the child for future life from the vocational point of view. That is why at the secondary level the Latin Grammar Schools lost their charm and Academies with their comprehensive and useful curriculum began to flourish.

In Academies, provision for subjects like philosophy, politics, and military studies was made along with vocational education. In this system there was a provision for women education as well. The management of these academies was democratic and semi-public. The expenditure was met by contributors from public and fees collected from boys and girls. By 1837, as the curriculum of New York Academies indicates, old languages like Greak, Hebrew and Roman were also included in the curriculum along with English literature and rhetorics. According to the needs of the people and the new traditions, the academies prepared students for higher education too. Hence provision was made for classical subjects in addition to geography, science and English.

The spread of democratic tendency created interest in women education. It began to be realized that women, too, had mental and physical capacities like men. Hence they must also get equal opportunities. So the academies got encouragement from the public and took a universal form. In this way eduacation developed in a democratic way even at the secondary level.

The Public Schools

The early part of nineteenth century witnessed movement against the colonial and conservative education started in U.S.A. During this movement the view gained ground that the secondary schools of U.S.A., should not be conservative and should impart education different from the useless, unnecessary and expensive education of Latin Grammar Schools. Hence it was thought that an integrated form of curricula prevalent in Academies should be introduced in these schools. So Public schools were established in New York in 1824 and in Boston in 1826. The Boston school was meant for women. The purpose of these schools was to impart college education at a certain minimum level and to provide useful education in conformity with the needs of the people. Thus, secondary schools started with the above aim in view, trained the minds of boys and girls.

In the latter part of the nineteenth century, the need of organising education at graduation level was stressed. Hence courses were started for awarding degrees through higher and college level education. The secondary schools thus aimed at providing educational background to students for further education of graduation level. Upto this level these schools were run by public contributers and were incapable of introducing curriculum of their own choice. Consequently, these schools could not gain further importance. In 1827 in Massachusetts State of U.S.A. an Act was passed to the effect that education should be universal and it should be available to all in every city with a population of over 500 families. Consequently, a state-wide revolution took place for making secondary education free and universal. This revolution effected various improvements in the existing conditions of schools.

In Michigan, the Kalamazoo case gave support to the cause of making secondary education free and spending government funds on it. It was decided in Kalamazoo that a tax should be imposed on the public for making secondary education free in school districts. The public opposed this decision and the case was referred to the Supreme Court. The Supreme Court upheld the decision stating that the local bodies and school districts could impose tax on the public for the progress of education beyong primary stage, if majority favoured the decision. Thus local bodies and school districts got the legal right of imposing tax on the public for the progress of secondary education and for making it free.

In the last decade of the nineteenth century, the newly developed schools followed the integrated form of curriculum and pattern of education prevailing in Latin Grammar Schools and Academies. The concept of social, religious, moral and intellectual development was taken from the Latin Grammar Schools and the educational programmes based on vocationalization and universalization of education were borrowed from the Academies. Yet some people persisted in their individualistic outlook, and wanted that these schools should cater to the needs of some special section of society as well. The Committee of Ten formed in 1982 presented a report in this connection which read "A part of total number of children whose guardians are capable of keeping them in schools and are desirious of higher education, should be provided all educational facilities upto the age of 18 years". This report greatly influenced the educational system. In some schools education was made compulsory upto the age of 18 years. But generally in all the states, education was made compulsory upto the age of 16 without much opposition.

With the beginning of the twentieth century, a change in social, political and individual conditions took place in U.S.A. as a result of new awakening. Industrial revolution promoted national prosperity. A need of skilled labour to work on machines was felt and the problem of unemployment of unskilled persons came to the forefront. The economic standard of people improved and they began to view secondary education from the point of view of economic gains. With the development of spirit of freedom, the need for able citizens having faith in democracy began to be felt for the service of the country. Hence schools began to be regarded as institutions for preparing capable and freedom loving citizens; their role of developing mental abilities and providing background for higher education was given up. Now it began to be realized that the aims of secondary schools should be education in citizenship, vocational training, control of fundamental processes, training in worthy home-membership, development of ethical character, healthy development and training in proper use of leisure time. Consequently, motivated by economic gains, people were attracted towards vocational training. The importance of schools providing professional training enhanced with the growing demand of professionally trained persons. The number of students getting admission to colleges came down to 25% from 75%.

Changes in the Organization of Secondary Education

In the middle of twentieth century, changes in the secondary education system began. It was felt that the period of eight years of primary eduation was very lengthy. Hence the last two years of primary education (class VII and class VIII) were attached to the four years (9th to 12th) of secondary level. Thus, the curriculum of primary level extended from 6 years to 12 years of age and that of secondary level from 12 years to 18 years of age. Another important change which took place due to the need for professional training was that the first two years of college stage were also attached to secondary stage extending the duration of secondary education from 4 to 8 years ranging from 12 years to 20 years of age. According to the first change, the sixteen-year education was converted into six year of primary education, six year of secondary education and four years of college education. But according to the second change, sixteen years of education were distributed into periods of six years, eight years and two years respectively.

According to the modern plan, it was realized that the 6 or 8 years duration of secondary education was very lengthy. So the tradition of breaking it into different groups was established. The first 6 years course of secondary stage was divided into two parts of three years each; the first part was called Junior High School education and the second Senior High School education. But for the distribution of the second eight-year course of secondary stage, two plans were prepared. According to the first plan the eight-year course was split up into 2 groups of 4 years each. They were called Junior High School education and Senior High School education respectively. But according to the second plan, eigth-year course of secondary education was split up into 3 parts in three years of Junior High School education, three years of Senior High School education and two years of Junior College education. The Junior College plan was first introduced in Illinois in 1902 and the first Junior High School was started in 1910 in the State of California.

Aims of Secondary Education

The Europeans who settled in U.S.A. had established Latin Grammar Schools in order to preserve their religion and to maintain the traditional literary and cultural environment. The aim of these schools was to prepare students for college education and to make the new generation devoted to their religion. Thus, the secondary education imparted in Latin Grammar Schools attracted people towards dignified posts and towards political, social and professional leadership. From administrative point of view, higher education was not suited to the needs of every student. But academies, modifying the curriculum of the Latin Grammar Schools, constructed a new curriculum according to the new demands thus providing education for future progress through vocational education.

In U.S.A., secondary education is mainly influenced by local environment and controlled by local public. But the system is based on the recommendations of national commissions on secondary education. In 1892, National Education Association appointed a 'Committee of Ten' which gave its recommendations for the improvement of programmes of secondary education with the view point that secondary education should prepare a social background for college education and that classical subjects and arithmetic should be included in the prevailing curriculum of secondary education. A 'Committee of Thirteen' was appointed in 1899 in order to give support to the recommendations of the 'Committee of Ten'. This committee was called 'The Committee on College Entrance Requirements.' This Committee made specific recommendations on programmes of secondary education. Likewise a 'Committee on the Articulation of High Schools and Colleges' was appointed in 1911, which made various recommendations and presented various schemes in order to make the prevailing system of secondary education more useful.

In 1912, National Education Association appointed a 'Commission on Reorganisation of Secondary Education'. After six years of intensive study and inspection, the Commission laid down some cardinal principles of secondary education. According to these principles the aim of providing opportunity of complete and worthy living to every citizen of U.S.A. after getting secondary education was accepted. Seven main aims of secondary education were accepted. These were as follows:—

(1) *Health Education*: This Committee recommended the inclusion of health education in the curriculum of secondary education for the improvement of physical and mental health. Health education aimed at arranging health programmes from time to time and providing opportunities for the improvement

of health as well as motivating students to fulfil their national, social, family and individual obligations and responsibilities.

(2) *Command of Fundamental Processes*: In order to make the education of secondary level more useful and progressive, efforts should be made for conducting necessary experiments in the education based on fundamental processes of elementary stage and for providing practice in them.

(3) *Worthy Home-membership*: Secondary education should be so adequate and effective that the children, after getting this education, may become dutiful and prove worthy members of the family by showing ideal behaviour in the family, and by developing such qualities as co-operation, tolerance and good will, which are necessary for worthy home-membership.

(4) *Vocational Education*: Vocational education and training should be given priority in the curriculum of this stage so that children may achieve success from the point of view of vocation. The future citizens, thus trained vocationally, will be able to contribute to the prosperity of the nation and will be able to raise their standard of living. This education should develop in them vocational interest, vocational efficiency and co-operative spirit.

(5) *Civic Education*: The education should be so organized as to make the future citizens of U.S.A. worthy citizens of the nation so that they may prove useful to the nation, society and the world. The modern citizen should help not only in the solution of national problems but also in the solution of problems of international importance.

(6) *Worthy Use of Leisure*: Secondary education should develop in children the capacity of using their leisure time constructively. The educational system should be so organized as to enable the children to use their leisure time for developing their personality and raising their mental and physical standard.

(7) *Ethical Character*: Those activities should be included in the educational programmes at the secondary stage, which may develop ethical character of students and create an ethical environment in the country.

All the schools tried to incorporate the above principles of organization of secondary education in their respective curricula and determined educational aims accordingly. An attempt was also made to socialize individualistic education.

In 1933, the need for reorganisation of secondary education was felt. A 'Committee on Socio-Economic Goals of America' was set up to look into the matter. The Committee appointed in 1918 had stressed the need of individual development on the basis of development of individualistic education. But this committee gave more emphasis on social development through the medium of social and co-operative educational programme. This Committee recommended that American education be made more social, economic and public. It laid down the following ten objectives for this socialy progressive education:—

(1) The objective of physical security.
(2) The objective of equality of opportunity.
(3) The objective of economic security.
(4) The objective of freedom.
(5) The objective of mental security.
(6) The objective of fair play.
(7) The objective of suitable occupation.
(8) The objective of an active and flexible personality.
(9) The objective of hereditary strength.
(10) The objective of participation in evolving culture.

In the same way the 'Department of Secondary School Principle' appointed a 'Committee on the Orientation of Secondary Education' in 1932, to study secondary education and to suggest suitable programmes for it. This Committee submitted two main reports and recommendations.

In the first report this Committee gave suggestions for creating a conducive atmosphere in the schools for the development of social membership, social ideals, abilities and character. This process was defined by the word 'Education' by this Committee. In this type of education, motivation for complete development of normal citizens and capacity of providing guidance to children were considered necessary. This progress was possible through secondary education alone.

Primary education could not provide any opportunity for such a progress. This education prepares students for future life and develops in them the ability to pursue study in Liberal Arts Colleges and Professional Schools of Specialization.

Functions of Secondary Education

The 'Committee on Orientation of Secondary Education' constituted by the 'Department of Secondary School Principals' suggested the following functions of secondary education:

(1) *Development of Knowledge and Integration*: It is the function of secondary education to develop the knowledge of students and its integration according to definite programmes, may be that those programmes are in a diminishing degree. The practice of all those programmes should continue so long as their increasing intellectual level does not imbibe desirable general ideals, tendencies, appreciation, knowledge and training, permanently.

(2) *Fulfilment of Probable Future Needs*: The re-organisation of secondary education is necessary in order to fulfil the probable future needs of the students by explaining to them the personal and social value of their needs, keeping in view their capacity, interest and maturity.

(3) *Knowledge of Traditional, Cultural, and Contemporary Social Duties*: Modern secondary education should be such as can cultivate progressive outlook as regards caste, creed, traditions, culture, society and the individual and through progressive programmes they should strive to fulfil their obligations to the above. The students should be inspired to achieve success in the fulfilment of their desired needs. They should be taught all about the opportunities that lead to success in life.

(4) *Awakening for Specialisation*: The secondary education should inculcate capacity for increasing specialisation and specific study.

(5) *Provision of New Knowledge Correlated with Previous Knowledge*: The outline of the new knwoledge based on previous knowledge should be so systematised that the students

are able to understand easily by learning the laws, principles and importance of knowledge. But they should not confine themselves to that knowledge alone, rather they should be curious for more knowledge.

(6) *To Create Interest in the Field of Human Activities*: The secondary education should create interest in the major field of human activities through personal happiness of students and social progress.

(7) *Use of Progressive Teaching Methods, Independent Thinking and Research Principles*: Educational programmes based on independent thoughts, principles of research, co-operative and personal intelligence and self-directed practice, should be implemented at this stage.

(8) *Retention of Students in Schools upto Diminishing Return Level*: The students should be retained in the school as long as they are ready for independent study and it is felt that the school is no more useful to them. In such a situation, it is necessary to send the student to some other training institution or school where he is able to study according to his personality and capacity.

In 1934, the Progressive Education Society was constituted but it did not present any solid suggestion upto 1942. Thereafter it suggested that the responsibility of secondary education be shifted to the States. It also expressed the opinion that the State governments should be free to formulate aims of secondary education. Similarly, for formulating educational policies for secondary education, Education Policies Commission was appointed in 1944. This Commission considered it necessarry to keep secondary education free from the distinctions of sex, colour, creed, environment, place or State and suggested that it be made well-balanced. In 1947, the Commission on Life Adjustment Education was appointed to re-assess educational aims. This Commission proposed the following suggestions for adjustment in life and recommended to conduct education on the same basis:—

(1) Secondary education, specially, should be able to provide worthy citizens.

(2) This education should acquaint the students with daily life activities.
(3) This education should provide worthy home-membership.
(4) This education should enable the citizen to utilise leisure properly.
(5) This education should familiarise the citizen with the fundamental tools of learning.
(6) This education should provide proper vocational training to the citizens.
(7) This education should inculcate power of appreciation of beauty in order that they are able to understand Art and Nature.
(8) Through this education, one should understand the significance and methods of science.
(9) This education should provide mental health and physical fitness.
(10) That education should be provided to boys and girls, which may cultivate in individuals the capacity for ethical thinking and evaluation of ethical principles.

The above recommendations for adjustment forced the administrator of every school to re-assess the organisation of secondary education. Gradually, 'adjustment for life' objective found an important place in the curriculum, educational policies and aims. The Commission advised that the prescribed policies be followed according to the local environment, needs and traditions. Various subjects were provided to satisfy the interests and needs of the students and accordingly buildings, teaching and learning facilities, means and teaching methods were provided. Inspite of various difficulties, the curriculum was framed for balanced and proper adjustment in life.

The Nature and Organisation of Secondary Education

The nature and organisation of secondary education has changed according to the recommendations of vairous commissions appointed from time to time. Ultimately, the nature of education has attained its present form.

Types of Institutions and their Classification

Secondary schools based on the earlier system were wide and comprehensive according to the peroples needs. Their courses, class-systems and nature continued to develop till the end of the nineteenth century. But during the twentieth century the secondary education continued to be re-organised according to the recommendations of the commissions and committees appointed from time to time. In the first half of the century, courses were changed and special courses were introduced. In addition to general education, secondary schools for special and vocational subjects were established, e.g.—Practical Arts High Schools, High School of Commerce, Technical High School, Manual Training High Schools, etc.

The nature and organisation of re-organised schools in U.S.A. are not similar. There is some similarity of types only. Ordinary secondary schools have four year course teaching classes from IX to XII. In re-organised secondary schools, classes from VII to XII are taught. The first three years of 6 years secondary school, i.e., classes VII, VIII and IX are known as Junior high school classes and classes X, XI and XII are called higher secondary classes. The above type of secondary schools on the basis of re-organisation were adopted very slowly during the first 12 to 14 years. The following data prove it:—

Years	*New system in Schools*
1922	11 per cent
1926	19 per cent
1930	26 per cent
1934	29 per cent
1935	30 per cent

The number of students in six year secondary schools was more than the number in four year secondary schools. Upto 1935, the number of students in both the types of secondary schools (having four year and six year courses) was 51 per cent, whereas in reorganised six year secondary schools alone it was 49 per cent. It is thus clear that though the number of re-organised secondary schools was less, yet they educated most of the total number of students. Only 2 per cent students got education in four year secondary schools. Now it has been noticed that if there are 266 students in re-organised secondary schools, only 85 students go to the four year secondary schools. Thus the number of students in new secondary schools is three time the number in old secondary schools. The data of 1934 has brought to light the following details:

1. The average number of students (boys and girls) in Junior High School class — 626 per school.
2. In Higher secondary classes — 983 per school.
3. In Junior and Higher secondary classes together — 314 per school.

The educational system of secondary schools in U.S.A. is not common on the basis of curriculum. In some schools, there is six year curriculum and in some schools it is for four years. These curricula have affected the duration of teaching in primary schools and colleges also. For example·

Primary state	*Secondary stage*	*College stage*
1. 6 years	4 years (classes VII to X).	4 years
2. 6 years	6 years (classes VII to XII) 3 year Junior high school 3 years Higher secondary	2 years
3. 8 years	4 years classes IX to XII	2 years

The recognised popular structure of education is of the second type in which the primary level curriculum is of 6 years and at the secondary level 3 years are meant for junior high school classes and 3 years for higher secondary classes. The remaining two years are spent at the college level.

The junior high school classes at the secondary level of American education were started for the reason that in every sphere of life and in the vocational sphere, skilled persons were required. It was possible to fulfil this need only through the re-organisation of educational system. At that time it was felt that junior high school classes (generally classes VII and VIII were included in the Primary stage) should be integrated with secondary classes and their curriculum should be different from that of primary classes. Thus through re-organisation of curriculum, more skilled citizens could be prepared. At the secondary level the 6 year curriculum, in which 3 years are meant for junior high school and 3 years for the higher secondary, is not universal. These provisions have been implemented in big cities or at those centres where all the secondary classes cannot be taught together for want of space in the existing buildings. The arrangements for junior high school classes and higher secondary classes are separate but they are complimentary to each other. In some places, the lower classes of the college level are included in the junior colleges and in some, they have been attached to the secondary level. Thus, inspite of the popular nature of secondary education sysem, it is not common.

Secondary education system in U.S.A. is still at the experimental stage. The organisation of schools has not changed suddenly and completely; gradual changes are made according to the time, need and philosophy of life. Educational provisions are made in the schools on the basis of local environment in order to meet the occasional requirements. In 1997, the data of different types of schools have been as mentioned below:

Total number of secondary schools: 50,000 in which

Junior High Schools	—	8 per cent	
Higher Secondary Schools	—	20 per cent	
Higher and Jr. High Schools	—	40 per cent	100 per cent
8-4-4 years System of Secondary Schools	—	32 per cent	

Organisation of Junior High Schools

The American educationists felt that the prevailing 8 years of primary education were not conducive to the mental and physical needs of the students (both boys and girls). The last two years (classes VII and VIII) did not fulfil the needs of young boys and girls. Along with it, the 4 year secondary curriculum was entirely new for the students who came after completing the primary education and they took much time in adapting themselves to the new curriculum. Therefore, it was felt that problem could be solved by including the classes of last two years of primary level in the secondary level. So, by including the 2 years of primary level in the secondary level 3 year junior high schools and 3 year higher secondary schools were constituted and curriculum was constructed according to their needs.

In 1880, President Eliot of Harvard University, criticising the 8 year education system of the primary level, suggested that it be made shorter. In 1888, with the start of elementary education re-organisation trend, efforts were made to reduce the 8 year curriculum at the primary level. In 1893, the Committee of Ten and in 1899 the College Requirements Committee suggested to change and re-organise the primary and secondary level curriculum into 6 years each. In the beginning, only classes VII and VIII were included in the Junior High School. Later on it was increased to 3 years. First of all, this re-organised system was implemented in Massachussets and Springfield. Later on in 1909 it was implemented in Columbia and Ohio and then in 1910 in California and Berkley.

The purpose of beginning Junior High School system was to create an intermediate standard between the primary stage and the higher secondary stage. In re-organisig the curriculum, preference was given to the fact that the new curriculum should help the students in learning difficult subjects after the integration (co-relation) of the primary level curriculum and the secondary one. It was hoped that this change would fulfil the physical, mental and social needs of the young boys and girls. The curriculum is important in as much as it points out the system of education and direction of life. So, we can call curriculum as the corner-stone because at the Junior stage, it provides opportunities to the students to understand their limitations and possibilities. The teacher, also, is able to get an idea of the individual needs, interests and capabilities of the students (boys and girls). The curriculum enables the students to develop their natural social tendencies, and at the same time their individual differences may be kept in mind while teaching. The inclusion of pre-scientific and pre-vocational subjects at this stage has produced novelty and vocationalisation in the curriculum.

The secondary Education Reorganisation Committee obtained official sanction in 1918 for the re-organisation of the proposed junior high school classes. It was accepted as the education unit between primary stage and the high secondary stage. The junior high school stage provides for the education of adolescents. Therefore, it may be called as school for adolescents. This system has been less influenced by the academic interpretation of higher education or university education than the pre-existing secondary schools. At this stage, the students are taught to adjust themselves to their private, social, civic, home, economic and vocational life. They are taught to adapt themselves in the complex world and adopt a healthy view of life by utilising their leisure hours constructively Thus the junior high school system fulfils a great need of the society and nation.

Adolescence begins at the junior high school stage. At this stage, the age of boys and girls is generally between 12 and 14 years. The curriculum of these classes is more developed, extensive and liberal than the curriculum of the last three classes of 8 year primary stage. In this curriculum gradual teaching-system has been provided by including combined subjects and fusion of subjects. Combined subjects are taught for a long period by the same method. In subject combinations, English, social studies and science are common. Additional subjects included are mainly home-economics, industrial art, music and art. In teaching, unit method and correlation of subjects are given preference. Most of the junior high schools have separate buildings from the higher secondary schools.

According to National Survey of Secondary Education, the characterstics of junior high school education are as follows:—

1. Progressive teaching—system.
2. Study observation.
3. Study-programme.
4. Admission and progress facilities.
5. Educational and vocational counselling.
6. Special subject-combination.
7. Organisation of extra-curricular activities.
8. Separate school-building and material aids.
9. Specially trained teachers.

Organisation of Higher Secondary Schools

According to the new grouping-system, classes X, XI and XII are included in this stage. Higher secondary system belongs to the type"6 - (3-3) - 2". There are no tests for admission to the higher secondary classes. But attention is paid to the individual interest, ability, capability and age of the boys and girls. It is also seen whether the education given would be useful for the boys and girls taking admission, for this the mental age of the students is ascertained. For assessing the students their recorded scores, teacher judgment and the findings of the intelligence tests are looked into. For admission, measurement process also includes weight, height, body-measurement and health-records. For measurement of their social age, their backgrounds are studied.

There are three types of higher secondary education system in U.S.A. The first type is 3 years junior and 3 years higher stage classification, the second type is 4 years junior and 4 year higher stage classification and according to the third classification the junior stage is of 4 years but the higher secondary stage is of 2 years. Separate provisions exist for 4 year junior and 4 year higher secondary schools. Although the 4 year higher secondary education system depends on local conditions, people's economic status and social outlook, yet it if fairly extensive. In States where junior and higher secondary stage is of 3 years each, the junior high schools, being a higher part of the primary stage and being correlated with high secondary schools, are completely free from the view-point of control and establishment, but they have to be related and affiliated to the elementary school districts. In the state of Illinois, higher secondary education has no relation with elementary school districts, rather its administration is in the hands of a separate education board. In such an organisation, the three year system cannot be conducted.

From the view point of curriculum, the provisions of 3 year and 4 year curriculum are sufficiently common. Those secondary schools, too, where junior and secondary stages are not classified, are quite advanced and liberal as regards educational aims, teaching methods, guidance philosophy, provision of teachers and students behaviour. Schools providing specialisation in certain sphere in addition to general education also exist. The notable institutions among them are Technical High School, Maimi, Florida and High School of Music and Arts and High School of Automotive Trade, New York. Besides these many other secondary schools providing vocational and industrial education also exist.

Classification of Secondary Schools According to Curriculum

On the basis of varied curricula the secondary schools of U.S.A. may be classified as under:

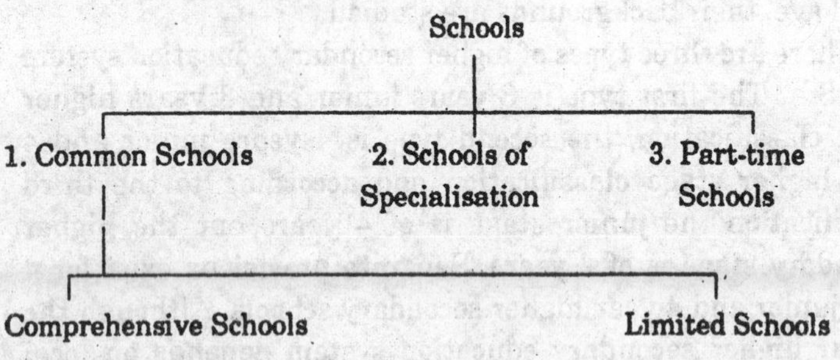

Common Schools

Comprehensive Secondary Schools: In American educational system, 4 year secondary schools belonging to 8-4-

4 year and 8-4(2-2) year type classification are called Comprehensive Schools. They are based on traditional methods. Admission to these schools is given after finishing 8 year primary education. These schools provide education from classes IX to XII. Various subjects are taught in these schools and, therefore, they are considered comprehensive. Efforts are made in this educational system to provide education for every phase of life. The following characterstics of universality and comprehensiveness may be found in these schools.

(1) *These Schools are Universal and Democratic*: At the time of admission, no importance is attached to the differences in sex, caste, class, colour and creed. Children of all communities may receive education in these schools.

(2) *Social and Free Education*: Children of all classes and communities are educated in these schools through collective programmes and without fees. Thus social feelings are developed and the students (boys and girls) develop the attitude of co-operation.

(3) *These Schools Provide Opportunites for Solidarity*: Because of their comprehensiveness, these schools lead to consolidation of interests of all, democratization of interests of all and solidarity.

(4) *Pleasing Teaching-methods and Interesting Organisation*: The curriculum of these schools does not present peculiar problems of teaching-methods and organisation and there are no diversities in them.

(5) *Economical and Useful according to Rural-Needs*: These schools are favourable and economical in those rural areas where there are no re-organised schools. These schools provide facilities for the teaching of even a few students in the rural areas.

(6) *Provision exists for Various Subjects but not Successful in Rural Areas*: In these comprehensive schools, provision for the teaching of a number of subjects exists. The students select the subjects according to their need, interest and capacity. As many as 200 subjects have been provided in these schools. Subjects related to art, vocations, commerce and agriculture

as well as those preparing for admission to colleges, are taught in these schools. But compared to cities these schools are considered deficient in rural areas. They prove more comprehensive and useful in cities only. The following deficiencies have been noticed in these schools of rural areas:

(a) *Shortage of Teachers*: Because of the large number of subjects, qualified teachers for teaching every subject are not available.

(b) *Lack of Contact between the Students and Teachers*: Due to the shortage of teachers, pupil-teacher ratio is very high and, therefore, the teachers are unable to establish personal contacts with their students.

(c) *Lack of Discipline and Control*: In rural areas there is less of eductional awakening in the people than in the people of cities. So, the schools lack discipline and proper control. Non-availability of sufficient facilities is also responsible for this indiscipline.

(d) *Mutual Contact amongst the Teachers is also Insufficient*: In re-organised secondary schools, there is more of mutual contact amongst the teachers but in these comprehensive schools, mutual contact among the teachers of different departments breaks down due to the large number of departments of different subjects.

(e) *Sectarian view is also prominent.*

(f) *These Schools Emphasise Classical Methods*: As a result the educational tendency remains tilted in this direction.

(7) *Defects of Co-education*: The boys and girls study together, leading to sexual attractions and the resultant complexities of organisation.

(8) *Education is very much Academic*: The impact of University-education system is found in these schools. So education here has too much of academic characteristics.

(9) *Educational Aim is Limited*: The students are prepared only for college education in these schools. This, however, should not be the sole aim of education.

(10) *Curriculum is Narrow*: The curriculum in these schools is not correlated with the needs of practical life. It is rather narrow.

(11) *Useless General Education*: These schools provide vocational and other specific training satisfactorily, but do not provide useful general education.

(12) *Not Suitable for Individual Teaching*: Educational provisions in these schools are not suitable for the students of different intelligence levels, abilities, capacities and interests.

(13) *Vocational and Co-curricular Activities*: Attention is not paid to vocational and co-curricular activities. Importance is not attached to modern languages, science, art and manual labour activities.

(14) *Modern Teaching-methods are not applied*: Scientific teaching methods are scarcely used.

(15) *Lack of Similarity of Teaching-methods like other Schools*: The new and useful teaching methods that are used in other schools are not applied in these schools. Hence there is no similarity in teaching-methods. Consequently except for sociability, the teaching remains backward from other view-points.

(16) *Lack of Recreation*: These schools are not quite attractive and enjoyable. Because of this, the boys and girls who get admissions in other attractive schools, leave these schools.

Limited Schools

These schools were established by the local people to fulfil their limited needs. Therefore, these schools do not provide education in all subjects and neither do they provide subject-specialisation and opportunity for subject selection. The size of the school depends on limited needs of the local people and their financial resources. But as the number of students goes up, provision is made for the teaching of other subjects and the size of school increases. Vocational training and subject-specialisation are provided in these schools. Facilities for general education are arranged and education in social studies, science and English is of a high standard. Schools providing specifiᴄ education are called technical schools or vice-techinical schools. Among such technical schools, Technical High School Ohio is famous.

Specialised Schools

These schools were established for providing speicalised vocational training. In these secondary schools, introductory training of a particular vocation is given, such as to provide specialisation in technical, commercial, arts and trade subjects. These schools have the following characteristics:

(1) Students of common interest receive education in these schools.
(2) Speical interest-based education accelerates the teaching process.
(3) Qualified teachers who provide external knowledge and practical training for specialisation, are available.
(4) By preparing the students for vocations, these schools create capacity for future life.

But these schools are not free from shortcomings. All-round development of students is not possible through these schools. The main defects are as follows:

(1) Vocational education is pre-mature.
(2) Education is not comprehensive. All the subjects are not taught.
(3) The teaching-methods are not based on democratic lines. Attention is paid to a particular subject and it is given undue importance.
(4) They create sectarian feelings.
(5) They are less important than the progressive re-organised secondary schools. Even then, their number is fairly sufficient.

Vocational and Industrial Schools

In 1906 some educationists and industrialists of America jointly established the National Society for the Promotion of Industrial Education for the development of industrial education. This Society suggested to include industrial and vocational training subjects in the curriculum of secondary schools and demanded that their proposal should get the Federal approval. Therefore, Smith Hughe's Act was enacted in 1917 and emphasis was laid on providing industrial and vocational education at the secondary level. Consequently, schools for vocational and industrial education were established.

These industrial and vocational secondary schools are established at vocational and industrial centres. This system is based on a separate organisational-pattern. Three to four periods are fixed for the teaching of industrial and vocational subjects. These schools fulfil the vocational and industrial needs of the society and prepare the students for their present and future life. These schools provide for the teaching of industiral and commercial subjects and for training in vocations.

Part-time Schools

These schools are established to provide education to those who remain engaged in some work throughout the day. The schools are of the following types:

(a) *Continuation Schools*: These schools are opened for 24 hours a day and all the year around for those boys and girls or adults who are unable to receive education because of being engaged in a job or who leave education before completing the secondary level. Teaching is done in these schools for about 3 to 4 hours per week. The organisation and management of these schools is quite different from that of the common schools. Provision exist for both vocational and cultural education in these schools. These schools are connected with adult education system.

(b) *Adult Evening Schools*: Evening Secondary schools have been established for those adults who are employed in some vocation and remain busy throughout the day. Efforts are made to make the adults efficient by giving them training in their related vocations and feelings of good citizenship are inculcated through general education.

Junior College System

Two views are current in U.S.A. regarding the junior college system. The first is that the secondary education should be raised by two more years and the classes of the first 2 years of junior colleges should be included in the secondary schools. Following this view-point in some places, the first two years of junior colleges have been included in the secondary schools and they are managed by the local secondary school managements. The second view-point is in support of keeping the two year education of junior college connected with higher education or college education according to the traditions of England, Germany and other countries. This type of education is under University administration and is considered as an inseparable part of higher education. These different opinions in U.S.A. reflect the free and local influence tendency in education.

In U.S.A., the suggestion of connecting the first two years of junior college with secondary level schools, was placed by Henry Tappen of Michigan in the year 1852. But this view-point was declared in the twentieth century. In the beginning of the current century, there began a movement that the 4 year education at college level was not suitable to meet the needs of the local people. It was not related to the life of the students and was useless. If the first two years of junior college were connected with the secondary level schools, the same would prove fruitful after being integrated with useful vocational education. This 4 year college education was unduly long. All the students could not complete that course. Hence it was considered worth while to connect the first two years of junior college with secondary level in order to provide social, vocational and utilitarian base to education. By adding the two years of college level education to the secondary level, it was made more progressive, mature and useful. It was re-planned and re-organised in order to give it a social and vocational form. This provision was first made in Illinois. Less number of junior colleges were established in eastern States, but they were developed speedily in the western and middle-west States.

The junior colleges increased in number under the Government Education Programme due to the fall in trade and commerce during the period of depression(1920-30). The third decade of this century proved crucial for the expansion of these colleges. After the World War II, there was such a huge crowd of young boys and girls returning from the war that the then existing colleges were unable to accommodate them. Consequently, the municipal boards and local education boards established new junior colleges. To meet the need of that time, many temporary junior colleges were established, the curriculum of which was influenced by higher education. But even the temporary colleges, established in California and Illinois taught progressive curriculum.

California has been most progressive in the establishment of junior colleges. The universities here have extended their full co-operation in the establishment of these colleges. The reason for this co-operation was that there was a fear of a large number of students seeking admission to the universities. The history of junior college movement makes it clear that mostly these colleges were established speedily around 1930. Private efforts contributed a lot in this movement. According to the data of 1950, there were 256 public junior colleges and the number of students studying in them was 1,87,659. Moreover there were 227 private junior colleges and the number of students enrolled in them were 55,045.

The financial support of private junior colleges and public junior colleges is different. So, these institutions have been classified on the basis of this finanical support. The public colleges get financial help in the form of Government grants and education tax. All the States do not have similar provisions. In California State, government grant is given on the basis of students attendance. But in Texas and other States, financial help depends on the education tax. In Northern Carolina, the court judgment on the dispute of 1930 that local townships were empowered to levy education tax for running junior colleges, proved very helpful. The court judgment also made it clear that necessary help could be taken from the local education tax funds. In most of the States, these examples led to the sanction by special legislations to impose education tax or take necessary help from it.

In European countries, 8 year curriculum, from junior high school to junior colleges, is prevalent. The same curriculum is found in American education system also. Here classes XIII and XIV are included in junior colleges. In these classes pre-vocational education is given and needs of the local society are met. With the establishment of junior colleges, the colleges of higher education which provided four year curriculum, improved their educational standards and most of them divided the curriculum into two years each. Junior colleges, being situated in the local areas, were near to the colleges providing four year curriculum. So the guardians admitted their wards in the nearly junior colleges instead of sending them to distant colleges. Thus the importance of junior colleges increased and they developed also.

The curriculum of junior colleges is very useful and modern. These colleges not only prepare the students for higher education through the teaching of general subjects, but they also provide industrial and vocational education which helps the students in earning a living. These colleges have gained importance because of their terminal functions. These colleges include all the educational groups—technical, scientific and arts. In the beginning, the curriculum at this level was neither useful nor utilitarian. But these courses have now become more flexible, progressive, varied and utilitarian because semi-professional and highly skilled subjects have been included in them. Private junior colleges create a better vocational atmosphere than public junior colleges do. For the sake of social services, adult education has been started in these colleges. These colleges provide supplementary education to adults through short-term education and arrangement of evening classes. In some places, junior colleges have been converted into community colleges, keeping in view the importance of adult-education. Post high school education is provided in these community schools. The importance of junior colleges has gone up for the following reasons:—

(1) Those persons or young boys and girls who do not get any job after secdondary education and are unable to enroll for 4 year higher education, take the benefit of these junior colleges.

(2) Those boys and girls who find it inconvenient to go to distant colleges for their education or find it difficult to take admission in colleges after the completion of secondary education or cannot bear the expenses of college education, take advantage of these junior colleges.

(3) The junior colleges provide opportunities of education to boys and girls of all communities and are educationally convenient also.

(4) The teachers teaching similar classes at the junior college level are more capable than the teachers teaching the same classes at the college level because their system of instruction is higher and more developed.

(5) These junior colleges have been made more useful for the public by introducing important programmes, supplementary education and terminal education from the civic and social point of view. These colleges are able to make those young boys and girls efficient, who do not want to study further.

Some people criticise the junior colleges because the money meant for secondary schools is spent on these junior colleges and these colleges usurp most of the help from education tax. These colleges are responsible for the increase in education tax again and again and are opposed to four year college education. But in fact, they are now complementary and not opposed to higher education and have become a necessary part of higher education.

Curriculum and Educational Programme of Secondary Education

Educational Programme: All subjects are compulsory at

the primary level but special classes have been provided at the secondary level. The establishment of these classes depends on the needs of local society and the size and area of the school. In civic areas the number of these classes is from 20 to 30. But in rural areas one class secondary schools are in sufficient number. Thus the secondary schools are more liberal from the viewpoint of curriculum and programme (and due to this their programme of studies is more liberal and useful).

Three types of courses are available in the secondary schools. The first one is compulsory for all boys and girls, the second includes semi-compulsory subjects which are not compulsory for all, but are compulsory only for those students who want admission in special classes related to those subjects and the third has varied subjects which provide free elective curriculum. The students have to select the subjects from the different subject-groups. Thus, in every secondary school, the number of subject and subject-groups is different according to the local needs. The subjects are selected either in the last year of junior high school classes or first year of secondary schools. In the four year secondary schools, the subjects have to be selected in the first year.

At the secondary level, the curriculum has been expanded because of re-organisation and to cater to the needs of the children. Provision of teaching upto 290 subjects exists at this level. About 100 subjects are available in a secondary school of a big city and the students select the subjects of their interest, capacity and need. In America most of the students leave their studies after the secondary level. Hence efforts are made to make them fit for some vocation. Therefore, basic training in agriculture, industry and commerce is given at this level. In the first year of this level, subjects like sociology, experimental science, physical education, mathematics and English language are mostly selected. However, out of subjects like handicrafts, metal work, electric-work, type-writer knowledge, animal husbandry, soil-conservation, manfacturing of musical instruments fashion designing, drawing and painting, home science or subjects of similar utility are chosen.

These subjects are classified according to utility and need.

Vocational, Cultural and Co-curricular Programmes: In most of the American schools vocational and general education are given simultaneously. In some cases, vocational and specific training schools are separate from general education schools. Joint system is advantageous because the students of art, science and comercial groups, by selecting useful vocational subjects, are able to find means of earning a living or for becoming more efficient and they go to specific vocational schools and thus adopt a suitable vocation for life.

In secondary schools, along with vocational and general education, co-curricular activities are also conducted. These programmes help in developing qualities of good citizenship. The students receive training in collective exchange of views, freedom of thought and expression and qualities of leadership through activities like discussions, students' self-government, and mock-parliament. Their student-life and activities prepare them for future life and behaviour. Students' administration committees by trying to amend the teaching-behaviour of teachers, provide opportunities for evaluation of each other's work. Various institutions are established for collective games and sports, literary projects, recreation and constructive utilisation of leisure. The students learn human virtues through constructive activities. The school provides various types of desired help, such as co-operation of the teachers and provision of buildings, etc. The students organise clubs according to their interests and needs, e.g., in music, literature, instrumental music, discussions, dramatics, news-paper publication, social behaviour, recreation, games and sports, etc. and related activities are also organised.

These co-curricular activities are all the more important at the adolescent stage. Schools, teachers, education department and administrators, all encourage such activities and make new provisions after evaluating the success of activities. Now all possible efforts are being made in this direction.

Summary

Latin-Grammar School System: These schools were established by Puritans for maintaining European language, literature and politics and religion. Because of the prominence of religious tendency, their influence remained upto nineteenth century. Now there have been a lot of changes and they have been replaced by academies.

Academies: Industrial development influenced education system since the middle of eighteenth century. So academies were established to help vocational and industrial life. In 1751 an academy was established in Philadelphia for the first time through the efforts of Benjamin Franklin. By 1830, the number of academies had risen to 500. Women-education, naval education, vocational education, politics, philosophy were the main subjects taught.

Public Secondary Schools: Along with industrial, political and social development, demand for free, universal, public educational system, had begun in the beginning of the nineteenth century. In 1821 first public school, in 1926 first public girls school in Boston, and in 1924 Public School in New York, were established. In 1847 after the judgement of Kalmanzoo case and on the basis of the report of Committee of Ten free and universal education was organised

Secondary Education Re-organisation: Considering 8 year education at the primary level too long a duration, the need of an intermediate unit arrangement between primary and secondary education, was felt. Consequently, class VII and VIII were joined with secondary classes and together with it the first two years of higher education were also added to the education of secondary level. The secondary level was divided into Junior High School-3 years. Higher Secondary School-3 years and Junior College-2 years.

Aims of Secondary Education: In the beginning, Latin Grammar Schools and educational academies were established in order to fulfil the needs of European religion, politics, education, literature, leadership in traditions and vocations. Later the nature of educational system changed according to the recommendations of education commissions and committees, appointed from time to time. According to the Committee of Ten in 1892, the aim of secondary education was not only preparation for college education but also utilitarian. Study of arithmetic was suggested along with classical subjects. In 1899, the Committee on College Requirements also supported the suggestions of the Committee of Ten. In 1912, the Secondary Education Reorganisation Commission suggested the following seven aims of secondary education:— Civil education, vocational education, command of fundamental principles, health education, worthy-home membership, ethical character and worthy use of leisure. Similarly, in 1933, 1936, 1942, 1944 and 1947 different aspects of educational aims were emphasised.

Functions of Secondary Education: Development of knowledge and integration, probable future needs, knowledge of traditional, cultural and contemporary social duties, development of specific ability, provision of new knowledge correlated with previous knowledge, tendency of taking interest in human activities, progressive teaching methods, independent thinking and use of research principles and checking students, before diminishing returns are the main functions of secondary education.

Nature of Secondary Education and Organisation

Types of Secondary Schools and Classification: There are two main classifications. In the first classification, the secondary stage is of 4 years (8 = 4 + 2 + 2) and in the second classification, the secondary stage is from IX to XII. In the second classification, junior high school is from VII to IX (3 years, higher secondary classes from X to XII (3 years) and the classes XIII and XIV are included in the junior college.

Junior High Schools: In some place these classes are included in higher secondary classes and in some places, they are separate.

Higher Secondary Schools: This is a supplementary provision for junior high schools. Classes from X to XII are included in this stage. Along with general education, provisions for vocational and industrial education and specialisation are available at this stage.

Classification of Secondary Schools according to Curriculum

(1) *Common Schools:*

(a) *Comprehensive Secondary Schools:* These schools are of 4 year duration. Various subjects are taught in these schools. They are free and universal. The number of subjects is about 200. They lack modern teaching methods. They are economical and convenient for rural areas.

(b) *Limited Schools*: Importance to vocational and special subects for local people. The choice of subjects is limited.

(2) *Specialisation Schools*: Elementary training of vocational education is given. Compared to general, vocational education is emphasised.

Vocational and Industrial Schools: These are established mainly in industrial and vocational centres and are similar to specialisation schools. More useful for the people.

(3) *Part-time Schools*: These schools are established for education of adults who are engaged in some vocation.

  (a) *Continuation Schools*: Provision of teaching for about 244 hours in a year and 3 to 4 hours teaching per week for adults.

  (b) *Evening Adult Schools*: Education facilities daily in the evening. Education according to the needs of the adults.

(4) *Junior Colleges*: The first two years of college stage, i.e., classes XIII and XIV are included in junior colleges. Mostly they are considered a part of college education but they are organised as a part of secondary education.

Secondary Education Curriculum and Educational Programme

Teaching Programme : Compulsory, semi-compulsory and optional subjects— three types of subjects. Semi-compulsory subjects are meant for skill in specific vocations. Optional subjects are given in groups. Students select these subjects according to interest and need. Provision depends on the size of the school and need of the place. More subjects in cities than in rural areas. Need for selection is felt in the last year of junior high school or first year of higher secondary school.

Vocational, Cultural and Co-curricular Programme: Alongwith general education and vocational education, constructive activities, literary meetings, discussions, games, and sports, recreational and swimming programmes are arranged under the guidance of teachers for worthy citizenship.

Exercises

1. Describe in brief the modern nature of the American Secondary Education, tracing the development of secondary education-system in U.S.A.
2. "The modern nature of American secondary education is the result of recommendations of various education Commissions and Committees." Comment on this statement.
3. Why did secondary education become important for the American people? Describe the aims of modern secondary education in U.S.A.
4. "Re-organised secondary education in U.S.A. is based on primary education but it is a basis for junior colleges." How?
5. What are the characteristics of re-organised curriculum of American secondary education? How does it lead to adjustment in life? Explain.

Chapter 12

Adult Education

An adult is mature in age and he is supposed to be mature mentally also. Mental development is in the direction of the progress made in gaining experiences in life. Hence an adult cannot cram like a child or a parrot. However, he may also be educated like a child. But an adult and a child cannot be taught by the same method. Adults do not take interest in learning through coloured, decorated pictures and material aids. They should be taught psychologically on the basis of their experiences. In U.S.A. much progress has been made in the field of adult education and efforts has been made to make teaching modern and psychological.

Learning is not the monopoly of children and youths alone. Learning is useful and easy only when the mind is mature and along with adult-hood there is an intellectual adult-hood and maturity. On the basis of modern researches and experiments, the educationists have come to the conclusion that adulthood is not only the mid-point of age, rather it is also the mid-point of efficiency, learning and thinking. Thus there is hardly any difference in learning between age limits of 30 to 40 years and 10 to 20 years. It has also been observed that specific intellectual ability is higher in adulthood than in youth. This is true of ability both from the general and practical point of view. An adult of 45 years of age (if he so desires), can learn more than a young man of 15 years of age.

The Meaning of Adult Education

Adult education is that active study programme in which people of more than general or compulsory schooling age participate. In this voluntary learning programme, the attitude of an adult is different and voluntary from that of a general young student. Therefore, the spirit of adult education in its multiple forms covers various points of view. Adult education is an effort to study by those persons who have not received any formal education or have left it incomplete. They, in order to enhance their ability and knowledge, want to learn through a continuous process. Adult education makes an adult capable of making himself free from narrow views and servitude even when he is engaged in his vocation or earning a living. Thus he may get rid of monotony and fatigue. Adult education enables persons, anxious of receiving continuous education, to inculcate human virtues like generosity, sympathy, co-operation by coming into contact with persons of various occupations. They make themselves cultured by learning the habit of right judgment and appreciation of values and thus become capable to contributing to the field of cultural development.

Development of Adult Education

The students receiving education through a continuous process get more facilities than the adults who are engaged in some occupation, try to be literate or educated for the satisfaction of their mental hunger. The youth is an age of carefreeness when a person can learn much. But an adult who leaves his education incomplete because of his concern for earning a living or due to non-availability of educational facilities, is unable to study. This does not mean that an adult has no tendency for mental development and a desire for the satisfaction of mental hunger. It has been observed that mature and busy adults are very much anxious to learn and for this they form various cultural, spiritual, social and voluntary associations.

There are many examples in the American history to show that the people have organised various voluntary, cultural, social and political associations in order to fulfil the educational needs of the adults. Such provisions existed since the beginning of the eighteenth century. But the nineteenth century presents a practical view of such provisions. In 1820 Lyceums evolved a formal system of education for the first time. This system was based on lecture method. This system took the shape of an Education Movement in 1826. This education movement is known as Lyceums Lecture Education Movement. This movement had spread throughout United States of America before the States Civil War began. As a result of this movement the lectures and discussions extended by the existing churches, mechanics institutes and Philosophical and Historical societies, could take a more developed form. It was estimated that about 4,000 such groups had been organising lecture and discussion programmes every week. A central organisation had been established to regulate and extend the movement.

New York Educational Efforts:

In 1874, inspired by Lyceums method, Chautauqua adult organisation was established at Chautauqua in Western New York for the first time. This effort is known as Chautauqua Institue Movement. It was in the form of a summer camp based on Lyceums method. In that camp along with out-door life activities, lectures, discussions, recreation, exhibitions, seminars, concerts, higher education classes, direction in home reading classes and other educational programmes were organised. Those programmes were full of recreational, attractive and interesting activities. Those programmes ended with concerts and games and sports in public places or parks while moving from one city to another. The American people took sufficient interest in those programmes. But with the beginning of the first World War, these programmes came to an end and new projects were executed.

Other Adult Education Efforts:

Leceums and Chautauqua movements had their effect on university education too. In 1820, some universities started correspondence education system. In 1892, the Chicago

University tried to educate the adults by organising lectures. It was the first effort and the system was influenced by the British University System. This effort influenced other universities too, and other big universities also adopted the the Lecture System for adult education.

During the transition period of the nineteenth and twentieth century, illiterate labourers from Europe migrated to America. Most of the labourers were totally illiterate. So, the problem of making them literate and increasing their efficiency emerged. It was considered necessary to educte them in American citizenship. As a result, public, community and individual institutions which undertook the responsibility of free adult education, were established. Such efforts benefited the semi-literates much and their working-efficiency also increased sufficiently.

In the beginning, the American people were of the opinion that adult education programmes should be organised for only those persons who could not receive any formal education during their childhood or youth and who are engaged in some occupation for earning a living. Thus, educational projects continued to be planned for such adults and youngmen. Such conditions continued upto the end of the nineteenth century. Later on, people realised that education was a continuous process that goes on form birth to death and a person continues to learn one thing or the other till one's death. Therefore, provision was made in the adult education plans for the education of infants, adults and old persons.

Adult education extended by various educational institutions could not be considered as a good system and it was demanded that adult education should be conducted by schools for adults, established solely for the purpose of adult education. Consequently in 1879, People's Institute of New York was established to impart an integrated education on the basis of Lyceums method and other social programmes. Finally, it was declared as an institution of adult education which began after the First World war. For the first time in 1924, an integrated and practical curriculum of adult education was started in Cleevland. At the same time, Department of Adult Education was established for the illiterate and semi-literate labourers migrating from Europe. It was only after the first World War that institutes of adult education or Lecture Institutes of Adult Education flourished. It was during this period that financially strong Brooklyn Institute of Arts and Science, New York, included vocational and social education in adult education. In 1839 Lyall Institute, which tried to arrange lectures on various literary, social and political subjects, was established in Boston.

American adult education developed speedily during the period 1925 to 1950 and subsequent years. During this period not only youths but adults and old persons also were inclined to receive education. The aims of Adult Education were revised and the modern needs were included in it. An attempt was made to make the individual an able citizen of the country by acquainting him with changes and developments in family, occupations, community, and country and the international affairs along with political, scientific and social changes. Reading rooms, libraries, museums and night schools were established in almost every city, town and village. Adult education programmes were organised in private, religious and public places.

Adult education movement is an important public movement in America because the American citizen is eager to learn more and adult education provides all possible help for preparing him for life. The adult education movement provides an opportunity to every illiterate and semi-literate child, youth, adult and old persons to receive adult education during leisure hours after the whole day's vocational labour. Both men and women participate alike in this movement. In the beginning the adult education system was something surprising for the foreigners but for them it was a medium for the fulfilment of their creative and functional needs.

Adult education department was established with a view to make the persons migrating from abroad, efficient Americans. This system provides them opportunities for leadership and success in life. Modern American adult education is very well developed. Besides receiving education in adult education schools, millions of people are utilising libraries, museums, religious places, reading-rooms and radio and television programmes for this purpose. According to the previously collected data, about 300,00,000 adults, busy in different professions, were receiving adult education in one school or the other. About five million adult men and women received adult education of the highest level.

Finance:

Both Federal and the States Governments provide periodical grants for the development and extension of adult education. About 45 States give grant-in-aid for adult education. This aid is only a part of the total expenditure. According to the Government rules, vocational aid is given to the full-time students in schools and to the adults engaged in vocations. The benefit of this aid goes mostly to the adults. About 65 per cent adults who out-number the regular students, get the advantage of such provision of grants. On the basis of the data announced in 1949, out of about three million students, about 2 million adults got that benefit. Apart from vocational grants, all State Governments undertake the responsibility of agriculture, buildings, commerce and trade, etc. and provide sufficient facilities to the adults.

Administration:

A director of vocational education is appointed for the administration of vocational training connected with adult education. America needs more money, trained teachers and instructors for conducting extensive adult education. This could have created a big problem. But adult education there is a well-planned and wisely co-ordinated affair. Firstly, whole time trained instructors have been appointed in many States. These instructors fulfil their duties devotedly and extend their full co-operation to the Government. Secondly, educationists, editors, professional experts, presidents of banks, dentists, skilled house-wives and other experts provide training in their subjects freely with a zeal and a sense of service. Mostly, adult education is free there. If there are any fees in some places, they are very nominal. The adult education system provides educational opportunities to the members of every class of society. Thus American adult education is universal, secular, free and economical.

Why and How of Adult Education

In order to know the why and how of adult education, we should understand the aims and functions of adult education. The aims of American adult education may be expressed in the following way:—

Why Adult Education?

After the literal meaning of the word 'Adult', it has been assigned meanings according to the need of the time and provision for the education of specified adults in order that—

(1) The American adults may understand their political, social, economic and family responsibilities and are able to shoulder the same successfully.

(2) Adults are able to imbibe qualities of good citizenship and are able to lead their life in a democratic way.

(3) They get facilities for learning throughout their life.

(4) They are able to get education in basic subjects like English language, literature, mathematics, geography and history; aesthetic subjects, such as, music, painting, architecture, science subjects, hygiene and other general subjects.

(5) They are able to get useful knowledge in home-art, home-science and home management for becoming worthy members of the family.

(6) They are able to learn social qualities imspite of their different cultural and social beliefs.

(7) They are able to become efficient and skilled in their related occupations and new vocations.

(8) They become familiar with national, interational and other problems.

(9) Disabled persons are able to get education, which would enable them to earn a living.

What does the Adult Education do?

Adult education has proved very beneficial because of its specific functions and importance. The functions of adult education are as under :-

(1) Adult education by providing opportunities for the utilisation of leisure, inculcates the spirit of inward communication, quiet reflection and dealing happily with occasional solitude.

(2) Adult education creates power of tolerence by inculcating the feeling of sociability in persons of different classes, groups of different social customs and persons of different religions. It is the function of adult education to develop the attitude of exchange of ideas and provide facilities of vocational and behavioural development.

(3) To make the people capable of dealing with occasional, immediate and personal problems and develop ability to gather necessary resources accordingly.

(4) To enable the people to solve problems connected with agriculture and commerce, such as, destruction of crops due to natural calamities, change in prices due to demand and supply, loss in agriculture because of political impacts like war and peace and also to provide vocational and agriculture extension education to the farmers.

(5) To provide education through art, literature, music, nature study, excursions, dramas and movies, etc. for making them well-versed in cultural and civilized behaviour.

(6) To arouse political awakening, civic sense and sensible thinking in adults so that they are able to express useful, unambiguous and sound opinion for the smooth running of administration and the Government.

The above aims and functions of adult education were formulated by Carnegic Corporation, established in 1941. This Corporation is the best institution for research in adult education. Its function has been to study the problems of adult education and to give useful suggestions regarding its organisation, methods, resources and material, training of workers, guidance, opportunity and research. Consequently, the Corporation established contacts with more than 400 adult education leaders after visting adult education institutions of about 80 cities, and then presented suggestions for the development of adult education.

Adult education, prevailing in America, provides for the utilisation of leisure by giving opportunities of life-long learning. This education is given after the formal education provided in schools.

The Nature and Organisation of Adult Education

Adult education system is sufficiently wide spread in U.S.A. It is found in two forms from the organisational point of view (1) Formal and (2) Informal.

Formal Education:

Institutions from primary to university level, such as Adult Education Extension Programme Institutions, Night Schools, Evening Schools, and various Education Extension Associations are included in this type of education. Some of these are:

(a) *School for Adults*: These schools conducted lectures and other social programmes in the beginning. But later on, they were declared regular institutions for adult education. First of all in the nineteenth century, New York People's Institute was established for this purpose. All other such adult schools are confined to adult education only and undertake the responsibility of continious education of adults. These schools are managed and organised by the teachers of universities and other educationists. Any person, of any qualification, can take admission in these schools.

These schools impart education through lecture method and other educational programmes for catering to the needs of local people, their occupations and specific abilities. These schools study the traditions and needs of the local people from time to time and try to fulfil them as far as possible. These schools maintain co-ordination in the educational programmes, curriculum and their organisation.

(b) *Institutes of Adult Education*: In 1839, Lowell Institute, Boston, based on the lecture system, was established. This educational institution seems to be an ideal institution. Apart form the lecture system, vocational and technical programmes are also organised here. This institution is very popular and thousands of people take the benefit of education there. Another notable institution of adult education is the Brooklyn Institute of Arts and Science. This institute was estabished in 1823, long before the Lowell Institute. This institute is financially sound. It has got separate departments for lectures on science, art, and literature. The music department here is one of the best in the whole of U.S.A. It is a unique institution for training in music. Children's Museum of Arts and Science and Botanical Garden are sufficiently interesting and famous organisations which benefit numerous children, young adults and the old.

(c) *New Schools for Social Research*: New schools for social research were established for adults receiving graduate and higher education. These institutions were established in 1919 for the first time. At that time, their aim was to conduct progressive and developing eductional and social programmes. This institution provides opportunities for new researchs on social problems through social studies and social programmes, discussion, lectures on related problems and projects. Main social studies subjects include—

history, social psychology, labour, behaviourism, policital science, criminology and mental hygiene. Lectures and correspondence teaching methods are employed for teaching. Learned men and women with social inclinations do much successful work in such institution.

Informal Education:

In the field of adult education, there is no provision for regular curriculum and its implementation in the informal system of education. In this system, adult education is imparted through Lyceums, public clubs, museums, libraries, reading rooms, dramatic clubs, radios, movies, press and various games and sports In 1914 following the Smith Lever Act, an effort was made by the Agriculture Department to implement Agriculture Agent System. Through this system provision for the education of farmers in rural areas was made in subjects like argiculture education, familiarity with modern scientific means, psychology, house-keeping and such other subjects for progressive social life.

Those adult education centres, too, which provide for continuous general education are also known as Informal Education Centres because their provisions are quite different from those of formal education system. In those centres citizens' committees, labour unions, commercial business firms and adults' clubs, mostly participate. These institutions try to give vocational training and increase professional efficiency through their co-operative and collective efforts. Such adult education is also known as labour education. Innumerable programmes related to adult education are broadcast by radio and television. The contribution of mass-media in the spread of informal adult education, is immense.

American adult education presents unique examples of public co-operation. People there seem to be quite alive to their need for education. There are many good public libraries and reading rooms. Similarly, there are about 70,000 rental libraries and reading rooms. Branches of libraries and reading rooms have been established in rural areas. For rural adult education or for agriculture education, magazines and journals, books, news pamphlets, documentary films and educational films are provided. Mobile libraries have been arranged for extension of education from one place to another. These mobile libraries distribute reading materials in various rural areas. Attractive programmes are organised in big reading rooms of public libraries. Attractive and interesting education is provided through discussion and book review clubs.

In cities, the functions and use of the museums seems to be more praise-worthy. These museums, by organising exhibits, archaeology, architecture, paintings, art and sculpture, bring educational revolution for millions of people. Various educational programmes continue throughout the year and adults of different groups gain useful knowledge through them.

Institutions of Adult Education

In U.S.A., various types of institutions provide adult education. Universities, junior colleges, labour institutions, correspondence educational institutions, adult education community projects and such other institutions are engaged in the task of providing adult education.

(1) *Universities and Adult Education*:

Universities provide education of the highest level. Adults who are keen on higher education receive higher education through universities. These universities are run by the State or public. Community institutions also contribute in their establishment. These universities occupy an important place in the adult education system. By 1992 there were about 250 university institutions and about 8 million adults received higher education in those institutions. New York Unversity has got an important place in the sphere of adult education.

New York University:

New York University is a representative institution for adult education system of U.S.A. Department of General Education organises adult education here. Fees are charged but certain departments such as industrial firms which send their employees for adult education pay full fees or part of it. Both vocational and general education are given in these universities. Examinations are held after the completion of the course. But there is no compulsion for appearing in the examination. No certificate is awarded after passing the examination.

Adult education programme may be classified into two types of courses:-

(i) Cultural Study.

(ii) Vocational Training.

The cultural course includes foreign languages, literature, philosophy of life, etc. and the vocational training course provides training in painting, typing, printing, electroplating, radio and television. Repairing and practical work are also done during training. Although there is a provision for multipurpose vocational training, yet not more than 40 per cent adults take part in them. Compared to cultural study, vocational training programme is more tiresome and hard. The provision of vocational, technical and craft subjects makes the curriculum of these schools truly utilitarian. Any adult, besides subjects of cultural study, may offer any of the vocational subjects, such as book designing, book binding, drawing and painting, printing, ink production, book publication, calligraphy, typography and lithography.

Department of General Education of the New York University is very important from the view point of adult education. The programmes related to labour, industry and specialisation are given an important place in this department. The department of labour acquaints the labourers with the history of labour, aims and philosophy and various other labour problems. Their relationship with the state, society, and country on the basis of labour is also explained to them. In the field of industry, provisions exist for industrial and vocational training according to their posts. Persons are trained for the post of instructor, supervisor and foreman. Many industrial units of New York send their labourers and other persons eligible for posts for training here and pay their tution fees. At the request and suggestions of industrial concerns, arrangements for training of their labourers and personnel are made from time to time. In 1992, 5000 adults, between the age of 20 to 50 years studied here. 20 per cent adults had received education upto Graduate and Post-Graduate level. This Univesity has become famous for education in accountancy, law and taxation. Teaching is arranged for these subjects under the guidance of reputed persons in the subjects concerned.

In the universities of U.S.A., good arrangement has been made for teaching the adults for degree courses. Nearly 75 to 80 universities and institutions of higher education train the adults in a wide curriculum. Besides these, there are 'credit and non-credit' educational institutions which provide education through correspondence.

(2) *Correspondence Adult Education Institutions*:

Adults who cannot go to schools for some reason, receive education through correspondence. There are about 3000 such institutions in U.S.A. Besides these, there are about 500 universities, colleges and institutions of higher learning which direct and guide through correspondence. Scranton (Pennsylvania) International Correspondence School is the most extensive and famous school which distributes about 9000 question-answer booklets daily and has educated more than fifteen million adults during the last 80 years through correspondence. This method is very popular in U.S.A. Pamphlets are published by subject specialists.

Correspondence education system adds to the specific ability of some persons and helps in the satisfaction of hunger for learning in many others. For some, it fulfils their educational aims and for others it is a source of recreation. This method provides facilities of education from high literary education to domestic general education.

(3) *Night Adult Schools and Education*:

These schools provide educational opportunities to persons

engaged in vocations and earning their livelihood. These institutions, run by collective and individual efforts, have adopted the form of community centres These centres manage successfully the teaching of all subjects from primary to higher education, such as vocational, commercial, literary, cultural, recreational, domestic, etc. These night schools make arrangements for training according to local needs.

(4) *Junior Colleges and Adult Education*:

In the United States of America, Junior College System is the contribution of re-oriented curriculum. In this system, the teaching of first two years of higher education is done in Junior Colleges. During these two years, provision of education, based on most recent nature of national needs and traditions, has been made. These colleges are very important in the Evening Teaching System. They are also community centres like Night Schools. These colleges have become so important that the number of students in the Evening Education System is more than in the day school system. A survey of evening education in the town of Modesto has revealed that one-third of the total adult population which was nearly 8000, took part in the educational programmes of Junior Colleges. Similarly, there was difference in the day courses, the number was 30,000 in evening classes. The junior college system have helped the expansion of adult education to a great extent. The number of such colleges is about 900. In these colleges all the social, cultural and vocational subjects are taught.

(5) *Labour Unions and Adult Education*:

In U.S.A. Adult Education System is not run by social institutions only. Labour Unions also have established various schools and colleges for labourers to take benefit of adult education. These schools, too, provide all types of vocational, commercial and general education. In 1921, the American Federation of Labour established Workers Education Bureau for adult education. The American Labour Education Service supplemented it. The famous industrialist, motor-car manufacturer, Henry Ford extended much co-operation in this direction. He created Ford Foundation Fund for adult education and made the education system financially sound. Along with it, he offered all financial assistance for the implementation of the curriculum modified by the labourers according to their needs in 1930 and this was implemented in many industrial towns.

The labour unions have been holding seminars and meetings at adult education centres for intensive study and performing other functions such as publication of books and reading materials, etc. These institutions have been organising education programmes for educating the labourers in specific technical changes, social securities, labour rules and legislations, international trade, etc.

(6) *Adult Education Community Projects and Their Organisation*:

United States of America, impressed by the adult education programmes of schools and other education institutions prepared Adult Education Community Projects and established community Adult Education Councils at different places with the view to run these projects according to local needs. The main function of these Councils has been the replanning of projects according to the interests and needs of the time after a careful study of local needs and interests. The members of these councils are elected representatives or leaders of non-educational or semi-educational institutions.

Mode of Working:

Community development educational projects are generally inspired by local education officer, public-library presidents, and influencial community leaders. Inspired by these persons, any person who is interested in adult education and possesses qualities of leadership, prepares general outlines of community programme for adult education after collecting community members interested in educational programmes. He presents his recommendations on the draft about the local needs after ascertaining the needs of the local people. After this, other dignitories are invited and a council is formed on the basis of majority votes or unanimously. This council, then, prepares community education projects according to the need of the local people.

In some places, the education superintendents with the co-operation of elected members and leaders of various institutions, prepare the general outline of the project and constitute the council by nominating its members. These members help in the development of adult education through their efforts for the implementation of the projects.

In the mid west area of Iowa, the community education projects have been conducted through recreational programmes for the last 55 years. Although they are organised on a small scale, yet they are very popular because of their utility. In some small towns educational projects are run with the help of as small a number as 40 citizens only, out of which 20 belong to the agricultural areas. Education superintendent, education board and adult education council co-operate from time to time. Small communities in American states follow this method. In the Olivet city of Michigan State, the community education projects have been organised successfully since 1946. Subjects specialists co-operate sufficiently in the implementation of projects. The custom of charging fees equal to the expenditure on teaching material is a fine example of economic justice.

Community projects of adult education are multi-purpose and extensive. The following subjects get priority in these projects:—

(1) Education for doing creative work with interest and recreation.

(2) Education for technical changes according to changed social needs.

(3) Education for the contemporary problems of American states, country and the world.

(4) Education of the disabled persons and of special communities.

(5) Professional education and training.
(6) Education for the labourers and labour education.
(7) Civil security education.
(8) Education for posts and promotions.
(9) Home-development and worthy home-membership education.

Precautions in the Implementation of Community Projects

The successful execution of community projects depends on the draft of educational projects. Certain precautions are needed in conducting them. They are as under:—

(a) *Inclusion of local, individual and social interests*: After surveying the interests of a particular society at a particular place, attention should also be paid to the interest of individual adults. It is possible that some might be interested in vocations, some in intensive study, some in art and some might be eager for the satisfaction of hunger for scientific learning. In such a situation attention will have to be paid to the compilation and implementation of projects according to the interests of different persons. So the programmes or the projects should include social needs, incorporating the interests of all the groups and individuals.

(b) *Precautions regarding duration of teaching and Organisation*: It is necessary that the duration of teaching in the programmes of the projects is not long and expensive. One day's teaching per week is sufficient for a course of 8 to 10 weeks. Adult education guides, leaders or co-ordinaters should also be trained on a short-term basis. The council should try to organise projects of few subjects or teacher-free subject programmes.

(c) *Precautions in the Provision of Finance and Teachers*: Adult education projects of small communities should utilise the services of energetic social workers rather than employing paid teachers. Paid teachers should be appointed by large communities. It will be better to appoint paid teachers on the basis of their maximum prescribed qualifications. The same precaution should be taken in the selection of the members of the Council.

Finance for Adult Education

The organisation of the adult education system requires sufficient funds. These funds are provided by the Federal government, State government, local community and individuals efforts.

(1) *Help by the Federal Government*: According to the provisions of the American constitution the Federal Government extends much financial help in supplementing the expenditure on adult education projects. This help is in millions of dollars. On the basis of this help adult education projects are implemented throughout the country. Acts passed from time to time have proved very helpful. Smith Hughes Act, George Barden Act and Smith Lever Act have been praiseworthy. The Federal Government spends money on the education of adult farmers under the Agriculture Extension Service for increasing crop prduction, storage, preservation, cattle-breeding, house-keeping, various vocational activities and cottage industries. This Agriculture Extension Service successfully leads to the social, national, home community, cultural and personal development of the farmers. The Federal Government provides financial help of nearly twentyfive million dollars for agriculture programmes to local leaders, agriculture development clubs, 4 H clubs, home demonstration agents, county agriculture agents and project councils. Community groups, leaders, government experts, local committees, and various agriculture development representatives whose number exceeds 6 thousand, go from village to village, trying to improve the social, national, home and personal life of the farmers. These workers make arrangements for imformation on modern agricultural researches, inventions, lecture on new agriculture methods, hold exhibitions, guidance programmes, etc., which benefit the rural adults to a great extent.

Radio, television and cheap publications are very important for adult education extension in U.S.A. They broadcast various literary, social, cultural, political and vocational programmes. The Federal Government bears the financial responsibility of radio, television education programmes and cheap publications. Such audo-visual aids might be helping about fifteen million adults every week. Discussions, lectures and question-answer programmes are also held. Some active workers get the summaries of these programmes published in order that cheap adult education literature may be available to the adults.

(2) *Help by the State Governments:* More than fifty per cent of the States of U.S.A. give financial help for adult education programmes. 15 States give partial help. California, Pensylvania, New York and 10 other States bear most of the expenditure incurred on adult education institutions. In California, 64 per cent adult education expenditure is met through grant-in-aid from the State Government, 20 per cent from the local sources, 2 per cent from fees and rest of the 14 per cent from other sources. In Michigan State, only 5 per cent of the expenditure is met from the State aid, 43 per cent from the local taxes, 42 per cent from fees. Thus the development of adult education is more in those States which spend more and less in States which spend less on adult education.

(3) *Public help on education*: Besides regular schools in U.S.A., there are many public institutions which provide adult education, such as religious centres, libraries, reading rooms, museums and clubs, etc. Their size depends on their financial conditions. Some evening adult education institutions provide training in specific technical vocations. City Evening Trade School, New York and Frank Trade School, Los-Angeles are such adult education institutions which along with training in vocational and commercial subjects, provide technical education from ordinary machines to heavy machines like aeroplanes. Instituions run by Education Boards are controlled by local education officers. Local, community, religious and commercial institutions, too, are influenced by the administrative and financial co-opertion of these education officers. Adult education institutions conduct their programmes successfully on the basis of local financial co-operation and facilities.

(4) *University help*: Adult education institutions fulfil their obligations at different levels. Here, higher education institutions and private universities provide higher education of graduate and post-graduate level. These institutions organise education of both short and long duration. These adult education institutions of the university level receive grants from the Federal and State Governments from time to time. The number of graduate level institutions is more than other adult education institutions. In 1992, there were about 800 adult-education institutions for higher education level which have been imparting education from general subjects to technical, industrial, vocational and specific ability subjects. Extension projects have led to sufficient development in rural areas. Agriculture-Extension programmes are successfully conducted under the Agriculture-Extension projects. Agriculture schools and Agriculture-Learning-Extension centres are run by the Agriculture Department and they receive help and grant from the Federal and State Governments. The Director of Extension Courses looks after the programmes of agriculture extension centres and schools. The Director of Extension Courses is considered to be the man who undertakes the responsibility of providing information on agricultural subjects to home life in rural areas.

(5) *Finances of Private, Community and other Adult-Education Institutions*: Mostly it is seen that these institutions are organised on the basis of contributions, donations and gifts. Their programmes and projects are like those of public institutions, but the expenditure on education programmes is sanctioned by the members of the Board of Trustees whereas in public institutions the expenditure on adult education is sanctioned by the Congress (parliament). If the funds sanctioned are insufficient, fees are charged by the institutions. In order to make the adult education programmes purposeful and successful, it is necessary to conduct them with combined effort of various agencies. In 1950, National Education Association of U.S.A. and American Association of Adult Education jointly sponsored adult education programmes. As a result of this joint effort, both the institutions were united

into the Adult Education Association of U.S.A. Now the papers and magazines published by this Association are called Adult Education Magazines. Such mergers and joint efforts have brought in uniformity and coherence in the adult education organisation.

In U.S.A., many adult education institutions provide education through correspondence only for the sake of earning money. These community adult education institutions organise adult education based on different methods and techniques. Harvard University Trade Union Fellowship programmes and Lusaville University conduct teaching programmes through radio and correspondence. Among the non-public institutions, New York University is the best in the adult education department.

SUMMARY

Development of Adult Education: Since the eighteenth century, social, cultural, religious and political associations in U.S.A., made efforts for teaching of adults through lectures, etc. Lyceums method of 1820 and Chautauqua Movement of 1874 are some such efforts. Adults were educated on the basis of lectures through recreational programmes. In 1890, some universities and higher education institutions conducted correspondence education programmes. Development in the field of adult education took place in 1925 after the World War I. During this period, reading rooms, libraries, schools and museums were established for the expansion of adult education. In 1950, more attention was paid to all such agencies. Sixty per cent of the States of America have public, extensive and universal adult education system, responsibility of which rests with State Governments. Other collective, individual and religious institutions get useful help from the Federal and Sate Governments. Along with the provision of constructive, commercial and cultural general education, there is a provision of necessary vocational education in the system of adult education. About sixty million people have benefited from this system of education. There is a provision of a full-time teacher for running the system successfully. Social-service educationists, leaders, subject-specialists and vocational experts extend full co-operation where full-time subject teachers are not available.

Why Adult Education? Adult education in U.S.A. has broad aims. Adult education is a strong medium of vocational, social, individual, cultural and economic development for the adults. This education helps in solving various economic, social and mental problems.

Forms of Adult Education: Adult schools and adult education institutions are established for the extension of adult education and its organisation. Provisions exist for education from the primary to the university level in these institutions. Art, science and vocational subjects are taught in these schools. Correspondence method seems useful for adult education. Among informal educational institutions, the Lyceums, reading rooms, libraries, museums, radio, television, movies, etc. are very popular. Agriculture programmes, too, are conducted through these mediums. Through them qualities of co-operation, sociability and morality are inculcated.

Finance of Adult Education: The Federal Government in America offers financial help and co-operation to adult education institutions. They encourage extension of adult education by giving grants worth millions of dollars every year. Thus various public, community and local institutions conduct adult education with responsibility and are obliged by the Government grants. State Governments, too, offer grants for expansion of adult education. The system of grant by State Governments is not the same in every State. Various religious, community and private and commercial institutions co-operate in the extension of adult education. Expenditure on adult education is supplemented by fees and local financial sources. The Federal Government undertakes the responsibility of expenditure on university adult education programmes and it is also supplemented by fees charged from adults. Private and community donations are also collected to meet the expenditure on adult education programmes.

Exercises

1. What is the meaning of adult education in U.S.A.? Why is adult education given there?
2. How did the modern adult education in U.S.A. evolve its present form? Explain.
3. How are Community Projects on adult education conducted in U.S.A.? How are the programmes under these projects organised?
4. Describe the organisation, management and control of adult education system in U.S.A. and explain the sources of its finance.

Chapter 13

Teacher Education

Development of Teacher Education

Teacher Training System in U.S.A. is not very old. The suggestion of teacher training was put forward in the middle of the ninteenth century and provision was made by some States for it. Earlier the status of the teacher was not very high in the eyes of the public. So learned persons were not attracted towards this profession. No learned person was prepared to join the teaching profession on such low salary and without any social status. Only people from the low strata of society took up teaching. In fact, it was not considered a good profession.

With the awakening for education, shortage of teachers began to be felt. Realising the seriousness of the art of teaching and its importance, there arose a demand for a system which could prepare skilled and capable teachers. Consequently, in Massachussets State a Government Teachers' Training Institution was established in 1839, for the first time. With the establishment of this institution, some other States, too, began to feel the need of one year Teacher Training Schools. In 1857, State Normal School at Lexington in Illinois State was established. The curriculum of this training school aimed at the training of teachers of both primary and secondary levels. In 1860, the one year course of Lexington Normal School was changed to two years course. By that time, mostly teachers for the primary level were trained and there was no prescribed qualification for admission. So the educated and eager persons were selected.

So far, teacher training was conducted by Normal Schools. Colleges of higher education and universities could not make any provision for teacher training. But with the awakened desire for education and the need of the time, the need for professional training for teachers began to be stressed. Consequently, the want of teacher training system was fulfilled by establishing education departments in the following universities:-

In 1873, short-term and part-time courses were started in the Educational Training Department of Iowa University. In 1879, the University of Michigan did praiseworthy work by organising full-time teacher training course. In 1887, Columbia University in New York, not only provided teacher training programme but also organised training for school managers. This provision proved very useful and this Teacher Training College made significant contribution for the development of teacher training.

During the second decade of the twentieth century, efforts were made by the educationists to give a technical shape to teacher training. Thus education was now treated as a subject of teacher education and it was compulsorily included in the curriculum of teacher training for making the teachers more capable and qualified.

Admission Requirement and Selection

Upto the first quarter of the twentieth century, there was no prescribed qualification for admission. The status of Normal Schools was considered equal to that of a secondary school. So, trainees with primary education qualifications were admitted to the Normal Schools. Upto 1920, 2 year training course was being conducted and in order to raise the standard of teachers, students who had passed two year course of secondary level, were admitted to a training school. Later, the two year course was changed into a 4 years course and the teaching methods were revised and modernised. In 1922, Columbia University revised teacher training methods and teaching techniques. There was more emphasis on the training of pupil-teachers. So, teacher training institutions and teacher education centres were established. Americal Association of Teachers and Colleges passed resolutions in favour of providing teacher education in most of the States. Such resolutions, along with increasing the number of teachers during the time of Depression, contributed significantly in determining a reasonable teaching standard.

In America, teacher training has been assigned vocational importance like other vocational training and minimum academic qualifications have been laid down for selection to the Teacher Training course as is the case for other vocational courses. For admission to Teacher Training course, attention is paid not only to the academic qualifications but other general considerations are also kept in mind. Recommendation of the head of the institution last attended, academic and character records, certificates of extra-curricular activities, intelligence, personal interviews, physical capacity, are mainly examined at the time of admission. The trainees are admitted after testing their teaching aptitude, phychological efficiency and professional informations. In the States, there is no prescribed qualification for admission to the training course. However, at the time of appointment, it is seen that the teachers teaching secondary classes should have received 4 year training after passing post-graduate examination, i.e., a master's degree. So for the teachers of this level, post-graduate qualification is necessary for admission to a training course. For teachers of primary level, 2 year junior college education is necessary for admission. In some cities a Ph.D. degree is necessary for secondary level teachers.

In 1938, the National Education Association stressed the need of appointing most qualified male and female teachers in national interest. This Association established an institution called Future Teachers of America. This institution, with a view to enlist qualified teachers for secondary schools, laid emphasis on establishing Clubs and Chapter at college level. The Normal Schools tried to implement the suggestion gladly.

The American citizens are very alive to the educational system. They know that the teachers are the makers of future citizens and there is always a demand for providing necessary facilities for their training. For admission to training, their personality, nature, religion, their socio-cultural and political beliefs are carefully examined.

Teacher Training Institutions

In the United States of America, individual and collective efforts in the field of education have always been very significant. The same is true of teacher-education system. Provision for teacher education through private efforts had been made before governmental efforts. In 1823, fifteen years before any governmental effort, a private Normal School had been established in Vermont. Similarly, in 1827 a Normal School had been established in Lancasters in Massachussets State. Upto the middle of nineteenth century, Normal Schools were established through public efforts. County boards had established Normal Schools for the training of teachers in their respective areas. Thus before the beginning of the twentieth century, 170 such Normal Schools had been established. All these efforts speak of the interest of the American people for the cause of teacher education. The establishing of these Normal Schools reflects the influence of European progress and environment but necessary changes in the system has been going on according to American environment and needs.

The following forms of teacher training institutions are available in U.S.A.:-

(1) Normal Schools.
(2) Teachers' Colleges.
(3) School of Education.
(4) Department of Education.

These institutions have been described in detail as below:

(1) *Normal Schools:* Expression of teacher education in

U.S.A. has been based on European traditions. 'Normal' is a French word which means 'according to rule'. So Normal Schools are those schools in which 'Rules of Teaching' are taught. Here, teacher education had been organised on the lines of the Report on Public Education in Prussia, presented by Victor Cousin. In the beginning, the duration of the teacher education course was of one year. But when the course was changed to two years, education was taught in the first year and in the second year, organisation of teaching was taught. Then, only those students who had passed primary education came for admission and after the training they could become qualified teachers for teaching primary classes. In fact, those Normal Schools provided education as in the lower secondary classes. At that time there was no provision of any specific teacher training, rather the courses of first two years of secondary education after primary level, were taught. In some places, even this education was not compulsory and one could become a teacher without training after completing the primary level course.

In U.S.A. during the first 25 years of twentieth century, it was customary for the Normal Schools to revise the subjects of primary level therefore, under teacher training, the two-fold programmes—(1) Teaching of Methods of Teaching and Principles of Teaching (2) Practice Teaching—were conducted. But on realising that for creating future citizens of the nation, better qualified teachers were required, more attention began to be paid on training in teaching methods and higher professional education, instead of education subject. In 1920, 2 year course in the Normal Schools was converted into 4 year course. Thus, by the end of the first quarter of the twentieth century, the training course became a course of 4 year duration and all the Normal Schools were changed into Teachers' Training Colleges.

(2) *Teachers' Training Colleges*: As has been said above, the curriculum of the Normal Schools had been changed into 4 year course and their form had been changed into Teacher Training Colleges; But even earlier there were Teachers'

Training Colleges besides Normal Schools. About 125 years before, in 1857, Government Teachers' Training College had been established in Illinois. This college provided higher professional training for college teachers. Upto the American Civil War, this college continued to give professional training to college teachers. At that time, some provision was made in the Liberal Arts Colleges for lectures on the art of teaching. In 1888, a teachers training college was opened in New York. The founder of this college was Nicholos Murray Butler. This teachers' training college was affiliated to the Columbia University, after it had worked for 10 years. By 1920, the number of these training colleges rose to 45. Afterwards, in the subsequent 20 years, the number of these colleges increased rapidly. During the subsequent 20 years, the number of newly opened teachers training colleges went up by three times.

The period between 1920 to 1992 has been a period of revolution and expansion for the system of teacher training. During this period, the importance of education as a subject was reduced and that of techniques of teaching increased. Thus, two levels—pre-service and in-service emerged in the field of teaching and nature of secondary level training changed into college level trainng. At that time, the training-curriculum was revised to include those courses which could make the prospective teacher skillful, efficient, humane, learned and of fine personality. So the curriculum included programmes like general education, specialisation, teaching professional education, teaching practice, etc. An effort was made to lay teaching foundation by including important subjects like humanities, departmental education, hygiene, social studies, natural sciences, art, educational sociology, education psychology, educational philosophy and principles of education. For increasing the specific ability of teachers, various programmes and courses were organised. By receiving such training, the teacher could attain professional efficiency. To-day, in order to make the teacher training more developed and utilitiarian, free opportunities, supervision by experienced supervisors and guidance by serious-minded counsellors have been provided. Practice-teaching system is changing according to national needs and is becoming more psychological and progressive day by day.

In U.S.A., the training colleges are run and managed by the State. The teachers for primary and secondary classes are awarded Bachelors degree after training. Some colleges, in order to add specialisation, are conducting five year courses instead of four years. These colleges award masters and doctorate degrees. These colleges have gained international reputation because of their special teacher training programme.

(3) *School of Education*: Schools of Education are like Teachers Training Colleges but they are affiliated to some University. In 1879, Michigan University, first of all, organised full-time teacher training. However, even before this, Michigan, Brown and New York Universities had started part-time training system. Michigan University awarded graduation degree after the completion of the teaching courses. In 1888, New York University also began to award graduate degree and modernised teaching profession by giving pedagogy, a vocational form. This policy affected teacher training schools and centres all over and all of them tried to raise the standard of teachers' training.

The nature of American Schools of Education is similar to the separate departments of education in Universities. These departments are completely independent in their organisation and administration. Admission to the education course is given after the completion of two year degree course. In the training curriculum, provision has been made for the teaching of general education, philosophy of education, psychology, language, literature and culture along with the education subjects. During teacher training, emphasis is laid on professional efficiency and skill. After the completion of the course, graduate degree is awarded. The courses in these Schools of Education are similar to those of Teachers Training Colleges.

(4) *Education Department*: In 1873, the Iowa University had started part-time teacher training programme, teaching science of education as a separate subject. Afterwards, the

Michigan University conducted full-time training course on science of education, in a vocational form. Thus many Arts colleges and Universities established separate Departments of Education, considering science of education as an independent subject and conducted teacher training course.

Discussions on the development of pedagogy continued in U.S.A. from time to time and new changes continued. Educationists and experts emphasised the need of making the training for teaching profession more technical under the science of education. Consequently, Arts colleges and Universities began to give professional training in the service of education by establishing separate departments of education. Chicago University established its independent departments. Advanced courses have been started for the training of School administrators and educational administrators. In these departments, provision has also been made for research in the science of education.

Curriculum for Pedagogy

As has been mentioned earlier, under the science of education, there is a provision for general education along with professional training in the science of education. Hence the courses may be divided into two parts:—

(1) General Education Course, and (2) Teacher Training Course.

Organisation of the Courses: Most of the States in U.S.A. run a 4 year Teacher Training Course. Some States have 5 year course. Such an arrangement of courses includes one year special professional training after the completion of the 4 year teacher-training course. There is no general sequence of general education and professional training during the 4 years. All the States have some difference or the other. In some states, general education and teacher-training go together during the 4 years and in others, general education or teacher-training is provided in the last two years of the course.

In U.S.A., there are about 1000 such institutions which try to make the professional training of teachers more efficient and create life-long interest in the teaching profession by providing advance degree courses. These institutions make the teachers capable of establishing contact and taking admission in higher degree courses. The teachers get a raise in pay when they obtain a higher degree. This encourages the teachers for getting the highest degree and they become more capable and learned. Organisers in the field, college presidents, administrative officers, teacher specialists and experts are provided opportunities for participating in the higher degree course in order to maintain the tendency of obtaining higher degree training.

In U.S.A., the period of four years of the teachers' training course is divided in the following way:— the first two years are devoted to liberal arts, and the last two years are meant for detailed study. Teachers training is given along with general education. General education includes the study of national and foreign languages, literature, mathematics, music, science, social sciences and economics, etc. Teacher training subjects are health education, education for mental hygiene, child psychology, education for internationalism and cultural subjects based on lecture and discussion methods. For practice in class-teaching, the trainees are familiarised with old and modern teaching methods and efforts are made for giving thorough practice in the methods.

In accordance with the democratic needs of the country, the teachers are trained for adapting themselves to the democratic atmosphere. And in order to give the trainees, a wholesome and social personality, additional programmes are arranged. Democratic virtues are inculcated in the male and female pupil-teachers by organising associations and committees on 'Federal Lines'. For community information and guidance, magazines and journals are published and facilities of games and sports are provided. The teachers are trained to work according to the atmosphere of the place where they are to work after training. Provision of music, vocal and instrumental, and dancing is made for recreation. Thus, the teachers there, are made to adapt themselves according to national, social and professional ideals.

Recognised Degree—Distribution after Training

The American people and administrators are known for their progressive attitude in the field of education. It is customary to appoint those teachers who have self-control and strong social sense. At the time of appointment, attention is also paid to their personality and modes of behaviour, the patience of the teacher, his strong, effective tendencies and sense of humour are carefully looked into. All these specialities are considered as the prerequisite capabilities of the teacher.

The qualifications of the teachers are not the same at different levels. About 36 States have different perscribed qualifications for male and female teachers even for the primary level. In some states minimum of 2 years study at the college level is essential, while in others completion of 2 year training course is necessary. And in the rest of the States, a graduation degree along with 4 year teachers training is required. In about 48 States, for the teachers of secondary class, a graduate degree together with 4 year teacher training, is considered necessary. The remaining States prefer specialised professional qualification after the 4 year teacher training. In some States, there is a demand for teachers, trained in nursery methods, kindergarten methods and Dalton Plan and some others demand specialists in guidance and counselling. At the time of appointment for the secondary level, special attention is paid to the teachers' special capability for teaching, additional training and higher degree. Generally, preference is given to the teachers with five year training.

The responsibility of distributing degrees or certificates after the training lies with the education departments, State Education Superintendents or State Boards of Education. Certificates are compulsory only in one third of the States in the country. In States where certificates are compulsory, the same are given after holding a test before appointment. Certificates are awarded on the basis of educational and graded ability of the teachers. In some places, certificates are given for the probationary period. And after the expiry of the period, the certificates are cancelled. Certificates may be awarded for life also. In some places, the certificates are conditional. Thus, the system of certificates is both probationary and conditional.

For University and colleges, teachers' certificates are not necessary. But they are required to have passed two years course after their college education. In some places, a post-graduate degree and three years of additional study is prescribed. And in some States, teachers with a doctorate degree are considered qualified for teaching at the University level.

Provision of Research in the Science of Education

Provision of research work is made for the teachers in order to make them well qualified and upto-date in knowledge. Universities provide research facilities to the trained teachers and refresher courses are conducted for those who are engaged in teaching work. Harvard University is doing pioneer work in this direction. This University provides opportunities for getting higher degree and professional qualifications under the supervision of learned and experienced guides (supervisors). It arranges special courses for those teachers of primary and secondary levels who could receive four year training but could not get specialised qualification of the fifth year. This training is considered equivalent to the five year training course. The Harvard University through its fellowship courses, tries its best to make the teachers well qualified, capable of following the national ideals and earn international reputation.

The Antioch College of Ohio State trains those teachers and counsellors who work in industrial or vocational areas instead of educational areas. These persons after teachers' or counsellors' training guide persons who are in search of a vocation or occupation and thus given vocational guidance. Such a provision embodies the feeling of social service that a person of any other sphere may give useful counselling and vocational guidance during leisure hours to other persons. It is a part of naitonal youth welfare plan in which a person gives the benefit of his abilities and skills to others. Thus the coming generation is able to get capability and direction for entering the vocational sphere.

This work is conducted through camp-system in which the teachers of Antioch College actively participate. The teachers move from one camp to another in order to fulfil their responsibility. Such work refines their attitude and feeling of service and opens avenues for solving the problems of the youth. This provision helps in the higher college education as well. According to the 'Camp System', the teachers are divided into two groups. If one group works at the camp centres, the other group conducts educational programmes in the college premises. When these groups have completed the assigned work, they replace each other and complete their respective assignments.

Condition of Teachers in U.S.A.

The American way of life has been materialistic from the very beginning. The status of a person is determined mainly on economic basis. The same basis is used for teachers also. In the beginning, the teacher had no social status because he was leading his life on a low salary. His services were not given any proper recognition even when he had tolerated economic and social depression patiently. But by the end of the nineteenth century, there was sufficient progress in the field of education and due to the progressive thinking, attention was paid to the needs, conditions and facilities required by teachers. As a result, the conditions of the teachers began to improve.

In the beginning of the twentieth century, along with eductional development, attention was paid to the academic freedom, service security, medical leave, weekly rest day, pension and other facilities for the teachers. The teachers began to be appointed on long-term contracts and gradually the appointments began to be made on permanent basis. The teachers, to-day are enjoying full facilities and are working in a very satisfactory atmosphere. They have their big associations like the workers in other professions, equipped with all facilities and service security rules.

In U.S.A.the services of the teachers are based on an

agreement between the management and the teacher and on the rules framed by the government. In about 45 States of the country, the services of the teachers are quite secure and may be terminated only under special circumstances. In all the States the services of teachers are permanent and there is one or the other statutory provision for their security of service and other facilities. In about 30 States, there is statutory provision for sickness leave and retirement.

The Federal and State Governments have not prescribed any universal law for the appointment of teachers as in France or Australia. After completing his training, the candidate sends his application to the teacher employment agencies. The agencies keep a record of the educational qualifications, training, abilities and experience of the teacher on the basis of which they contact the local education control units for their needs and select the teachers according to their demand. In some places, the teachers directly send their application to the local education control units. These units send their applications to the employment agencies for selection according to their needs. The employment agencies forward the application according to the need of the units and on the recommendations of the local education superintendent, the local units appoint the teachers. Teacher employment agencies are private, community, governmental and public. Some agencies are governed by teachers' associations and training institutions.

As has been discussed, the status of the teachers is determined on the basis of their salary scales. The salary scale of the teachers depends on the economic status of the local bodies. These local bodies prescribe the salary scales of teacher according to their economic condition and need. The scale of the teachers of rural areas is less than that of the teachers of urban areas. So the teachers of low salary scale migrate to the areas of higher salary scales. Very often, the scale of teachers salary is determined on the basis of average State income and the number of children of school going age. In the salary scale, no importance is attached to the time scale or efficiency bar. Increase in pay depends on the increase in State income. With the increase in State income, the salaries of the teachers are also raised. Most of the expenditure on salaries is met from the funds of the local units.

The minimum salary is always fixed. Accordingly, no teacher of a prescribed qualification, whether of primary or secondry level, can be paid less than a fixed amount of salary. According to rules as existed in the middle of the current century, the prescribed salaries are approximately as under:—

(1) University Chairman and local Education Superintendent - from 12000 dollars to 25,000 dollars per year.

(2) Teachers with post graduate degree - from 5000 dollars to 7000 dollars per year.

(3) Teachers with Bachelors' degree- from 2400 dollars to 5000 dollars per year.

(4) Teachers with Bachelors degrees but having 10 years experience - from 4000 to 5000 dollars per year.

(5) Head of the Department in Universities and Directors - 7000 dollars to 12000 dollars per year.

Besides these salary scales, teachers who retire after serving upto a definite period, are given annual pension also. In places where the minimum scale is not fixed, the average of the annual salary is also different, e.g. in 1950 when the average of annual salary in the whole country was 3010 dollars, in Mississipi. In 1954, the national average increased and became uniform but 'he average of salaries at the State level remained different.

Condition of Work for Teachers: American schools have vacations of two days - Saturday and Sunday every week. The session is of 9 months. Working days are between 160 and 200. The teachers are not assigned more than 35 periods in a week. The number of students in the class is usually 25. After teaching work, the rest of the time is utilised in preparing the class for the next day, coaching of the backward and dull students in order to bring them at par with other students, and other programmes, instructions and guidance.

The teachers try to solve the problems of the students by establishing contact with their parents. Now the post of the teacher is considered honourable and dignified. The teachers take interest in working with young boys and girls and utilise their leisure in soical and public relation activities. They exchange views with the honourable members of the society and community on educational problems and projects and organise meetings.

American teachers mainly consist of ladies and young girls. They are occupying higher posts in educational services, outnumbering male teachers. Traditionally, every unmarried girl considers it a privilege to work as a teacher for two years before marriage. There is no distinction of sex in salary scales and service opportunities. Both get equal honour, status and salary, following the democratic ideals of the country. On the basis of available data in 1949, there were 7,06,084 women teachers, out of the total number of 8,78,720 teachers. Thus the number of women teachers is more than the male teachers. National Association of Education has been organised for teachers of all levels. Fifty per cent teachers are the members of this association. Male and lady teachers of all levels are represented on it. The function of the Association is to undertake developmental-programmes conforming to the professional and philosophical outlook of teachers. Unions have been organised at different places in order to work for collective progress and security of teachers. A national institution named American Federation of Teachers tries to fulfil its obligation in co-operation with other trade unions.

Summary

Development of Teacher Education: The development of Teacher Educattion in U.S.A. is not an old one. The status of the teacher depends on his salary scale. Low salary attracted very few people to this profession. In 1839, a Normal Training School was established in Massachussets for the first time. In 1857, first Normal School in Illinois was established. In 1873, Iowa University started part-time teacher training programmes. In 1879, Michigan University established Departments of Education and in 1887 the Columbia University established its Department of Education and started conducting teacher training programmes.

Admission Qualifications and Selection: In America, there was no prescribed qualification for admission. In the beginning two year study at the secondary level after the education of the primary stage was considered sufficient. As soon as the duration of the training was changed from 2 year to 4 years, minimum qualifications for admission were also raised. Information regarding the trainees' health, educational qualification, character record, teaching aptitude and behaviour, etc. is obtained through interview at the time of admission in a normal school, training centre or training college. Importance is attached to the recommendation of the principal at the time of admission. At the time of appointment of teachers, attention is paid to the different needs at different levels. There is no uniform pattern for selection in all the States. Generally for the primary level, teacher training is necessary, along with 2 year college education. For secondary level, 4 year teacher training certificate with graduation degree is required. For selection to post, attention is paid to the temperament of the teacher, his health, religion, political views, his philosophy of life, etc.

Teacher Training Institutions: (1) *Normal Schools:* Generally, normal schools were considered equivalent to secondary schools because in the beginning, 2 year secondary level education was given after the primary stage education. In 1925 the need for trained and qualified teachers was felt and efforts were made to maintain some standard in the field of education. Consequently, the educational qualifications of teachers and training courses were widened. Thus all the normal schools were converted into training colleges.

(2) *Teachers' Training Colleges*: In 1988, a training college was established in New York. Upto 1920, ordinary training colleges which gave education in the science of education were established. The number of such colleges upto 1920 was about 45. Afterwards science of education was given a vocational form and along with general education, provision was also made for professional training of teachers.

(3) *Schools of Education*: The institutions which provided an integrated curriculum for general education and laid special stress on the science of education, were named schools of education. These schools are affilitated to some University. In these schools philosophy of education, different languages, literature culture, etc. are taught

along with science of education. The courses are similar to those of training colleges.

(4) *Departments of Education*: These departments are a part of Universities or Liberal Arts Colleges in the form of departments of education. These departments lay maximum emphasis on professional training of teachers. Here higher professional courses are conducted and provision is made for research work.

Education Courses: Four year training duration is divided into—(1) general education course and (2) professional training course. There is no common pattern of implementation of courses in the country. In some places first or last 2 years are devoted to teacher training and in other places general education and training courses are run together during all the four years.

Provision for Research in Education: In U.S.A., after the 4 year teacher training course, there is one year specialisation course. Harvard University conducts country-wide special training for trained and in-service teachers. Antioch College is a pioneer in this respect. Several centres and camps attached to this college have been established. In these camps, teachers in service increase their knowledge by doing research work and social service. After the completion of this 1 year course, the training is considered equal to 5 year teacher-training.

Distribution of Certificates after Training: The degrees and certificates are arranged by local education boards or departments of education. Professional training degree is awarded by universities and training colleges. The ordinary lower level certificates are given for a fixed period on certain conditions. After the expiry of the period, the validity of the certificates ceases. In some states, a test is held before awarding the certificates. Through these tests, the teachers of different levels are examined and certificates are awarded accordingly.

Service Conditions of the American Teachers: The American teacher gets pension, sickness leave and medical facilities like the workers in other professions. His services are permanent and secure. The appointment of teachers is made by local education boards through teacher employment agencies. The teacher sends his application to the agencies or boards directly. The salary of the teachers depends on the funds of the local boards and the number of students in the schools concerned. The salary of the teacher is increased with increase in national income.

Exercises

1. "The condition of the teachers is satisfactory in U.S.A.' Comment on this statement.
2. How did the teacher education develop in U.S.A.? What type of institutions train teachers in America today?
3. What efforts are made in United States of America for maintaining higher standard of teachers? What qualities are considered important for admission of trainees and appointment of teacher?

Chapter 14

University and College Education

The Fundamental Philosophy of Higher Education in U.S.A.

In the beginning, the nature of higher education in U.S.A. was like the higher education in Europe. Both the educational systems were dominated by specialisation and research methods. But the American philosophy of life changed with the needs of the time and so the aims of higher education also changed. Consequently, a vast difference in the nature of European and American education now exists.

Higher education being specialised and research oriented was non accessible to all. So it proved purposeless for persons with vocational interest. Hence stress began to be laid on making higher education utilitarian and accessible to all. In 1949, in New York and New Jersey States, laws were passed against prohibiting any person on the basis of caste, religion, sex, nationality and class from receiving higher education. According to these laws, all such entries which required information regarding the above were removed from admission forms. Although this statutory provision was made only in higher education, soon it began to be followed at other levels of education also.

University education connected with specialisation and

research was useful for brilliant students only. Average student was neglected at university level and he was neglected by the teachers too. But by making higher education easily accesible and utilitarian, average students were able to get higher education and the teachers had to change the methods of teaching and their attitude towards students.

As a result of equal educational opportunities in 1992, the number of Universities rose to about 250 and that of colleges of higher education to about 2500. The number of students in Liberal Arts Colleges increased to 100,00,000. The number of students in 1992, receiving education in professional schools and separately organised schools, which are about 3000 in number, is about 40,00,000. Increase in population and the need of education has affected all levels of educational institutions. Out of the total number of higher education institutions, about 40 per cent are government and the remaining are individual, collective, community, denominational connected with Municipal boards and private institutes. Inspite of the sufficient number of higher education institutions, there is a large crowd for admission and problem of lack of seats usually arises.

The changed system of higher education in America, has affected the aims of the life of the graduates. A graduate who previously wanted to be a research scholar and go in for specialisation, now tries to be an able teacher through research work alone. Although, this has lowered the standard of education to some extent, yet it has made education practical and useful. As regards the problem of admission to higher classes, terminal education, provision of supplementary courses and additional special provisions may be made. By making the admission-test easier and simpler, the problem related to admission may also be solved. Now it may be noted that a reorganisation of the curriculum is necessary for saving the standard of education from deterioration and it is the duty of the teachers to provide education according to the needs and interest of the students and make the teaching more interesting. Multi-purpose subjects should be introduced in the colleges. Provision of useful and practical education should be made according to the individual capacity of the students and their educational courses should be divided into units for successful evaluation of educational standards.

Kinds of University

There are two kinds of Universities in U.S.A. as under:—

(1) Private Universities, and

(2) State Universities.

(1) *Private Universities*: These universities are based on old and conservative traditions. Their traditions have been mainly influenced by European traditions. System of specialisation and research work are prevalent in these universities and as such, only brilliant students can take admission in them. Because of the limited number of students and want of State Control, these universities have to face the problem of shortage of funds. This is made good by fee from the students. So, fee charged from the students is also high. The result is that the common man cannot educate his wards in these universities. Stanford, North Western, John Hopkins, Columbia, Prinston, Yale and Harvard are some such universities.

(2) *State Universities*: Indiana, Ohio, Minnesota, Wisconsin, California and Michigan are some of the main State Universities. These Universities are aided and controlled by the State. Therefore, the number of students is more and fee charged is less than that in private universities. Only those students who come from other States for education in these universities, pay more fee. For them the fee is almost five times. The students of the concerned State are given preference at the time of admission. These universities provide education according to new and revised curricula based on national ideals. There is full co-operation and contact between the affiliated colleges which make joint efforts for making higher education useful, practical and public. The tendency of specialisation and research work is vanishing form these universities.

Sources of Income of Higher Education

Sufficient income is required of meeting expenditure on the

salaries of teachers and ministerial staff, construction of buildings and their maintenance, expenditure for laboratories, instruments and material aids, expenditure for inventions and research, scholarships, loan scholarships, games and sports and such other expenditures. The following are the sources of income for American universities-

(1) Private income and (2) State income.

(1) *Private sources:—*

For the development of higher education in America, the following sources have been utilised. The sources of income are meant for running private universities and colleges.

(a) *Endowment*: The State grants permission for establishing private universities and colleges for higher education on the basis of movable and immovable properties attached to them. The institutions have their own endownment and they get private help and donations from time to time. The endownment may be increased when needed but other sources such as tution-fee cannot be increased. Consequently, these institutions reduce their expenditure.

(b) *Tution Fee*: Private Universities and colleges charge more fees than the State or public universities and colleges. This tution-fee is annual. Private educational institution fix these tution-fees after much deliberation. While fixing the fees, importance is attached to the number of students taking admission, standard of education, financial status of the local people, the reputation of the institution, etc. If in a private institution the tution-fee is raised too high, the student begin to move to other educational instituions. Therefore, if the enrolment falls, the institution has to reduce its expenditure which results in falling education standards. Higher fee leads to a high standard of education. If the tution fee charged in private institutions is between 1000 to 1500 dollars per year, it is about 800 dollars annually in State educational institutions. In private institutions, in addition to tution-fee, reading-room fee, class-maintenance fee, light, refreshment, meals, conveyance fee, etc. are also charged.

(c) *Donation for Immediate Expenditure*: Private institutions receive donations from the public from time to time. These donations are known as gifts. It is in two forms-(1) Investment gift or endowment which is given by the public for increasing the endowment and (2) Indirect gift which is given by the public which may ultimately accumulate to a much bigger amount. This gift or donation is given to meet immediate expenditure. The amount donated may be from 1 dollar to one million dollars. The American people give these donations when there is a rise in their finanical status or at the time of some function or for providing educational facilities to some member of the family. This voluntary donation may be given for University reading room, library, lecture-theatre, laboratory, etc., or it may also be given without expressing any special reason. This donation is spent by the President and the treasurer of the University who are free to spend that donation. To-day, memory-donations have become customary. People donate annually in the memory of their dear ones at the time of birth or death and this donation continues indefinitely. Various scholarships, known as memory-scholarships are given from this fund. This donation is given to private universities by commercial and industrial concerns. These commercial and industrial institutions help the universities in their financial stringency from time to time. These educational institutions extend their co-operation in training and educating the employees of these commercial and industrial concerns.

Although the American private universities are entitled to

get State financial help and grants, these universities hesitate in taking that financial help from the State lest the State control should restrict their autonomy. Even then, they continue to get State help indirectly in various forms. No tax is levied on endownments and donations. During 1992 annual income of about 1500 dollars, collected from endowments and memory scholarship was exempted from income tax. Guardians spending about 1200 dollars annually on the education of their wards, are exempted from paying income-tax. The student, after his education, when he begins to earn, also pays annual donations as a matter of duty to the institution.

(2) *Sources of Income of the State Educational Institutions*: Universities and colleges run by the State receive their income from the funds of the municipal boards and public income-tax. Most of the universities are run by the State Governments. Nominal fee is charged in these universities from resident students. Although the States have provided various sources of income to these universities, still sometimes they face shortage of funds which is supplemented by donations, gifts and fees. These gifts and fees are charged more from those students who come from other States to take admission in State-run educational institutions.

Organisation of Universities

Universities in America have been established to satisfy the public thirst for knowledge. Whatever knowledge is gained through public efforts, it is diffused in the Universities for development through researches and is made available for the good and welfare of all. Educational plans related to culture, sociology, science and even atomic research are implemented in the autonomous system of universities. Although these universities are prominent in specialisation, priority is given to novelty in their educational efforts.

Central Administration of the Universities

The head of the central administration of the university is known as the president. The president of the university is elected by a board of trustees, constituted by politicians, teachers and recognised citizens. The term of the president is indefinite and he continues unopposed for several years. Sometimes, the president of the unversity is less educated than many professors whom he heads. He looks after the financies of the university and solves related problems. He tries to maintain contacts with registered graduates who have been educated in the same university. He also maintains contact with local administration, state administration, traders, industrialists and other generous institutions in order to get donations when needed to meet the financial shortage.

Faculties in the Universities: The administration of the university is divided into various faculties. Every faculty has a dean who tries to solve the financial and individual matters from legal point of view. He is also the head of the department of the subject concerned in the affiliated college. In some universities, the Dean is not the head of the department of the affiliated college, but the college has a separate head of the department. Sometimes a faculty has to look after two colleges with a common curricula, e.g. the medical department of Harvard University supervises the School of Dental Medicine and Medical School both. Liberal Arts Colleges and Graduate School of Art and Sciences are run under the supervision of Science and Arts faculty. The main problem in this system is that the teachers take interest in the education of graduate colleges and neglect the student in other colleges. This attitude is harmful. To solve this problem, Columbia University has entrusted the colleges of two levels in the charge of different faculties. Provision of separate teachers has been made for the two levels. This system seems expensive and there is always a fear of the one over looking the interest of the other.

The above university faculties are wholly responsible for the education of the concerned students. They are responsible for the admission, examination, formulation of educational policy, vocational and citizenship guidance and counselling of the students. The guidance of the faculty is praise worthy for the success of student life. Universities with large faculty spheres are divided into administrative divisions for the sake of administrative convenience and are thus given the form of sub-faculties. These sub-faculties undertake the responsibility of related financial provisions and annual budgets. In Chicago University, faculties have been broken into sub-faculties for running the adminstration.

Organisation of Inter-faculty Programmes: Whenever a programme related to the different sub-faculties is organised the dean calls a meeting of the assistant deans to discuss about the implementation of the programme. But when the programme concerns the different faculties separately, the dean of the university conducts the programme with the joint efforts of heads of departments.

Head of the Board of Trustees and Departments

The members of the board of trustees are traders, politicians and legal advocates, etc. This board controls the university affairs. The President of the university or vice chancellor is the representative of the board. The board extends its full co-operation to the president. The board of trustees has satisfactory relations with the heads of the departments (deans). The deans are directly concerned with formulation of educational policy but the board has no such direct obligation. So there are no chances of any conflict between the two.

University Curriculum: In the university curriculum 4 years are required for a Bachelor's degree, 1 year for Masters degree and at least 4 years are needed for obtaining Doctorate degree Three years are spent at the under-graduate level. Thus the university curriculum is of 12 years.

Affiliated Colleges: Colleges affiliated to the university are of three kinds:-

(1) *Liberal Arts Colleges*: These colleges award Bachelor's degree and are mostly run by religious institutions.

(2) *Under-graduate Colleges*: These colleges are independent and separate from the university system; but within the university itself, there are

some autonomous colleges, eg. Fine Arts College, Agriculture College, Music College, Home Science College, Hygiene Gymnastics College, etc.

(3) *Graduate Colleges*: Only the student with a Bachelor's degree may be admitted to a graduate college. There are different colleges of this kind, such as, Law College, Medical College, Arts and Science College. The administration and control of such colleges is collective and separate both. Collectively, it is administered by a university office. The Registrar is the head of this office.

The Place of Students in the University Administration

The students do not interfere in the administration of the university. They can simply give suggestions. Every university makes provision for the teaching of a number of interesting subjects and every student is free to select subjects of his choice. The deans give due consideration to the annual report presented by the Students' Union of the Liberal Arts College. The old students of the University may demand accounts of expenditure when they collect funds for the institution.

Provision of Adult Education by the Universities

The university academic session generally begins in the last week of September and ends in the middle of June. The rest of the summer time is utilised for adult-education. Day and night classes are held for educational counselling, medical arrangements, vocational guidance, and teaching of English to foreigners. The teachers and students get opportunities for the revision of the knowledge gained by them.

Student Life at the Higher Education Stage

Educational philosophy determines the educational aims and educational system depends on the educational aims. The educational system affects a student's life. Therefore, a student's life may acquaint one with the American philosophy of education.

Students live in hostels for their physical, mental, social and spiritual development. There is no provision of hostels in some municipal-colleges, otherwise all the universities and colleges are residential. The hostels are equipped with bed-rooms, dinning halls, libraries and play-grounds and two students live in one room as co-partners and learn to live in harmony. The entire hostel system is based on one-family attitude. The daily activities are performed in a co-operative atmosphere. This system is very expensive and therefore, it is not meant for all. Those students who cannot bear the hostel expenses, live in rented houses or rooms in the adjoining areas. For them a community centre is established where all the facilities like a hostel are available.

Courses and Holidays

The students are free to select subjects of their interest. Three periods per week are assigned for the teaching of one subject. The duration of the period is 50 minutes. In addition to class-periods, every student gives at least 2 hours per week per subject for self-study. At the graduate level a student has to earn regular credit of 120 periods of class-teaching. Since more time is required for laboratory-work, the number of periods are increased. The number of periods for all the subjects may go upto 40 per week. One term is of 15 weeks. There are vacations of one week in the month of April and of two weeks at Christmas.

Teaching

In one of the methods, the teacher reads his lecture before 500 students. This teaching-method is not considered a good method. In another method, the lecture is delivered before 15 to 20 students and there is a discussion afterwards. This method is more expensive. And therefore a third method in between the two methods has been evolved. According to this third method, the teacher reads his lecture before a large number of students once or twice a week. The students then divide themselves into small groups and discuss the subject with assistant teachers who themselves are students, holding graduate degrees. This system is found in affiliated colleges. In Liberal Arts Colleges more attention is paid on finishing the courses; whether the student has learnt anything is not a consideration. In American colleges, the laboratory system is prevalent everywhere. They have language-laboratories and workshops where tape-recorders are used.

Transfer of Students

At the higher education level, both colleges and affiliated college systems are in vogue. The number of students in the colleges is less but the teachers there are not qualified. Even then the students have sufficient contact with their teachers and they are able to learn. In the affiliated colleges, the teachers are well qualified but because of the large number of students, student-teacher contacts are less frequent and hence the guardians are always in two minds regarding the admission of their wards in affilicated colleges.

The standard of degrees of the above two institutions is also not the same. But every institution tries that its educational standard does not fall and the value of the degree awarded by it, is maintained. So the students are losers if they change or get themselves transferred from one institution to the other because of the difference in standards. Both the institutions admit the students on the basis of prescribed minimum qualifications. The degrees of the two institutions have got state and vocational recognition.

System of Examination and Grades

The examination system is the same at all places. After finishing half of the courses, subject-wise written examinations are held. At mid-term exams the question-paper is of one hour duration. At the end of the whole course, question paper of three hours duration are given. For evaluating specialisation in different subjects, an additional examination is held after every four or five years. Inspite of taking all possible precautions, some students are caught and punished for using unfair means during examinations in America.

At the time of evaluation, along with marks, grades are also assigned:

Grade A - for students getting 90 per cent marks or above.

Grade B - for students getting between 80 per cent and 90 per cent.

Grade C - for students getting 70 per cent to 80 per cent.

Grade D - for students getting 62 per cent to 70 per cent.

Grade E - for student getting 62 per cent or less.

The student getting less than 60 per cent marks are considered to have failed.

Women Education System

In the beginning co-education was not prevalent. Even today, Wellesly, Sweet Briar, Vasson, Mount Holyoke, Mills, Bryn, Mawan and Smith colleges admit only women students. Similarly, Williams, Amberst, Bowdin, Kenyon and Dart Mouth colleges are meant for male students only. But as a result of country-wide movement co-education has become common now. As regards hostels, mens' hostels have better facilities than womens' hostels. The girl students are kept under strict supervision in junior classes and even in senior classes they are not permitted to go out after 10 o'clock at night.

Fees, Scholarships and Other Facilities

The tution fee of state residential colleges is about 1800 dollars annually, but private residential colleges charge from 6000 dollars to 9000 dollars annually. Hostels are more expensive. Poor students get scholarships. The students are given scholarships on the basis of their physical and mental ability, character, and other skills. Some students are paid remuneration for their extra-service (labour) rendered in the college. Loans from different funds are provided through Higher Education Assistance Corporation. Foreign students get loans for twelve months. Education is cheap in community colleges. Loans are repaid in instalments. Very nominal interest is charged on such loans.

Games, Sports, Gymnastics, Clubs and Various Committees

are organised for the all-round development of students. Co-curricular activities are conducted. Convocation is the most important function of the year for the students.

SUMMARY

1. *Fundamental Philosophy of University Education*: In the early years, university and college education was mainly dominated by specialisation and research as in Europe. But by 1949, the tendency to make education useful, accessible and utilitarian crept in and got statutory recognition.

2. *Sources of Income*: There are two kinds of sources (1) Private sources and (2) State sources.

(1) *Private Sources*: Endowments, fees, donations for immediate expenditure, donations and gifts in the form of scholarships and other such amounts.

(2) *State Sources Income*: State grants, land grants, income tax, nominal fees, and private donations are the State sources of income.

3. *Sources of Income of Private Universities*:

(a) *Endowment*: Received in the form of movable and immovable property and money received as a result of increase in production from time to time.

(b) *Tution fees*: Tution fees are higher in private colleges than in State institutions.

(c) *Donations for immediate expenditure*: Money paid by guardians for the education of their wards, donations given in memory of loved ones, and annual scholarships.

Organisation of University: The representative elected by Council of Trustees is the President or Vice-Chancellor of the University. Formulation of all the financial and administrative policies is done under his presidentship.

University Faculty System: Every subject has a faculty. The chief of the faculty is the dean. The faculties are some times divided into sub-faculties and divisions and the programmes of these groups and divisions are conducted by inter-faculty and inter-sub-faculty incharges.

University and College Systems: Liberal Arts Colleges, under-graduate colleges, graduate level colleges fall under this system.

Administration and Students: The head of the department pays attention to the report of students' union in Liberal Arts Colleges. Old degree-holder students of the college are informed of the annual accounts of income and expenditure.

Students Life: Student life depends on educational aims according to the educational atmosphere. Hostels are provided for the all-round development of students.

Courses and Holidays: Courses are wide. There is a freedom of choice of subjects. Semester is of 15 weeks.

Examinations and Grades: Evaluation is on the basis of marks obtained but grades are awarded on the basis of marks obtained, e.g. the grades A, B, C, D, E are based on percentages of marks.

Women Education System: In the beginning co-education was not common. Even now there are separate institutions for boys and girls. Now co-education is prevalent.

Fees, Scholarships and Other Facilities: Scholarships, remuneration and loans are customary in America. The students are free to do extra work.

EXERCISES

1. What is the fundamental philosophy of higher education in U.S.A.? What are the problems of professional education at the University level there?
2. What are the sources of income at the higher education level in U.S.A.? Describe the different private sources of income.
3. The teaching profession is the most attractive profession in U.S.A Why? Explain the system of teachers' training and the status of teachers in U.S.A.
4. How far is the American tradition of University education worth following? What is the place of University President in the administration? Describe the various organisational provisions in the University in U.S.A.

PART III

British Education

15. Life and Character of the British People and their Education.
16. Control of Education in Great Britain.
17. Events Leading to the Growth of Primary Education.
18. Events Promoting the Growth of Secondary Education.
19. The Education Acts of 1944, 1946 and 1948.
20. British University Education.
21. Modern Secondary Education.
22. The Modern Pre-primary and Primary Education.
23. Teachers' Training and their Condition.
24. Further Education.
25. Technical Education.
26. Adult Education and Youth Welfare Services.
27. Special Services in Education in Great Britain.
28. Meanings of Some Terms of British Education.

Chapter 15

Life and Character of the British People and Their Education

Education plays a very important role in the development of a country. In fact, one influences the other. As geographical conditions, racial character, historical and cultural traditions influence the life of a people, similarly, they have their inevitable impact on education as well. This can be said about any country and Great Britain is no exception to it. The climate of Great Britain is generally healthy. The sea-coasts are open throughout the whole year due to the warm gulf-stream. Therefore, there are many good harbours which function as good means of transport with other parts of the world. The good climate of the country has made its people industrious. Thus trait of industriousness is inculcated in boys and girls as is evident from the curriculum of the school. The co-curricular activities also develop industriousness in children. The informal agencies of education, too, provide opportunities for development of knowledge in children who, industrious as they are, derive full advantage.

Great Britain is an industrial country with big industrial towns. Hence, its culture and civilisation are derived from the same. Because of industrial development of the country there are many technological and professional institutions, spread all over the country. These institutions are situated mostly in towns. The life style of the people of this country is ever developing because of these various types of educational institutions.

Many couples in Great Britain are employed in factories and other industries. They are busy earning money to the maximum with aview to raise their standard of living very high. As a result, many children have to be in pre-primary schools and at other educational centres while their parents are away from home and working in offices and factories. Thus, the schools and teachers have to shoulder a great national responsibility in giving education to a huge number of young children. Because of this feature the British people have shown tremendous faith and loyalty to teachers who enjoy great respect in society. The British government too is trying to improve the conditions of teachers. Consequently, teachers in Great Britain enjoy a better social status and prestige than any other country in the world.

Some of the racial character traits of the British people may be clearly noticed in their educational systems. One of the character-traits of the British people is that in them we find a judicious blend of new and old tendencies. By nature they are conservative, but in ideas they are progressive. However, any newness does not tempt them to discard the old traditions wholly. Due to this progressive attitude great changes of far-reaching importance are introduced in the educational system but the people because of their conservative nature, have also always staged opposition to the same. Ultimately, they accept the new ideas but never permit the undermining of their own old traditions. The education Act of 1944 is an example of this tendency. This Act has prescribed new types of school buildings but the public has not accepted them in entirety. Even to-day many schools are found in their old patterned buildings. Though, this is against the law, but the government has to accept this situation. Similarly, the Act has emphasised the opening of new secondary schools but even to-day there are many old secondary schools still functioning with the government approval.

The love of freedom is a great character-trait of the British people, so they never like any state interference in their freedom. Consequently, the impact of individualism is very well marked in the educational system of the place. Because of their love for freedom many educational systems have refused government help, thinking that the same will result into state interference in their work. In 1833, many educational institutions accepted state help, but they refused to accept any restrictions placed by the government. Evidently, the British people have great love for their individual freedom and they cannot lose it at any cost.

Another trait of the British people is that they cannot tolerate centralization of powers in any individual or group. They do believe in partnership among powers, but they cannot accept the full ownership of the same by any other authority or individual. They have great regard and faith in their king or queen (Crown) but they believe in democratic traditions and practise the same. They consider the Parliament responsible for everything. They do not want that the implementation of a plan or policy should be entrusted to the authority of a single individual. Hence the same is decentralised in various communities. This tendency is seen in the British educational system as well. The educational powers are not concentrated in a single individual. The Education Minister is responsible to the Parliament and the Local Education Authorities are responsible to the Minister. The various education officers in carrying out their responsibilities have to depend upon other officers and committees. This feature is found in the organisation of schools and committees. The principal and teachers are mutually inter-dependent and so are education committees and related officers. Thus, co-operation and division of responsibility in carrying out a task may be regarded as a special trait of the British people.

In the development of education, the various religious organisations have played a very important role. This is quite evident in the progress of education of the country. This fact is indicative of the tendency that the British people are very devoted to their religion. Although secularism is emphasised in the country, yet religion plays an important role in the educational system there. Each student is devoted to his own religion but respects the religious faith of others. The country schools and voluntary schools have been classified on religious grounds, simply because the religious sentiments of each other should be respected. Thus, the life and the character of British people have their inevitable impact on education.

SUMMARY

The geographical conditions, racial character-traits and social and cultural traditions influence education in a country. Great Britain is no exception to it.

The sea-coasts of the country are open throughout the whole years. The climate is healthy. Therefore, the people are laborious. The trait is visible in their educational organisations as well. The children are eager to learn and are industrious.

There are big towns in the country. Most of the educational institutions are in cities. Parents are busy earning money. Children have perforce to be in pre-primary schools. Teachers bear a great national responsibility. They enjoy great respect in society.

The British people are freedom-loving. They cannot tolerate state interference. Therefore, many state laws have been ignored by many educational institutions.

The British people, though having full faith in their Crown, believe in democratic traditions. Their democratic traditions are seen in educational organisations as well.

The British people are religious. Each child get religious education but each shows respect to religious faith of others as well.

EXERCISES

1. How do the geographical conditions and social traditions influence the educational system of a country? To explain this give examples from Great Britain.
2. How have the British character-traits influenced the British educational system? Explain with examples.

Chapter 16

Control of Education in Great Britain

The well-organised system of educational control and administration has been of great help in the development of education in Great Britain during the present century. In Great Britain the various committees in educational areas, centres of education and citizens at large consider themselves as equal partners in the development of education in the country. Their attempt has always been to develop the capacity of various types of educational agencies, devices and equipments. The role of various units that are responsible for control and administration of education in Great Britain is of great importance.

Powers and Duties of the Education Minister

The Education Minister in Great Britain is responsible to the British Parliament which makes Acts and rules for regulating the educational affairs in the country. The Education Minister presents before the Parliament data about the achievements and failures in education each year. On this occasion the House of Commons has a full debate on the issue. In addition, any member of the Parliament may discuss any educational issue in the House. The Education Minister proposes to the Parliament to pass certain rules and regulations for the smooth running of educational system in the country.

The Parliament has 40 days to debate on the proposals. The members of the Parliament may question the Education Minister on the proposals and may demand the withdrawal of any proposal presented by him. Thus, the Education Minister has to honour the wishes of the Parliament. In fact, it is the Parliament which controls the educational organisations of the country. But the Parliament has no right to pass any rule to bring about changes in the curriculum, text books, methods of teaching and related matters. This responsibility lies with the Local Educational Authorities, principals and teachers.

The Act of 1944 has defined the educational powers of the Education Minister. Below we outline the Education Minister's duties which he performs according to the accepted democratic traditions as laid down in the Education Act of 1944:—

The Education Minister should formulate a national educational policy for England and Wales. All the educational institutions and Local Educational Authorities that come under him have to work-out this policy. The Education Minister has to see that the same is implemented. In the performance of his duties, the Education Minister is influenced by his political party. He seeks advice from the Prime Minister and other Minister-colleagues about his educational policies. Although, the Education Minister is the final formulater of the educational policies, but he has to seek advice from the Chancellor of the Exchequer who is the Chief of the Finance Department. The Education Minister consults other officers of his department, Local Educational Authorities and representatives of teachers. Thus, ultimately he places his proposals before the Parliament. The Education Minister is the head of the Education Ministry and for the implementation of the proposals passed by the Parliament, he is responsible to the government.

In the country the Education Minister represents the Parliament. His powers are limited to secondary education alone. He cannot interfere in university affairs. The universities in England and in Wales are independent in their affairs and do not look to the Education Minister for financial grants.

They derive direct grants from the Chancellor of Exchequer. Besides the universities, Juvenile Delinquents Schools, Elder Delinquents Schools and Armed Forces and Auxiliary Services Schools are also beyond his control. The Armed Forces and Auxiliary Services Schools are directly controlled by admirality, war-office and air-force.

The Education Minister does not interfere in day-to-day working of the schools. He has no concern with the appointments and resignations of teachers. He has nothing to do with selection of text-books and material-aids meant for schools.

The Education Minister neither controls public libraries, museums and art-galaries nor recommends financial grants. But, such public institutions as museums which are considered of national importance are placed under his control and he recommends financial grants for them. Bethnal Green Museum in East London, the Science Museums of South Kensington and Victoria and Albert Museums are under him.

The committee appointed in 1951 lays down the following six subjects which come under the direct control of the Education Minister:—

1. The Education Minister should pay special attention to the organisation of educational facilities.
2. He has also to see that all the educational institutions are functioning smoothly. For this he should provide them with the necessary educational implements.
3. He should see that only those teachers and medical officers should be appointed in schools who can look after the needs and the interest of students satisfactorily.
4. He should pay adequate attention to maintaining reasonable standards of education.
5. The Education Minister should see that students are charged reasonable fees and teachers are given adequate dearness-allowance and salaries.
6. The Education Minister should see that teachers, guardians and other persons related with educational affairs enjoy appropriate freedom.

The government has accepted the above recommendations and the Education Minister acts accordingly. The Education Minister is responsible for formulation of the following nine rules:—

1. Rules for determining educational standards within the school limits.
2. Rules for primary and secondary institutions.
3. Rules for Further Education.
4. Rules for Local Educational Authorities.
5. Rules for facilities for milk and lunch in schools.
6. Rules for education of the handicapped children.
8. Rules for scholarships and other benefits.
9. Rules for teachers' training.

Besides, the Education Minister may form some other rules as well. Hence, he makes about 20 other rules which include affairs pertaining to registration of students and state scholarships. The Education Minister can modify his own rules. He issues circulars for clarifying his rules and policies. The educational institutions and education officers are not compelled to follow the points in these circulars because they are not issued as orders. They are just 'advices'. However, the decisions taken by the Education Ministry are to be followed by the educational institutions. But, such decisions are not published in the circulars issued by the Education Minister.

In addition to the above circulars the Education Minister issues some administration memoranda as well. These contain direction for the daily routine of schools. The decisions taken by the Ministry of Education are also published in there.

The Units Helping the Education Minister

There is a Parliament Secretary to help the Education Minister. He is a member of the Parliament and also the Junior Minister of the Crown. There is a Parliamentary Private Secretary also to advise the Education Minister. Under the Education Act of 1944, the Education Minister is empowered to appoint an Advisory Committee for giving him advice from time to time. Besides, there are other Committees as well, such as Secondary Schools Examination Council, National Advisory Committee for Teachers, Under Training and National Advisory Committee on Education of the Industry and Commerce. The Education Minister, if necessary, may appoint any other adhoc committees. Under the Education Ministry there are civil servants and Her Majesty's Inspectors of Schools and Executive Officers. Branch Officers of Education Ministry are located in London and at other places throughout the whole country. The main Education Ministry is on Curzon Street, London.

There is a permanent Secretary of the Education Ministry who inspects the working of the various departments of the Education Ministry. There are Deputy Secretary and Under Secretary and Assistant Secretary as well.

Her Majesty's Inspector of Schools

Her Majesty's Inspectors of Schools occupy a very important place in the whole educational set-up of the country, particularly upto the secondary stage. They are appointed by the Crown and not by the Education Minister. The Senior Chief Inspector of Schools and a Member of Civil Service Commission send to the Crown a list of names for appointment as Inspectors of Schools. The Crown arranges for the training of the Inspectors. Each Senior Chief Inspector of Schools has six Inspectors of Schools under whom the following six departments are placed:—

1. Primary and Special Education Department,
2. Secondary Education Department,
3. Vocational Further Education Department,
4. Non-vocational Further Education Department,
5. Teachers' Training Department, and
6. Education Development Department.

To facilitate the inspection work, England is divided into ten divisions. The Divisional Inspector of Schools is the Officer of his division. Each divison has been sub-divided into districts. Her Majesty's Inspector of Schools is the inspection officer of his district. The Regional Inspectors of Schools are transferred from time to time and one place to another.

For Wales there is a separate Inspectorate. The Chief Inspector is its officer in charge.

The Functions of her Majesty's Inspectors of Schools

Her Majesty's Inspectors of Schools perform the following three types of functions:—

1. To inspect educational institutions and to evaluate their achievements.
2. To represent the Education Ministry from the administrative point of view.
3. To give theoretical and practical advice on behalf of the Education Ministry.

The function of the Inspectors of Schools is limited to inspection only. The Inspector cannot give any order to the teachers, but he may praise or criticise their work and advise them at times. He inspects an educational institution from all points of view before giving his report to the Board of Inspectors.

The school-in-charge decides whether the report is just or partial. The inspection report is treated as confidential. Before preparing it the Inspector obtains information from the head-master and other staff. Therefore, generally his report is just and reliable. The copy of this report is kept in the school. Teachers may be criticised in it and they may get permission to study the same. A teacher after studying this report may give his explanation. The Inspector alone may choose to make any change in his inspection report. The Inspectors of Schools, besides inspection, perform some other constructive functions as well. These are as follows:—

1. Every year to formulate refresher course and short-term course for teachers.
2. To collect bulletins published by the Education Minister for the guidances of teachers.
3. To function as Liaison Officers between the Education Ministry and educational institutions and to participate in meetings and committees held on educational matters.

Local Education Authorities

For England and Wales, besides the Education Minister, Ministry of Education and Inspectors, there are about 146 Local Education Authorities to look after the educational affairs in their respective areas.

There are about 129 Local Education Authorities for England and about 17 for Wales. Under these 146 Local Educational Authorities there are 62 Administrative Committees, 83 County Boroughs and a Joint Board of Representatives. Evidently these 62 Administrative Committees, 83 County Boroughs and a Joint Board of Representatives make 146 Local Education Authorities. These Administrative Committees are of different sizes depending upon the population and financial resources of the areas concerned. For example, the area of London Council is about 303 square kilometers and that of Lancashire country council is about 5,200 square kilometers. From the latest data it is understood that educational expenditure and population of London Council is much higher than those of Lancashire County Council.

The Organisation of Local Education Authorities (Councils of Counties and County Boroughs)

The citizens and rent-payers of these respective areas elect these bodies. Their representatives consider all matters that fall within their local autonomies. However, it is not necessary that these representatives understand their problems of education. Keeping this fact in view, a Chief Education Committee is organised; and, if necessary, this committee is further sub-divided into sub-committees for considering matters pertaining to primary, secondary and higher education separately. The members of these committees and sub-committees generally have some experience of educational affairs and understand the related problems. In certain matters these sub-committees take decisions on education matters and the same are honoured by the Chief Educational Committee. But, in certain contexts, these sub-committees function only as advisory bodies. The approval of the Education Minister is necessary on the decisions taken by these Local Educational Authorities. The elections in Councils of Counties and County Boroughs are organised on political basis. Hence, they have a direct bearing on the national educational policy. It should be kept in mind that irrespective of control exercised by a particular political party within the area of a certain Education Authority it is extremely difficult to effect a basic change in the educational policy already implemented.

Evidently, the Local Education Authority, anywhere in the country, has to function in the strict adherence to the general educational policy laid down by the Parliament. The Local Education Authority organises an education office which is manned by persons belonging to the area autonomy. The Director of Education is the Chief Education Officer. Besides, there are other administrative and executive officers to perform certain duties with the help of clerks. This education office has departments for Primary, Secondary and Further Education. The Education Minister has a hand in the appointment of the Chief Education Officer, i.e. the Director of Education. The Education Minister examines the particulars of all those candidates who are aspirants for the post of Director of Education. The Education Minister has a power to reject the candidature of any person who may be considered as unfit. It is a constitutional necessity that there will be a Director of Education, a Chief School Medical Officer and a Chief School Dental Officer appointed by the Local Education Authority.

The Method of Work of Local Education Authority:

For deciding any matter the Local Education Authority places it before the Education Committee which in turn sends it to a sub-committee for remarks. This sub-committee studies it carefully and sends it back to Education Committee with its recommendations. The Education Committee may accept, modify or reject the same. The decision of the Education Committee is treated as a decision of the Local Education Authority. The decisions on financial matters have to be approved by the County Council or Council Boroughs. Some Local Education Authorities may appoint architects for construction of some buildings. They may also appoint some local inspectors. The number of workers in the various Local Education Authorities is not identical.

The Ministry of Education and the Local Education Authorities:

The purpose of the Ministry of Education and the Local Education Authorities is related with national educational policies. The relationship between these two authorities is generally very intimate and cordial. In the Education Ministry there are some officers who are called territorial principals who generally look after the workings of some Local Education Authorities. A territorial principal may be in-charge of one or more Local Education Authorities. Each Local Education Authority continues to supply educational informations to its territorial principal who scrutinises them in order to see if the national education policy formulated by the Education Ministry are not contravened. If the Local Education Authority violates any rule, it is advised to correct its mistake. In case of some differences between the territorial principal and the Local Education Authority, the matter is referred to the Education Minister. But this happens very rarely. The territorial principal is the real liaison officer between the Education Ministry and the Local Education Authority.

For maintaining a close relationship, at times the members of the various departments of the Education Ministry organise meetings and conferences amongst themselves and the local education authorities.

County Education Authority and its Divisional Executives

Before the Education Act of 1944 there were about 169 Municipal Boroughs in England and Wales. These Boroughs and urban districts used to look after primary education in their own areas. These organisations were considered as Part Third Authorities. The Education Act of 1944 tried to remove these authorities. This feature of the Act was vehemently opposed by the people. Because of this opposition in the Education Act of 1944 the counties were divided into Divisional Executives which were entrusted with the responsibilities of looking after primary and secondry education on behalf of the Local Education Authorities.

The Education Minister has the power to prevent the Local Education Authority from making Divisional distributions. But at the same time, the urban District Council and the Municipal Boroughs have also been given the power not only to execute the plans of the Local Education Authority but also request it to originate new divisional plans. However, two conditions are placed with such a request. These conditions are as follows:—

1. The population of the county and Borough should not have been less than 60,000 in 1939 and the students in primary schools should not have been less than 7,000.
2. For the above request the permission should have been obtained before 1944.

Accordingly, 15 Municipal Boroughs and Urban District Councils applied for this concession. Consequently, 1962 Divisions were constituted.

Local Education Authority, Board of Managers and Board of Governors

According to the Education Act of 1944 for those primary and secondary schools which are wholly run on financial grants received from the Local Education Authority, Board of Managers and Board of Governors, have been organised. Such schools are termed as 'Maintained'. The Board of Managers should consist of at least 6 members. But the number of Broad of Governors is not fixed. Generally, the Board of Governors has more members than the Board of Managers. The Local Education Authority appoints members of Boards of those primary schools which are under some Minor Authority. But the Local Education Authority can select only one third members of the Boards of these schools. For those primary and secondary schools which are governed by voluntary organisations, two third members of their Boards of Managers and Boards of Governors are appointed by the Local Education Authority, whereas, one third of the members are appointed by the voluntary organisation concerned. According to the Education Act of 1944 from the practical point of view, a Board of Managers or a Board of Governors may have more than one school under them. It is also seen that those sub-committees of Local Education Authorities which are related with primary and secondary schools, also function as Boards of Managers and Boards of Governors. But this is done in a very unusual situation.

The Board of Managers and Board of Governors function under strict limitations placed on them. Such powers as appointment of teachers and acceptance of their resignations are under the Local Education Authority. However, the Local Education Authority may choose to invite the members of the Boards of Managers and Boards of Governors at the time of the appointment of teachers. The voluntary, controlled and Special Agreement schools co-operate in the appointment of reserved teachers for religious education. But none of these can accept resignations of teachers. In Aided Schools the appointment of teachers is effected by the Local Education Authority, Board of Managers and Board of Governors according to the government rules.

The Board of Managers and the Board of Governors co-operate with each other in the development of education. These boards function as the connecting link between the schools and the Local Education Authority. Generally, the members of each board and their chairmen participate in the various school functions in order to encourage principals and teachers.

The head-masters and the teachers play a very important role in schools. They prescribe the daily school routines and perform their duties on strict moral principles. No Board and Local Education Authority can interfere in any manner in the curriculum and teaching methods.

Thus in principle, the Education Minister is wholly

responsible for the education in the country. But he can never ignore the Co-operation of the Local Education Authorities, Boards, Organisations, head-masters and teachers.

SUMMARY

The Education Minister: According to the Education Act of 1944 the Education Minister is the supreme authority of education in England and Wales, and he is responsible to the Parliament. The other organisations and authorities are responsible to the Education Minister. Headmasters and teachers enjoy full autonomy in curriculum teaching methods and daily routines. The Education Minister has no relationship with universities. Exchequer gives grants to universities directly. The Education Minister determines the national education policies. Primary and secondary schools receive grants from the Education Minister.

Her Majesty's Inspectors of Schools: An Inspectorate. The Inspector is responsible to the Education Minister. They inspect schools.

Local Education Authorities: County Boroughs and Councils are under the Local Education Authorities. A Chief Education Officer is the principal spokesman of the Local Education Authority. Voluntary organisations, Minor Authorities, Board of Managers, Board of Governors and Divisional Executives are very helpful in the development of education.

EXERCISES

1. Discuss the role of the Education Minister in the organisation of Education in England and Wales.
2. Describe the powers and duties of Her Majesty's Inspectors of Schools.
3. Discuss the role of the Local Education Authorities in education in England and Wales.

Chapter 17

Events Leading to the Growth of Primary Education

In this chapter we propose to point to some of the outstanding events of the history of primary education in England and Wales during the eighteenth and nineteenth centuries.

During the later part of the eighteenth century there were some Private Day Schools and Common Day Schools in England and Wales. Strict disciplinarians were working in these schools as teachers and they followed cruel unpsychological methods. Some ladies also were managers of these institutions. Some tution fees were charged per week. The conditions of most of these schools were not satisfactory.

The Development of British Education in the Eighteenth Century

The Common Day Schools and the Dame Schools: The Common Day Schools were meant for older children and Dame Schools for younger ones. These schools charged nominal fees. Still, the wards of poor guardians could not get educated in these schools. Therefore, for poor children there were Charity Schools run on charities received from benevolent people.

The Charity Schools: In 1698, some Charity Schools were established for imparting knowledge of Christianty to poor children. The teachers of these schools were generally very generous, religious and were members of some established church. Since charity was the only source of income, the condition of these schools was not satisfactory.

Curriculum of the Charity Schools: Religious education, reading, writing and arithmetic formed the major structure of the curriculum of these schools. The children were also taught ploughing fields, gardening, spinning, weaving and sewing with a view to give them some practical skill in order that they might take up some work as labourers after leaving schools.

The Financial Arrangement of Charity Schools: Most of these schools did not have their own buildings. So the classes were held in church galleries. Students were not charged any fees. Hence they had to depend entirely on charities received from the public. From these Church galleries the teachers used to place demands before the public. During Sunday prayers charities were received from the public for these schools.

Importance of Charity Schools: Since these schools served poor children, the general public had great faith in them. These schools were established generally in those areas where the people were very poor and illiterate. From the beginning of the nineteenth century some of these schools were patterned on the monitorial system. These charity schools served the public very well. The Pretism Movement of Germany drew inspiration from this sytem and many Charity Schools were established in Germany also. By 1760 there were about 3,0,000 students in the Charity Schools in England but gradually their number fell.

Besides the above mentioned Charity Schools, there were some other schools running on charities, but they had no relationship with any Church. These schools were run by Non-confirmists and Roman Catholics. There was no central committee or authority to look after these schools. Hence towards the close of the eighteenth century they were bitterly criticised. Because of their bad condition, the people disliked them. Hence their decline began.

The Industrial Schools

The children of persons working in small industries received education in these schools. They were established due to the Industrial Revolution. The children in these schools received free education and were taught such practical skills as spinning, weaving, sewing and gardening, etc. The articles produced by the students were sold to meet a part of the expenditure of the schools. The students were given religious education and were also taught reading, writing and arithmetic. They were also given meals in the schools. These schools gradually received the attention of the Government. In 1769, the Pit Government suggested that students should seek admission in these schools. But owners of industries had begun to employ children on wages. The guardians of working children found the money earned by the children a big help. Therefore, these guardians, instead of sending their wards to Industrial schools, began to send them to these industries. Consequently, the Industrial schools had to undergo a great loss.

An attempt was made by an Industrial School Society to improve the conditions of the Industrial schools and to give special facilities to their students. An ideal Industrial School was established in 1786. However, inspite of this reform, by 1804 there were only 20,336 students in these schools. The age of the students ranged between 5 to 14 years. By and by the development of such schools stopped.

The Sunday Schools

Due to the Industrial Revolution in the country many children began to serve in industries on wages. Hence it was necessary to find a solution to the educational problems of these children. These children worked for 6 days a week. Sunday was the only holiday. So for them, Sunday Schools were opened. In 1785, Robert Raikes opened such a school for children working in industries near Gloucester. A Sunday School Society was also established for organising such Sunday Schools. In 1803, this society was called "Society for

Establishment and Support for Sunday Schools."

The purpose of these schools was to promote the religious and social development of children. So, besides teaching, reading, writing and arithmetic, religious eduation and handicrafts were also taught. Some higher class people sympathised with these schools and gave them financial supports. In the beginning the teachers of the Sunday Schools were given some remuneration. But as the number of volunteer-teachers increased the number of teachers working on remuneration decreased.

Importance of Sunday Schools in Elementary Education: The main importance of these schools was that they made a beginning in free and universal education. Gradually, these Sunday Schools became a meeting ground of mill-owners, workers and foremen of industries. In 1787, there were 2,50,000 students in these schools. Out of these, there were 1,56,000 students in these schools in London alone in 1801. The generous nature of some mill-owners was responsible for the development of these schools. Consequently, the lives of children working in industries also improved. Thus the Sunday Schools contributed a great deal towards the development of elementary education.

The Circulating Schools

In 1737 these schools were establihsed by Griffith Jones in Carmarthen of Wales for teaching Bible to poor children through their mother tongue. He wanted to teach the Bible through catechism. When he saw that Porochial Schools of Wales were not fulfilling this objective, he established Circulatory Schools. These schools were called Circulatory because their teachers used to go from one place to another for teaching work. The teacher used to remain at one place for three to six months and taught in some vacant buildings. These schools were run during the day and in the evening. Both children and adults received education in them. These schools were supported by charity and the grant received from the Society for the Promotion of Christian knowledge. Due to the indifference shown by the successors of Griffith Jones, these schools began to fade away and the Sunday schools replaced them. Their period of success was later half of the eighteenth century to the first half of the nineteenth century.

The Monitorial System

The Monitorial System was borrowed from the Indian system by Andrew Bell and Joseph Lancaster. This system was adopted in order to make education available to poor children as well. In this system the senior students used to teach the junior ones. Thus the problem of lack of teachers was partially solved.

Andrew Bell and Joseph Lancaster

Andrew Bell (1753-1832), and Joseph Lancaster (1778-1829), were the members of the Peace Committee. Andrew Bell had worked in Madras (India) as a headmaster. In Madras he tried to educate some children and adults through the Monitorial System. He successfully introduced this system in England as well. Lancaster, too, conducted school in South Work on the Monitorial system. This experiment succeeded and under the control of only one teacher a number of senior students used to teach a large number of junior students successfully.

Evaluation of Bell's and Lancaster's work

Through their Monitorial System both of them promoted the cause of elementary education. Thus a new system of elementary education was started. However, this system resulted in falling of educational standards. The teacher lost his contact with his students and it was not possible for the senior student to give new knowledge to junior students whom they taught. However, this system brought the senior and junior students together.

Robert Owen, Wilder Spin and David Stow

Like Bell and Lancaster, these three presons also furthered the cause of elementary education.

(i) *Robert Owen (1771-1858)*: Robert Owen was a practical man. He organised the Ignorant Factory Community. The children who had attained the age of at least 10 years were employed in industries. For the labourers' children between the age of 5 and 10 years free schools were established by Owen. These schools were run in the beginning on the Monitorial System. But later, this system was changed and sufficient number of teachers were appointed.

(ii) *Wilder Spin (1792-1866)*: He established a number of Sunday Schools in 1816. But, these schools did not succeed. So, in 1826 he established the Glasgow Infant Society for teaching infants. Through his efforts infant education was promoted in Scotland.

Development of Elementary Education in England and Wales during the Nineteenth Century

The experiments conducted by Bell, Lancaster, Robert Owen, Wilder Spin and David Stow in the field of elementary education did not succeed much because of prevailing conditions of the country. We hint at these conditions below:—

1. All the people did not encourage elementary education. Particularly, the upper class people did not want to educate poor children of the lower class for they thought that they would lose hold on the poor if they got educated as they were likely to claim equal rights.
2. The capitalists and businessmen thought that by receiving education the poor children would not work in their industries and workshops.
3. The stands of various Churches in the context of religious education were contradictory to each other and were unhelpful in the development of elementary education.
4. The Monitorial System was criticised as a bad tool for promoting elementary education, as it emphasised rote memorisation rather than the development of the child as a whole.
5. The State was not taking interest in elementary education, as it did not like to interfere with the private efforts in the field.

The State and Education

Upto the eighteenth century the State did not take any special interest in the elementary education. But due to the Industrial Revolution the people became conscious of the need for education and the State thought that it was no longer possible to ignore the cause of elementary education. Many lovers of education drew the attention of the State to the cruel behaviour to which the children in various industries were subjected. This state of affairs necessitated interference by the Parliament.

Robert Peel's Bill of 1802:

Robert Peel presented a Bill in the Parliament in 1802 in connection with the cruel behaviour and expolitation practised by the mill-owners against the employed children. The mill-owners and many members of the Parliament vehemently opposed this Bill. But the Bill was passed under the name of Factory Act. Although, the scope of this Act was very limited, but it influenced elementary education. This was the first bill against the evil practices followed by the mill-owners. Many other Acts were passed in due course which were a boon to the children against exploitation. The Factory Act as passed through the efforts of Robert Peel included only the child-labourers of those work-houses and apprenticeship which were connected with cotton and wool factories. This Act included the following important reforms:

1. The child-labourers will not work for more than 12 hours a day and they will not work at night.
2. The mill-owners will always maintain healthy atmosphere for their mills by ensuring fresh air and sufficient light in the work-houses.
3. The children in apprenticeship will be taught reading, writing and arithmetic for some time.
4. The children in apprenticeship will receive religious education for an hour every Sunday and they will be sent to Church at least once a month.

The Factory Act proved very helpful and it served as a base for the Education Act of 1870.

The Parochial School Bill of 1807:

White Bread proposed the Bill in the Parliament. This Bill stood for two year-provision of free education to the rural children between 7 and 14 years of age. But the capitalists and the Churches opposed this Bill. Therefore, it could not become an Act.

Sir Robert Peel Bill of 1815:

In 1815 Sir Robert Peel introduced a Bill in the Parliament for improving the conditions of the children working in mills. The House of Commons established a secret committee to study this Bill. This committee found that the children working in mills were subjected to inhuman treatment. They had to work for 16 hours a day. Somewhere the children were compelled to work for 100 hours a week. On committing mistakes they were given cruel punishments. They were not given adequate leisure for taking meals or for rest. The House of Commons in 1819 accepted the Robert Peel Bill with some modifications. But this Act, too, could not be implemented and was neglected like the Act of 1802. The Act of 1819 was limited only to the Cotton mills. According to this no child below 9 year of age could be employed in a mill and no child between 9 and 13 years of age could be forced to work more than twelve hours per day.

The Parliamentary Committee of 1816:

Samuel White Bread had started a popular education movement. After his death Henry Brougham (1778-1869) took up this movement in the Parliament. Due to Henry Brougham's efforts the Parliament appointed a Parliamentary Committee in 1816 for inspecting the educational institutions meant for the people of Lower Order. This Committee reported that the children going to schools were not given full facilities. Their attendance, too, was not regular. Henry Brougham demanded that endowments of schools meant for Lower Order should be inspected. He contended that good utilisation of endowments facilitated the work of education. By doing so it would not be necessary to levy new taxes. Many schools opposed this move.

But Brougham brought this Bill before the Parliament in 1820 under the name 'Parish Schools Bill.'

The Parish Schools Bill, 1820:

This Bill was introduced in the Parliament by Henry Brougham for making a national system of education available to the poor children of England and Wales. But the Roman Catholics and other churches opposed this Bill tooth and nail. Consequently this Bill was withdrawn. But it was again taken up by John Arthur Roeback.

John Arthur Roeback and Popular Education:

John Arthur Roeback argued that only organising the means of education was not the development of education. He held that the purpose of education was to develop the moral and intellectual qualities of children. Acquiring informations could not be considered education unless the same were properly utilised in the right context. He advocated the establishment of four types of schools, viz., 1. Infant schools, 2. Schools of Industry 3. Evening schools for Adults and Adolescents and 4. Normal schools for Training of Teachers. Roeback emphasised that through endowments, taxations and schools pence (i.e. tution fees) the financial arrangements for running schools might be made. The whole country should be divided into school districts and the people of each school district should elect a school committee. The whole education should be under the control and supervision of the Education Minister of the Cabinet. Most of the people supported the Roeback's views. Still, the Bill could not become an Act.

The Progress of Education between 1833 and 1859

There was good progress of education during this period, as the Government started giving financial assistance to educational institution. In 1833 the Government sanctioned a grant of £20,000 for school buildings for the first time. Afterwards such State grants gradually increased. In 1846 it was raised to £1,00,000 and in 1859 to £8,36,000.

The Elementary Education Enquiry of 1833

This Enquiry was instituted to study the elementary

educational facilities available in the country. This enquiry revealed that good schools did not exist. The big cities had fewer schools. Only ten per cent of the children were receiving good education. Twenty per cent of the children were attending unsuitable infant schools, thirty percent were receiving education in private schools and the remaining forty per cent were not receiving any education at all. The people who were very interested in the development of education were known as the 'Education Mad Group'. The findings of the enquiry shocked them. They demanded immediate establishment of State schools. They held that there should be a central education authority in the whole country for distributing grants and levying taxes for the development of education. They also asked for opening a Central Teachers' Training College and a model school for training teachers. They also suggested that religious education should be organised into two parts viz., 1. Denominational (Special) and 2. Undenominational (General).

In the first group those persons would teach who were given the right for imparting religious education and were secretaries of various religious organisations. For the second type of religious education all the teachers were considered as suitable. In 1836 the Central Society of Education was established. This Society was empowered to work for the implementation of the above suggestions.

The Committee of Privy Council of 1839

This Committee was appointed by the Queen. This committee considered all matters that affected the development of elementary education. The inspection of the utilization of the endowments was also included in the purview of the committee. Inspite of vehement opposition from many groups, the proposals forwarded by this committee were passed and a Central Administrative Authority was established.

The Factory Bill of 1843

For improving the condition for the poor, House Secretary, Sir James Grahns prepared a Factory Bill which included the following main points:—

1. The children within 8 to 13 years of age working in

work-houses or in Cotton Factories will not work for more than six hours a day and will definitely be given education for at least 3 hours each day.

2. The Schools Trustées may appoint teachers but the same must be approved by the Bishop. The clergyman of the rural area and the director of the church will also be the members of the School Trust.
3. The students will have to receive religious education under the Church of England and they will have to be present in the church every Sunday.
4. The financial necessity of the schools will be fulfilled through State loans and school fees and school buildings will be constructed with State loans.

The above points indicate that the church had a special place in the educational system. The church wardens opposed this move. They were given the option that they could keep their children away from Catechism. But due to strong opposition the Factory Bill could not be passed and it was withdrawn.

The Voluntarists Movements

Some voluntarists opposed the move for State interference in education, but they accepted religion as the basis of all education. They wanted to apply the Principle of Free Trade in the field of education as well. According to them freedom and competition were necessary for reforms in education. They collected money from the public and established schools. They did not take any help from the State. By 1851 there were 364 such schools. Gradually, people realised the inadequacies of these schools and the non-denominational people doubled their success.

The Kay Plan of 1846

Dr. Kay prepared a plan in 1846. The Committee on Council of Education announced this plan. The following were some of the more important aspects of this plan:—

1. The pupil-teachers, chosen for five years of apprenticeship should be given stipends.

2. Her Majesty's Inspectors of Schools should inspect the pupil teachers.
3. The colleges training pupil-teachers should be given grants.
4. After working as an apprentice for 5 years, the pupil-teacher should be allowed to sit at the Queen's Scholarship examination.
5. In the State training college teachers should be given proficiency grants.
6. After having worked for fifteen years teachers should be granted pensions, if they choose to retire.
7. The training colleges should be given annual grants.

The above plan got much support. A sum of £1,00,000 was granted for educational development. Within two years (1848-1850) this grant was raised to £1,25,000. Thus the Government helped the cause of education.

W.J. Fox Bill of 1850

Some persons without any religious bias prepared a Bill which W.J.Fox presented in the Parliament in 1850. In this Bill no place was given to any denominational school. The Bill suggested that unequivocal rights be given to tax-payers of those areas where schools were urgently needed. The Bill further provided that the tax-payers who wanted to arrange for free and non-denominational education should be empowered to levy education taxes in their areas. But this Bill could not be passed because of the majority of the church and denominational members in the Parliament.

Establishment of Education Department

The Government realised the necessity of the development of elementary education. So in place of the Committee of Privy Council, it established a Department of Education 1856 on the basis of the Council Order of February 26, 1856. The Chairman of the Committee of Privy Council (usually a Lord) was made the Chairman of this Department. A Vice-chairman was also appointed. This Vice-chairman was a member of the

House of Commons associated with the party in power. The Vice-chairman was responsible to the Parliament on financial matters.

The Royal Commission of 1858

Under the Chairmanship of the Duke of New Castle, a Royal Commission was appointed in 1858 with two main purposes in view. The first was to study the prevailing condition of elementary education in the country, and the second was to suggest measures for making elementary education healthy, cheap and available to all. The Commission began its work with above two purposes in view. Some of its major recommendations were:—

1. The grants given in 1833 could not give desirable results. Therefore, these grants were not adequate. So adequate grants should be given by the State for the expansion of elementary education.
2. The educational system prevailing in 1833 was defective, but still useful.
3. The prevailing system of education should be made easier and it should be given a clearer form.
4. It was good to give financial grants on the basis of examination results.
5. The Commission recommended that the schools which were found satisfactory after inspection by Her Majesty's Inspectors of Schools should be given grants, but such grants would be additional grants if pupil-teachers were getting some grant from else where.
6. The local grants to be given to counties and boroughs should be prescribed.
7. The amount of the grant should not be higher than the total income accrued from fees and charities.
8. The Commission recommended starting the system of tution fees and urged that the Boards of counties and boroughs should be empowered to administer the local grants. But these boards should neither interfere with the school affairs nor with religious education.

The above recommendations were just suggestions, but due to opposition none of them could be implemented.

Principle of Free Trade in Education

Robert Lowe was appointed the Vice-chairman of the Department of Education in 1869. He believed in the principle of independent working. So he wanted to apply this principle in the field of education as well. Thus educational affairs gradually came into the hands of those persons who were against the principles advocated by Dr. Kay. Thus the system of evaluating a student's merit on the basis of examination was started. This increased the importance of examinations. In 1859 the local examinations of Oxford and Cambridge were started. In 1865 examinations in science and other subjects were started. Competitions for Civil Services were started in 1855. On the basis of the principle of supply and demand Robert Lowe wanted that popular education should remain denominational. He did not like to give educational grants on the basis of the recommendations of the Royal Commission.

The Act of 1870

The Liberal Party again came into power in the Parliament in 1855. Great changes were introduced in elementary education by this party. School Boards were encouraged in their efforts to spread elementary education. At that time school boards and voluntary organisations were organising elementary education side by side. In fact, the voluntary organisations had more schools under them than school boards had. In 1870, out of 17,614 elementary schools, 14,181 were under the voluntary organisations and only 3,433 schools were under the boards. In spite of the great changes effected in the schools under the voluntary organisations, by 1879, there were more students in them than in schools under the Boards. But in course of time the administration of schools under the boards were improved and the number of students also increased in them, and by the end of the nineteenth century only 46 per cent of the students continued in the schools under the voluntary organisations. The schools under the boards benefited immensely from the grants. The taxes were not so helpful to them. Thus the schools under the voluntary organisations lagged behind.

The Public Elementary Schools

The code of 1882 effected many changes in the grant system. According to this code the grant was to be determined by the average attendance of the students in the schools. The report received from His Majesty's Inspectors of Schools was taken as the basis for giving grants. The inspectors used to report on the following:—

1. The organisation and discipline in the school,
2. The methods of teaching, and
3. The general standard of the school work.

The Inspector was to give 'fair', 'good' or 'excellent' as his remarks about a school. According to the report to the Inspector, the school used to receive two types of grants, merit grant and fixed grant. The schools under the boards were receiving more grants than the schools under the voluntary organisations. The schools under the boards were better from all points of view and generally the standard of school under the voluntary organisations began to fall. There were very few schools under the voluntary organisations which could be regarded as excellent. Hence most of them were receiving lower grants.

Establishment of Kindergarten Schools

In 1854 a Kindergarten school was established in Bloomsbury by one of the followers of Froebel. Then it was only after twenty years that some other Kindergarten schools were established in other parts of London. Children of rich people only could get education in these schools. In 1874 Maria Grey founded the Froebel Society and many Girls' Public Day Schools were opened. With each of such schools, a Kindergarten school was also attached. Croydon's High School was one of such schools. Encouraged by the success of these schools, many other persons also opened such schools. Now the children of middle and upper class also began to join such schools. In the beginning Froebel's methods were not rightly followed in these schools. But gradually this defect was removed.

The Royal Commission of 1886

This commission was appointed under the chairmanship of Sir Richard Cross in order to evaluate the working of elementary schools. After two years' labour this commission submitted its reports in two forms—the Majority Report and the Minority Report. About religious education all the members were unanimous in their views.

Some schools boards were conducting higher grade schools, which were secondary schools. The Minority Report was in favour of giving grants to such schools as well, but the Majority Report opined that the public funds should not be used for such schools, because most of the students in these schools came from rich families. Therefore these schools should organise funds by fees.

The Implementations of the Recommendations of the Royal Commission of 1886

Many reforms were introduced in elementary education according to the recommendations of the Commission. Grants given on the basis of reading, writing and arithmetic (three Rs) were stopped. Thus the system of grants for result got a set back. Now grants were to be given for teaching of elementary science, physical geography and also for those subjects which were taught to senior children. Teachers' Training Colleges were established in universities or in colleges affiliated with universities. The other recommendations of the commission could not be implemented as they were regarded as controversial.

Summary

The Development upto the Eighteenth Century: Boys Day schools and Infant Day schools. Fees charged.

The Schools Based on Charity: To teach poor children the three Rs, religion and industrial education. Public Charity received Monitorial system followed.

The Industiral School: Free education in religion and small industries.

The Sunday School: For children working in factories, to teach three Rs, religious education.

The Circulatory School: Mother tongue the medium for teaching the Holy Bible. Teachers going from one place to another to teach poor children.

The Monitorial System: Andrew Bell and Joseph Lancaster. Senior students teaching the junior ones.

Robert Owen, Wilder Spin and David Stow: Contributed to the development of elementary education

Development during the Nineteenth Century: Due to the Industrial Revolution, children between the age of 10 and 14 working in factories. The capitalists and the higher class people opposed their education.

State and Education: Act of 1802 Apprenticeship; Rural School Act, 1807; Robert Peel Bill, 1815; Parliamentary Committee, 1816; Parish Act 1820.

Privy Council Committee of 1829: To look after the use of grants and education of the general public. Dr. Kay.

The Voluntary Organisation Movement: No State interference accepted. Principle of Free Trade in education to be followed.

The Establishment of Department of Education in 1856:
Replaced the Privy Council Committee.
The Royal Commission of 1856.
The Education Act of 1873.
The Schools under the Boards.
The Public Elementary schools.
The Kindergarten schools.
The Royal Commission of 1886.

Exercises

1. Trace briefly the development of elementary education in England and Wales upto the eighteenth century.
2. How did the State interfere in elementary education in England and Wales during the nineteenth century? Illustrate your answer by drawing attention to some important events.

Chapter 18

Events Promoting the Growth of Secondary Education

The Endowed Schools or Grammar Schools

Some Bishops established these schools in the beginning. For sometime the City Livery Company or Guild contributed towards the establishment of some Grammar Schools. Endowed schools are called Grammar Schools as well. They existed during the Roman period also. Classical languages were taught in these schools. During the Tudor period in the fourteenth and fifteenth centuries some businessmen had helped the establishment of these schools. Later on, the general public had also become interested in their establishment. Individual efforts had special importance in their establishment. For example, Lady Manner's Schools in Bakewell was established by the generosity of the lady. Winchester Public School was established in 1382 by William of Wikeham and Eton Public School was established by Henry VI. Both these schools are still running as boarding schools since their inception. Because of this characteristic these schools are different from other Public Schools. The Rugby, Harrow and Shrewsbury are Public Schools of this type.

The Organisation of Grammar Schools

The following points are worthy of mention about the organisation of Grammar Schools:—

The Teachers: Persons having teaching licence alone could be teachers in these schools. This was compulsory upto the eighteenth century. But the indifference shown by the churches in the teaching licence was not considered as adequate. Later, the Bishop alone could grant teaching licence on the basis of teachers' efficiency, morality and religious outlooks.

The Curriculum of the Grammar Schools: In the beginning the word Grammar was used for establishments where classical languages were taught. Therefore, classical languages were given special place in its curriculum. These languages were considered as keys to further knowledge. In England, Latin occupied a special place in the curriculum. Upto the eighteenth century there was not much difference between the curriculum of Endowed and Grammar Schools. In both such schools Latin and Greek enjoyed a special status. But in the Merchant Taylors School Hebrew, too, was taught. Later, an attempt was made to change the curriculum of these schools. In 1805, it was decided that a modern language and subjects like mathematics will be taught in the Grammar Schools of Leeds. But inspite of the Grammar School Act of 1840 no changes could be effected in the curriculum. According to the Act of 1840 the headmaster was empowered to introduce any subject in the curriculum. But he had no power to compel the teachers to teach them. This was one of the reasons due to which the Grammar Schools were subjected to bitter criticisms. Sidney Smith and Locke drew the attention of the public to the defects of Grammar Schools.

Discipline in the Grammar Schools: The discipline in the Grammar Schools and their management were not satisfactory. Hostels and their kitchens were not well organised. Discipline was maintained through fear. Strict corporal punishment was given. The headmasters of these schools were famous for inflicting cruel punishments. There was no good arrangement for physical and social development of the students. The students were not helped to use their leisure hour in healthy pursuits. Some boarding houses had become centres of gambling, drinking and other corrupt practices. Of course, some Grammar schools were free from these evils.

The Private Schools

Inspite of the Grammar Schools, the necessity for some other Private Schools was also felt because of the following reasons:—

1. It was not possible for children of poor families to get admission in Grammar Schools.
2. Because of the defective environment of the Grammar Schools many families did not want to sent their children to them.
3. Some families did not like that their children should come in contact with children of business-class people who were studying in the Grammar Schools.
4. Private schools were much better in discipline and organisation than the Grammar Schools. More subjects were taught in these schools. History, geography and modern languages, mathematics and art were the additional subjects taught in them. English and French occupied a special place in them. The interests and aptitude of students were developed by giving them opportunities to take up such subjects as music, painting, modelling, printing and surveying. Thus the students got opportunities for their natural development.
5. Private Schools were very carefully maintained and latest, progressive teaching methods were used in them. They had also become centres for experimental and research work.
6. The Private Schools followed the democratic principles in maintaining discipline, as the students themselves were made responsible for the same. For maintaining discipline the students used to select a committee which formulated discipline rules. All the students were compelled to follow these rules. The defaulters were presented before the Jury presided over by a Judge. The Judge and the members of the Jury were students

themselves. The defaulters were sometimes deprived of certain facilities or were closed in dark-rooms for sometime. Similarly, there were many other committees consisting of students themselves to look after various affairs relating to students. But the critics criticised this excellent system on the ground that it made students adults prematurely.

Girls were also educated in Private Schools. The aim of their education was to make them good house-wives. Hence, in the curriculum subjects pertaining to domestic arts, instrumental and vocal music, painting and embroidary, French and Italian and general knowledge were included.

Upto 1840, not much improvement could be effected in Endowed and Public Schools. But due to the views of Bentham, Jermy and Mills people began to criticise these schools. Bentham and Mills were for utilitarianism which these schools did not promote. The Missionaries also criticised the curriculum of these schools. Due to the Industrial Revolution a special class of middle class people came up. These people stood for individualism which the Endowed and Public Schools did not follow. Hence the time was ripe for the reforms of these schools.

Reforms of Public Schools

Samuel Butler, the headmaster of the Shrewsbury Public School and Thomas Arnold, the headmaster of the Rugby Public School, struggled for the reforms of public schools. First of all, an attempt was made to introduce the necessary changes in the old curriculum and the stereotype methods of teaching. Thomas Arnold stood for adopting progressive methods of teaching with a view to give ample opportunities to the students for self-expression and self-activities. To him the teaching of classical language was of great importance, but he wanted to change their traditional methods of teaching. He considered these languages necessary for the study of history, political science and philosophy. He advocated the teaching of Christianity and wanted to make it as the basis for general education.

The Royal Commission of 1861

A big exhibition organised in 1851 indicated to the British people that France and Germany were much more progressive in the areas of primary, secondary and technical education. The British public felt great resentment and unrest because of the existing poor educational conditions in their country. Thomas Arnold had not succeeded in effecting any reform in the public schools. Consequently, the Prime Minister, Lord Palmerston, appointed a Royal Commission under the Chairmanship of Lord Clarendon in 1861 in order to look into the financial matters, curriculum, methods of teaching and the general organisation of Eaton, West-Minster, Weinchester, Harrow, Charter House, Shrewsbury, Rugby, Merchant Taylors and St. Paul public schools. The Commission submitted its report in 1864. In its report the commission considered only the curriculum and the teaching methods as defective and other matters were regarded as good.

The Recommendations of the Royal Commission of 1861

The Commission recommended that the existing curriculum and the Governing Bodies of the public schools should be re-organised either on the pattern of German classical secondary schools or on the style of the gymnasium. The Commission supported the teaching of classical languages and religious education, but recommended also the inclusion of arithmetic, science, German and French languages, nature study, music and art in the curriculum. In the Public School Act of 1868, these recommendations of the commission were duly included. Except in St. Paul and Merchant Taylor's public schools, the provisions of this Act were to be accepted by all other public schools. The Governing Bodies of these schools were reorganised on the new representation basis. Those bodies were empowered to appoint and remove headmasters, to construct the curriculum and to prescribe fees. The headmaster was made responsible to his Governing Body. The headmaster was given the power to appoint his assistants. His decisions about his assistants were to be final.

The School Enquiry Commission of 1864

This commission was appointed under the chairmanship of Lord Taunton to enquire into the schools other than the public schools. These schools were those about which the New Castle and the Clarendon Commissions had not recommended any thing. This commission visited 800 Endowed and 942 other schools and submitted its report in 21 parts in 1868. It gave certain recommendations for three types of schools which were as follows:—

1. The schools meant for children of rich people.
2. The schools meant for children of the guardians with limited means of livelihood, but desirous of giving their children some vocational education.
3. Schools meant for children of poor labourers, farmers and ordinary businessmen.

For the first type of schools the Commission emphasised the teaching of classical languages, modern languages, arithmetic and science. Eighteen or nineteen years of age was accepted as the school leaving age for such schools.

For the second type of schools the Commission recommended the teaching of English, arithmetic, nature study, modern language and Latin. The school leaving age for these schools was 16 years.

In the curriculum for the third type of schools, besides English, one more language, nature study and mathematics were included. Religious education was recommended for all the three types of schools, but any guardian was free to withdraw his ward from religious education, if he so desired. It was recommended that the restrictions placed on the members of the Holy Orders as regards teaching should be removed.

Organisation of Secondary Education

The Commission recommended that the organisation of an Administrative Board should function as a Central authority for secondary education. The Commission opined that this board might be constituted in two ways. Firstly, the powers of the charity commission may be widened in order to enable it to function as an administrative board for secondary education. Secondly, an altogether new board might be constituted. The administrative board was empowered to appoint inspectors for inspection of Endowed secondary schools. Its scope was limited to the Registrar General Division and his officers which would inspect the Endowed secondary schools atleast once every three year and submit their reports about the conditions in Endowed secondary schools. Such officers would be called the District Officers.

Some special recommendations were made about Private Schools. Accordingly, Private Schools were empowered to have their own Governors who would appoint the headmasters who would give the final touch to the curriculum, and would also arrange for finances. They would be under the Local Education Authorities and enjoy full freedom in internal matters. The trustees may interfere atleast with these schools. The Parliament should make laws for the utilisation of Endowments. The necessary educational facilities should be organised from the Endowments. The Commission also recommended that the Governors should prescribe the minimum fees. Only those students should be given free education who could utilise the same.

The Teachers of the Secondary Schools

The salary of the teachers should be improved in order to attract better talents. The Commission further recommended that on the basis of the examinations, teaching certificates should be granted and a register of the grantees should be maintained. There should be a medical register for recording names of teachers who have availed medical help. The age of retirement should be fixed 60 or 65 years of age.

Examinations

The Commission recommended for the reorganisation of an Examination Council. But this was not implemented. The Commission emphasised the necessity of inspecting a school at a definite time through the Central Administrative Board which would appoint an inspector on its behalf for the task.

The Endowment Schools Act of 1869

Gladstone Government passed this Act for regulating the affairs of Endowed Schools. No attention was paid in this act on the recommendation made by the Inquiry Commission. For the utilisation of Endowments, the appointments of three special Endowment School Commissioners was recommended. The Act further required that for the education of girls the Endowments should be fully utilised. The Commissioners should control the Endowments of those schools which were less than fifty years old. This power could be utilised by the commissioners only when the Governors permitted the same. The Commissioner had no control over the elementary and secondary schools. The Parliament did not help these commissioners in any way. There was no system for registration of teachers. Thus the Public Schools Act of 1868 and the Endowed Schools Act of 1869 could not accomplish much, because the work could not be done according to the recommendations of the Royal Commission and the Enquiry Commission. Any way, the above Acts succeeded in creating an interest in the public for secondary education.

Secondary Education after the First World War

The First World War affected the educational system of England and Wales badly. However, the elementary education was not so much affected as the secondary education. During the course of the War many school buildings and equipment were damaged. Hence the schools had to face a financial crisis. Many teachers had to join war services. This affected the efficiency of the teachers and also their number.

In a way the World War had a good effect on the elementary education, the teachers and students of the elementary schools got opportunities to serve the society in many ways in the crisis the nation was facing. They co-operated in agricultural activities as well. The public was very much impressed by these services and it became convinced that all efforts should be made to produce such conscientious citizens by educating children.

The Fisher Act of 1918

The Parliament passed the Fisher Act of 1918 on August 8, although the war had not then concluded. Fisher was the Chairman of the Education Board. This Act had a special place in the national system of education of the country. This Act made elementary education free and emphasised the necessity of reorganising grant system, tuition fees and local education authorities. This Act accepted only that money as legal which was determined and accepted by the Education Board. It was also decided that the local education authorities would receive at least fifty percent of their total expenditure as a grant. The local education authorities were empowered to initiate any plan of education and send it to the Education Board for approval. In this plan the method of execution of powers by the various units and officers of education would have to be explained in order that the Board of Education might see as to what extent the provision of the Fisher Act have been honoured. Thus with the prior approval of the Board of Education the local education authorities could organise school camp, physical education centre, school swimming pool, play-centres and day or evening centres of social and physical training.

The Fisher Act laid down that no child below the age of twelve years could be employed on wages anywhere. Rules for employing children over 12 years of age were prescribed. The local education authorities were directed to prescribe the maximum age limit for Day Continuation Schools and compulsory full time schooling. This age limit was respectively prescribed as 18 and 15. For boys and girls education was free till the age of 16 years in the Day Continuation schools and students had to attend the schools for 320 hours during the year. The local education authorities were empowered to reduce 320 hours to 280 hours during the first seven years. This plan stressed the need for bringing the schools and work-houses nearer to each other, because the child while working in a work-house could receive education in a nearby continuation school.

The provisions of this Act could not be fully implemented because of the following reasons:

1. The teachers and school buildings were not sufficient in number.
2. The industrialists had no sympathy with the education reforms initiated.

However, the Fisher Act drew the attention of the people to the importance of Nursery schools and day continuation schools. Due to this Act, the age limit for going to school was increased.

Labour Party and Education

The Labour Party came into power in 1924. It tried to implement its education policies. The party wanted to make secondary education universal as it regarded education as a very important measure for social reforms. It considered elementary and secondary education as two inter-connected stages of the same education process. It advised the consultative committee of the Board of Education to make the necessary investigations and experiments for post-primary education at the primary education stage itself and to submit a report for its curriculum and nature of education. This report was not to be related with the prevailing system of secondary education. This report was to consider with necessary educational system for children under 15 years of age. The part wanted to realise two objectives through this report:—

1. To provide for adequate general education of the nation and,
2. To device various types of curriculum according to interests of children.

The Hadow Committee Report of 1926

W.H. Hadow was the chairman of the Consultative Committee in 1926. Hadow was entrusted with the responsibility of giving suggestions for educational reforms.

The committee under him submitted its Report in 1926 regarding the education of juveniles. At that time, only 10% of the children of the country were receiving secondary education. The Committee recommended that all the children between the age range of 11 ot 15 years should receive secondary education. Upto 11 years of age each child should receive post-primary education after completing his primary education. For this the necessity of establishing more secondary schools was emphasised. These schools were termed as Modern Schools, Grammar Schools, Senior Classes, Junior Technical Schools and Trade Schools. Science or literature was given the necessary place in these schools. Modern schools were established according to the selective or non-selective centre schools. They were established in 1911 and 1912 respectively in London and Manchester. These schools were established for those children between 11 and 15 years of age who came from Preparatory Schools. The Hadow Committee especially emphasised the establishment of these schools, because their curriculum was industry-centred and not narrow. The Hadow committee suggested that this curriculum should be of four year duration. The Committee recommended that at places where Preparatory Schools could not be established, Senior Classes should be opened. Some Public Schools were also advised to run Senior Classes. The Hadow committee also recommended for opening some Technical Schools and Trade Schools for giving special industrial and vocational education. In these schools children of 13 years of age or over, alone could get admission.

This Committee also suggested that in place of elementary education the word primary education should be used. Primary education should be compulsorily given upto the age of 11 years. For this, establishment of selective and non-selective centre schools was considered. The Committee further recommended that a written entrance examination should be taken for admission of 13 years old children in Junior Technical Schools. If possible, an oral examination should also be taken. All the Post-primary Schools should be called Secondary

Schools. The Committee also provided for the provision of the School Leaving Examination for admission in Selective Centre Schools, Non-selective Centre Schools and Senior Classes.

Implementation of the Recommendations of Hadow Committee

The recommendations of Hadow Committee proved very useful, as, since 1926 an attempt was made to make secondary education more popular. The Board of Education published a Pamphlet entitled "The New Prospects in Education in 1928" in which it inquired about the difficulties experienced in the recommendation of Hadow Committee. There were many difficulties in the field of expanding secondary education. There was a necessity of constructing many new buildings. But this was extremely difficult to accomplish because of financial crisis. The Second alternative was to use buildings of the existing schools but this could not be permitted by the authorities concerned. The grants that the Local Education Authorities used to receive from the Exchequer since September 1,1919 was completely stopped in 1931 because of national financial stringency. However, much development could be achieved in the field of education. About 63.5% of the children over 11 years of age were receiving post-primary education, while before 1926 this percentage was only ten. Voluntary Organisations were made responsible for constructing new buildings for schools, but this was not possible then.

Both the old and new types of schools were imparting education in the country. It was difficult to start the new system of education in the rural areas. All Standard Church Schools and Senior Church Schools in England continued to function. The All Standard Church School was transformed into Junior School. Thus, the children of 11 years of age who after passing this schools were admitted to the Senior Church School were now refused admission in Senior Church School. Such children were compelled to seek admission in the post-primary council school. Such a situation was not healthy.

The Education Act of 1931

This Act was passed for finding solutions to the problems experienced in the implementation of the recommendations of the Hadow Committee. According to this Act the school leaving age was made 15 years since September 1939. But any child, after attaining the age of 14 who was employed in some profitable job was exempted from this rule. But because of the outbreak of the Second World War the provisions of this Act could not be implemented.

The Spens Report of 1938

Sir Will Spens was the chairman of Consultative Committee in 1939. He prepared a Report in 1938 for organisation of secondary education for children above 11 years of age. In the Report it was observed that secondary education should be organised according to various interests of students. The Report further observed that in the existing old Grammar Schools major attention was paid to the fulfilment of the requirements of the certificate. However, like the Hadow Committee Report, this Report, too, recommended the continuance of these Grammar Schools and suggested the establishment of Secondary Technical Schools. The Junior Technical Schools might be permitted to continue but it was necessary to establish Secondary Technical Schools for children over 11 years of age with 5 years curriculum. This recommendation was bitterly criticised as it was thought that an 11 years old child was not suitable for technical education.

For children over 13 years of age the Report stood for liberal education. The Report suggested the introduction of School Leaving Examination for children over 13 years of age in technical schools with a view of facilitate the transfer to Grammar Schools from other technical high schools. Like the Hadow Committee Report this Report also suggested that the post-primary education should be of secondary education standard. This change would bring all types or schools into prominence. No doubt, the recommendations of the Spens

Committee were of great value, but it was extremely difficult to implement them.

The Norwood Committee of 1941

A Committee was appointed under the chairmanship of Sir Cyril Norwood in order to consider the recommendations of the various committees. This committee submitted a report outlining the nature of secondary education for the whole country. This Report was published in 1943. It classified the students into the following three groups:—

1. The students who are specially interested in practical work.
2. The students who took interest in applied art and applied sciences.
3. The students who acquire knowledge for the sake of knowledge. They want to understand the root of the things before them.

The Committee recommended that different types of schools should be established according to the tastes of the above three groups of children. Modern Secondary School was considered suitable for the first type of children, Secondary Technical School for the second group and the Grammar School for the third type. The Committee thought that the teachers of the primary schools were quite competent to form the above three groups according to the interests of children. The use of Intelligence and Performance tests was also recommended for this classification.

Similar to the Spens Committee, this Committee also recommended that the children over the age of 11 years and 13 years should be taught the same curriculum in all the schools in order to facilitate transfer from one school to another. A Lower School should be opened under a single teacher (male or lady) who would be responsible for the classification of children.

Critics of the Norwood Committee Recommendations

The critics of the Norwood Committee held that the implementation of these recommendations would create social disparities. The recommendations were criticised on the basis of physiology as well. The critics held that the children should not be classified into three different groups at the premature age of 11 years. But the classification of schools into three categories was accepted.

The Fleming Committee of 1942

Lord R.A. Butler was the President of the Board of Education in 1942 under the chairmanship of Lord Fleming. This Committee was requested to find out ways and means for establishing a close relationship between the general education of England and Wales and Public Schools. The Committee studied the condition of the Public Schools and gave the following recommendations:

1. The students should be given admission in Public Schools in terms of their abilities and interests. The financial position of the guardians should not be an impediment in their admission to Public Schools.
2. The Committee recommended that the various schools should be classified into two groups - 'A' and 'B'.

Under the 'A' group were to be placed those schools which obtained direct State grants. Board of Education should recognise these schools as Associated Schools. These schools should be made either free or the fees for students should be determined according to the financial position of the guardians. The fees for Boarding Houses, too, should be decided likewise. The Local Education Authorities may get certain seats reserved in these schools and should pay the fees for them. This rule should be followed in connection with reservation in the Boarding Houses also. The Local Education Authorities reserving such seats in 'A' type of schools may also get atleast one third seats reserved for them in the management also.

Under the 'B' group were kept all the ordinary types of Public Schools. All these Public Schools were required to teach according to the national policy of general education. If need be 5 per cent of the seats should be reserved for graduates of those primary schools which had received grants atleast for two years. The Board of Education started a system of giving bursaries to the students of 'B' type schools. These bursaries were to be decided by a Provincial Committee. The bursary for a student was adequate to meet all his expenditures in school. But this bursary was to be awarded only when the guardian was prepared to pay his usual contribution. The guardian could try for admission of his ward in any 'B' type school. Through the Local Education Authorities some seats could be got reserved in the 'B' schools for the students of the 'A' type schools.

Thus the Fleming Committee did not try to introduce any new system of education. It only tried to bring in a harmony between the old and new schools. However, the public was not satisfied with this arrangement, as it still thought that the Public Schools were available only for a privileged few. The introduction of the bursary system worried the schools which were conducted by the State as they thought that the more intelligent students would be a financial loss to them. So the provision made by the Fleming Committee were bitterly criticised. Thus the objectives with which the Committee was appointed could not be achieved.

Summary

Endowed and Grammar Schools: Teaching licence necessary for teachers. Classical languages were emphasised. The method of teaching unpsychological.

Private Schools: Modern languages, mathematics, art, history and geography, etc. in the curriculum. Progressive methods of teaching. Students were made responsible for maintaining discipline. Education in domestic skills as well. Samuel Butler and Thomas Arnold tried to introduce reforms in Grammar Schools. Arnold wanted to make the teaching method more psychological.

The Royal Commission of 1861: To suggest means for reform of nine Public Schools.

The Public School Act of 1868: Accepted the recommendations of the Royal Commission.

The School Enquiry Committee of 1864: Submitted its report in 1868. Three types of schools to be established. Reorganisation of secondary education, Teacher's Training and examination system.

Reorganisation of Secondary Education: The Royal Commission and Enquriy Committee emphasised this.

The Endowed Schools Act, 1869.

The Effect of the First World War.

The Fisher Act of 1918: Changes in the grant system, fees and Local Education Authorities. The industrialists did not co-operate. The Act could not succeed.

The Labour Party and Education: To bring in social reforms through education.

The Hadow Committee Report of 1926: Secondary Education for all the children between 11 and 15. Emphasised the establishment of Grammar Schools, Modern Secondary Schools and Senior Classes.

The Education Act of 1936: To implement the recommendations of the Hadow Committee Report.

The Spens Report of 1938: Classification of students on the basis of intelligence and performance tests.

The Norwood Committee of 1941: Secondary education for all children of the country. Classification of students into three groups for giving education in three types of schools. Social disparities feared. Hence criticised.

The Fleming Committee of 1942: To bring in harmony between general education and Public Schools which were to educate most children of all classes. 'A' and 'B' types of schools. The public was not satisfied.

Exercises

1. Describe the nature of Grammar Schools of England and Wales. What reforms were introduced in them from time to time upto the middle of the 20th century?
2. How were the Public Schools Great Britain better than the Private Schools? Explain how some committees tried to reform them.
3. Write a short note on the development of secondary education in Great Britain during nineteenth and twentieth centuries.

Chapter 19

The Education Acts of 1944, 1946 and 1948

The Education Acts of 1944, 1946 and 1948 are of great importance in the development of education in Great Britain. We shall study the principal features of these acts.

The Education Act of 1944

R.A. Butlar, the President of Board of Education, placed a bill before the Parliament in 1944 with a view to introduce reforms in education. This bill was passed. It is called the Education Act, 1944. It is popularly known as Butlar Act. The purpose of this Act has also been to introduce some reforms in the political, social and economic conditions of the country. Some of its main features were:

1. The Board of Education was merged into the Education Ministry. The office of the President of the Board of Education was merged into the office of Education Minister.
2. The Education Minister will look after the working of the Local Education Authorities. He will determine a national policy of education and submit an annual report on education to the Parliament.
3. The Education Minister will appoint a Parliamentary Secretary and other Officers. He will appoint a Central Advisory Council for England and another for Wales.

4. Local Education Authorities of counties will be termed as County Councils and those of the county Boroughs as County Borough Councils.
5. The purpose of education will be to promote the physical, mental, moral and spiritual development of children. The Education Authorities (i.e. County Councils and County Borough Councils) will be chiefly responsible for this. They will arrange for the Primary, Secondary and Further education. Elementry education will be called now Primary education. Primary education will be for children between 5 to 11 years of age, Secondary education for children between 11 to 15 years of age and Further education for boys and girls between 15 and 18 years of age. Primary and Secondary schools conducted by local education authorities will be called county schools. The manager of the Primary school will be called the Manager and that of the Secondary School, Governor.
6. Educational arrangements will be made according to the age, needs, interests and capacities of children. Primary and Secondary education will be given in separate buildings. The children between 2 and 5 years of age should be given Nursery education. Local Education Authorities should be responsible for the education of backward children.
7. Arrangements for hostels should be made.
8. The Local Education Authorities should send their education plans within the fixed time to the Education Minister for his examination.
9. Those schools which will not be under the control of Local Education Authorities will be called Voluntary schools. There will be three types of schools:

   (1) Controlled (2) Aided and (3) Special Agreement Schools.

   The Local Education Authorities will control the Controlled schools, but their Managers and Governors will be free in internal school matters. They will be free to appoint teachers and in matters of religious education. The Aided schools will receive 50% help from the Local Education Authorities and their Managers and Governors will also be free to appoint teachers and in matters of religious education, The Special Agreement Schools will receive partial grants for repairing their school buildings.

10. The Education Minister will frame rules for the size and site of school buildings.
11. For those persons who have crossed the compulsory school age-limit, part-time and full-time Further Education will be arranged. The Local Education Authorities will be responsible for this.
12. From time to time the students will be medically examined. Distribution of milk and provision of lunch in the schools will be compulsory. Poor children will be given clothes free. At all the stages of education opportunites will be given for physical and social development and for recreation. The Local Education Authorities will ensure all these.
13. The children coming from distant places will be given transport facilities.
14. Education will be arranged according to desires of the guardians.
15. The Education Minister will appoint a Registrar for inspecting voluntary schools.
16. Students will be given scholarships and other help.
17. Arrangements will be made for research in education. The research centres will receive financial assistance from the Local Education Authorities.
18. Teachers will receive salaries according to the recommendations of the Burnham Committee.
19. The compulsory school age-limit will be raised from 15 to 16 as soon as the necessary facilities are available.
20. Mass-prayer and religious education will be compulsory for each child.
21. The Local Education Authorities will send the

education budget every year to the Education Minister.

22. The institutions and schools giving Further Education will be given appropriate help.

The above provisions of the Act were openly criticised by the public. However, they have introduced good changes and reforms in education.

The Education Act of 1946

In order to clarify some of the provisions of the Education Act of 1944 the government passed another Act of 1946 on May 22. The following are some of the more important features of this Act:

1. The Local Education Authority may provide temporary accommodation to voluntary schools.
2. The Local Education Authority will be responsible for the construction and repairs of the buildings of Controlled schools.
3. The children of the Maintained Boarding schools and Nursery schools will be given free clothes.
4. If voluntary organisations rent their school buildings, the Local Education Authorities will receive these rents.
5. The mass-prayer will be held on the school campus. If notice is given fourteen days in advance its arrangement will be made outside the school.

The Education Act of 1948

This Act was passed on June 30,1948. This was made for changing the compulsory school age of primary and secondary education. The age limit for primary education was fixed at ten and a half and it was prescribed that secondary education will begin from the age of ten and a half. Many did not agree with this age limit.

Summary

The Education Act of 1944: Board of Education merged into the Ministry of Education. A Central Advisory of Committee Controlled,

Aided and Special Agreement Schools. Controlled under Local Education Authority, Aided under voluntary organisations, Special Agreement schools got grants for buildings. Primary Education between 5 and 11 years of age, Secondary Education between 11 and 15 and Further Education betwen 15 and 18 years of age. Local Education Authority to be responsible for lunch and milk. Separate schools for backward children. Religious and physical education compulsory.

The Education Act of 1946: The Local Education Authority to give temporary grants to schools under voluntary organisations and grants for buildings to special Agreement schools. Free clothes to poor children.

The Education Act of 1948: 10 years the maximum age limit for primary education. 10 years of age starting point for secondary education.

Exercises

1. Discuss the provisions of the Education Act of 1944.
2. Write short notes on the Education Acts of 1946 and 1948.

Chapter 20

British University Education

Development of University Education

By the middle of the present century there were 12 universities in England, 4 in Scotland and one in Wales with 4 associated colleges and one in Ireland. By the beginning of the nineteenth century there were only 2 famous universities, Oxford and Cambridge. These two universities are the oldest universities of England. Later Durham University was opened in 1832 and London University in 1836. During the later half of the nineteenth century other universities were established. In the beginning there were some university colleges associated with universities. Later, towards the beginning of the twentieth century these were made universities.

Universities of Birmingham, Bristol, Leeds, Liverpool, Manchester, Nottinghem, Shefield and Reeding were established in the twentieth century. Therefore, the British universities are considered as a contributon of the twentieth century. Queen's University at Belfast in Ireland was established in 1909. The Glasgow, Aberdeen and St. Andrews of Scotland were established in the fifteenth century and in Edinburgh, the fourth one, was opened in 1583. It may be noted that the number of universities in Great Britain increased with the increase in population.

General Nature

The British universities are autonomous. The State does not interfere with their internal and administrative affairs. In appointment of teachers and in financial matters the universities are wholly independent. The State gives them financial and other help for their smooth working. The universities are voluntary organisations.

The universities may be classifed into the following four groups:

1. Oxford and Cambridge Universities imparting traditional and high class education.
2. Universities in Wales, Ireland and Scotland which work as Central Universities.
3. University of London.
4. Universities in England, Manchester, Birmingham and other provinces.

More universities are needed in the country, as all the above four types are not able to cope with the ever-increasing crowd of students seeking admission. Hostels are very few. Only 25 per cent of the students enjoy hostel facilities. There is a provision for various types of stipends for helping the poor and meritorious students. More than 50 per cent of the students enjoy some kind of financial assistance. Most of the universities attract foreign students. Many universities have affiliated colleges in foreign countries as well.

The General Administration

We have already noted that the British universities are autonomous. Now we shall understand the nature of their management and finances.

The Management

There is a senate house which controls the general management. For administration a governing council or governing court is organised. Heads of various departments are members of the senate house. Some other teachers also are enlisted as members. The Senate House makes the educational plannings, and programmes and advises the Governing Council or Governing Court. The members of the council or court are generally other than the members of the Senate House. The Council or Court is free to take decisions on matter that fall within its jurisdiction. The State can interfere only when the interference is invited. On demand, the state may appoint a committee or commission to enquire into certain matters. The recommendations of this committee or commission are generally implemented.

The Financing

The university enjoys adequate financial assistance from the State and the Local Education Authorities. Sometimes this assistance is to the tune of 50 per cent of the total expenditure. There is a University Grant Commission to decide about the nature of financial grant to be given to the university. The members of this commission are not related with the Education Ministry in any way. Hence they are in a position to exercise their free judgment. However, in order to allow the government representation, one or two government persons are also included in the commission. The university grant commission examines the demands of each university and sends its recommendation to the government. Besides the grant from the government, thus received, a university organises its finances through fees, endowments and direct donations. The tuition fees cover about 33% of the income and the rest of the income is gathered from other sources. Now the Government grant given to a university is being increased every year, because its other sources are dwindling away.

The Curriculum

The graduate curriculum is generally of three years' duration. At the graduate level, there are B.A. or B.Sc. (General) and B.A. or B.Sc. (Honours) courses. In the Honours course there is a provision for some specialization. In the area of arts in England, there are more Honours students than in science. In Scotland about 25% students study Honours courses and the rest go for general courses. There are provisions for Honours courses in engineering, physics, mathematics, chemistry and natural sciences. In the art group one may take Honours in law, history, English and classics. In the B.A. (Honours) courses more attention is paid to incorporating utilitarian aspects of human life rather than studying the particular subject only. In this process an attempt is also made to emphasise the importance of various sciences on human society. To the science Honours students the importance of citizenship and sociology is emphasised. Both the arts and science students have to study the 'philosophy of nature' and 'philosophy of man'.

The B.A. general course includes English language and literature, modern languages, history, economics, mathematics and other subjects. Variations are found in the general and honours courses of different universities.

The examination council of the university conducts examinations. The heads of departments and teachers of the university are members of this council. External examiners are also appointed in order to maintain a balance.

For the post-graduate students there is a provision for research leading to Doctor's degrees. The research course is usually of 3 years' duration.

The Teaching Methods

Teaching methods vary in different universities. The Oxford and Cambridge universities have organised tutorial system in order to maintain contact with affiliated colleges. Lecture-method is generally followed. Tutorial classes are held once a week for arts students. For science students, in place of tutorial classes, demonstrations are organised.

For post-graduate students, in place of tutorial-in-charge teachers, supervisors are appointed. These supervisors maintain contact with the students and try to solve their study and research difficulties.

The Research

Research work is considered as indicative of the right of

knowledge that a teacher possesses. With this belief in view, in British universities particular attention is paid to research work both by students and teachers in arts and sciences. Even citizens are encouraged to do research work by utilizing the research facilities available in a university. Study apartments and sophisticated laboratories are provided in the universities for doing research. A researcher is encouraged to give lectures on his research work to groups of students and teachers.

The Student Life

There are residential and non-residential students in the universities, because hostels are not available for all except in Oxford and Cambridge. For non-residential students community centres have been organised for giving them some study and recreational and cultural facilities. The residential students come in contact with foreign students in their hostels. This widens their outlook. Various types of cultural activities, such as — music, drama, dancing and debates etc., are organised in hostels. Thus the residential students get better cultural education. In Oxford and Cambridge universities the students' day is distributed over four types of activities:—

(1) Attending lectures and study; (2) Sports and games; (3) Study in libraries and reading-rooms; and (4) To participate in group activities. The universities are co-educational. There are separate hostels for girl students. Some variation in the curriculum is allowed to suit the particular needs of girls.

Summary

Development of University Education: 18 universities in the country. All are autonomous. They affiliate colleges as well.

Four types of universities: (1) Oxford and Cambridge, (2) Belfast and Scotland, (3) London and (4) Other universities.

Administration: Senate House, Governing Council and Court. No State interference. Government grants, fees, endowment and donations.

Curriculum: General and Honours course. Facilities for research.

Students' Life: **Residential and non-residential students. Foreign students. Hostels. Community life. Library and reading facilities.**

Exercises

1. Describe the nature of university education in Great Britain.
2. Give a critical account of the curriculum and teaching methods as current in the universities of Great Britain.

Chapter 21

Modern Secondary Education

The modern secondary education in England and Wales are the result of the Educational Act of 1944. The maximum age limit of secondary education is sixteen years. We should pay special attention to the provisions of the Education Act of 1944 in order to understand the nature of secondary education. We have already hinted in an independent chapter to these provisions.

The Education Act of 1944 and the Local Education Authorities

The credit for establishing a form of universal secondary education goes to the Education Act of 1944. According to this Act, the Local Education Authorities are made responsible for establishing primary and secondary schools. These local authorities have to make sufficient efforts for the development of education in various areas.

The Types of Modern Secondary Schools

The education Act of 1944 has placed all secondary schools under three categories:— (1) Grammar Schools (2) Modern Secondary Schools and (3) Technical Secondary Schools. The current types of secondary schools in England and Wales are:

Bilateral and Comprehensive Schools

After 1950, there has come a tendency to incorporate the

essentials of any two types of such secondary schools; as Grammar School, Modern Secondary School and Technical Secondary School and establish a Comprehensive Secondary School. Thus an attempt has been made to establish a secondary school which may be of more practical value for the children concerned. In addition to these new types of Bilateral and Comprehensive Schools, The Grammar, Public and other types of secondary schools are also quite popular.

In the Bilateral schools there are two types of secondary schools—recognised and unrecognised. These Bilateral Schools are not much different from the Grammar, Modern and Technical Modern Schools. Many Modern Secondary Schools had accepted a Grammar School curriculum. The number of such Bilateral Schools is not very large. In these schools students were educated for the examination of General Certificate of Education. These schools were unrecognised. In 1959, out of thirteen thousand Modern Secondary Schools only one thousand appeared for this examination. These students were taught a mixed curriculum incorporating the essentials of the Grammar schools. From 1955, the number of Bilateral Secondary Schools recognised by Education Ministry increased, but this number was lower than that of the unrecognised schools. These Bilateral Secondary Schools were regarded as comprehensive, but really speaking they were not so. In fact, only those schools are regarded as comprehensive which impart general education to boys and girls, according to their individual needs, interests, and capacities. But these so called comprehensive schools did not have this feature. Some of these schools admitted either only boys or girls. Even to-day there are some guardians who like to send their wards to Grammar Schools and not to Bilateral Secondary schools, simply because they do not meet their needs.

Multilateral and Other Secondary Schools

Besides Bilateral Secondary schools, there are many Multilateral Secondary Schools as well. They are called Multilateral, because they incorporate in their curriculum the essentials of Grammar, Modern and Technical Schools. Such schools are not well equipped, because it is difficult to organise the curricula of many types of schools in one school.

In addition to the above Bilateral and Multilateral Secondary Schools there are other types of secondary schools as well established at various places. Such schools are Intermediate Schools, Central Schools and Area or High Grade Schools. According to the Ministry Report of 1958 these schools have been classified thus. Boys and girls are admitted to these schools on merit. The curriculum of these schools is less academic than that of the Grammar School. These schools also teach combined courses of Grammar, Modern and Technical schools - the three types of curricula. In England, under some Local Education Authorities there are some other types of secondary schools as well. These are Junior Comprehensive Schools and Higher Grade Comprehensive Schools. Junior Comprehensive Schools admit students after they have completed primary education and they are giving education upto 14 or 15 years of age. These are called High Schools. In the Higher Grade Comprehensive Schools those boys and girls are admitted who want Further Education after having completed the course of Junior Comprehensive Schools upto the age of 14 or 15 years. These two types of schools are regarded as good because they are able to enlist the services of well trained teachers and by studying in them the Eleven plus Examination is not considered as necessary. However, the Grammar Schools, the Modern Secondary Schools and the Technical Schools are still considered as superior to these.

The Grammar Schools

These schools were started in the seventeenth century. They are the oldest type of secondary schools in the country. In these schools English language and literature, modern foreign languages, such as French, German, Italian, Spanish and Russian; applied and pure mathematics, chemistry, physics, botany, zoology, history, geography, art, music and carpentary are taught. These schools prepare students for university education. Girls are taught domestic science also. Religious education is compulsory for all. Students are given practice in metal work. All these schools have provisions for health education, sports and games. For girls, lawn-tennis, basket-ball and hockey are arranged. Boys play cricket and football also. In Grammar Schools many voluntary clubs and societies are organised. These pertain to literary debates, dramatics and other cultural programmes. There are circle-clubs like those of mountaineering, chess, French and German. These clubs and societies do not interfere in any manner with the academic activities of the schools. They are organised after the school hours and ordinarily students are responsible for them. In the Grammar Schools some students are taught special courses for the examination of General Certificate of Education. This General Certificate is of three types—Ordinary, advanced and scholarship. These three types have different subjects of examination. Students may appear for any of these. The minimum age for appearing in this examination is 15. On the recommendation of Head Master some students could appear for the examination of General Certificate earlier than 15 years of age.

Importance of General Certificate of Education

By passing this examination, one is exempted from appearing at the preliminary examinations of Universities or some principal vocational organistions. But for obtaining admission in a university or in some special vocational organisation, the student should pass the General Certificate Examination in the same area in which he seeks admission. For admission, a certificate of the desired standard should also be obtained. In a university one has to study English and 4 or 5 other subjects. So far as admission in a university is concerned one must pass the General Certificate Examination in at least two subjects. This is also applicable for determining the grant of scholarship.

Secondary Modern Schools

The existing Senior Primary Schools of England and Wales

were transformed into Secondary Modern Schools in 1945. These schools have progressed much because of the co-operation they received from the public, as they have tried to cater to the needs of children with varying capacities and aptitudes. These schools offer both part and full-time special types of vocational courses, such as - Art and craft, home-craft, needle-work and design, practical craft, craftmanship, mechanical trades, house maintenance and furnishing, automobile engineering, rural science, agriculture, gardening, nursing, music, seamanship, social and commerical education. These schools prepare students for such examinations as school certificate, commercial certificate and technical certificate conducted by the Royal Society of Arts. These schools also prepare candidates for the General Certificate of Education examination. Some Secondary Modern Schools prepare candidates for such examinations as those of Armed Forces, H.M. Dock yards and Apprenticeship, Local Leaving Certificates, Northern Counties Technical Examinations.

The four types of Modern Secondary Schools may be found. These are as follows:—

(a) *Modern Secondary School of General Courses*: In such schools special emphasis is placed on art, craft and social and moral activities in addition to other general courses.

(b) *Modern Secondary Schools providing General and Special Education*: In these schools for the first two or three years, general education is given and afterwards students are given some special education.

(c) *Modern Secondary Schools resembling Senior Primary Schools*: In such schools, the curriculum of the senior primary school was generally taught with some modifications.

(d) *Modern Secondary Schools giving Advanced Education in Some Subjects*: In these schools the principal subjects are taught, but in one or two subjects, advanced education are also given.

Now many Modern Secondary Schools have become Bilateral Comprehensive Schools.

Secondary Technical Schools

These schools are not as popular as Grammar schools. The establishment of Bilateral and Multilateral Comprehensive Secondary schools have marred the progress of Secondary Technical Schools. Moreover, the public considers the Grammar Schools more important than Secondary Technical Schools, although the Ministry of Education has proclaimed that the children with the same intelligence quotient (I.Q) may be admitted either to Grammar or Technical Schools. But the public sends its children to the Secondary Technical Schools only when they are not accepted in the Grammar Schools. Another factor which makes these Secondary Technical Schools less popular is that the admission age in these is 12 years whereas, in other secondary schools it is 11. Another reason for their less popularity may be that they have begun to hold their classes in Technical Colleges as well. In these classes, technical tools meant for adults are used and their teachers are required to co-operate in expansion of adult education. Consequently, these Secondary Technical Schools have not built their own buildings and they still suffer for want of teachers. This feature has reduced their attraction for the public.

An Evaluation of Modern Secondary Schools

Few Secondary Technical Schools have been popular. They have made no appreciable contribution in the development of Secondary Education. These schools have developed scientific and technological education upto considerable extent. They prepare students for General Certificate of Education Examination and also for admission to Universities, Royal Society of Arts and Technical and Commercial Certificate Examinations. Students receiving education in Technical Colleges are generally graduates of Secondary Technical Schools.

Summary

The Education Act of 1944 and the Local Education Authorities: 15 years the maximum age limit. L.E.A. made responsible for primary and secondary education.

Types of Secondary Schools: (1) Grammar (2) Modern Secondary schools (3) Technical Modern School, (4) Bilateral Schools and (5) Multilateral Schools.

Exercises

1. Describe the nature of secondary education in England and Wales.
2. How is a Grammar School different from the Modern Secondary School in Great Britain? Discuss the specific nature of each.
3. Why is a Grammar School more popular than any other Secondary Schools in England?
4. Describe the nature of Bilateral and Multilateral Secondary Schools in Great Britain. Why have they not become popular?

Chapter 22

The Modern Pre-Primary and Primary Education

The Present Nursery, Infant and Junior Schools

There are three types of primary schools in England and Wales. The Nursery and Infant Schools may be grouped under pre-primary education. However, they cannot be separated from primary education as they are just complementary educational arrangement leading to primary education. We find three stages in primary education in England and Wales. These are as follows:—

1. *Nursery Schools or Nursery Classes*: Children of two years of age are admitted in these and receive education upto three or four years of age. Attendance is voluntary, and not compulsory.

2. *Infant Schools*: Children of five years of age are admitted in these schools and receive education for two years, i.e., upto seven years of age. Attendance is compulsory.

3. *Junior Schools*: Children of seven years of age are admitted in these schools and receive education upto eleven years of age. Attendance is compulsory at this level.

If a child passes through all the above types of schools he is considered to have passed primary education. We shall study the nature of the three stages.

Pre-Primary Education

(i) *Nursery Schools*: There are two types of Nursery Schools in England and Wales. Under the first category come those schools which receive full financial grants from Local Education Authorities. These are called Maintained Schools. Under the second type come those Nursery Schools which receive only partial grants. In a Nursery School there are about sixty to eighty students. In a class there are about twenty students. The age limit is 2-4 years. The teachers are mostly ladies. They try to improve the behaviour of children. They teach the children to dress themselves. They arrange for their food. They teach them many useful things through plays. These schools are generally situated near cotton mills. Mothers working in these mills leave their children here before going for work. No formal education is given in these schools. Through playing, singing, painting, dancing and modelling an attempt is made to promote their physical, mental and social development. As a result, children become self-reliant. Constructive plays and activities involving good behaviour and good healthy habits are the essential parts of curriculum. According to the stage of development of child the school buildings and equipments are organised. Most of the Nursery Schools are independent and some of them are connected with Infant Schools.

(ii) *Infant Schools*: Children of five years of age are admitted in these and receive education upto seven years of age. Reading, writing and arithmetic are principally taught. Thus formal education begins here. The Montessory and Kindergarten methods are followed. Children are given opportunities in different types of play-activities. At some places the Infant Schools are connected with Junior Schools and at other places they are connected with some other schools. An attempt is made to explain to the children the relationship between the given knowledge and life. An interesting and free environment is created in these schools. Proper attention is paid to the development of various senses, power of observation and vocabulary. There is co-education in these schools. The power of self-expression is developed through singing and use of mother tongue. Attendance is compulsory.

Primary Education Junior Schools

Junior Schools are established for given primary education. The admission age is seven years and the children remain here upto eleven years of age. There is co-education. Attendance is compulsory.

These Junior Schools may be independently established or may be connected with Nursery and Infant Schools. Nature study, mother-tongue, mathematics, science, history, geography, music, gardening and health education are the various stubjects on the curriculum. Some changes may be introduced in this curriculum according to the local needs. Thus there is no uniformity in the curriculum of these schools.

The children have full freedom within the school campus. For self-expression, dramatisation and story-telling are encouraged. The power of observation and practical skills are developed. The children are also taught spinning, basket-making, clay work and handi-crafts. The educational activities in these schools are better organised than in nursery and infant schools. The maximum number of students in a class is forty. Both men and women are employed as teachers.

SUMMARY

Primary education divided into three stages:— 1. Nursery School 2 to 4 years of age; 2. Infant School 5 to 7 years of age; 3. Junior Schools 7 to 11 years of age.

Pre-primary Education

Nursery Schools: Attendance voluntary. To teach how to dress, take food, play and behave. No formal education. Schools near mills and factories.

Infant Schools: Attendance compulsory. Teaching 3 Rs, singing, dancing, painting and clay work. Montessori and Kindergarten methods. Sense training, power of observation.

Primary Education—Junior Schools

Attendance compulsory. Dramatization, story-telling, nature

study, mother tongue, mathematics, arts, geography, history, health education and gardening. 40 students in a class. Curriculum flexible.

EXERCISES

1. Discuss the nature of pre-primary education in England and Wales.
2. Describe the nature of primary education in England and Wales.
3. How is pre-primary education in England and Wales complementary to primary education?

Chapter 23

Teachers' Training and Their Condition

About a century ago, teaching work was not regarded professional work like medicine and legal practice. At that time teaching was regarded as personal work for which no standard was prescribed. Hence, the teacher was not under any one's control.

With the development of education the importance of the teacher naturally increased. The Royal Society of Teachers of England has contributed a great deal for making the position of teachers stronger. This national voluntary organisation is working for raising the status of teachers. This society has emphasised the training of teachers and has prescribed a minimum standard for teachers at the various stages of education.

Educational developments have necessitated the growth of science of teaching. The public wants that the children should be taught by able teachers. Various government commissions and committees on education have prescribed qualifications and standard of teachers for each stage of education. To-day all the schools in the country insist on trained teachers.

Teachers' Training

Before the Education Act of 1944, teachers' training in

Great Britain was controlled by voluntary organisations. At that time the Church or some religious organisation controlled teachers' training. Now local Education Authorities are generally responsible for organising training of teachers. It is the responsibility of the Education Ministry to prescribe the minimum standard of ability of teachers. A National Advisory Council of Education is appointed by the Education Minister for solving problems pertaining to teachers' training. The Education Ministry generally looks after the following:—

1. To prescribe qualifications for admission in teachers' training institutions and to determine their curriculum.
2. According to the needs of the various schools in the country to distribute teachers' training facilities.

It is a national responsibility to arrange for teachers' training in order to maintain a high standard of education. An Institute of Education is regarded as the leading centre of teachers' training. All the teachers' training institutions are affiliated to it. Two types of training institutions are found:—

1. Teachers' training institutions controlled and supported by Local Education Authorities.
2. Teachers' training instituions controlled by voluntary organisations and supported by public funds.

For the first type, the Education Ministry gives a partial grant and for the rest of the expenditures Local Education Authorities are made responsible. For the second type of institutions, the Education Ministry gives 50% of the grant and the remaining half of the expenditure is shouldered by the voluntary organisations. Pupil-teachers have to pay some tution-fees.

There are teachers' training departments in many universities for training of teachers. For each university there is an Area Training Organisation which looks after the training of teachers. The Area Training Organisation consists of representatives of Local Education Authorities, training colleges and training schools.

At present there are about 250 training colleges and schools of all kinds training about 35,000 teachers every year. Training of teachers for Nursery, Infant and Kindergarten schools has also become quite popular.

Classification of Teachers

Four types of teachers according to the various stages of education may be mentioned. They are as follows:—

1. Nursery and Primary school teachers.
2. Secondary school teachers.
3. Teachers for specific subjects and for art and vocational schools.
4. Teachers for Further Education.

Primary School Teachers:

These teachers are trained in training schools. General Certificate of Education is the minimum qualification for the admission. The minimum age for admission is 18 years. The duration of the training is of two years. Besides professional subjects, education is also given in general courses. Training is necessary for teaching in a nursery and primary school.

Secondary School Teachers:

For these teachers, training is compulsory. These teachers are called trained graduate teachers. After training they may teach in a secondary school or in a university. The duration of training is of one year. Teachers' training departments of universities usually train teachers.

Teachers of Specific Subjects and of Arts and Vocational Schools:

Separate training institutions are organised for giving training in such subjects as arts, painting, music, dancing, physical education and domestic science. The certificate received from the Royal College of Music and Royal College of Arts are considered equivalent to certificates received from training institutions. The duration of training of these subjects is not the same. For physical education and domestic science three years' training and for arts and music fours years' training are required. The General Certificate of Education is a minimum qualification for admission.

Teachers For Further Education:

For such teachers experience in work concerned is considered as equivalent to training. Experienced persons in various industrial and commerical institutions are appointed as teachers for Further Education in the related subjects. For this, special training is not necessary. Experience in work is especially emphasised. According to the advice of National Advisory Council, the Education Ministry has prescribed the minimum qualifications for teachers. This minimum qualification for teachers is only the work-experience in the subject concerned.

Selection of Trainees

There is no formal method for selection of trainees. The women-trainees for specific subjects are selected from women who have completed their general education and have worked for one or two years in the industrial and commercial organisations concerned. The male trainees are directly selected after they have completed their minimum general education. The teachers' association also co-operates in the training of teachers. This association organises counselling for prospective trainees.

Appointment of Teachers and Their Service Conditions

The appointment of teachers in Great Britain is neither made by the Education Ministry nor by the Local Education Authorities. It is true that the Local Education Authorities give grants to Endowed and Aided schools, but they do not interfere with the appointment of teachers. Generally, the managing committee of a school appoints a teacher on the prescribed service conditions. In the aided schools the manager appoints the teacher, but in the school under a voluntary organisation the teachers are appointed by the managing committees. Local Education Authorities and Associations of Teachers co-operate in the formulation of service rules which are determined in terms of the recommendations of the Burnham Committee. The Education Act of 1944 has already incorporated the recommendations of the Burnham Committee. Thus teachers' position is generally very safe. Ordinarily, Local Education Authorities make service rules which the teachers accept. On three months notice a headmaster and on two months notice a teacher may be removed from service. But, before removing from service approval of the Local Education Authorities is necessary. Generally, a teacher is removed on certain charges only at the end of the session. The whole removal proceedings are kept secret till the decision is finally approved by the Local Education Authority concerned. The removal of a teacher is never advertised. This is just to help the removed teacher to get a teaching job elsewhere easily.

A teacher is removed only when his activities are not in the interest of the school. At first the teacher is warned, and if the warning does not lead to change of attitude in the teacher, he is charge-sheeted. If the teacher fails to give satisfactory explanation, he is removed from the service. The Teachers' Association, too, does not want that an undesirable teacher should remain in the school. The Education Ministry also acts against such a teacher and cancels his licence.

If some injustice is done against some teacher, the Teachers' Association fights against it. The Local Education Authorities also fight against the injustice done to a teacher. Thus, it appears that the service conditions of a teacher in Great Britain are quite satisfactory.

The teacher gets three months vacation during a year and he gets medical leave with pay. If necessary, the medical leave may be extended on the recommendation of the Local Education Authorities. The teachers is granted loan as well.

Teachers' Salary

According to the Act of 1944, the Education Ministry prescribes the salary. There are some salary advisory committees to advise the Education Ministry about fixation of salaries. There is a committee represented by Teachers'

Association, training colleges, education departments and Local Education Authority to advise on the salary of teachers of training colleges and universities. Sir Henry Pelham, Secretary to the Education Ministry, was the president of this committee. Recommendations of this committee have been accepted for future guidance.

There is a little variation in the salaries of headmaster, male-teachers and lady-teachers. The salary is fixed on the annual basis which is divided into 12 parts, one part for each month. On acquisition of some special qualifications teachers are given some additional increments. There is a little difference in the pay of headmasters of rural and urban areas. There is a difference between salaries of training college teachers and university-teachers. The Burnham Committee has done much to remove the disparity in salaries of teachers.

Summary

Teachers enjoy great respect. Their services are secure.

Teachers' Training: Formerly, voluntary organisations engaged in teachers' training. Now universities, training colleges, and training schools provide teachers' training. They receive government grants. Local Education Authorities also responsible.

Classification of Teachers:

1. *Primary School Teachers*: General Certificate of Education. Minimum age 18 years. Two years' training.
2. *Secondary School Teachers*: One years' training in universities and training colleges.
3. *Teachers of Special Subjects*: Separate training. Certificates from Royal College of Arts are also accepted.
4. *Teachers for Further Education*: Experience is their training.
5. *Selection for Training*: Through Teachers' Associations. Direct from schools and colleges as well.

Appointment of Teachers: Manager appoints teachers in schools run by voluntary organisations. Local Education Authority appoints in Aided institutions. On three months notice a headmaster and on two months notice a teacher may be removed. Approval of Local Education Authority for removal is necessary.

Emoluments: Headmaster enjoys higher salary. Male teachers enjoy higher salary than female teachers. Medical leave with full pay. Loan granted.

Exercises

1. Describe the nature of teachers' training in England and Wales.
2. Write a short essay on teachers' status and service conditions in England and Wales.

Chapter 24

Further Education

Further education occupies a special position in education in Great Britain. Its nature has been determined by the fortieth clause of the Act which means that full time or part-time Further Education will be arranged for those who have crossed the compulsory school age and are desirous to develop their various capacities in terms of their needs and aptitudes. Thus Further Education is somewhat different from secondary, technical, teachers' training, and adult education. Higher Education as conducted by the Local Education Authorities does not come under its purview. Under this educational arrangement come those persons who are engaged in some profitable vocational area and have crossed the compulsory school age limit and want to develop their abilities further.

Local Education Authorities and other organisations arrange for Further Education. But principally, Further Education is under Local Education Authorities which arrange Further Education or give financial assistance to other institutions for the same. About 60,00,000 persons in 1993 acquired Further Education in about 11,500 institutions. Some institutes organise longer courses than others. Out of these students about 50,00,000 studied in evening classes, 3,00,000 in full-time classes and about 7,00,000 in part-time classes.

There are many semi-independent and voluntary organisations which provide Further Education. These organisations receive grants from the Education Ministry. There are some private institutions as well which provide Further Education, but they do not receive any grant.

Nature of Further Education

The nature of further education is incorporated in the following three types of education:—

1. Vocational Education;
2. Formal adult education; and
3. Social and cultural activities.

According to the Education Act of 1944 formal educational institutions are required to arrange for formal and informal Further Education. According to the Act formal Further Education will be both full-time and part-time and informal Further Education through vocational education during leisure-time. There is little difference between these two types of formal education. For example, in the modern languages class are to be found students of vocational education and of other subjects. In Further Education institutions organised by Local Education Authorities mostly students of vocational education seek admission. For some industrial workers technical education is arranged from vocational point of view in some technical colleges. But in this technical Further Education boys and girls of other subjects also study. In this context, indeed, it is difficult to define the word 'technical'.

Technological Institutions

According to the plan of 1960 technical and technological education is arranged both at the elementary and advanced level. This plan is implemented throughout the country. There are about ten classes of elementary level in Further technical education. There are colleges of advanced technology established since 1956 for preparing students for degree in technology. Regional colleges of technology are larger in number and they prepare students for diplomas and Higher National Certificates. They give education in scientific and technological subjects. The colleges of advanced technology prepare students for post-graduate and research degrees. They are separately established. Regional colleges of technology function independent of colleges of advanced technology.

The third type of technical colleges prepare students for technical education of the intermediate standard. They prepare students for Ordinary National Certificates and certificates awarded by London Institute of City and Guilds. The Ordinary National Certificates are given through part-time education. Therefore these certificates are also called Certificates of Technicians. These certificates are awarded by the Education Ministry and also by the concerned industrial institutions. These industrial institutions approve the curriculum prescribed by the colleges and appoint persons for examinations on the basis of which certificates are awarded.

Certificates are awarded on the basis of the examination result of the prescribed curriculum. For the Ordinary National Certificate one should be of at least 18 years of age and the duration of the course is three years. For the Higher National Certificates one has to study for two years more.

From 1938 to 1997 the number of students has roughly increased from 12 to 160 times or even more.

Number of Students	1938	1997
1. Ordinary National Certificates	3, 393	90,000
2. Higher National Certificates	1, 137	50,000

The part-time education system in Great Britain has been more successful than the full-time. The full-time students in the National Certificate Course are give education in electrical, mechanical, mining, architectural and production courses. In 1992 there were more than 15,000 students studying these subjects for the National Certificate.

The London Institute for City and Guilds prepares students for various trades and awards certificates of intermediate standards and final certificates of a higher standard. These certificates are recognised in foreign countries as well. For the Intermediate Certificate one has to study for 2 years and for the Final Certificate one has to study for 2 years more. Besides these two types of certificates, the London Institute for City and Guilds awards many other kinds of trade certificates. These trade certificates are awarded on the basis of one year study after the Final Certificate course.

The London Institute for City and Guilds generally awards certificates to those students who are working as apprentices in the related trades. For this education the mill or factory-owners give their employees leave for one working day per week. From 1950 to 1992 the number of such students has increased about 40 times. The government wanted that by 1992 their number should have increased 50 times. Some mill and factory-owners do not give leave to their apprentices for this education. In addition to these certificate-courses, the technological colleges prepare students for other examinations such as—General Certificate of Education (G.C.E.) of London University Examination for the Membership of Vocational Institutions and Diploma of National Bakeries, etc. Some commercial colleges prepare students for National Certificates of various types of vocational abilities related to different trade organisations.

Colleges of Arts

In addition to technological colleges there are some Arts Colleges which prepare students in various subjects of arts for the award of the certificate by the London Institute of City and Guilds. Besides Arts Colleges, some technical schools also prepare students for certificates in arts subjects. For example, technical schools prepare students for such arts subjects as printing and glass technology. But, printing and decoration are taught by Arts Colleges only. In 1958, the Education Minister appointed a National Advisory Council to advise the Government on education in arts. Two types of awards are given on the basis of the examinations:—

1. Intermediate certificates in art and architecture.
2. National Diplomas.

For Intermediate diplomas the course is of two years duration of full time in any Arts College. The minimum age for this certificate is 18 years. For the National Diploma the minimum age should be 19 years. The course is of two years of full-time duration or three years of part-time duration. Two types of examinations are taken for the National Diploma awards. One in special subject and another in the main subjects. There are about 30 main subjects. The number of additional subjects is quite large. The colleges concerned arrange for examinations on the approval of the Education Ministry.

Agricultural Education

Responsibility for the development of the agricultural education is placed on the Education Minister since April 1,1959. Agricultural education is both part-time and full-time. Farm institutes give full-time education and part-time is given by technical colleges and other educational organisations engaged in Further Education.

Administration of Technical Education

The Education Minister is the highest administrative officer of technical education in England and Wales. But there are certain committees for advising them. There are 9 Regional Advisory Councils in England and one Joint Education Committee in Wales for advising the Education Minister on technical education in their respective regions. The Local Education Authorities organise and support these councils and committees. The Education Minister has appointed a National Council of Education to inspect technical education work and give advice on the same.

The Education Ministry awards some scholarships in order to make technical education more attractive and easier. Only students experienced in some work and of less than 20 years of age are given scholarships. In 1975, about 500 such scholarships were awarded. For these scholarships generally students of Further Education Colleges with two years full curriculum or students working for higher national certificates are considered.

Technical education, adult education and youth special services pertaining to Further Education will be covered in separate chapters.

Summary

Provision for Further Education has been defined in clause 40 of the Education Act of 1944. Full-time and part-time education for those who have crossed the compulsory school age-limit. Local Education Authorities, semi-independent, voluntary and private organisations engaged in Further Education. Semi-independent institutions receive full grant and voluntary organisations 50% grant.

Nature of Further Education

1. Vocation education.
2. Formal adult education.
3. Social and cultural activities.

Technical Institution: 1. Advanced technical and technological education, 2. advanced technology of the second grade, 3. technical education for Intermediate Certificate and Higher National Certificate and 4. technical education of the elementary level. The first type of education can be obtained in universities and colleges of Further Education of post-graduate and research level. The second type in Regional Technical Colleges of the first degree standard. The third type in Regional Colleges of diploma and Intermediate certificate standard. The fourth type of education is organised by the Education Ministry and related industries. London Institute of City and Guilds also awards certificates.

Arts Colleges: Further education in arts subjects. They prepare for certificates of London Institute of City and Guilds. Technical Colleges also give education in arts.

Agricultural Education: Part-time and full-time. By technical and Further Education Organisations under the supervision of Education Minister. A National Advisory Council.

Exercises

1. What is Further Education in England and Wales? Describe its various forms.
2. Describe the nature of the organisations engaged in Further Education.

Chapter 25

Technical Education

We have already hinted at the nature of technical education in the previous chapter. However, we shall study this aspect of education again for the benefit of the readers. There are so many technical educational organisations providing part-time and full-time courses so that any employed person may further develop his technical efficiency. Full-time education is generally organised during the day and part-time in the evening.

Junior Technical Schools and Trade Schools

There are junior technical schools and trade schools for children at least 14 years old and who have passed primary education. Engineering, architecture, weaving, sewing and shoe-making, etc., are taught in the junior technical schools. Book-keeping, short-hand and related subjects are taught in trade schools. In technical schools for girls, pre-nursing and house-wifery are taught.

These schools prepare candidates for the examinations conducted by Royal Society of Arts or any other organisation of the same nature. Only few schools charge fees. Some general education is also given in these schools.

Evening Classes

Provision for technical education in Great Britain has been very much developed through evening classes. Generally mechanics institutes run evening classes. Evening and continuation schools also provide technical education. Evening classes are of junior and senior types. Due to the organisation of colleges of Further Education the importance of evening classes has declined. However, many evening-class schools are still preparing candidates for commercial diplomas.

Higher Technical Education and Institutions

Royal College of Science, Central Technical College and Mining School have contributed towards the growth of higher technical education in the country. The Board of Education was very much impressed by the work done by these institutions in their respective areas. A Departmental Committee under the chairmanship of Lord Haldane was appointed to look into technical education. On the recommendations of this committee a Royal Charter was issued for the establishment of the Imperial College of Science and Technology. This was later affiliated to London University which has contributed a great deal to the development of higher technical education in Great Britain.

The Technical Education Teacher

The teacher of the junior technical school enjoys the same salary and other emoluments as a secondary school teacher. No specific qualification is laid down for the technical education teacher. His experience in the areas is considered as necessary. The McNair Committee has given some suggestions for the training of technical school teachers. It was laid down that if not for full-time some part-time training should be given to technical school teachers.

Summary

Full-time and part-time provision for children of at least fourteen years of age who have passed primary education. Full time in Junior Technical Schools, Trade Schools and Technical Schools. Part-time in colleges of Further Education.

Junior Technical School: Full time. Admission age 14 years. General courses as well.

Evening Technical Classes: Night classes, continuation classes and Further Education Colleges.

Higher Technical School: Lord Haldane Committee. The establishment of the Royal College of Sciences and Technology and Imperial Colleges of Science under the Royal Charter.

The Technical Education Teacher: Emoluments like those of the secondary school teacher. No training. Work experience is required. McNair committee.

EXERCISE

Describe the nature of technical education in England and Wales.

Chapter 26

Adult Education and Youth Welfare Services

Adult education and youth welfare services are just a part of Further Education, as we have already remarked.

Adult Education

The organisations engaged in providing Further Education make arrangements for adult education. The organisations that are engaged in adult education in England and Wales are:-

1. Local Education Authorities,
2. Responsible Bodies,
3. Her Majesty's Forces, and
4. Voluntary Organisations.

Local Education Authorities give adult education by organising some sort of vocational education with the co-operation of bodies giving Further Education. Many Local Education Authorities give grant for Further Education. Becoming formal members of the National Institute of Adult Education of England, the Local Education Authorities shoulder the responsiblity of adult education.

Under the responsible bodies are the universities of Bristol, Hull, Leicestor, Nottingham and Southampton which run departments of Adult Education. These universities, for the purpose of Adult Education, received assistance from the

Workers' Educational Association. This association has more than 60,000 members and more than 4,000 adult education institutions support it. The education minister recognises this association as a responsible body. Each responsible body for adult education organises some form of adult education with its area. These programmes are both individual and co-operative. These programmes consist of single lecture and terminal course of at least 10 meetings, sessions courses of 1 year and tutorial courses of 3 years organised by universities. The Workers' Educational Association organises various kinds of adult education programmes for industrial organisation. In the lecture programme some time is allowed for questions and answers also. Universities and Workers' Educational Association organise three years' tutorial course in co-operation with each other. This course is of the university standard. But these courses are available for a few students only. Each responsible body has to send its programme and budget to the Education Minister for approval.

Admirality, War Office and Air Ministry provide adult education to the members of H.M.Forces. The members of H.M.Forces may take part in any adult education programme organised by L.E.A., Workers' Educational Association, voluntary organisations and Universities. The service departments organise some correspondence courses of adult education for the members of H.M.Forces. There is a Central Committee of Adult Education for advising on adult education of the members of H.M.Forces. Representative of L.E.A., Universities, Service Departments and voluntary organisations are members of the Central Committee.

Voluntary organisations giving Further Education are very well developed. These are Learned Society, Youth Organisations, Churches, Trade Unions and the associations promoting Appreciation of Arts.

There is a National Institute of Adult Education which serves as a connecting link between the various organisations working for adult education. This Institute functions on the annual grant received from the Education Ministry, membership fees and royalty money received against its various publications. Universities and Local Education Authorites are also its members.This Institute gives advice and necessary information to all bodies working for adult education. It publishes a directory enlisting the names of all the bodies working for adult education. It publishes bulletins, organises libraries and research work in the area of adult education. Thus adult education is very well organised in England and Wales. Consequently percentage of illiteracy is very low there.

Youth Welfare Services in England and Wales

In 1939 the Government decided that the Board of Education would shoulder the responsibility of Youth Welfare Services in co-operation with Local Education Authorities and voluntary organisations. The Government formed a National Youth Committee and advised the Local Education Authorities to form such committees in their own areas. These welfare committees do not themselves organise activities for youth welfare. But they advise how the officers should run the various activities.

According to the Act of 1944 the youth welfare services were made a part of Further Education. The clause 41 of the Act mentions this. A Youth Service Department has been opened in the Education Department. The Department advises the Education Minister regarding policies and grants to be given to Local Education Authorities. The Local Education Authority give grant for Youth Welfare Services out of its block grant received from the Government. The Education Ministry gives grant to some voluntary youth organisations directly. The Local Education Authorities organise youth committees in their areas. Minor Local Education Authorities, some local citizens and teachers, voluntary youth committees, church organisations, Youth Employment Services, health services and people from industrial areas are represented on the Youth Committees. Local Education Authorities appoint some Youth Officers. They look after the Youth Welfare Services in their own areas and draw attention of the authorities to related problems. They choose youth leaders for training. They try to organise clubs and maintain voluntary centres for teachers.

Institutions for Youth Welfare Services

The Institutions related with Youth Welfare Services giving Further Education are the following:—

1. *Local Education Authorities*: The Local Education Authorities establish their own centres and even construct buildings for Youth Welfare Services. Generally these centres are opened in schools. It is not compulsory for youths to participate in the programmes of these centres. The youths are free to participate as they wish. At most of the centres such cultural activities as arts, music, sports and physical training are organised.

2. *Uniform Voluntary Organisations*: Under these come Boys Brigade, Girls Guide, Boys Scouts Association, St.John Ambulance Brigade, British Red Cross, and Junior Section. Amongst these, Boys Scouts Assoication and Girls Guide are more popular. There are senior and junior sections in these. In the junior section, children within 8 and 11 years of age are admitted and in the senior section, children of 15 years of age are admitted. In both these junior and senior sections there are such classifications as Brownies, Rangers, Rover-scouts and Wolf cubs. Boys Brigades are very popular in Commonwealth and other foreign countries. Denmark and Holland too, have patronised them. The programmes for Boys Brigades are organised from centres in Great Britain. In these centres there are more than 2,00,000 members who participate in the various programmes. The purpose of these centres is to expand the Kingdom of Jesus by teaching obedience, respect for elders, self-discipline and self-respect.

3. *Non-uniformed Club Organisation*: There are two types of such organisations, one for providing general facilities and the other for special facilities. Organisations giving general facilities are B.C., G.C., N.A.M.C., Y.M.C.A., Y.W.C.A., Girls Guildary, Girls Friendly Society and Boys Work Section.

Organisations giving special facilities are co-operative Youth, National Federation of Young Farmers Club and Welsh League of Youth.

The representatives of all the above organisations form an organisation named Standing Conference of National Voluntary Youth Organisation. This organisation protects the objectives and programmes of all the voluntary organisations and conveys their ideas to the Education Minister. Thus, these organisation function as a connecting link between the Education Minister and voluntary organisations.

Causes of the Failures of Youth Welfare Services

Sir W.A. Lester has been the principal critic, in Great Britain, of the workings of the Youth Welfare Services. According to him now these organisations do not retain their previous enthusiasm due to paucity of funds. The State Exchequer does not give them adequate financial support. Lack of adequate leadership has been another cause of their failure. Too much expansion and over-emphasis on vocationalisation are the other causes of their failure. In 1958 a committee was formed under the Countess of Albermarle to suggested a 10 year programme under the responsibility of Education Minister. The Government accepted this recommendation and tried to implement it.

Summary

Adult Education: 1. L.E.A., 2. Responsible Bodies, 3. H.M.Forces, 4. Voluntary Organisations.

Youth Welfare Services: The Government took its responsibility in 1939 for the first time. The Education Act of 1944 made it an essential part of Further Education.

1. Local Education Authority organise fine arts, music, physical training and sports and games in schools.
2. Uniform Voluntary Organisations, such as — Boys Scout Association, Girls Guide, Boys Brigade, British Red Cross, Junior Section, St. John Ambulance Brigade.
3. Non-uniformed Club Organisation.

Causes of the Failure of Youth Welfare Services: 1. Paucity of funds, 2. Lack of enthusiasm, 3. Lack of good leadership.

Exercises

1. Describe the nature of Adult Education Programme in Great Britain.
2. How are the Youth Welfare Services organised in Great Britain? Why have they not succeeded?

Chapter 27

Special Services in Education in Great Britain

1. *School Health Service*: According to the Education Act of 1944 the Local Education Authorities have to organise health service for students in schools. Thus, children get free medical help. According to the National Education plan of 1948, children are now given more medical facilities. Medical examinations of children is done at the prescribed time and dental treatment and other medical facilities have been better organised.

2. *School-Meal and Milk Arrangement*: In England and Wales arrangement for school meal and milk is made for those children in schools who do not get balanced diet at home. The Local Education Authorities appoint a manager for this purpose in each school.

3. *The Special Services for the Physically and Mentally Retarded Children*: According to the Education Act of 1944, the Local Education Authorities and Education Ministries have to make arrangements for special schools throughout the whole country for deaf, dumb and retarded children. Separate schools are maintained for children suffering from epilepsy and gonorrhoea. Special schools are provided for children with speech defect and for problem children. Specially trained teachers and medical officers are appointed for such schools.

4. *Psychological Clinic*: Local Education Authorities have established psychological clinics where qualified psychologists have been appointed. These clinics are meant for problem children. With the co-operation of Chief Education Officer, psychologists treat problem children and render necessary advice to parents and teachers.

5. *Research Work in Education*: The Local Education Authorities for improving educational standard give financial assistance to training colleges, university departments of education and other institutes of education.

6. *Youth Employment Service*: Through the co-operation of the Education Ministry and Labour Ministry employment services are organised for boys and girls studying in schools. For each area a Youth Employment Officer is appointed. For helping youth to get employment according to their needs, interests and aptitudes, this officer maintains a list of youth seeking jobs. He acquaints the youths with various industrial and business organisations. He provides the necessary informations to schools about the requirements of various types of services in order that the teachers may prepare the youths for the same.

7. *Education Welfare Service*: This service is considered necessary for bringing the schools and community nearer. This service is also intended to see that the compulsory school attendance law is not violated. Because of this service, industries, business-concerns and social homes become aware of the compulsory attendance law. Due to this service maximum number of children attend schools and delinquent children improve their behaviour. This way parents also become conscious of their responsibility.

Summary

School Health Service: Local Education Authorities responsible. Periodical medical examination by appointed medical officers.

School Meal and Milk: Arranged by Local Education Authorities.

Special Service for Physically and Mentally Retarded Children.

***Psychological Clinic*:** Chief Education Officer, psychologists, problem children and delinquents.

***Research Work in Education*:** For improving standards of education.

Youth Employment Service.

Education Welfare Service.

Exercise

1. Describe the special services in education organised in England and Wales.

Chapter 28

Meanings of Some Terms of British Education

In this chapter we shall briefly explain some of those important terms of British Education which are generally used in various contexts, but are sometimes misunderstood.

Advisory Council: There are separate Central Advisory Councils for England and Wales.

Aided Schools: They are established by voluntary organisations. Their managers have a free hand in religious education and appointment of teachers. The L.E.A.s give them 50% of expenditure incurred on construction and repairs of school buildings.

Board of Education: It was established in 1889. In 1944 this was transformed into Education Ministry.

Burnham Scale: The prescribed pay scale for teachers is known as Burnham Scale. The Burnham Committee has been represented by L.E.A.s and teachers.

Camp Schools: These are established in rural areas and sea coasts. The children from cities go to them for education during summer.

Certified Teachers: Those teachers who are approved to teach in recognised schools.

Chief Education Officer: The highest salaried officer of the L.E.A.

Community Centre: This is run either by L.E.A.s or a voluntary organisation for providing social, recreational and educational facilities to adults.

Consultative Committees: According to the Education Act of 1889, this was established to advise the Board of Education.

Controlled Schools: These are established by voluntary organisations. They receive full grant from L.E.A.s for repairs of buildings. In lieu of this grant the managers or governors of these schools lose their freedom in religious education and appointment of teachers which are controlled by L.E.A.s.

County College: This is established by L.E.A.s giving part-time and full-time education facilities to boys and girls within 15 to 18 years of age.

Day Schools: Schools which have no hostel facilities.

Development Plan: The plan which is sent to the Education Minister by L.E.A. for the development of the primary and secondary education.

Direct Grant School: Those schools which receive direct grant from the Education Minister, such as nursery schools, Grammar schools or any other special school.

Emergency Training College: It is established by Education Ministry and is managed by L.E.A.s. It gives training to men and women having rendered national service.

Evening Institutes: They give vocational and non-vocational further education to youths.

Excepted Districts: Those borough and cities which have powers for regional administration and are free from the control of L.E.A.s.

Fisher Act: The Education Act of 1918.

Free Place Pupils: Those students who receive free education in Grammar schools directly receiving grants.

Further Education: According to the Education Act of 1944, post-secondary education. This is meant for those boys and girls who have left schools before completing secondary education. Vocational and technical education is also given under it.

Governing Body: The managing committee of the high school.

Grammar Schools: Those secondary schools, after passing from which students are directly admitted into universities or get good jobs. They are based on good old traditions.

Hadow Committee Report: This is an advisory Committee report published in 1926. This publication was entitled Education of the Adolescent. This report has suggested the establishment of separate senior schools for those children of primary schools who were of over eleven years of age.

Her Majesty's Inspectors of Schools: He is appointed by the Education Ministry. He tries to establish co-operation between L.E.A.s and educational institutions.

Higher School Certificate: This is also called Higher Certificate Examination. This certificate is given to students passing the last class of the Grammar Schools.

Higher Education: Before the enactment of the Education Act of 1944, secondary education and Further education.

Independent Schools: The school which does not get any grant from the Education Ministry and the local Education Authority.

Infant School: Primary school for children between five and seven years of age, nursery schools for children between three and four years of age. These nursery classes are found in primary schools as well.

Junior School: Schools giving primary education to children between seven and eleven years of age.

Local Education Authority (L.E.A.): This is responsible for providing education facilities at all levels within its jurisdication. The County Council, County Borough Council and Joint Education Board also function as L.E.A.s.

Managing Body: This body manages a primary school.

Maintained Schools: The school which gets full support from L.E.A.

Modern School: Those secondary schools which have come into existence after amalgamating the previously run senior elements.

Non-Provided School: The old name of the Voluntary Elementary School.

Nursery School: The school meant for children between 2 to 5 years of age.

Nursery Class: The affiliated class with primary schools for children between 3 to 5 years of age.

Part II Authority: County and County Borough Boards which were responsible for primary education under the Act of 1902. But there were many primary schools outside the control of county boards.

Part III Authority: Municipal Boroughs or City Districts responsible for elementary education before the Act of 1944.

Preparatory School: A boarding school in which children between 8 and 14 years of age receive education for preparing for admission to public schools.

Primary Education: That state of education which includes Nursery school and Junior school education. At this stage children upto 12 years of age receive education.

Private School: A voluntary school run by any individual or group.

Provided or Council School: The Public Elementary School run by L.E.A.

Public Elementary School: The schools for compulsory attendance before the Act of 1944.

Public School: The Direct Grant Grammar School under which come Grammar Schools and Boarding High Schools.

Secondary Grammar Schools: See Grammar Schools.

Secondary Modern School: See Modern School.

Secondary Technical School: That secondary school where technical training or business-related education is given.

Special Agreement School: According to the Act of 1936 and as modified by the Act of 1944 that school which receives full financial assistance for construction of building from L.E.A.

Special School: The school meant for physically and mentally handicapped children.

State Scholarships: The scholarships given by the Education Ministry for university education after Higher

Certificate Examination.

Supplementary Teachers: Those less qualified teachers who impart education in rural areas on special salaries.

Technical College: College for Further Education.

Uncertified Teachers: The teacher for primary education without necessary qualification but having received permission from Education Minister.

University Training Departments: The University Education Departments giving training to Graduate teachers.

Voluntary Schools: A voluntary organisation runs such a school. It gives religious education also. But the special agreement voluntary school receives grant from L.E.A.

Work School: An employer establishes such a school for giving part-time education to his workers.

Youth Centres and Youth Clubs: The recreational centres established by an L.E.A. or voluntary organisation for youths of 20 years of age having crossed the compulsory education age. At such a centre youths spend their leisure time.

Youth Committee: It is established by the L.E.A. for organising activities at youth centres.

Youth Service: The necessary service organised by Education Ministry, L.E.A. and voluntary organisation for helping youths to utilise their leisure hours. The youths have to be within compulsory school attendance age.

PART IV

Problems of Indian Education

Chapter 29

Problems of Pre-Primary Education

The pre-primary education owes its origin to the famous German educator, Froebel. He introduced this type of education by setting up a Kindergarten school in Blakenberg in 1837.

The people in India did not attach any importance to this system for a long time, although even in ancient Indian books it has been said that Abhimanyu learnt the art of smashing the Chakravyuh (a circular formation of an army in the battlefield) during his pre-school days. Even then no attention was paid in India towards the pre-primary education of the child. After Independence in 1947 some private efforts were made to develop pre-primary education and give it a definite pattern and shape. With the inspiration drawn from foreign countries, pre-primary education took root in the Indian soil. This system for the first time came into existence in Germany and it has come to India from there. As such, for its proper study it is necessary to have a glimpse of its progress in the Western countries.

Pre-primary Schools in the West

In the Kindergarten school set up by Froebel, children of four years of age were admitted and they were taught things relating to personal conduct through play and games. Besides, some practical knowledge was also imparted to them in a psychological manner. This system introduced by Froebel proved very successful.

Mrs. Margaret Macmillan, keeping in view the proper physical, mental and intellectual development of children started nursery schools. The main aim of these schools was to keep babies in the care of efficient matrons in the school and give them proper guidance. These institutions provided fresh and healthy atmosphere to children living in slums and in densely populated areas. Children between the ages of two and four years were kept in these nurseries.

Later, Dr. Maria Montessori established Montessori schools where the Montessori system of education was introduced. The child in a Montessori school is provided with equipments and he himself learns independently with the aid of these equipments. In this way children from two years to six years of age received pre-primary education.

The importance of pre-primary schools should be realized and the responsibility that rests on a country and society in relation to pre-primary schools. Pre-primary is that stage of education which leaves its mark on the entire life. It is because of this that lot of care is taken in developing children in a psychological manner. Out of the three, i.e. the Froebel, the Nursery and the Montessori systems, any one may be adopted. These schools provide an all-round development of children, i.e., they try to develop a child mentally, physically and morally.

Regular medical examination takes place in the pre-primary schools for ensuring proper physical development. Children are given ample opportunity to enjoy fresh air and ample sunshine. They are given nourishing diet. Good habits are developed in them to ensure good character. In order to develop their personality and infuse in them a sense of respect towards the society they are taught how to live and adjust themselves in society during the play hours. Besides, their relations with their families are strengthened. In this way while engaged in play, the child builds his character and develops his personality. He is given education in arts, language, arithmetic and music in a psychological manner.

Pre-primary Education in India

There were 330 pre-primary schools in India in 1951-52 but in 1957 this number was almost doubled and now over four hundred schools or more are being opened every year since then. In these schools the Montessori or the Kindergarten system is adopted along with games and sports. But the government has always been apathetic in this sphere. The pre-primary schools lack equipments due to shortage of funds. The pace of progress being slow, there is a dearth of trained teachers and child literature in this field of education.

Development Efforts

It is difficult to deny the importance and value of pre-primary education. Pre-primary education may be regarded as pre-requisite to primary education. So proper arrangement should be made for it. The efforts of Dr. Montessori and the recommendations of Sargent Scheme have attracted some persons in the field of pre-primary education in India.

New Experiments and Researches:

In view of the importance of pre-primary education, educationists in India have begun to pay some attention to this vital stage of education. So far the pre-primary age for children in India has been from three to six years. But now the educationists have divided it into four stages; (1) pre-natal period, (2) upto the age of two and a half years from the day of birth, (3) from two and a half years to four years, and (4) from four to six years. The child remains solely in contact with his mother since conception to the age of two and a half years. As such, there is a need of maternity welfare centres attached with pre-primary schools. After this age, the child may receive education independent of his mother in schools. During this period the teacher is required to study minutely the child's tendencies and aptitudes and create accordingly an atmosphere for his education and all-round development. Careful handling and regular medical examination is needed to ensure his proper physical development. He is taught language, art, arithmetic, science and music in a psychological manner through the medium of play.

Teaching

So far we have had to adopt the foreign system in the sphere of pre-primary education such as Froebel, Montessori or play-way systems. But now efforts are being made and new researches are being conducted in order to evolve a pattern suiting the Indian atmosphere. Now a mixed system comprising of Montessori and pre-basic system has been adopted by many schools in our country. The Bhav Nagar Bal Shikshan Sangh is evolving a new system by incorporating the good qualities of both the above mentioned systems. There, therefore, appears to be a bright future for pre-primary eduction in India.

Summary

There are some practical difficulties in providing pre-primary education in India. In fact, the financial difficulty is the major difficulty. Pre-primary education is mostly related with the family and its environment. The Government has always been apathetic to the problem of pre-primary education in our country. It is mostly managed in our country by private agencies and individuals. Froebel, Montessori and play-way methods are usually followed. The age for admission in a pre-primary school is two and a half to three years. This education is continued upto six or seven years of age. Homely atmosphere is provided to each child. Special care is taken of his health.

Exercise

Discuss the nature of pre-primary education in India.

Chapter 30

Problems of Primary Education

Out of the various major problems that India faced at the time of attaining independence, the one was of illiteracy of the masses. The progress and the prosperity of a country mostly depends on the education of its masses. In order to eradicate this evil the Constitution has laid down that each state would try to spread education in its area through Five Year Plans. According to statistics available at the time of the beginning of Five Year Plans educational facilities were available for 42 per cent of children at the primary level. It was, therefore, decided that education facilities at the primary level should be provided to 60 per cent of children in the First Plan and 100 per cent in the Second Plan. Besides, it was also decided that education should be made free and compulsory for the children in the age group of six to eleven years. The progress of the Plans has revealed that the targets could not be fulfilled in both the plans. In fact the fixed targets have not been attained in any of our seven Five Year Plans so far.

The basic reasons for this partial success are many. We will look into some of the main problem areas.

Natural Difficulties

Hilly tracts, deserts, rivers, plateaus and forests are some of the natural factors that have created difficulties in the attainment of targets. The pattern of houses, commerce, communication etc., are all governed by them. The masses in India live in far flung villages away from each other. There are also mountainous regions and dense forests in the country. Due to natural difficulties and lack of money, means of communication have not been developed sufficiently. As such, there existed many regions which had no primary schools for miles around. According to statistics collected for implementing the Plans it was estimated that 22 per cent of education facilities were to be provided in dense forest areas and 82 per cent in agricultural areas. But the difficulty that arose was that majority of teachers did not prefer to go to rural areas and it was also found difficult to open schools in forest zones.

Political Difficulties

Primary education could not spread due to political factors as well, besides natural difficulties. The British government during the pre-independence days remained indifferent towards education. The result was that the primary education prevailing during those days became conservative in outlook. The Government of India after independence considered the basic education system for primary education useful and now it is trying to spread its modified forms through various plans.

But there are some lapses in the present government efforts, too. Firstly, all the organs of the government machinery are not equally active or involved in achieving the fixed targets. The policy adopted for the expansion of education is defective and unrealistic. Secondly, the responsibility of primary education rests on local bodies like Antarim Zila Parishad (interim district council), corporations, municipal boards etc., which are unable to co-operate with government officers entrusted with the control and expansion of primary education. The third cause is that the officers of the government officials and non-officials responsible for expansion of education indulge in partiality and irresponsibility. The result is that proper survey and allotment is not made for opening new schools. Schemes are fully implemented in some areas, while in others sufficient attention is not paid. Another reason relates to the general public which is still conservative in its outlook. Instead of extending co-operation and help for expansion of education, it does not even associate itself with this work. The result is that even minor taxes levied for expansion of education are opposed and even after much persuasion people do not send their children to schools.

Thus it is evident that there are many difficulties in the way of expansion of primary education. Sufficient money and adequate co-operation are necessary for introducing basic education. The local bodies need money for the development and expansion of education. But for fear of local opposition they do not feel inclined to propose any kind of education tax. The government-controlled inspection machinery is not adequate for the purpose. The educational policies are not free from local and regional partialities or favouritism. Public co-operation exists in name only. Moreover, in a majority of schools there is a dearth of teachers.

Social Difficulties

In the sphere of social difficulties come the prevailing conservative outlook of the people, illiteracy, communalism, favouratism and personal prejudices, etc., which create obstructions in the development programmes of education. Some people having faith in a particular religion seek separate school facilities. A large number of illiterate persons think it futile to educate their daughters and even boys after a certain age. Some people of lower social status even hesitiate to send their children to common schools. Persons speaking different languages suffer from, linguistic partiality. Separate schools are demanded for girls even at the primary stage. In the face of so many social problems the opening of an independent primary school and running it smoothly is not an easy job. The number of educational officers is not adequate therefore they are not able to establish personal contacts with all the guardians and solve these problems.

Financial Difficulties

The economic condition of a nation mostly depends on its national income. Despite the per capita income of a nation being satisfactory, in the absence of its proper distribution, public life cannot prosper. The distribution of national income in India cannot be called rational and based on equality. As a result, there are many families in India whose members despite full day's hard labour, do not find it possible to make two ends meet. The children of tender age in these families have to work for their living. The other difficulty that comes in the way of education is educational expenses. There are many families which, although are in a position to feed their children, but are unable to pay for their education. As such, in the absence of proper facilities these children do not get primary education. The statistics of expenditure on primary education reveals that inspite of growing public consciousness, the percentage of national income spent on primary education remained the same even in the middle of the century (1950) as compared to what it was in the beginning (1901). Thus, in the absence of lack of finances the expansion of education also remained stagnant.

Difficulties of Education System

The pattern of education and the educational institutions ought to be so attractive that both public and students get drawn to it. The other important consideration relates to its utility so that it may be in accordance with the regional needs and fulfil its natural aspirations. The present system lacks in these qualities with the result that the students after receiving education shun hard work. The parents do not show enthusiasm in educating their children because instead of helping them in their family trade the children show disinclination to join their traditional profession. Due to proverty some parents from the very beginning introduce their sons to their trade and keep them along with themselves. Now-a-days such a system of basic education has been adopted in primary schools which, it is hoped, will prove more attractive and useful than the previous system, but due to lack of proper buildings and trained teachers it has not yet achieved the desired objectives.

Programmes of Educational Reform

In the Constitution of India instructions have been laid down that within ten years, i.e., by the end of the Second Five Year Plan compulsory and free education would be provided to all boys and girls between the age group of six to fourteen years. Accordingly, provision for compulsory and free education should have been made throughout India at the junior secondary stage. The Planning Commission after taking the difficulties and shortcomings into consideration, came to the conclusion that it was not possible to fulfil this objective within a period of ten years. As such, the age group and the education standard has been reduced to six to eleven years at the primary stage. But even this target could not be achieved by the end of the Second Plan. So the period of providing free and compulsory education upto the primary stage for boys of 6 to 11 years age group has been extended till the end of Third Plan. Similarly, the period for providing free and compulsory education to boys of 6 to 14 years age group upto the junior secondary stage has been extended in all the successive Five Year Plans. In this connection it was taken into consideration that by achieving the targets of primary education by the Third Plan a large percentage of students having completed the primary education will join the junior secondary classes and in this way targets fixed for the junior secondary education in the constitution will also be achieved, but all these expectation have been belied.

Some other difficulties will crop in achieving the targets of pilot programmes and it will be necessary that efforts are made to solve them side by side with the expansion of education. These difficulties relate to pattern of education, courses of studies, school management, finances and administration. These aspects should also be considered in connection with primary education.

School Management

It is necessary to increase the number of primary schools for the expansion of primary education. Education at this stage will succeed only if schools are situated near the residents of students and there are no natural obstructions in their coming to schools. This does not mean that schools should be opened in each village. India has over five and a half lakh villages and although it is not impossible to provide each village with a school yet it is extremely difficult. The other thing to be considered is that one-teacher-schools will not meet the requirements of primary education on the basic pattern. Before opening a school it should also be taken into consideration whether according to the capacity of the school, students will be available in the area or not. The population of about 65 per cent of the village in the country is below 500 persons per village. As such for a reasonably useful arrangement it is desirable to examine the area and the number of students likely to come forward before opening a school. This problem is not faced in cities.

The rural public has some of its own special problems. Some people, due to ignorance, do not attach much importance to education, while others consider it an obstruction in their professions. Some people, despite their desire, fail to send their children to schools due to poverty and put them to work in their trade. Some attach more importance to their trade and consider it more profitable to give the boy training of their vocation instead of education. It is, therefore, necessary to change the pattern of education and make it more attractive so that parents get interested to educate their children. Primary education should be based on the local conditions. In rural areas, besides education, vocational training should also be provided so that the boys may help their parents while pursuing studies. Interest in the rural public will increase only when these reforms are introduced. Personal contact and persuasion by educational officers and teachers with the ignorant masses which do not understand the worth of education will be necessary to convince them to send their children to schools.

Due place has to be given to the local or regional traditions in primary education. Persons speaking some particular languages and some belonging to particular religions and sects are more attached to their mother tongue and faiths and although the partiality towards a particular group is not in keeping with national sentiments, even then, some such arrangements should be made so that these persons may feel at home in primary schools. There is no basic need for separate schools for girls at the primary stage, but some particular section of the society must have the freedom to establish schools of their own choice. Particular emphasis and priority should be given on the opening of primary schools in industrial, tribal and back-ward areas. Some attention has been given to these areas during the seven Plans and many voluntary organisations, too, are making efforts to spread primary education in such areas.

Teachers

There is an acute problem regarding the availability of trained teachers for certain areas. Educated men and women do not want to live in villages. There is a shortage of trained teachers in the country. A large number of teachers is required to implement the programme of compulsory education. The teachers generally do not take equal interest in all the subjects in the single-teacher-schools. Education suffers in the class when the number of students is very huge.

It is necessary in the interest of the development of primary education to look into these problems. Residential facilities should be provided in villages for keeping the teachers there. The teachers living in the villages should be posted near their homes. It is estimated that about 50 lakhs of teachers will be required to implement the programme of compulsory education throughout the country. The present strength of the teachers is only 20 lakhs. As such, it is difficult to train such a large number of teachers in a short period. One of the ways to meet this shortage is that men and women who have received education upto the secondary stage should be appointed as teachers in primary schools and they should be gradually trained in shorter courses after dividing them in groups. In this way, teachers will be available for primary schools and the problem of unemployment of educated persons, too, will be partially solved. The single-teacher-schools should be provided so that a teacher may not have to teach more than two classes. If the number of students is large in a class, it should be divided into sections. This system has been adopted at the primary stage almost in all the developed countries of the West while introducing compulsory primary education. Equitable and proper distribution of teachers is essential for the expansion of primary education and the number of students will be increased in the class, if one teacher is entrusted with the responsibility of teaching only a single class.

Courses of Study

Educational development schemes and changes should be implemented at the primary stage in the first instance. In the present condition, education based on local requirement is the best. So there is a need to change the current courses of study. The basic education enunciated by the Education Ministry of the Government of India (now known as the Ministry for the Development of Human Resources) was considered to be more useful and the Government made efforts for its expansion. But the problems could not be solved by introducing basic education at the primary stage alone. The courses of study in the primary schools, besides considering the local needs, should have also taken into account the teaching of hygiene and civics. They should also try to develop a constructive attitude in the students.

There is a difference between the educational needs of rural and urban areas. In accordance with the prevailing atmosphere provisions should also be made for the teaching of some vocational course in the urban schools, while emphasis may be laid on including subjects like argiculture and horticulture in the courses to be studied in the rural schools.

The teaching of a local industry, simple general science, arithmetic, social science and the national language should be common in both rural and urban schools. The basic education scheme of the Education Ministry has been a fairly good scheme, but it involved huge expenditure and despite the assurances of the Central and the State Governments to provide financial help, its success has never been satisfactory. Due consideration should be given to the expenditure likely to be incurred in the above proposals. The help of craftsmen in the urban areas for giving guidance to boys in industrial teaching and farmers in the rural areas for teaching agriculture and allied subjects may easily be secured.

Buildings

There is a shortage of suitable buildings for primary schools. The primary schools should be housed in well-ventilated and spacious buildings. These buildings should possess open fields so that the boys may have full opportunities for games and exercise and also for some industrial and agricultural training. More spacious buildings and open land attached to them will be needed in future to implement the basic education programmes. This will be a difficult job. Spacious buildings are neccessary for basic education, but that does not mean that in their absence the education expansion programmes be shelved. Our national aim is to introduce free and compulsory education throughout the country and we should remain active to achieve that goal even if there is a shortage of buildings and open land. To begin with, primary schools, should in the meantime, be opened in public buildings like Panchayatghar (Building for village council), Dharamshalas (rest houses for travellers) or private residential houses and gradually proper buildings and equipments may be arranged.

National and Local Arrangements

The co-operation from both the public and the Government

is needed for the expansion and development of primary education. The Central and State Governments have been particularly active in this direction, but they have not achieved much success. There are two main reasons for this failure. Firstly, the various parts of the government machinery are not functioning efficiently and the system of their working is defective. Secondly, there is a lack of public co-operation and whatever co-operation had come forth has not been properly utilised. Changes are needed in the present system for overcoming these shortcomings. The Central Government in co-operation with the State Governments should formulate a plan which should not suffer from the prevailing defects and through which maximum co-operation of the public should be secured. The first necessity is that of effecting changes in the rules relating to compulsory education. In the present system, the relations of educational officers with teachers and public has been bitterly criticised. The relations between them should not be that of a ruler and the ruled. Instead, it should be based on comradeship and mutual respect. Public and teachers' distrust of the education officer and their indifference towards education is the result of improper behaviour of education officers. It is the duty of education officers to develop contacts with the public, understand their needs, provide education accordingly and secure their co-operation in the expansion and development of primary education.

The public co-operation has been found of immense value in the expansion of primary education. Where, on the one hand, it created public interest, on the other, the public itself provides some facilities. There are hundreds of examples of money, land and building donations. The officer staff and teachers connected with primary schools should, besides establishing contact with the public, also make efforts to create interest in the public. When the local public, realises that schools are for its welfare, they will participate fully in their development and a stage may be reached when the public will itself contribute in the establishment of more primary schools.

Research Work

Many other problems relating to the development of primary education may crop up. It is better to examine, discuss and conduct researches to improve the pattern of education and to solve problems relating to buildings, and curriculum, etc. This work may be successfully taken up in training colleges and universities. The Ministry of the Development of Human Resources of the Government of India and education department of State governments should establish special committees and institutions on a large scale in order to take up the research work.

Apparently, the problem of removing illiteracy from the country is a difficult job. In order to achieve success in this sphere, an education-expansion movement should be launched with the co-operation of the government and the public. The examples of various countries are there to guide us and this work, although difficult, is not impossible to carry out. Eighty per cent of illiteracy has to be wiped out from the country with the help of various plans. It is a national obligation in which every citizen has to participate. The financial difficulties, too, will be solved if proper and enough enthusiasm is generated.

Summary

The national objective relating to primary education could not be solved due to some basic difficulties. In the absence of means of communication in forests and hilly tracts, spread of education became difficult. Public indifference towards education, conservative outlook, defects in governmental machinery, lack of co-ordination in the public and government organisation, favouritism and partiality of educational officers and their irresponsible attitude, etc., were some other difficulties. Among the social difficulties were favouritism in public, sectarianism, conservatism, etc. Financial obstacles also arose due to small national income. The prevailing pattern of education is defective and not suitable to local conditions. On account of these obstacles, only partial success could be achieved against the targets of the various Five Year Plans.

Schemes of Educational Reforms: The fixed targets having remained unfulfilled in the first two Five Year Plans, Planning Commission decided to achieve them during the other successive Plans. It has, therefore, become necessary to think over some main problems. The schools should be started after a proper survey and nearer to localities. The education should be in accordance with the local needs and many-teacher-schools should be opened instead of single-teacher schools. Untrained teachers should be appointed in place of trained as long as the shortage of trained teachers exists. These persons may gradually be trained. The teachers should be posted nearer their homes. The schools should be held in two shifts, if the number of students is large. In the absence of proper buildings the schools may be opened in any building that may be available. Subjects relating to local industries should find place in the course. The teachers should be given education in citizenship and social science, besides other subjects. The educational officers while behaving with the public in a cordial manner should also make efforts for enlisting their co-operation. Necessary reforms should be introduced after research. Thus, introducing changes in the existing pattern and with the help of government and public co-operation, the targets of primary education may be achieved.

Exercises

1. What are the main problems of primary education in India today? Explain briefly.
2. Suggest measures for reforms of the current system of primary education in India.

Chapter 31

Wastage and Stagnation in Primary Education

Wastage in Primary Education

The Indian Government, after the attainment of independence, stressed the need of primary education and provided funds for its development, but a scrutiny of statistics reveals that the desired success has not been achieved due to certain reasons. It has been observed that some children give up primary education before completing it. As such, the money spent on them during the early years goes waste. Along with the money the labour and time of both the teacher and the taught are wasted. This is what we call wastage. The available statistics reveal that till 1992, 40 per cent of the children have dropped out before completing primary education. Some of the reasons for this wastage are given below:

(1) *Lack of Proper Arrangements*: In the absence of proper arrangements there is a shortage both of proper buildings and trained teachers. Besides, there is also a dearth of reading materials and equipments for healthy entertainment in schools. In this condition of scarcity the parents feel that the present education is simply a burden. It is futile to imagine that this sort of education can foster the mental, physical and moral development of children. Therefore, many children give up study before completing primary education.

(2) *Illiterate Guardians*: The statistics available in 1992 reveal that about 70 per cent population of India is illiterate. Illiterate guardians who do not understand the value and utility of education are not inclined to send their children to schools. Moreover, how can they be persuaded to send their children to schools which do not impart education that can fulfil one's daily requirements? The result is that they initiate their children in some vocation even before they complete their primary education.

(3) *Unsuitability of Administration*: Much of the money that has gone a waste on primary education in India has been due to mal-administration in this sphere. Under the educational expansion scheme the number of teachers, inspectors of schools and administrative officers was not increased in proportion to the increase in the number of school. The result is that neither the teachers are able to give enough time to students nor do the inspectors have enough time to inspect the schools. The administrative officers have no time to plan and act. Lack of means of communication and other facilities of inspection are responsible for waste of money.

In most of the States of the country there are no fixed rules for joining or leaving a primary school. The students are free to join any class and fill in any birth date. They can leave the school whenever they desire. In this way there arises a difficulty in teaching when the children in the same class differ in age-group and mental standard. Besides, the students who do not do well in their studies are psychologically badly effected. The unsuitability of atmosphere in the class-rooms encourages students to remain absent from the class and finally they leave the school. The reason for students remaining away from the class is poverty of the parents and bad spacing of holidays. Agriculturists are generally more busy during crop-sowing and crop harvesting seasons. At such time the children have to help their parents in their work and therefore cannot attend classes. Thus their is interruption in their education and after some time becomes the cause of waste. The administrative officers should, therefore, keep the needs of the parents in view while preparing the list of holidays for primary schools.

(4) *Unsatisfactory Financial Conditions*: Poverty of Indian masses is a stumbling block in the development of primary education in the country. What to say of providing books and stationery to their children, the poor parents find it difficult even to provide two meals per day. They, therefore, stop their children from attending school and instead introduce them to some vocation to supplement their income. In this way many children give up primary education half-way and money spent on their education proves to be a mere waste.

(5) *Defective Curriculum*: Many primary schools have not so far been converted into basic schools and their curriculum is one-sided and still devoid of interest. The children of tender age neither find it interesting nor attractive; on the contrary the curriculum seems burden-some. As they get into higher classes, their burden increases and a stage comes when not being able to cope up with it any more, they leave the school.

(6) *Conservatism and Social Practices*: India, traditionally, is a conservative country. Even till this day people follow some such social traditions that can only be called bad social practices. Despite the efforts of social reformers and some legislations, the practices of child marriage, indifference and contempt towards girls, 'purdah' system, etc., still prevail in many sections of the Indian society. Many do not favour co-education even in primary classes. The result is either the girls remain uneducated or the money on their education is wasted. One reason why people do not favour girl education is that they do not consider it economically profitable because in a traditional Indian family male members feel that the responsibility of earning and feeding the family rests on them alone. These evil social traditions are proving costly to primary education.

Suggestions to Remove the Wastage

(1) *Improvement in the Curriculum*: In order to remove the non-interesting and non-utilitarian aspect of primary

education, some useful vocational training or handicraft according to local demands should be introduced in the curriculum and its superfluous parts deleted. The courses of study of boys and girls should differ and made purposeful keeping in view their different tastes and responsibilites. The curriculum should be flexible so that according to needs it may be made attractive, interesting and purposeful. The introduction of a suitable handicraft is essential for the development of their creative and constructive instincts.

(2) *Changes in the Educational Pattern*: Following are the factors that cause wastage in education:—

(a) Lack of suitable reading material,
(b) Unsuitable atmosphere of schools,
(c) Dearth of stadiums, play grounds and equipments for healthy entertainment, and
(d) Shortage of trained teachers.

Due to the above difficulties the all-round development of children is not possible and schools appear to be confining like prisons. Under these circumstances to expect that a student will leave school after completing his education will simply be fanciful. The condition of single-teacher schools is deplorable due to shortage of trained teachers. If due to some reason the teacher fails to attend the school the class turns into a noisy market and no guardian likes indiscipline and noise in the school. Besides, to think that the same teachers will teach with equal zeal and efficiency all the classes is to expect too much from him. The wastage in education can, therefore, only be checked when these defects are removed.

(3) *Educating the Parents*: Another important reason for wastage in education is the illiterate parents. Being unaware of the importance of education in human life, the illiterate parents do not send their children to school or even if they do send them, they remain indifferent towards the educational progress of their children which in turn causes wastage. As such, part-time educational institutions should be set up to create interest in the parents towards education. The government is making some efforts in this direction.

(4) *Due Change in the Administration*: Adequate reforms have to be made in the administration of the Education Department in order to check the wastage. This can be done by increasing the strength of inspecting staff, introducing a better inspecting system and providing more reasonable facilities. Besides, a definite education policy should be formulated and rules should be framed regarding age, efficiency, capacity and admission of children. Emphasis should be laid on regular attendance and standard of education should be raised. Local voluntary bodies should take keen interest in the sphere of educational development and administration.

(5) *Removal of Social Evils*: The main social evils that stand in the way of development of education are child marriage, indifference towards female education and narrow outlook towards co-education. Revolutionary steps to eradicate these evils will neither be proper nor practical. As such, the educated citizens of the country should patiently and steadily work for the removal of these social evils.

(6) *Solving the Financial Difficulties*: Ever since the country attained freedom, the Government of India has been consistently making efforts for the economic development of the country. Some success has been achieved during the various Five Year Plans in this sphere, but it has not been adequate keeping in view the present needs and requirements. India is an agricultural country and as such, besides industrialising the country, efforts are also being made for the development of agriculture and cottage-industries. It is hoped that by the end of the 8th Plan when various schemes relating to economic development are completed, the economy of the country will improve considerably. Recent statistics reveals that the average income of an individual has increased by 18 per cent but the cost of living has increased more than four hundred per cent. Under these circumstances, it is wrong to think that the 18 per cent increase in income will solve our economic problems. It is, therefore, necessary that while we complete our development plans we should also make efforts to check the inflationary trends.

Stagnation in Primary Education

By stagnation we mean that a student continues to remain in one class for more than a year or the prescribed course is not completed within the alloted time. Stagnation is a major factor responsible for wastage in primary education, both directly and indirectly. If a student completes five years' course in seven years' time, it naturally means that he has wasted two years' time and labour. Besides, if the student consistently fails in a class he loses interest in studies. The parents also get discouraged and lose interest in the child's education. Generally, in the end the child gives up studies and either gets into some trade thereby helping his parents to supplement their income or turns a vagabond menacing the society and thus increasing the burden on the nation. In this way stagnation damages the primary education to a great extent. Statistics reveal that the percentage of stagnation is high in the early primary classes. The average of stagnation rate for all the five classes comes to about 40 per cent. Only 60 per cent children make full use of the money spent on them. Hence it is necessary to seriously deliberate over the causes of this stagnation.

A. Causes of Stagnation

The following are some of the main causes of stagnation:—

(1) *Heavy and Uninteresting Curriculum*: The children studying in the primary classes are mostly in the tender age group of six to eleven years, and they have to study five subjects including arithmetic and science which are uninteresting for the children of this tender age. So they find it difficult to complete this huge and un-absorbing curriculum within the prescribed period. They therefore, fall victim to stagnation.

(2) *Absence of Definite Admission Rules*: There are no definite rules regarding admission in primary classes. Any child of any age within the age group may seek admission in any class. The result is that there is no co-ordination and balance between one's age and mental development and consequently the child may have to repeat a year.

(3) *Unsuitable Atmosphere and Conditions*: Mostly two different types of atmosphere are faced by the student when he gets admission in the class. The first is that of his family or locality and the second is that of the school which comprises of children of various families and different social strata. It is generally not possible for all the children to strike a balance between the two. This maladjustment sometimes not only causes stagnation but also becomes responsible for juvenile delinquency. Delinquency being an easy way out of the problems faced by the young students, does spread fast among children at this vulnerable age.

Sometimes the atmosphere at schools, or the home being unfavourable for education causes stagnation. Many children do not get sufficient time to study at homes with the result that neither they complete the home-task nor the prescribed course within the expected time. Hence they do not achieve success in the examination. The stagnation is, therefore, natural in their case.

(4) *Physical Weaknesses of Student*: A healthy body possesses a healthy mind. Our children do not get a balanced diet with the result that their physical development gets retarded. The mind and the memory, therefore, do not develop to the desired extent and the children fail to cope-up with their course within the prescribed time.

(5) *Social Evils*: Sometimes some evil social practices also become major hurdles responsible for stagnation. Even to-day early marriages take place and the boys and girls get involved at a young age, with married life. They lose interest in studies and therefore, they fail in examinations. Besides, on boys falls the responsibility of supporting the family and therefore they leave studies to take up a trade. Girls in particular are forbidden to pursue their education after marriage. Moreover, they have to, at their tender age, begin to house-keep and rear a family.

(6) *Defective Education Systems*: Due to shortage of teachers, a teacher has generally to take many classes and teach various subjects. Under these circumstances it is simply

a folly to expect that the students will be able to complete their courses in time. Lack of trained teachers, dearth of educational material, unsuitable school buildings are some of the other causes responsible for stagnation in primary classes.

(7) *Defective Pattern of Examination*: Through the present examination system efforts are made to assess the knowledge gained by the student in a year within a few hours through some questions. Not the least importance is attached to the work a student does throughout the year. If due to any reason the student, despite knowing the subject matter, fails to answer in a particular fashion his entire year is lost and he once again has to repeat the class. Thus, the prevailing system of examination, besides being full of defects, also helps to increase stagnation.

B. Some Suggestions For Preventing Stagnation

We have acquainted ourselves with some of the causes of wastage in education and are responsible for stagnation. Now we have to deliberate on how to free education from the causes that are responsible for wastage and stagnation. Some suggestions to remove these causes are mentioned below:

(1) *Improvement of Curriculum*: It is necessary to effect changes in the tough and burdensome curriculum in order to avoid stagnation. Stagnation may be avoided by making the subjects of science and arithmetic light and more interesting. The method of teaching these subjects should also be made attractive and the number of subjects should also be reduced.

(2) *Regulation of Admission Policy*: The administrators and the inspectors should formulate a uniform policy and strictly observe it. Stagnation may be checked by framing rules regarding the age and the stage of mental and physical development for the purposes of admission.

(3) *Improvement of Atmosphere:* Changes in the home, society and school atmosphere should be made in order to stop stagnation. The changes made should aim at improving and making the atmosphere healthy. To achieve this, it is desirable that the public, the teachers and the government should co-operate. It is necessary to remove the evil social practices and

false values. Restrictions should be imposed on indecent films, film-songs, etc. Much success in this sphere may be achieved by providing healthy entertainment to children under the supervision of teachers and adult education to the illiterate parents.

(4) *Improvement of Health*: Physical development is necessary for mental development of students, but the tragedy is that most of the parents in our country are unable to provide nourishing food for their children. In view of the helplessness of the parents it is the responsibility of the State to take over the charge of providing food to the future citizens of the country. Indifference of the Indian Government towards this problem when other nations are paying so much attention to the development of their man-power, may prove harmful for the nation. It is, therefore, necessary to provide milk and other nourishing foods to the school-going children. This is necessary for removing stagnation and for building up healthy citizens.

(5) *Improvement in Teaching Method*: The Prevailing teaching methods being unpsychological and unattractive cause stagnation. The problem of stagnation may be solved to a large extent if psychological systems prevailing in other developed countries are adopted in this country, too. In adopting these systems we will face the difficulty of financial resources and sufficient number of trained teachers. This difficulty may be overcome if love for education is created in rich persons.

(6) *Stopping Child Marriage*: Although child marriage has been proclaimed an offence under the Act of 1930, and other Amendments to the Act yet this social practice coutinues. Unless the society looks down on this practice with contempt, it will not be stopped. As such, it is the duty of the public and leaders to put an end to this practice. The government, too, should take effective steps to ensure the implementation of the Act.

(7) *Reforms in the Examination System*: The system of examination should be based on the principle that education is imparted for success in examinations. The system, therefore

should examine the whole year's work and promotions should be given after testing the real knowledge acquired during the period of study.

Summary

Wastage in Education: Wastage in primary education takes place when students leave the school without completing the full course. By leaving the education mid-way all money and labour spent on education is wasted.

Causes of Wastage: The following are the main causes of wastage:—

(1) Lack of proper arrangements, (2) Illiteracy of parents, (3) Improper and unsuitable administration, (4) Poor finances, (5) Defective curriculum and (6) Conservatism and evil social practices.

Some Suggestions to Check Waste: (1) Improvement and revision of curriculum, (2) Effecting changes in the education pattern, (3) Educating the parents, (4) Effecting changes in administration, (5) Removal of social evils and (6) Solving financial problems.

Stagnation in Education: Stagnation means not completing the [illegible] within the prescribed time. Indirectly, it is a wastage. The main causes are: (1) Heavy and uninteresting curriculum, (2) Flexibility of school admission rules, (3) Unsuitable conditions and atmosphere, (4) Physical unfitness, (5) Evil social practices, (6) Defective educational pattern and (7) Defective examinations.

Suggestions to Check Stagnation: (1) Revision and improvement of curriculum, (2) Formulation of a definite admission policy, (3) Reform and improvement in atmosphere, (4) Development of health, (5) Changes in teaching methods, (6) Ending the practice of child marriage and (7) Changes in the examination pattern.

Exercises

1. Explain the causes of wastage in primary education in India. How can we remove it?
2. How can we check stagnation in primary education in India? Explain.

Chapter 32

Compulsory Education

In 1950 the Indian Constitution specified that free and compulsory education through out the country would be provided to all the children upto the age to 14 years. Accordingly, the state governments were directed to achieve this objective within the following ten years. This national effort was in keeping with the needs of the country. Under the circumstances when only 16 per cent of the population was literate, introduction of compulsory education upto a certain limit was particularly desirable. For a country having pinned its hopes on a democratic system, it was necessary that its people be given compulsory education in order to instil in them a sense of national responsibility and citizenship. Education was also necessary for success of democracy and providing it stability. Equal opportunity to every one is the basic principle of democracy and there should be no partiality in its implementation. The success of democracy is possible only when a citizen is aware of his responsibility, rights as well as his duty towards others. This required a positive change in the mental outlook of the people. The Second World War had shown that the members of the so-called civilized and cultured society, if misguided, could commit brutal acts that would put to shame even the barbarous communities of the past. This can only be called social backwardness or lack of social sense. Conduct occupies an important place in society.

Despite being civilised, people generally do not understand their duties and responsibilities nor do they make proper use of their rights. All this leads to the conclusion that in his basic attitude man possesses instincts similar to the instincts of an animal. It is only by his refined conduct that man can make a civilized society. A cultured person will pay due regard to the feelings of others. And in order to adopt this civilized attitude man has to be educated. Thus, it is clear that the provision in our Constitution for educating every-one upto a certain age is a national necessity.

Primary Education Before It Was Made Compulsory

Before the establishment of the British empire, the old and traditional education system prevailed in the country. But foreign rule over a considerably long period so much affected and discouraged the education system that it lost its finer points and by the end of the 18th century it almost became a nonentity. But while the adverse circumstances stopped its development and then destroyed it, Indians' intense love for their traditional education system did not fade away altogether. It remained deeply associated with their social and cultural life. In spite of the expansion of British empire after the Battle of Plassey in 1759 some Indian educational institutions made valient efforts in the field of expansion of education. Nearly one lakh primary schools were being run in Bengal alone.

Despite such efforts the ancient system of education could not progress. The main reason for this decay was the empire-building policy of the British according to which they tried to stabilise their supremacy by modifying or overhauling the social, literary and cultural values of the conquered country. So the Britishers in order to give a permanent footing to their political supremacy, besides introducing Western pattern of educational system and culture, tried to discourage the Indian method of education. They succeeded in their policy. Because of these destructive blows since the beginning of the nineteenth century, decay set in gradually in the Indian traditional educational system. In destroying the traditional Indian education, the Christian missionaries played a more important role than the East India Company did. They established primary, secondary and higher schools on the Western pattern with the aim of spreading Christianity.

The British Parliament under the Charter of 1813 authorised the East India Company to spend rupees one lakh yearly for the education of Indian people, development of scientific work and the progress of Indian literature. But due to the indifference of the Directors and Officers of the Company, the order remained completely un-implemented for about ten years. The main interest of the Company in India was trade and earning more and more profits. Hence, it considered the efforts of the missionaries sufficient and showed indifference towards the development of education. There was also the practical difficulty in following the Charter in the true spirit because the sum of rupees one lakh was too meagre in view of the vastness and large population of the country and it was difficult to decide on which particular sphere this money should be utilised. These problems were reviewed in 1824 and it was decided to spend a certain percentage of the allotted money on primary education.

During the rule of the Company upto 1857, the efforts in the sphere of education remained completely unsatisfactory. In the Wood's Despatch of 1854, while criticising the educational activities of the Company, it was admitted that the Company had completely neglected education in India. Accordingly, the Despatch urged that the responsibility of encouraging the Indian schools, expansion of primary education, proper financial assistance and provision of useful and practical education for the Indian people should be the duty of the Company. But during the Company rule prior to Indian revolt of 1857, financial help was given only to higher and secondary education. No expansion of primary education worth the name took place.

After the revolt of 1857 the rule of the Company ended and the British Parliament took the administration of India directly in its own hands. The direct rule by the British Parliament was better organised. The next 30 years were particularly important in the history of primary education. In the Stanley Charter of 1859 it was announced that the responsibility of primary education in India would be the direct responsibility of the Indian administration. The right to tax the Indian public for expansion of education was given to the Government of India. By 1882 nearly 29,000 primary schools with the capacity to teach 21 lakh students had been established in the country. For the expansion of primary education this provision was so inadequate that only 1.2 per cent children could be made literate.

Despite the patronage extended by the Government during the nineteenth century, proper expansion of education in India could not take place. This was even accepted by Lord Curzon, the then Viceroy of India. Lord Curzon held the view that primary education whose object was to educate the common people in the local or mother tongue, should be fully developed and available to every one. Full patronage of the Government was necessary for primary education. The then Government in order to free itself from this responsibility took an inadequate step and without considering the recommendations of the Indian Education Commission of 1882 transferred the responsibility of primary education to local bodies. It was expected that this step would help the expansion of primary education but due to wilful indifference of the government the local bodies had to face financial difficulties in this task. Lack of finances was a major obstacle in the progress of primary education and despite continuous efforts of the local bodies, its progress remained unsatisfactory. The result was that during the period of 20 years from the year 1882 to 1902, an increase of only 66 lakhs of students could be recorded at the primary stage of education.

Lord Curzon, the Viceroy of India, made commendable efforts for the expansion and development of primary education. As a matter of fact, the Curzon era could be called the first stage in the development of primary education. Lord Curzon gave much encouragement to the Indian people in the sphere of education. For the first time, without any fear the people asked the Government to discharge its responsibilities towards primary education. It was also expected that primary education would make much headway during Curzon's regime, but Lord Curzon's unfortunate policy of the partition of Bengal made all his reformatory efforts seem insignificant. The public rose against Lord Curzon's policy. The Indian National Congress held its session at Calcutta in 1905 and strongly criticised the government policies.Under this adverse and unfavourable situation neither the governmental nor the non-governmental policies, despite their importance, could be successfully implemented. Inspite of all the controversy the primary education took root during this period.

Efforts To Make Primary Education Compulsory

The British Government gladly transferred the responsibility of primary education to local bodies. It believed in the policy that in the sphere of education in India its duty was confined only to guidance; but some educationists like William Adam, Captain Wingate and T.C. Hope of England in their letters to the Government emphasised the need of declaring primary education compulsory. Although their representation did not succeed in moving the Government, yet they gave much inspiration and encouragement to the Indian people. The result was that the Indian leaders gave education an important place in their national struggle and this gave rise to educational movements. The credit for giving birth to this movement goes to Sir Ibrahim Rahimatulla Khan and Sir Chiman Lal Setalwad, the dedicated educationists from Bombay. As a result of their demand, the Bombay Government appointed a committee in 1906 to look into matters concerning education. The Committee after examining the demands and enquiring into the issues, observed in its report that the general public was not prepared to accept the policy of primary education. As such, the old policy continued.

The Liberal Policy of the Baroda Ruler

In view of the utility of primary education, Maharaja Sayaji

Rao Gaikwad, the ruler of Baroda State, introduced compulsory primary education in some 52 villages of his State. An Act was also passed in 1906 for the expansion of this scheme under which primary education was made compulsory for boys in the age group of seven years to twelve years and for girls in the age group of seven to ten years.

Efforts of Gopal Krishna Gokhale

Inspired by the efforts of the Baroda ruler, Gopal Krishna Gokhale submitted a proposal in the Central Legislature to make primary education free and compulsory throughout India, but this proposal remained shelved for nearly a year. Consequently, Gokhale introduced this proposal in the shape of a bill in the Central Assembly. The idea behind the bill was that with the sanction of the Government, the local bodies should make primary education for children of 6 to 10 years of age compulsory in those regions where the fixed number of children were available. Unfortunately in the absence of majority vote the bill could not be passed.

Efforts of Vitthal Bhai Patel

The famous leader Vitthal Bhai Patel introduced a bill in the provincial legislative assembly of Bombay to make primary education compulsory within the municipal limits in Bombay province. This bill fortunately got through and became an Act in 1918. The Act made its impact throughout the country and by 1930 primary education was made compulsory for the children between six to ten years of age throughout India. The entire responsibility of compulsory education was handed over to local bodies and they were given the right to levy tax to meet expenditure on education.

Expansion of Compulsory Education

The development of primary education took place at a rapid pace after the implementation of Primary Education Act. Primary education further received impetus due to the then prevailing political and social condition and national awakening. The reasons for this rapid expansion were:—

(a) More State help came for education due to the formation of popular provincial ministries.

(b) As a result of awakening of masses in India, an all-India Women's Educational Conference was organised in 1927. The women, in this Conference, announced their determination and right to have equal facilities for education as were enjoyed by men.

(c) As a result of the efforts of Mahatma Gandhi and Dr. Ambedkar, a new wave of awakening overtook Harijans (Scheduled Castes). They became aware of their right to receiving education and were trying to achieve it.

(d) Besides the above reasons, the Acts passed by various State legislatures making primary education compulsory also accelerated the expansion and development of primary education.

Slackness in the Pace of Expansion

The development of primary education went on unobstructed and at a rapid pace till 1930; but unfortunately the Hartog Committee in its recommendations suggested that the number of schools should not be increased. Instead, in order to improve the quality, the schools should be better equipped. This recommendation was accepted by the Government. Consequently slackness came in the speed of expansion.

Reorganisation

The pace of progress of primary education did not remain obstructed for long. In 1937 popular Congress Ministries came into power in six provinces and once again the pace of expansion gathered speed. In the Congress provinces more emphasis was laid on the establishment of primary schools in rural areas for making compulsory education available to the common citizen. As a result of this emphasis, compulsory primary education became available for children of 10,017 rural areas and 229 towns by 1947. Besides, arrangement of primary education for girls existed in 1,404 villages and 10 towns.

Development of Compulsory Education After Independence

After attaining independence, the administration of the country came in the hands of the people themselves. Due to the adoption of the democratic system, the responsibility of the reconstruction and all-round development of the country became the responsibility of the new administration. The national leaders realised that the success of democracy was only possible when the entire population was educated and understood their duty, rights and responsibilities. Therefore, the national Government under Article 45 of the Constitution declared the principles of compulsory education and based its detailed educational programme on these principles. The Central Government started to meet 30 per cent of the expenditure incurred on education by the State Governments for the expansion of compulsory education. Primary education was not only made compulsory but also free for children in the age group of 6 to 14 years. Although the financial condition of the nation was weak, a target for educating 60 per cent and 19 per cent children was fixed for the age groups of 6 to 11 years and 11 to 14 years, respectively in the Second Five Plan. Although a number of difficulties were faced by the Government in achieving this target, the progress achieved was not too bad.

Problems of Compulsory Education

1. *Neglect of Education by the Foreign Rule*: The British Government needed clerks in India for their commercial establishments and Government offices. So the education system that they introduced in India geared only for producing clerks. They feared that the mass education would expose their selfish policies and the common man would rise to oppose their unjust acts. Under such circumstances they would not succeed in making India a market for English goods. The Foreign Rule therefore, always neglected compulsory education.

2. *Political Problems*: As a result of centuries of exploitation, India's condition at the time of independence was

very pathetic. The last blow was inflicted on the country by the Britishers through their policy of divide and rule. Their policy inflamed communal passions in this sub-continent and the Indian leaders, since the first day of independence, had to mobilise their entire resources in tackling the problems of communalism. Although they achieved some success, but after paying heavily in men and material. The huge problem of refugees confronted them. Besides, the national leaders had to make all out efforts for solving the problems of Indian Princely States, abolition of 'Zamindars' (feudalism), the problem of linguistic states. Thus, there were problems relating to Kashimir and China. Consequently, proper attention could not be given to compulsory primary education, its development and expansion.

3. *Lack of Practical Knowledge in Administrative Policies*: Two main problems related to education cropped up before the country after independence. The first was the introduction of compulsory education for the children of 6 to 14 years age group and the second related to the transformation of traditional primary schools into basic ones. Although the first problem of compulsory education was covered in the Constitution, yet due to financial stringency, the achievement of the fixed target remained an impossibility. Another main reason for its failure was the implementation of basic education. Under such circumstances, when in the absence of required financial resources and political conditions far from being favourable, both these educational plans of the administration remained almost buried in the files. Even to-day the pace of their implementation is not totally satisfactory.

4. *Lack of Teachers*: Shortage of teachers is a prominent factor in the slow expansion of compulsory education and this is due to poor remunerations. Due to poor salaries, no highly qualified person likes to take up a teacher's job in a primary school. So far as the urban areas are concerned, the shortage of teachers is not so acute due to other available resources for supplementing the teacher's income, but in rural areas where such avenues of supplementing income do not exist, the

shortage of teachers is keenly felt. This problem is even more serious as far as lady teachers are concerned. This situation is all the more harmful for India, a country comprising of villages mostly. The dearth of training schools for teachers is also responsible for non-development of compulsory education to some extent. But these problems have been tackled to some extent now.

5. *Shortage of Funds*: The burden of primary education is being shouldered mostly by local bodies since the British rule. The British adopted this policy simply to misguide Indians, but it is regretted that the same policy is still being followed. The only change that has occurred since the establishment of democratic rule in the country is that the percentage of financial help for educational purpose to local bodies has been raised from 30 per cent to 33 per cent. It is simply impossible to expect that the local bodies with their poor financial resources would go on implementing successfully the compulsory primary education scheme. But happily now since about fifteen years, i.e., from 1975 the state governments have been made responsible for paying salaries to primary school teachers.

6. *Defective Educational Administration*: The burden of primary education in almost every State rests on local bodies, that is, on municipal and district boards. Constitutionally, pressure for the development of primary education could not be applied on district boards. Besides, the chairman and members of these bodies are the elected representatives of people. They do not want to further tax the already poor public and lose their votes. So these bodies generally fail in expanding compulsory education. In the sphere of the expansion of primary education, although the number of schools have increased, there still continues to be a shortage of good administrators and shortage of reading materials and necessary school equipments. Consequently, compulsory primary education has not made the desired progress. But by the end of 1992 almost all the state governments in the country have taken the responsibility of promotion of primary education on themselves.

7. *Unsatisfactory Teaching Standard*: The inadequacy of training schools and poor pay scale has been responsible for not attracting efficient teachers to take up jobs as primary school teachers. In most cases teachers in primary schools have studied only upto the middle high school level. Moreover, equipments and reading materials, too, are insufficient in primary schools due to shortage of funds. Consequently, the standard of primary education is very low.

8. *Defective Curriculum*: The old curriculum of primary schools was defective. It had no scope for the development of the student's creative and constructive faculties nor did it help him in acquiring paractical knowledge. Although the primary education has now been given the shape of basic education and the course of study has been changed accordingly, yet its implementation has not been satisfactory as it involves huge expenditure. Consequently, the desired success in this sphere has not so far been achieved.

9. *Difficulties in Constructing School Buildings*: It is a complex problem to open schools in villages and unfortunately most of the Indian people live in villages. In this period of financial stringency, the problem of constructing school buildings is a difficult one. Moreover, the population in villages being small, it is all the more difficult to select a village for the construction of the school building for enabling sufficient number of students to be benefited.

10. *Stagnation and Wastage*: Figures indicate that only 43 per cent of the students who join primary school complete the full course. Inadequacy and unsuitability of reading materials, unattractive school buildings and difficult curriculum are some of the reasons responsible for not attracting sufficient number of children to schools. Besides, the poor parents in order to supplement their income induct their children into family business at an early age, and either they do not send the children to school at all or make them leave school before completing the full primary education. In this way wastage of money and stagnation prove a hurdle in the way of achieving the goal.

11. *Shortage of School Buildings and Their Unsuitabi[illegible]*. Due to shortage of funds the programme of construct[illegible] of school buildings could not keep pace with the expansi[illegible]n of primary education. Consequently, in many places arrangements for teaching have been made in places like temples, public buildings and the houses of teachers, etc. Needless to say that this state of affairs is entirely unsatisfactory. Such schools have neither play ground nor is their environment healthy. Unsuitable buildings and crowded and noisy atmosphere have severely impeded the growth of primary education.

12. *The Problem of Language*: Like many other problems facing primary education, the one concerning the medium of instruction is also a major one. In the section of the Indian Constitution dealing with the languages for compulsory primary education, 15 lanugages (according to the Amendment made in 1992 for including Nepalese also), have been mentioned, but in India as many as 845 languages and dialects are spoken. Some of these languages are spoken by thousands of persons, but they do not have any script or their own literature. Under such circumstances, it becomes a problem to choose a language as medium of instruction at the primary stage.

13. *The Problem of Social Values*: Although every nation or society observes its traditions and practices, yet in India due to deep ignorance, the traditions and practices rule the lives of our people. Among these traditions and practices are some like child-marriage, religious fanaticism and caste-discrimination. These have proved obstructive in the expansion and development of primary education. Although the laws have been made to eradicate these evil practices, yet social practices proved more forceful than laws. Even to-day efforts are made in some schools to avoid admission of Harijans (Schedule caste and Tribals) students on some pretext or the other. Early marriage causes dislocation of education. After marriage boys and girls do not get opportunity to pursue studies. Moreover, it becomes imperative for boys to begin

earning. Many people frown upon co-education even in primary classes. Under such adverse conditions, how can one expect adequate expansion of compulsory education?

14. *Georgraphical Conditions*: India is a country which abounds in rivers, mountains and forests. In the hilly areas the villages are small and scattered at a great distance from each other. Due to shortage of funds it is not possible to open schools in every village. Parents do not like their children to walk through difficult hilly terrain in order to attend schools situated far away from their homes. The same difficulty is faced in crossing rivers and forests which are really a very great hardship for children of tender age. Under such circumstances, to expect successful implementation of compulsory education throughout the length and breadth of the country will simply be an act of over expectation.

15. *Poverty and Ignorance*: Even to-day the financial condition of the country is not such as to provide full meals and adequate clothings to each and every citizen. Even now a family of as many as ten members depend for their bread on one of its members. In many homes it is generally against social custom for the womenfolk to earn some money even when the entire family is unable to get two meals a day. Besides, the majority of the people, being ignorant, do not realise the importance of education. Therefore, many parents, instead of getting their children admitted in schools, try to introduce them to some trade at a tender age in order to supplement their income.

Due to the above factors primary education has not made much progress and the achievement of tragets appears a difficult task. Some suggestions for solving the above problems are given below.

Some Solutions of the Problems of Primary Education

1. *Solution of the Financial Problem*: Poverty of the masses is the greatest hurdle in the expansion of compulsory primary education in the country. Shortage of funds is responsible for lack of reading materials and equipments in schools, dearth of

efficient teachers and insufficient number of school buildings. With this in mind Gopal Krishna Gokhale pleaded for not spending money on the qualitative aspect of primary education but for opening primary schools in greater number and making the primary education available to every one so that ignorance might be wiped off from the country. He, therefore, argued for making primary education compulsory. For achieving success in this objective he suggested reducing expenditure on the process of changing the old primary education into the basic one. In order to ease the financial condition some educationists suggest for reducing the curriculum from five to four years. They also advocate that tuition fees should also be charged from the children of well-to-do parents. The Government should postpone the programme of introduction of basic education for some time. They should first make primary education compulsory and banish illiteracy and ignorance from the country. Money should be generated for primary education by heeding to the suggestions of eminent educationists.

2. *Change in the Administrative System*: In order to ensure progress and development, some reforms in the present educational administration is necessary. The Government should, in the first instance, take over the entire responsibility of meeting the expenditure on primary education. It is not possible to achieve the desired progress by merely giving grants to municipal and district boards. So far, as the administration is concerned it will be proper to leave this responsibility on local bodies only when a central committee is formed which should be in a position to force the local administrative set-ups to make arrangements for compulsory primary education. The local bodies will have no hesitation in carrying on the instructions of the central committee when the entire expenditure is met by the Government. Only under such an arrangement the development of compulsory education will go on unobstructed.

3. *Firmness in the Educational Policy*: The Government policy of compulsory education is not so much paractical as it is idealistic. It is due to this reason that it has not been able

to achieve solid results. Changing of traditional schools into basic ones and introducing compulsory education without taking into account the prevailing dearth of equipments in schools has crushed the Government objectives under the burden of financial expenditure. It would have been more proper to have introduced compulsory education first and later on it should have been given the shape of basic education.

4. *Provision of Teachers*: In view of the heavy demand of teachers for the implementation of the policy of compulsory education it has not been possible to obtain the necessary number of trained teachers. Consequently, the shortage of teachers has also affected the pace of progress of compulsory education. It cannot be considered a wise step to postpone or slow down the programme of compulsory education till enough trained teachers were available. To meet this difficulty untrained teachers possessing average efficiency may be employed to start the work. These untrained teachers may be gradually trained and their teaching standards may thus be raised. To bring better qualified persons in this profession it is desirable to raise the pay scale and the social status of the teachers.

5. *Shift System*: In view of the shortage of teachers and school buildings it is desirable that the shift system be adopted in India as is done in some other countries like Germany, United States, Japan, China, Denmark, Australia, etc. and classes be held for some children from 7.30 a.m. to 11.30 a.m. and for others from 1.00 p.m. to 5.00 p.m. This kind of shift-system will prove helpful to farmers and labourers also. Their children will get time both for education and for helping their parents in supplementing their incomes. No doubt the work to teachers will increase but they can be satisfied by providing extra-pay. In adopting the shift system attention will have to be given in fixing the school hours. In deciding school hours seasons and facilities of parents and teachers will have to be taken into consideration.

6. *Special Type of Schools*: In India there are nearly 12 crore people of scheduled castes and nearly 5 crore tribal

people. These people have remained cut-off from education since long. Now some emphasis is being given on their education by the Government. Provision has been made to give them some grants for purchasing books, besides stipends and scholarships. The government have made provisions for opening special types of schools in the areas where scheduled caste and tribal people mostly live. Even then public co-operation for the education of these people is very necessary.

7. *Reforms in Curriculum*: It is also necessary to introduce reforms in the curriculum of primary education along with the efforts to develop and make it compulsory. The traditional and unilateral course should be changed and a local craft should be included in it so that it may become more interesting and helpful to children. Although this is one of the main features of basic education, yet till all the primary schools are not converted into basic ones it will be desirable to include a local craft in the primary schools.

8. *Increase in the Number of Schools*: Most of the Indian population lives in villages which are small and situated at great distances from one another. It is not possible to open schools in every village due to lack of funds, therefore the compulsory education is receiving a great set-back. But to check the expansion of education due to these difficulties will simply be against the objective of education programme. Under the circumstances, it is desirable even to open schools at places like temples, mosques, churches and other public places etc., in the interest of education, keeping in view that India is a place where the Ashrams (forest schools) of Rishis in ancient days and Shantiniketan[1] in the present days have remained ideal places of learning. India can surely succeed in achieving its objective of the expansion of primary education by benefiting itself from some of the old ways of imparting education. It is worth mentioning here that in earlier days due to shortage of school buildings schools were held under bridges in England.

---

1. Abode of Peace - a name given by Tagore, Rabindranath to his open-air school.

9. *Five Year Plans and People's Co-operation*: Five Year Plans occupy an important place in the development of education in India. The expansion of education even gets help and co-operation from other development plans. Geographical factors obstructing the progress of education could be solved to an appreciable extent through the development of means of communication. With the successful implementation of the plans, the per capita income will increase and people will be in a better position to bear expenses on education. This will in itself help the expansion of compulsory education. In this way the progress and development of education is linked with the success of Five Year Plans and it is the duty of the people to co-operate in the successful implementation of the Plans. It is well known that for the success of democracy people's co-operation is a necessity. If our Plans succeed through public co-operation, the achievement of our objective of compulsory education is a certainty.

10. *Increase in Teaching Load*: Although it will not be proper to increase the work-load of teachers who are poorly paid, yet in the interest of the country they will not mind if their work load is increased for some time. This happened in foreign countries like England, Italy and China. The number of students in a class may be raised to 60 from 33; but care will have to be taken to see that under these conditions a teacher is not asked to take too many classes at a time. It is hoped that by acting on the above suggestions, success may be achieved in fulfilling the objectives of quantitative expansion of primary education.

Summary

Compulsory Education: It is necessary for the success of democracy that each citizen is an educated person. As such, provision has been made in the Indian constitution to make the primary education compulsory.

Historical Background: Education in India was neglected during the British regime. The East India Company Government paid some attention to education after 1813 but it neglected the primary education. The British Government paid attention to primary education after 1857. Lord Curzon accepted in his statement that British Government should not show indifference towards primary education in India.

Compulsory Primary Education: The British Government remained unmoved despite the efforts of the Indian National Congress, and some eminent educationists. Gokhale introduced a bill relating to compulsory education in the Central Assembly in 1911. But it could not be passed. The ruler of Baroda had earlier in 1906 introduced compulsory primary education in his state. This gave impetus to the public and the national leaders. In 1918 an Act was passed by the Bombay legislature introducing compulsory education by law in all the provinces where Congress ministries were formed in 1937.

But many difficulties were faced in making primary education compulsory even after India became free. Some of these difficulties are:

Problems Facing Compulsory Education: (1) Political problems (2) Government policies lacking practical touch (3) Shortage of teachers (4) Shortage of funds (5) Defective administration (6) Unsuitability of standard of education (7) Defective curriculum (8) Difficulties in the opening of schools (9) Stagnation and wastage (10) Shortage of schools buildings and their unsuitability (11) Problems of medium of instruction (12) Problem of social values (13) Physical Problems (14) Problems of poverty and ignorance.

In order to accelerate the pace of progress the following suggestions are made to solve the problems mentioned above.

Suggestion to Remove Difficulties: (1) Solving the financial problems (2) Change in administrative system (3) Firmness in the policy of education (4) Provision of teachers (5) Adoption of the shift system (6) Opening of special types of schools (7) Reforms in the curriculum (8) Increase in the number of schools (9) Public co-operation and success of Five Year Plan (10) Increase in teacher's work load.

Exercises

1. Discuss the main problems of compulsory primary education in India.
2. Give suggestions for removing difficulties in introducing compulsory primary education in India.
3. Describe the efforts for introducing compulsory primary education in India during the 20th century.

Chapter 33

Problems of Secondary Education

Present Secondary Education

Education after primary stage and prior to the university level is regarded as secondary education. The present system of education which originated in pre-independence era has been a conservative one. It has divided secondary education into many parts, which have been known as vernacular, middle, matriculation, entrance, high school, intermediate, etc. A relative study of the educational systems current in other advanced countries reveals that broadly speaking there are only three divisions of education namely the primary, secondary and higher education. The scope of each of these divisions differs in foreign countries. Generally, the primary stage lasts upto class VIII and higher education (university education) starts from class XII or XIII. In this way the three or four years of education between classes IX and XII is called secondary education.

During the foreign rule in India, enough importance was not attached to education and the government classified education from classes one to five as primary and from 13th class and above as higher education. The classes between the two came to be known as secondary education. With some changes the secondary stage was further sub-divided.

Accordingly, the first three years' programme (from classes VI to VIII) was known as junior secondary, the next two years as higher secondary and the last two years as intermediate education. According to the latest step the intermediate education has been included in the secondary education. But this step has not been given a final shape because a large number of students leave studies after high school and many schools have been recognised upto high school because of the lack of students. Now class XII has been included within university education. Thus the duration of secondary education has been reduced to three years duration in many states. But in U.P. Class XII still exists under the secondary education group, although here (in U.P) also three year course for Bachelor's degree has been accepted and implemented.

Objectives of Secondary Education

Secondary education is sure to be affected by the expansion of primary education. Accordingly, the number of students in secondary classes has gone up and the main objective of secondary education at present is to make available more facilities in high and higher schools. The number of students in secondary classes is fifteen times more than what was in the beginning of the century. But with the fulfilment of the objective of compulsory primary education, the number of students in secondary classes will increase so much that the present institutions will not be able to admit majority of these students. The number of secondary institutions even at present is not adequate and students face difficulty in getting admission. In view of the forthcoming increase in the number of students, efforts should be started right away to open more and more secondary schools.

In majority of the advanced countries various vocational trainings start at the secondary stage of education. The relative utility of the present secondary education is self-evident as can be seen at the time of selection for a government or non-government post. A large number of boys after finishing secondary education seek jobs, which cannot be created in proportion to the students passing the secondary classes. The present-day education has developed in the young boys an apathy towards their hereditary professions. They are neither inclined nor have the ability to pursue their family vocations. Consequently, an acute problem has arisen in the country in the shape of unemployment of educated youths. In the present atmosphere, the secondary education should be in accordance with the needs of the people and also useful for various vocations. Therefore, reforms are needed in the education system and this reformed system besides fulfilling the vocational needs should also help in the intellectual, physical and moral development of students.

Organisation of Special Institutions

It will be necessary to bring about changes in the shape and constitution of the present institutions in order to convert secondary education system into the basic one. In accordance with the recommendations of the Secondary Education Commission (1952-53), the Government of India had made schemes to convert the secondary schools into higher secondary schools, make them multi-purpose schools and establish new multi-purpose and higher secondary schools. Another scheme has also been prepared to establish and increase the number of such secondary schools in rural areas that relate to agriculture and village atmosphere. The Secondary Education Commission and the Ministry of Education are conscious of the importance of single purpose schools. In some countries, like England, more importance is attached to single purpose schools as compared to multi-purpose schools. Much thought and reason form the background of this ideology. Absence of specialised education is generally found in multipurpose schools. There is also some difficulty in getting efficient teachers for multi-purpose schools, because ordinarily such teachers are not available who have specialised training in more than one subject. Because of the diverse subjects, unity of thought is also absent in the students and the school atmosphere is less social as compared to other common schools.

The pace of progress also does not gather momentum because of undefined aim of education. It is because of these reasons that preference is sometimes given to single purpose institutions so far as subjects like literature, commerce, and engineering, etc., are concerned.

The provision of agricultural and village industry in schools is of great value to India. About seventy per cent of the people live in villages in India, but the statistics reveal that the progress of schools teaching subjects of rural importance had been very slow. Provision of only 84 institutions for imparting education on subjects like agriculture, cottage industries, animal husbandry and horticulture could be made in the First Five Year Plan.This effort for a predominantly agricultural country like India is far from satisfactory. Indifference in the rural areas towards these subjects cannot be appreciated. Establishment of institutions teaching these subjects is required on priority in pilot projects. The provision of junior basic education at the junior secondary stage will be beneficial from the above point of view.

Multi-purpose Schools

The Secondary Education Commission (1952-53) has recommended the establishment of multi-purpose schools. Some practical difficulties were faced in opening such schools during the First Five Year Plan. It is an expensive set up, because for a multi-purpose school a big building, different kinds of laboratories and workshops, adequate fertile land for agriculture, a rich library and other educational facilities are needed. In view of the poor financial condition of the country, these institutions cannot be expected to be set up at different places in the country. It is not easy to arrange for the study of three or more vocational subjects in one institution. There is a shortage of adequately trained teachers in vocational and technical subjects. The other difficulty is that for the teaching of different subjects, separate sections have to be opened according to the subjects. So it is necessary that these schools are set up in places where sufficient number of students may be available to make the best use of the money spent on these institutions. All this is possible only when the government makes a complete survey in this connection for finding out suitable sites for these schools. The other important aspect of these institutions is that being so expensive, it is only possible for the government to run schools and provide all the needed facilities. It is difficult for private and aided schools to provide complete equipments. The expenses in laboratories and workshops can be cut down to some extent in industrial and commerical areas with the co-operation of industrial and commercial institutions.

Despite these difficulties, it goes without saying that multi-purpose schools have their points and will prove of great utility in the present conditions of the country. This kind of training, besides developing vocational efficiency, is also intellectually beneficial and students can switch over to other subjects, if necessary. From the social point of view, it is also important if different students study different subjects, because it does not allow the feeling of sectarianism or groupism to grow. The feelings of social differences and barriers in students also grow weaker if students of different social status and vocational standards study together. Inspite of these good points the experiment in the field of multi-purpose schools, has not been successful so far. In a separate chapter onwards we shall deal with Multi-purpose schools.

Higher Secondary Schools

These institutions owe their origin to the three years' pre-degree course and three years' degree course schemes of the Government of India. The three years' course scheme have now been given a practical shape in all the states of the country.

Courses of Study in Secondary Schools

Prescribing the curriculum is of particular importance for the development of education. In view of the varying needs of different areas in the country a uniform pattern of curriculum which may prove helpful everywhere cannot be prescribed. Even then, the Central Government after obtaining the views of state governments is trying to prepare a central curriculum. The All India Secondary Education Council in its resolution on secondary education has suggested compulsory teaching of some subjects in every part of the country. The course of study may be divided into many sections or groups according to the needs of the state.

The decision regarding the language of the subjects is particularly important. The knowledge of the national language should be compulsory in every part of the country. But opposition may be voiced in non Hindi speaking areas that injustice is being done to the languages of the minorities. The other important thing is that due to advantages derived from the knowledge of English language in pursuing higher studies and also because of its international popularity, many people in every part of the country are still attracted to it. Besides, attachment towards Sanskrit is also found in many people in the country. Therefore, for safeguarding the interest of as many languages as possible, it is proposed to teach two or three languages in schools. Under the two languages, the first will be the national language Hindi or the regional language (in non-Hindi speaking areas) and the second the national language Hindi (if not opted in the first) or some other Indian language (including Sanskrit) or any Western language for the teaching of which arrangements exist. Under the three language groups, the first two groups would be as stated above except that the Western language has been separated from the second group and in the third group a Western language or Sanskrit or any other Indian language (which was not opted in the first and second group) may be made compulsory. The provision also exists that according to local or regional interests, any student, despite having two compulsory languages, may also study any other Indian or Western language.

In deciding upon the courses of study some efforts have been made to bring uniformity and unification. Other important aspects are the choice and interests of the students and regional demands, mother tongue to be made the medium of instruction, provision for advice and guidance and adoption of right pattern in the direction of curriculum. In the sphere of secondary education atleast two basic subjects like general science and social science have been suggested as compulsory in the resolution for the introduction of basic education pattern. Besides keeping the utility of secondary education equal for those students who leave study after this stage as well as for those who continue further studies, efforts have been made to help students to choose subjects according to aptitude and develop their constructive and artistic tastes. The introduction of technical and industrial subjects at the secondary stage is desirable for fulfilling the present needs of the country. According to these suggestions, in the junior secondary curriculum three languages, regional language in Hindi or non-Hindi speaking areas, some other Indian language in the Hindi speaking areas or two basic subjects along with English; general knowledge, social science and other optional subjects like mathematics, agriculture or some other arts subject according to local demand, art or music and cultural, physical or entertainment programme should be provided.

In the higher secondary stage according to the resolutions of Secondary Education Commission besides the above compulsory subjects, languages, basic subjects and various industrial subjects should also be introduced side by side so that the students may make use of their knowledge in their lives after completing education of the higher secondary stage. In view of the interest of even those students who go on to further higher studies after completing the higher secondary stage, the introduction of greater number of subjects is desirable. The resolution has also accepted the need of many-sided curriculum from the second year of higher secondary education and wider course of study from the third year. Many States in the country have not accepted the type of organisation of courses as suggested above.

Character-Building

The present system of examination creates hurdles in the student's character building programmes. Particular attention has to be given to the building of the student's character. But in our schools passing the examination has become the sole purpose of both the students and the teachers. Changes have to be made in the present educational system in order that character-building programmes are given due attention. We have to produce worthy citizens for upholding democracy and for the progress of the nation. In view of these objectives our education should not be limited to books only. For building the character of the future citizens efforts have to be made for their physical, intellectual and moral development. Only then we shall have citizens who will live a healthy public life. The students should, therefore, be encouraged to work independently in various fields, think independently, grasp knowledge and understand their responsibilities and duties.

Examination System

The present system of examination cannot be accepted as the true test of one's ability and efficiency. The real purpose of education ought to be the all-round development of a person and not only passing the prescribed examination. But it is also true that the system of examination cannot be abolished. The present system of examination which aims at the classification of students on the basis of the relative merits of students cannot be of any help in the progress of students. The system needs changes. In fact, the ability and efficiency of students should be judged from their work and conduct throughout the year. For this a record of the student's work should be maintained. In this connection the suggestions—like the consideration of the year's account of work in the annual examination, consideration of marks obtained in monthly tests before final assessment, and selection of questions on the new objective test pattern—will prove useful.

Management

Both government and private secondary schools are found in the country. Some schools are run by local bodies, but they have not been very successful. The secondary schools according to the present government policy should be run by independent or voluntary organisations. The schools receive from the government from time to time non-recurring and casual grants.

The Government pays salaries to all the teacher in many states. The government has decided to keep under its control the technical and women's education at the secondary level, although voluntary organisations connected with these subjects also exist. According to a survey the financial condition of these voluntary-organisation-controlled institutions is very bad. If in some there is a shortage of students, teachers or funds, in others either the atmosphere is unhealthy or the buildings are dirty, old and unsuitable. If one area abounds in such schools, the other has not even sufficient number of schools. There are also some schools which have no proper recognition. In voluntary schools, management and organisational problems are generally quite acute.

Administration

The administration and inspection system in the secondary schools is not good. For administration purposes, the education department in every State has central (at headquarters), regional and district level units which in local matters of their respective areas, function as independent units. Moreover, for the secondary schools there is a secondary education council in each state which supervises works relating to courses of study and examinations. Double control on the same level of education sometimes results in double administration. Therefore, some uniformity is needed. The education department should look after the works that have been entrusted to secondary councils. Side by side the education department should also endeavour to get the co-operation of other related departments, like agriculture, industries, labour, etc., for the success of education.

Inspection

The treatment of inspection authorities of secondary school teachers is not always cordial. Their attitude needs to change. The co-operation of both school inspectors and teachers is necessary for the development of education. The school inspectors should give proper guidance to teachers. This is possible only when the school inspectors themselves are aware of the latest developments in education. The education department should hold refresher courses for school inspectors from time to time. The number of inspectors should also be raised. It has also been suggested that in training colleges along with teacher's training, research should also be conducted in inspection and administration system in order to find out remedies for effective necessary changes in the present set up of education department.

Lack of Finances

The economic condition of the majority of non-government secondary school is far from satisfactory. Although the teachers of all the recognised schools receive their salaries from the government, yet their finanicial condition remains unsatisfactory because they have generally no other source of income. Moreover, the new educational schemes of to-day are expensive. Therefore, because of shortage of funds many schools fail to introduce new and useful subjects. Bad economic condition of schools is an important problem which needs help both form the government and public. The state government can improve the conditions by imposing an education tax as is done in U.S.A. The public should also be encouraged to donate generously to schools by taking such steps as exempting the donations to schools from income taxes, and providing some other such facilities.

For adopting modern educational system, making it useful according to the local needs and converting secondary schools into higher secondary schools, sufficient money will be needed for the salaries of teachers, buildings, laboratories, etc. It is necessary to take these factors into consideration before making changes in the system of education.

Summary

Current Secondary Education: The education in the classes from six to twelve have been divided into junior secondary, secondary and college education in the 3,2,2 groups. In the new basic system the junior secondary and secondary education have been divided into two groups of 3-3.

Objectives of Secondary Education: For the development of national citizenship, secondary education should develop the students mentally, physically and morally.

Organisation: Efforts were made in the country to introduce basic education system. Till complete change takes place, co-ordination between the existing system is desirable.

Specialised Schools: Provision of special schools is necessary for specialised education. According to local and regional needs, agricultural and industrial schools should be established. To make education useful for the common people multi-purpose schools should be opened. The pace of setting up higher secondary schools is rather slow due to the indifferance of universities and lack of adequate funds. The state governments, too, are not showing enough enthusiasm.

Courses of Studies: On the national level, three languages at the junior and higher secondary level national language, local language, and Western language and subject of general knowledge and social sciences are proposed to be made compulsory. More subjects are proposed to be introduced in higher secondary education. The curriculum should strive to develop constructive and artistic faculties of students. The examination system should be changed so that more emphasis is laid on character building.

Management and Administration: According to the present values the government should provide for women's education and industrial education. The other schools should be governed by voluntary or independent organisations. The conditions of the non-government schools should be improved and changes should be made in the administrative and inspection systems. The secondary schools should get economic aid both from government and public in the interest of education.

Exercises

1. Give your evaluation of the current secondary education in India.
2. Suggest measures for the solution of any two problems of secondary education in India.
3. What should be the aims of secondary education in the emerging democracy in India and why?

Chapter 34

Diversification of Secondary Education Curriculum

Secondary Education prior to Independance

The birth of secondary education took place during the British rule to meet the needs of the Government. The secondary education at that time had two aims, first to produce ordinary clerks for the commercial establishments of the East India Company and the second was to meet the requirements of the administration, and to enable students to get admission in universities. The result of this policy was that although it benefited the Government, the country had no special gain. Gradually, secondary education expanded. Larger number of students sought admission in universities, because the number of jobs did not increase in proportion to the number of students educated in secondary schools. Many were absorbed into Government offices. Even then, a large number of students faced unemployment. The main reason of unemployment was the one-sided aspect of the education. The medium of education was English. English, mathematics, history, geography and an Indian language were the compulsory subjects. Besides, two to four optional subjects were included in the curriculum. Sanskrit, Arabic, Persian, science and drawing were the optional subjects. But the entire curriculum was devoid of technical or vocational subjects. This only led to increase in unemployment.

Secondary Education in Free India

The shortcomings of secondary education in India came to light after the Second World War. India became free two years after the Second World War was over. Despite many changes effected in the education system, the pattern of education generally remained unchanged, even after India's independence. Consequently, the students, still, were not given the facility of opting for subjects of their interest because of narrow and unbalanced curriculum. Secondary education only enabled students to get admission in universities. In practical life this education proved of no help. Consequently, the Government appointed a number of committees and commissions with the aim of reorganising secondary education. The diversification of the curriculum has been made on the basis of the recommendations of these committees and commissions. Some of these committees and commissions, along with their recommendations for the reform of secondary education are discussed below.

Narendra Deo Committee, 1939

The appointment of this Committee was made during the British period and it was this Committee which, for the first time, recommended diversification of the curriculum. The Committee recommended that the students be given the facility of opting for subjects of their interest. In order to make the curriculum practical and helpful in life, the Committee recommended its classification into four groups so that every student may get an opportunity to develop his knowledge of the subjects of his liking. These four groups are (a) literary (b) scientific (c) constructive and (d) aesthetic. The students can opt for any one of these groups. The committee also suggested to examine the aptitude and fitness of a student for a particular subject.

Tara Chand Committee, 1948

The Tara Chand Committee made the following two important recommendations:—

(1) Secondary schools should be made multilateral, and

(2) Appointment of a commission to examine the entire secondary education structure.

The Committee, in view of the local conditions and time also recommended that indifference should not be shown towards unilateral schools.

Narendra Deo Committee, 1952-52

The recommendations of the Committee headed by Acharya Narendra Deo were as follows:—

(1) Multi-purpose secondary schools should be opened in large numbers for providing facility of studying subjects of one's choice.

(2) In order to make secondary education more useful, the curriculum should be made more practical.

(3) The Committee suggested the expansion of technical education for the economic development of the country.

(4) The Committee gave important suggestions for psychological examination of students and their guidance.

Appointment of Secondary Education Commission (1952-53)

The Union Government appointed the Secondary Education Commission in 1952, under the chairmanship of Mudaliar on the suggestion of Tara Chand Committee and Central Education Advisory Board. Named after its chairman, this Commission is also known as Mudaliar Commission. The Commission thoroughly examined the then prevailing secondary education system and gave a number of suggestions for reforms. Important ones among these were the diversification of the curriculum, and setting up a large number of multi-purpose schools. The courses of study provided in these schools should aim at fulfilling the different aptitudes of the students.

According to the recommendation of the Mudaliar Commission, the outlines for the diversification of curriculum were decided upon. Accordingly, the study of some compulsory subjects was made necessary for all students. Besides, the optional subjects were divided into seven groups for enabling students to get an opportunity to study as many subjects of their liking as they desired. An outline of this curriculum is given below:—

Compulsory Subjects:

(1) Regional language or mother tongue or a combined course of classical language and mother tongue.

(2) One of the following languages:

(A) (a) a classcial language (b) besides Hindi one more Indian language (c) Advanced English (for those students who had earlier studied English) (d) Elementary English (for students studying it at the secondary stage) (e) besides English, another modern foreign language. (f) Hindi, (for those students whose mother tongue is not Hindi.)

(B) (a) Curriculum of General Science with arithmetic for the first two years only.

(b) General course of social sciences for the first two years only.

(C) One of the following vocational subjects:- (1) Carpentry (2) Gardening (3) Printing (Spinning and Weaving), (5) Modelling (6) Laboratory test (7) Embroidery (8) Tailoring, embroidery and cutting and (9) Smithy.

Optional Subjects:

Optional subjects have been divided into seven groups. It has been made compulsory for a student to study any three subjects of a group. The groups and their subjects are as follows:—

1. *Science Group:* The following subjects have been included in this group:

   (1) Chemistry (2) Physics (3) Biology, Zoology or Hygiene (4) Mathematics and (5) Geography.

2. *Humanities Group:* (1) Mathematics (2) Home Science (3) Music (4) Geography (5) History (6) Economics or Civics (7) One language not taken from the group of

compulsory subjects or a classical language and (8) Psychology or Logic.

3. *Home Science Group:* This group has been prescribed for girl students. It is compulsory to offer three out of four subjects. The subjects are as under:—
   (1) Home Nursing (2) Home Economics (3) Maternity and Child Welfare (4) Nutrition and Cookery.
4. *Commerce Group:* (1) Commercial Geography or Economics and Elements of Civics (2) Commercial Practice (3) Short-hand and Type-writing and (4) Book-keeping.
5. *Technical Group:* (1) Practical Science (2) Elements of Electrical Engineering (3) Geometrical Drawing and Applied Mathematics and (4) Elements of Mechanical Engineering.
6. *Agricultural Group*: (1) Botany and Agricultural Chemistry (2) Animal Husbandry (3) Gardening and Orchard keeping (4) General Agriculture.
7. *Fine Arts Group:* The following six subjects have been included in this group:
   (1) Painting (2) Photography (3) Drawing and Sketching (4) Dance (5) Music and (6) History.

Advantages of Diverisfication of Curriculum

Some of the main advantages accruing from the diversification of curriculum are as mentioned below.

(1) *Facility of Desired Education to Students*:

The introduction of a number of subjects in the secondary schools will lead to the all-round development of the country. The students should get an opportunity to study subjects according to their abilities, tastes, aptitudes and capacities. In many States provision has been made for free education upto class sixth with the result that larger number of students will seek admission in secondary schools. The tastes, aptitudes and capacities of students differ. In this way the facility to choose subjects of one's liking is possible only through diversification of the cirriculum.

(2) *Availability of Subjects according to Mental and Physical Ability of Students*

Due to the different physical and mental calibre of students, it is necessary to provide different types of subjects for their education. All students do not possess a uniform standard of physical and mental ability. If some students are lean and thin, the others are more stout and healthier. Some are brilliant, while some are dullards. Similarly, their taste of subjects also differs. If some like science, the others are interested in literature. This problem of catering to different needs can only be solved through the diversification of the curriculum.

(3) *Full Development of Student's Personality*:

Full and proper development of student's personality is possible through the diversification of the curriculum. The Commission has included practical subjects in the curriculum because it is through them that the personality develops. Bookish knowledge alone is not sufficient for this purpose. The Commission holds the view that organised practical activities of various types, develop the student's personality more than the traditional subjects.

(4) *Provision of Education according to the Changed Outlook*:

The outlook on education has now entirely changed. Earlier, it was believed that what was being taught to the students was uniformely beneficial for all the students. But now, this view has completely changed. Researches made in the field of psychology have clearly shown that students have different inclinations, likings, aptitudes, tendencies and energies. So different types of curriculum are needed for them.

(5) *Fulfilment of the Social Needs*:

Every individual can not meet his daily requirements of life without the help of other members of society. Hence the progressive society has to meet many of his needs. The increasing needs of a society indicates its developing character. If all the members of the society engage themselves in the same type of work, it would then be impossible to fulfil the various needs. Therefore, members of a society engage themselves in different types of work. Similarly, if all the students who are the future mainstays of society study the same subjects, it will not be possible to meet the diverse needs. It is necessary for the all-round development of the society, that the younger generation be given education in various subjects in general, practical and commercial—so that various needs of the society may be fulfilled. The Commission emphasised the need of diversification of curriculum with this end in view.

(6) *Producing Efficient Workers:*

Efficient workers may be produced through diversification of the curriculum. Our country is passing through a stage of transition. There are a number of development plans before the country and efficient and trained workers in different fields are needed for successfully implementing them. The Government have opened a number of technical institutions for achieving this aim. Secondary schools prepare students for these technical schools. So the inclusion of practical and technical subjects is necessary in the curriculum of secondary schools. By the study of only literary subjects, the schools will become unilateral and there will be no multilateral development. Keeping this purpose in view, the Commission recommended the inclusion of various types of subjects.

Importance of Diversification of Curriculum

Now having known the benefit of diversification of the curriculmm we have see the importance it has in the context of the present condition of the country.

(a) *Easing the Problem of Unemployment:*

Due to expansion of education, the number of students has increased rapidly and since the number of jobs did not increase in the same proportion, unemployment has increased. This problem has now taken a serious form. One of the main reasons for unemployment has been the unilateral system of education. That is why, the Mudaliar Commission recommended the diversification of curriculum. According to this system of education, the students can pursue the study subjects of their choice in the technical, vocational, commercial and literary groups and learn handicrafts as well, in order to earn their living after leaving school. The diversification of curriculum in this way can help in solving the problem of unemployment.

(b) *Helping the Cultural Development*:

To-day, the definition of culture has now taken a wider form. In the secondary schools due to non-availability of technical education, mere bookish knowledge retards the all round development of a student. The teaching of technical subjects along with the traditional subjects is necessary for the full cultural development of the student. The Commission, therefore, has recommended the inclusion of technical subjects in the curriculum.

(c) *Love of Dignity of Labour*:

One of the main drawbacks of the system of acquiring knowledge merely through books has been that the student does not give due recognition to the dignity of labour. It is because of this tendency that students prefer to work on lesser emoluments in offices where they can wear good dresses than in places where manual labour is required, though the emoluments may be comparatively much higher. This happens because students do not appreciate manual labour and do not understand its dignity. It is felt that in the diversified curriculum, the students through the study of technical and vocational subjects will also realise the dignity of labour and have respect for it. This will also help the problem of their livelihood.

(d) *Solving the Problem of Employment*:

Due to unfavourable economic conditions, a large number of students give up their study after High School and try to enter some profession. But it is not possible to provide jobs for all of them. They have to choose some alternative. It is due to this reason that the teaching of handicraft has been included

in the curriculum, besides technical, vocational and commercial subjects. The students who learn handicraft do not depend for their livelihood on others, because they may set up their own enterprises.

SUMMARY

Secondary Education Prior to Independence: The secondary education during British regime was unilateral. Consequently, there was an increase in unemployment.

Secondary Education After Independence: After the attainment of freedom the problems of secondary education were seriously studied and a number of committees and commissions were set up. Some of them were: (1) Narendra Deo Committee, 1939, (2) Tara Chand Committee, 1948 (3) Second Narendra Deo Committee, 1952-53, and (4) Secondary Education Commission, 1952. All these committees recommended diversification of the curriculum and stressed the need of vocational and technical education. Handicrafts and teaching of technical subjects have been made compulsory. In the optional subjects, seven separate groups have been formed. These were science, humanities, home science, commerce, technical, agriculture, and fine arts.

Advantages of Diversification of Curriculum: The students get the facility of studying subjects of their liking. They get an opportunity to opt for subjects in accordance with their pyhsical and mental capacities. It helps the proper development of an individual's character. It meets the needs of the society in various ways.

Besides the above advantages, the diversification of the curriculum is also needed for the students' cultural development removing unemployment and establishing the dignity of labour.

EXERCISES

1. Describe briefly the nature of current secondary education in India.
2. Discuss the importance and advantages of diversification of courses at the secondary stage of education in India.

Chapter 35

Multi-purpose Schools

As is apparent from the name, the aims of multi-purpose schools is to provide various types of education to children having different aims and aptitudes. The Secondary Education Commission of 1952-53, in order to make secondary education more adequate and effective stressed the need of setting up multi-purpose schools in large numbers throughout the whole country. The Commission accordingly prepared an outline of a curriculum, wherein secondary education was divided into seven groups of optional subjects. In these groups efforts are made to meet the different aims, needs, abilities and aptitudes of students. The Commission has defined a multi-purpose school as an institution which caters for students of different tastes, objectives, etc. and provides courses of studies suiting the students and enabling them to develop their native capacities and potentialities in order that an all-round development of their personalities may take place.

Importance of Multi-Purpose Schools

We already know the kind of educational system prevailing in India prior to independence. We also know how far it was successful in helping and safeguarding the interest of the people. After independence the educationists in the country paid attention to the problems of education and effected some changes and improvements. Keeping in view the shortcomings of the old secondary education, the Secondary Education Commission, popularly known as the Mudaliar Commission, recommended revolutionary changes in the secondary education curriculum. This Commission laid particular emphasis on the opening of multi-purpose schools with different groupings in the curriculum.

The opening of multi-purpose schools is a very important step in view of the present educational set up in the country. Some handicrafts are taught to children at the primary school level, that is, in the Basic Primary schools, children are given training in some basic handicrafts. But due to lack of provision for continuing training in handicrafts in higher classes, whatever the student learns in the basic school proves of no help. This naturally means the misuse of basic education. Therefore, provisions have been made for training in different crafts in multi-purpose schools. Thus the wastage in primary education may be checked and each student may get opportunity to profit by his earlier basic education through the multi-prupose schools.

Students come to secondary schools from different primary or basic schools. There is a vast difference between their tastes, abilities and objectives. Some favour mathematics and science, while others have a liking for literature. If some have a liking for learning biology, many other prefer fine arts. Evidently, students have different aptitudes and interests and they want to study subjects accordingly. Under these conditions it is simply unwise to compel students to pursue a uniform pattern of course of study. This proves harmful to the native faculties of the students and retards their development. The only course open to educate students of different tastes is to open more multi-purpose schools in order that they may study subjects of their liking and develop their personality all round.

Many children generally reach the age of pre-adolescence by the time they finish their primary education. This age is very crucial from the point of view of their development. Their likings, inclinations and tastes are not very clear at this stage. Hence, it is very important to guide them carefully for their future growth. At this stage whereas subjects of their likings and taste accelerate the pace of their development, the subjects forced upon them against their choice retard their natural growth. Therefore, the multi-purpose schools alone can help them to promote their natural development.

Besides, these multi-purpose schools will create love for manual labour in the children. Some people hold the view that technical and arts schools should be opened separately as is the practice in some Western countries like U S.A. etc., which means that instead of multi-purpose schools, two different types of schools should be opened. But it may be inferred as what would have been the fate of technical and vocational schools in India where since times immemorial mental labour had always been considered superior to manual labour. Even in some progressive countries like U.S.A. where manual labour is accorded a high place, technical and vocational schools do not enjoy that much of respect which other institutions command. Hence in the development of our country, multi-purpose schools have a vital role to play.

Objectives of Opening Multi-Purpose Schools

The objectives of the Mudaliar Commission in recommending variety of courses for secondary schools was to help the all round development of our students' personalities. The Commission has recommended the opening of these schools in order to fulfil the following objectives:—

(1) Every student may become self-supporting after finishing secondary education. In order to achieve this objective the Commission has recommended the introduction of a compulsory craft subject so that the student, when the need arises, may be able to earn his livelihood.

(2) With the establishment of multi-purpose schools the defects of unilateral schools will be overcome. Every student gets an opportunity to select a subject of his choice from the long list of subjects taught in the school. This is necessary for the proper and full development of his personality.

(3) Multi-purpose schools will produce able citizens. The inclusion of literary and practical subjects has been done with the sole purpose of enabling the student to acquire both the types of education so that along with his cultural and social development he may also develop his personality and become a responsible and worthy citizen.

(4) It has been stressed in the scheme of multi-purpose schools submitted by the Mudaliar Commission that the students after the completion of secondary education should become self-supporting. They should in no circumstances be parasities. They should acquire the knowledge of a subject to the extent that they could easily earn their livelihood by practising it. But it should be borne in mind that the ultimate aim of multi-purpose school is not to make students into artisans and mechanic. Therefore, a proper place has been given in the curriculum to other subjects besides the vocational and technical ones in order to ensure proper and all-round development of a student. Care has also been taken to see that cultural and mental development take place along with the other aspects of student's personality.

The Nainital Educational Seminar of 1957 also discussed this important question of the setting-up of multi-purpose schools. It came to the conclusion that the following objectives might be fulfilled through such schools:—

(a) Interest towards co-operation should be developed amongst students through these schools by providing them with education in constructive, productive and other beneficial works for the society. Students will then stand on their own feet.

(b) Through proper planning and adjustments the multi-purpose schools may create in students love for acquiring knowledge of different subjects and act independently in accomplishing the related work.

(c) The students through these schools may be inspired to add to national assets. They may be inspired to uplift the national character.

(d) It is expected of these multi-purpose schools that they will enable the students to acquire efficiency in a vocation to an extent which will enable them to earn their livelihood easily.

Utility of Multi-Purpose Schools

A study of the objectives of multi-purpose schools clearly shows that in the present condition in India they are very useful.

Respect for labour and self-support may be created among students by training them in some vocations and handicrafts in these schools. The trained students of these schools will make substantial contributions in the technical, industrial and commercial undertakings of the country. Students of different tastes and aptitudes will have an opportunity of studying subjects of their choice. This will help in the development of their personality in a natural way. Besides, the students in these schools will have ample opportunity to prove their merits, because they will have the facility of studying subjects of their liking. Further they will remain engaged in the pursuit of knowledge of various other subjects also.

In educational institutions where facility for various optional subjects is not available, the students have to study only those subjects that are taught there. The result is that most of the students become very weak in some subject. Such students are looked down on by teachers and parents. Furthermore, because of their bad results they find it difficult to get admission in other schools. Such situations are not likely to arise in multi-purpose schools because of the facility of opting for many subjects.

The problem of changing schools arises when students do not find subjects of their choice in a school. Change of institution becomes a serious problem at certain stages. This problem may be easily solved in multi-purpose schools by changing the subject group of the student.

Development of Multi-Purpose Schools

The Government of India opened some multi-purpose schools in the year 1954. First of all some high schools and higher secondary schools were converted into multi-purpose schools. The foundation of nearly 250 multi-purpose schools was laid in the First Five Year Plan. This number was to be raised to 1,150 by the end of the Second Plan. In the Third Five Year Plan it was proposed to set up 1,000 more multi-purpose schools. But due to certain circumstances provision for only two kinds of groups has so far been made in these schools. In view of the importance and utility of the multi-purpose schools, the pace of progress so far maintained cannot be regarded as satisfactory. Some reasons for this unsatisfactory progress are given below.

Some Important Problems of Multi-Purpose Schools

The most important problem facing the multi-purpose schools is the non-availability of efficient teachers.

1. *Unattractive Pay Scale*: The pay scale of a vocational or science teacher is so low that able and qualified persons are not attracted towards its teaching profession. They try to find jobs in other departments and join professions where they get higher emoluments. It is, therefore, necessary to raise the pay scales of teachers. Moreover, the Education Department does not provide them with those facilities which are available to them else where. In private educational institutions whose financial position is sound and which are not under the full control of the Government, the services of teachers remain on the mercy of managers or managing committees. Thus the teacher's services are not very secure in private institutions. Consequently, only ordinary persons who fail to secure better jobs else where generally come to the profession of teaching in schools.

Under these circumstances it is necessary that the pay

scale of teachers be adequately raised and facilities necessary for decent living be provided. The teachers should also be given opportunities to add to their qualifications and knowledge. It should be the duty of the Government to inspect the private schools at regular intervals. The Government should compel private institutions to pay the teachers according to the prescribed pay scales. A training college should be set up in every State where refresher courses be held for teachers, headmasters and principals of the multi-purpose schools. They should be kept abreast with the latest developments and researches in this sphere. Guidance officers and Career Masters should also be appointed in every state.

2. *Lack of Suitable Text-Books and Problem of Preparing Time-Table*: There is an acute shortage of text-books of technical and scientific subjects taught in the multi-purpose schools. Whatever books are available are not of the required standard. Therefore, the Government should get text-books prepared by experts on reasonable terms. There is one more difficulty facing these multi-purpose schools. This is the problem of the time-table. Due to a number of different subjects, the headmasters find it difficult to prepare a thoroughly satisfactory time-table. The headmasters, having no specialised knowledge of technical and scientific subjects, fail to give enough time to these subjects. It is, therefore, necessary that the headmasters of the multi-purpose schools possess some understanding of the subjects taught in the schools. It may also be suggested that a number of time-tables be got prepared by different experts and the best of these should be used by the schools.

3. *Problems of Opening and Conversion of Schools*: Along with many other problems, the setting in of a multi-purpose school is itself a problem. To implement this scheme, it was decided that some new multi-purpose schools would be opened and some of the secondary schools be converted into multi-purpose schools. But no scheme was drawn up indicating either the names of places where new schools were to be opened or the names of secondary schools which were to be converted.

Although over a thousand such schools were opened during the Second Five Year Plan, yet in the absence of prior planning, their utility had remained doubtful. In order to make the multi-purpose schools more useful only such secondary schools should be converted which have a sound finanical position. Their conversion should be based on local needs and should be situated at places where adequate means of communication are available. They should be fully equipped. The school buildings should be such as to permit extension when required. It will not be to any use to open new schools without keeping in view the above mentioned factors.

4. *Difficulty in Completing Vocational Curriculum*: Many multi-purpose schools in the country due to shortage of funds do not possess good equipped laboratories and workshops. So it is no wonder that the course of vocational, technical or scientific study remains incomplete. This problem may be solved through government grants but the financial position of the Government itself is not so good as to undertake this work. Hence practical training of the students should be carried in nearby workshops as is the practice in many Western countries. The students will acquire in such workshops practical knowledge. Thus, the complex problem of providing workshops to multi-purpose schools will be solved automatically.

5. *Difficulty in the Selection of Curriculum*: The main feature of the multi-purpose schools is the varieties of subjects, but unfortunately provision has not so far been made for the study of all the prescribed subjects in these schools. Only seven optional subjects have been included in the curriculum, but by permitting the multi-purpose schools to provide any two groups of subjects, the sphere of utility has been narrowed down for the students. In this way the multi-purpose schools differ from the ordinary schools in as much as there is only one group of subjects in ordinary schools and the multi-purpose schools possess two groups. It is also worth mentioning in this connection that the limits of the subjects have not so far been indicated in all the schools. Although some states have with the help of the All India Educational Council fixed the studies

in subjects according to classes, yet in these fixations the local needs have not been taken into account. Moreover, there is no similarity in the standards laid down by different States. Under these conditions, it appears that the country will not derive full benefit from these multi-purpose schools.

In order to remove the above difficulties and to derive maximum benefit from multi-purpose schools, it is necessary to include at least three groups in all such institutions in the country. It is also desirable to prescribe a uniform standard of similar subjects in all the multi-purpose schools of the country and reorient the curriculum according to local needs. While according to the recognition of groups the situation of the schools and local needs should also be taken into consideration. This will prove helpful to the school also, besides increasing the facilities for the students. By receiving training in local crafts the students will easily get employment in the factories and establishments situated there. Consequently, the problem of unemployment will also be eased. Moreover, the required number of trained workers and officers will be available for the various development projects in the country.

6. *Problem of Parents' Dis-satisfication*: This is a problem due to which students do not get education of their choice. This problem mostly arises due to the ignorance of parents. For example, keeping in view the efficiency and aptitude of the student the teacher recommends the study of humanities while the parents, motivated by their own ideas and concepts want their child to join some technical group. This problem may be solved by proper guidance and efficiency test. The parents should be told about the importance of these tests.

Due to such difficulties we are yet not deriving the expected benefits from multi-purpose schools. It is, therefore, the duty of the public, government and private institution to contribute their full might in making this important and beneficial scheme a success and help in building up a prosperous India.

SUMMARY

The Nature of Multi-Purpose Schools: Multi-purpose schools as defined by the Mudaliar Commission are those schools which cater for different tastes, aptitude and objectives of the students by providing study in various subjects. This helps in the natural and all-round development of the students' personality.

Importance: Multi-purpose schools have a vital role to play in the present set up of the country. These schools allow students to opt for subjects according to their likings. Consequently, their emotional and psychological development will take place in a natural manner. They will understand the dignity of labour. They will have opportunity to widen their knowledge of crafts learnt in primary or basic classes. Some defects of secondary schools will find remedy in the multi-purpose schools.

Aim: The aim of multi-purpose schools is to eradicate the evils of unilateral schools by allowing the students to select and study various subjects of their choice so that they may become self-supporting, practical and worthy citizens.

Utility of Multi-purpose Schools: The provision of study of various subjects will remove the need of change of schools. The education system will be given a democratic spirit. Trained students of these schools will prove assets in the various development plans of the country. Due to the study of different subjects the personality of a student will develop in a balanced manner.

Development of Multi-purpose Schools: The Government of India introduced this scheme in October 1954 for the first time. The number of these schools which was 250 in the First Five Year Plan rose to more than a thousand in the Second Plan.

Some of the problems facing Multi-purpose Schools: (1) Shortage of teachers (2) Dearth of suitable text-books and unsuitability of time-table (3) Problem of opening new schools and difficulty of conversion (4) Difficulty in providing complete technical curriculum (5) Difficulty in the selection of curriculum and (6) the problems of parents' dissatisfaction. Only by solving these problems we can derive the maximum benefit from multi-purpose schools.

Exercises

1. Discuss the importance and objectives of multi-purpose schools in India.
2. Discuss the problems of multi-purpose schools in India.

Chapter 36

Problems of Women's Education

Historical Background

The foreign rule in India, and particularly the Muslim rule, had adversely affected the growth of Indian womanhood as a result of which they fell a prey to various conservative traditions and in the end found themselves confined to the narrow four-walls of the home. The last one hundred and fifty years of the British rule in India are important from the point of view of women's progress. The credit for bringing the Indian women out of their narrow precincts goes particularly to the foreign missionaries who rendered valuable service by setting up educational institutions for women. The first educational institution for women was established in the country in the year 1849 by Mr. D.W. Bethune, the then legal adviser to the Government of India. He donated a major part of his earnings to this institution and thus encouraged others to contribute towards this noble cause. Gradually, different missionaries opened institutions for women's education. By 1851 nearly 371 educational institutions had been opened in India of which 86 were residential institutions. In this way, during the first half of the 19th century, that is, prior to the revolution of 1857, facilities for the education of as many as 11,193 girls existed in the country.

After the revolution in 1857 the pace of women's education expansion slowed down and no remarkable progress was made. In the year 1882, having realised the need of women's education, the Government of India started giving grants to women's educational institutions on the basis of the recommendations of Education Commission. This step strengthened women's educational institutions and more new schools came into existence. The number of women's institutions and girl students rose to 6,107 and 4,47,470 respectively, by the beginning of the 20th century. These institutions, besides primary schools, included 467 secondary schools and 12 colleges. The first 15 or 16 years of the 20th century are particularly important from the point of view of women's education. In 1904 Mrs. Annie Besant established the great institution named Central Hindu Girls School at Varanasi and in 1916 the first women's college, namely the Lady Harding Medical College, was opened at Delhi. Both the Government and the public showed keen interest in women's education. The public started sending girls to schools and the Government extended financial help to girls' schools, scholarships and facilities for transport. With the opening of government girls' schools, inspectresses for them were also appointed. In this way, till the First World War (approximately till 1917) there were 18,827 girls institutions with 12,30,419 girls on their rolls. Of these, besides primary schools, there were 689 secondary schools, 12 colleges and four commercial schools.

After the First World War and till India's independence there has been a revolution in the sphere of women education. Mahatma Gandhi and other leaders and some prominent women organisations continued to agitate for more education and freedom to women. Their efforts produced good results and at the time of independence as many as 32,14,860 girls were receiving education in the undivided India. Of these, 16,284 were studying in the ordinary colleges while 40,843 were studying in industrial and medical colleges. Thus the pace of progress of women education remained satisfactory and the number of school-going girls increased three-fold during thirty years.

After the attainment of freedom the expansion of women's education became an important national responsibility. The government made consistent efforts to discharge its duty and the public, too, showed keen interest in giving education to girls. This created a favourable atmosphere for the expansion of women's education. At the beginning of the First Five Year Plan 16,951 educational institutions were imparting education to 35,50,503 girls. During the Five Year Plan the increase in the girl students in higher classes was comparatively more than those in the primary or secondary schools. Vocational and other specialised institutions also made some progress. Comparatively more girls opted for these subjects. The statistics reveal that by the end of the First Five Year Plan 26,425 institutions were imparting education to nearly ten million girls. By the end of the 7th Five Year Plan, i.e., by 1992, about 2 crores were receiving education in nearly 43,735 institutions. In view of the progress made during the First Plan further good results were expected in all the successive Plans.

The Importance of Women's Education

Although since independence some progress has been made in the field of women's education, but we cannot be satisfied with this progress, as much has yet to be achieved. The Indian women at present are far behind when compared to their counterparts in U.S.A., Russia and Germany. Much of the responsibility for this state of backwardness rests on the society. The only way to remove this social evil is to encourage women's education so that they may realise their responsibility and make efforts to regain their proper place in society. Despite shortcomings and difficult conditions the present educational systems has produced some Indian women who are far ahead when compared to women in many other highly advanced countries. It shows that what is needed for the progress of Indian women is education, and through its help, they can achieve their lost position in the society.

The Education Commission has stressed the need of women's education at all stages. The Radhakrishnan Commission (1948-49) in its reports has laid particular emphasis on women's education and has observed that Indian women can work like men in all spheres. Various scientific and psycholgocial experiments have proved that men and women can do equally good work in many spheres. The cause of backwardness of Indian women lies in the inherent flows of the Indian society and its conservative outlook. So the society has to be purged of these evils and thus reformed early. A large section of the Indian society considers the home to be the only field of women's activities. Some people hold the view that unemployment will increase if women's education spreads. All these views are misleading. For the national development along with the women's education, the old values of society will have to be changed. It is also necessary to change the present system of women's education and make it more fruitful.

Women's Education and Its Administration

According to the Indian Constitution the development of women's education is the Central Government's responsibility. But as women's education is a part of general education it is the State Government which is really responsible for proper educational arrangement. Like other spheres of the education the Government also is connected with the expansion, progress, inspection and financial help for women's education. In the early years of women's education the Education Department carried out all these functions through the local educational officers. This system of administration continued even after the appointment of inspectresses of schools. In States the supervision and administration of women institutions are carried on by the Director of Education with the help and advice of the Deputy Director of Education (Women). Regional inspectresses of schools and Inspectresses of schools have been appointed for the various educational regions and districts. But the number of women officers is insufficient and, moreover, due to double control, the work is not being carried on efficiently. This administration hardly reaches the girls schools in rural areas.

Provision for proper management, supervision, advice and guidance of schools should be made by the Government for the development of women's education. The Government of India appointed in 1958 a Naitonal Women's Education Committee and on the basis of its recommendations established a National Women's Education Council for the study of problems related to women's education and proper guidance. Hopes have risen high with the setting up of this council. According to the recommendations of this council the setting up of a separate unit of women's education in the state education department, appointment of a Joint Director of Education for Women and the establishment of an advisory council on women's education have been some of the major achievements in the development of Women's education.

Higher Education for Women

Some progress has been reported during the First Five Year Plan in the field of higher education for women. The number of students which was 14,754 prior to the Plan went upto 34,856. While satisfaction may be expressed on this achievement, but it cannot be called enough as this number is only one percentage of the total strength of women in that age group. More progress has been made during the successive Plan periods, and by the end of 1992, the number of girl students in higher educational institution rose to 61.97 millions. In future more subjects of women's interest will have to be included in the curriculum of women's higher education for the sake of expansion of women's education. At present colleges teaching domestic science, music, dance and other vocations comparatively attract more students. More such institutions for women are needed in the country.

Secondary Education for Women

More success has been comparatively achieved in the field of secondary education. With the opening of new schools the number of girl students has gone up. Whereas before the implementation of the First Plan the number of schools and girl students was 2,863 and 9,08,775, respectively. It rose to 3,920 and 13,40,071 respectively at the end of the Plan. The percentage of girls in this age group also rose from 29 per cent to 40 per cent. But even in this age group the conservative thinking of the society obstructed the growth of education. Only 3 per cent of the girls in the age group of 14 to 17 years could receive education. During the 7th Plan, i.e., by the end of 1992 nearly 13,417 girl schools were imparting secondary education to about 21,79,368 girls. For the future development of women's education changes in the subjects along with changes in the social outlook are necessary. The curriculum should include subjects of women's interest.

Arrangements for Women's Education

The growth of women education on different higher levels depends on more and more development of education at the primary stage. Setting up of different targets for boys and girls under the compulsory education at primary stage as envisaged in the First Plan was not quite adequate. The statistics available after the end of the First Plan reveal that out of 39,276 villages and 1,083 towns selected for compulsory primary education only 8,959 villages and 284 towns could introduce compulsory primary education for boys only. Some of the reasons could be social compulsions. But it is a national need to place boys and girls at par in the educational sphere. During the Plan period the number of girls getting education at primary stage continued to increase. Whereas 25 per cent girls in the age group of 6 to 11 years were receiving education before the First Plan, the percentage increased to over 33 per cent at the end of the First Plan and the percentage was likely to go upto 40 per cent at the end of the Second Plan. The perentage by 1992, i.e., at the end of the 7th Plan has been 60. But the main hurdle in women's education is the conservative outlook due to which the percentage of girls gradually goes down as their age advances and by the time they reach class V, 45 per cent of the total girls getting education in the first few classes drop out.

Vocational, Specialised and Adult Education for Women

It was been observed that now women are taking more interest in vocational subjects than ever before. The desire to have economic independence and of earning money appears to be in the background of this growing trend for vocational education. Even in grown-up women there is an inclination to gain for utilitarian and social education. All this indicates a social awakening and this opportunity should be utilised for providing facilities for more and more vocational education. Although girl students are found almost in all vocational training, but mostly they are found taking training in the teaching profession. After the profession of teaching comes the subjects of fine arts, nursing and medical education. Despite many facilities the number of students is less in these areas due to difficulties of admission. We need vocational schools and specialization institutes and special subjects should be in large numbers to meet the growing need. It is desirable to extend the facilities of subjects of social and domestic interest to the adult women in rural and urban areas. Women are showing great interest in trainings related to community development and social services. Many government institutions in India are giving this type of training. With the help of this type of training facilities, the social status of women may be raised.

Main Problems of Women's Education

In the present progressive age it is desirable that men and women hold the same status in society. A new awakening is developing in the women of Western countries. They are proving as efficient as men in various fields of activities. Those Indian women who got the opportunity to study and develop, are not lagging behind in any way when compared with their counterparts in other highly advanced countries of the world. It is evident that Indian women simply need an opportunity to develop themselves and broaden their outlook. But while making efforts to bring our women at par with the Western women we should not sacrifice our culture and heritage. Indian culture and traditions differ from the Western ones and possess something of their own which is unique.

The system of women's education, its curriculum and programme are the same as prescribed for men's education. The progress so far achieved clearly shows that still greater success could have been attained if the subjects of study were changed to suit the taste and temperament of women. Women's education has some of its own problems at each stage and their solution is very necessary.

No parents should have any objection to co-education at the primary stage. Even then, for adopting an education system suited to women's need more and more girls' schools should be opened in the country and particularly in rural areas.

Difficulties may arise in co-education at the secondary stage, because many parents do not consider it proper that adolescent boys and girls should study together. So separate education of boys and girls is a social necessity. Many parents are indifferent towards the education of their adolescent girls. There is also a section of people who despite their desire to educate their girls do not think it proper to send them to schools because their social norms forbid it. The ideas of such persons should be changed. Besides, such arrangements should be made as to enable these girls to receive education at their homes and appear for examinations. Women who, due to some or the other reasons cannot get education and those housewives who want to earn a living or supplement their income through education will also derive benefit by such an arrangement.

Educational facilities need expansion in the sphere of higher and vocational education, too. The strength of various services is increasing and opportunity exists for the absorption of more and more women in these services. There are a number of government and non-government services for which only women are found suitable. According to the targets fixed under the national development plans a large number of women's services are needed.

A large number of trained lady teachers will be required for the expansion of women's education. Trained lady teachers' services will also be required in vocational training. For meeting this huge demand of trained lady teachers, institutions providing higher education and training should be established soon. It is also to be noted that lady teachers have been found to be more suitable than the male teachers in teaching boys and girls of tender age. This is because lady teachers handle young children with great care as it suits their natural temperament. The result is that in the nursery and primary schools the demand of lady teachers has gone up. Necessary arrangements should, therefore, be made to provide more facilities for trained lady teachers for this particular job.

Reasonable pay and facilities should, therefore, be provided to attract more educated women to the profession of teaching. Proper residential arrangements should be made for women teachers in rural areas so that they may not remain indifferent towards the education of girls studying in rural areas. Adult women may easily be employed to teach in rural areas after they have been educated and trained for the job. Besides, earning money, education will help women to discharge their duties towards the family, society and the country in a more efficient manner.

SUMMARY

Historical Background: The foreign missionaries started to help the cause of women education in India from the early 19th century. The development period of women education during the British period may be divided into three parts: 1851 to 1881, 1882 to 1927 and 1928 to 1947. Despite special efforts the pace of the progress has remained slow. Since independence there has been a considerable increase in the pace, but even then greater efforts are needed.

The Importance of Women's Education: The object of women education is to achieve literacy and the social development of women. While making efforts to raise the standard of Indian women to that of women in other advanced countries, we should have to pattern their education in such a way that they do not develop contempt towards our cultural traditions and heritage.

Women's Education and Administration: Although according to the Indian Constitution, the education of women is a national liability, yet in actual practice the State Governments look after it. In the State a number of women educational officers like the Additional Deputy Director Education (Women), Regional Inspectresses and Inspectresses of Schools have been appointed.

Arrangement for Women's Education: Expansion at the primary stage will pave the way for expansion at higher stages. In 1950, 1956, 1961 and 1992 the percentage of girl students in primary classes was 25, 33, 40 and 60 respectively. But the percentage of girls who reach class V is only 30 per cent of the number that joined the school in the nursery classes. At the secondary stage the number of girls and schools in 1956 was 13,40,071 and 3,920 respectively, but the percentage of those in the 14 to 17 years age group was only 3 per cent. At the higher stage of education much development has not taken place. There is a shortage of subjects suiting the taste and temperament of women. Proper vocational training facilities as well as facilities related to adult education need expansion.

Main Problems of Women's Education: The system of education and curriculum of Women's education should differ from that of men's education. Arrangements of private education should be made for those young or older women who due to some reasons cannot go to schools. Special arrangements should be made and facilities should be given for training in teaching profession in view of the fact that lady teachers have proved more suitable for teaching young children.

EXERCISES

1. Discuss the importance of women's education in India and criticise the nature of prevailing women's education in the country.
2. Suggest measures for reforms of women's education in India.
3. What are the main problems of women's education in India? What should be done to solve these problems?

Chapter 37

Problems of University Education

Present University Education

In the absence of adequate facilities for the development of primary and secondary education, the education at the univeristy stage, too, could not develop much. At the time of achieving independence (1947-48), the number of students pursuing higher studies was about 1,80,000 according to available statistics. In view of the huge population of the country this figure of students is obviously unsatisfactory. The national government, after independence has tried to provide facilities for higher education. But the difficulties experienced by students in seeking admission to universities indicate that the progress has not been satisfactory.

During the post-independence era many new colleges and universities have been set up and grants are sanctioned for admitting more students. As the result of these efforts the number of students had risen to about six and a quarter lakhs within the period of ten years, i.e., upto 1958. Although this progress may not look impressive yet in view of financial difficulties satisfaction may be expressed over it. But during this period the desire to get higher education had become so strong amongst students that it became a problem for the nation as to how to make provision for every one who desires to pursue higher education. However, by the end of the 7th Plan, i.e., by the year 1992, nearly 21 lakh students had been receiving education at the various levels of higher education.

Due to inability to admit all students in universities the practice of granting affiliation to colleges has been revived. Prior to independence, during the early period of development of higher education there were some colleges affiliated to universities. But later on this practice was given up by many of the universities, but now this practise has been revived. The system of granting affiliation has to be revived for the expansion of higher education and even the Government administered universities have also been permitted to grant affiliation to colleges falling within a certain area of the university jurisdiction.

Besides the system of affiliated colleges, another scheme for establishing unitary universities has been implemented. Such universities are being established in bigger cities. With the establishment of such universities, whereas on the one hand, proper educational atmosphere, extra-curricular activities, better character building, closer relationship between the teacher and the taught will develop, on the other hand, there is a likelihood that other bigger colleges in the vicinity will suffer. As such, while establishing these unitary universities it will be desirable to turn big colleges themselves into such universities so that its establishment may not adversely affect other colleges.

In view of the present great demand and the development of secondary education facilities for higher education will have to be extended. Hence new colleges are being opened and they are being granted affiliation by the various universities in the country.

According to the recommendations of Rural Higher Education Committee, the proposal to turn some rural institutions into rural universities has been accepted. In such cities where a number of colleges are running successfully, it has been proposed to establish federal universities. Some universities like the Agriculture Universities, Rudrapur,

Sanskrit University, Varanasi, Sanskrit University, Mithila Engineering University, Roorkee, Agricultural Research Institute, Delhi and others have been established for pursuing the study of specialised subjects. It is envisaged that more universities of the nature will be established in the near future. For this purpose places like Ahmedabad, Tatanagar, Sewagram and some others have been considered suitable.

University Education and Administration

The majority of the people support the view that universities should enjoy autonomy in their internal matters. To-day the view is expressed that uncalled for interference is made by the Central and State Government in matters concerning univerities. Some Vice-Chancellors and educationists have voiced their opposition for making Governors the Chancellors of universities. Opposition is also voiced against some government provisions like making the mother language as medium of education and regarding publication of books. The Government action taken at the time of indiscipline and disorder in some university campus has also been criticised on the ground that political pressure increases in the universities by such actions. All these lead to a misunderstanding on the subject of university autonomy.

It is a recognised fact that the basis of education in universities is independent teaching, guidance, study and thinking, etc. In the absence of freedom of thought healthy education system cannot survive. But some disorder created due to autonomy in universities indicates a lack of experience in good administration and management of affairs. In the absence of proper control and due to sectarianism, mob-mentality and inter-rivalries among the teaching staff, the standard of education has gradually gone down.

On the other hand, if the universities are under the state administration rigidity enters in its organisation. The university authorities have to seek guidance and obey government orders and directives. They have to carry out these orders in the spirit of the letter and the government orders do not generally take into consideration their effect on any rule or constitution of the university. By a critical study of pros and cons of the Government interference we draw the conclusion that it is desirable to have government's involvement only to a certain limit.

According to the Indian Constitution the university education is the responsibilty of the State Government, but in India, Government relations with the university are not like those in other foreign countries like U.S.A., Britain and other European countries where either they are fully independent or completely under the control of the government. Finance is the main problem of a university and it receives economic help from the government in the shape of grants. The other main aspect is the framing of rules, regulations and defining of the rights and privileges and this is under the government directive. Sanctioning of grants and framing of policies is the right of legislature. In fact, it is the legislature that sanctions the opening of a new university. The university enjoys autonomy on all other matters.

According to the Indian Constitution the responsibility of the Centre in the sphere of higher education is only to bring a uniformity in the standard of education, encourage and develop research work, and arrange for technical and specialized education. Besides a few other national scientific and technical institutions, the universities of Delhi, Varanasi, Aligarh, Osmania (Hyderabad) and Viswa Bharati and many others are under the direct control of the Central Government. In special circumstances the Central Government has to co-operate and share the responsibilities of the State Governments as regards the university expenditure. Due to their financial responsibilities towards primary and secondary education and some other integrated schemes, the State Governments often find it difficult to meet their financial commitments. The Central Government, therefore, from time to time extends financial help to State Governments. Under these circumstances the implementation of schemes relating to higher education becomes doubtful. The setting up of University

Grants Commission is a noteworthy step on the part of the Central Government. The Central Government does not want to take the rights of the State Governments. The Central Government is always making efforts to promote co-operation between universities and national laboratories, extend special facilities for conducting scientific surveys and implement national policies, etc,

The Economic Set-up In Universities

The main source of income of an university or college is the tuition fees and donations, but the spheres of expenditure are so many that the income in many institutions hardly covers half of the expenditure. The income from donations is never known in advance. As a result, the financial position of higher institutions is always a matter of constant worry. They cannot run efficiently without the help of the government. With the expansion of higher education and the increase in the number of institutions the government grants have also gradually increased. According to the statistics of University Grants Commission the amount of money given as help to institutions has also rapidly increased. In 1954-55 this amount was Rs. 178 lakhs, it increased to Rs. 266 lakhs in 1955-56 and swelled to Rs. 341 lakhs in the year 1956-57 and by 1992 it has gone upto about Rs. 1,337 lakhs only. On the other hand, despite the increasing number of students, the income of higher institutions has proportionately gone down. In 1954-55 the income was Rs. 3,182 lakhs, in 1955-56 it was only Rs. 3,782 lakhs and in 1992 it happened to be only Rs. 8,763 lakhs.

The Radhakrishnan Commission (1948-49) and the Commission of 1964-66 after the study of economic conditions of various institutions suggested that the aid given by the government should be utilised only in certain spheres like the pay of teachers, study leave, pension, expansion of educational implements, buildings, hostels, libraries, laboratories, scholarships, vocational and technical training, etc. The government has started the implementation of some of these proposals. During the last few years grants were given for some of the spheres mentioned above and also for three years' degree course and for extension programmes. The government policy of sanctioning grants and aids needs some changes in order to effect some reforms in the set-up of higher institutions. The institutions should be informed about the amount of grant to be allotted at the beginning of the session so that they may prepare their budgets accordingly. While sanctioning grants provision should also be made for casual and unforeseen expenditure along with the permanent heads of expenditure. Besides, for settling the financial disputes of private institutions a definite outline should be indicated to the managing body and in the case of a university, a non-official independent judicial committee should be constituted.

Problems of Admission

To-day it is with great difficulty that students get admission in universities or affiliated colleges. A large of students do not get admission and are disappointed. Not only their future plans are disturbed, but the money that has been spent on their pre-university education is also wasted. This is a national waste. With the expansion of primary and secondary education and the implementation of three years' degree course the problem of admission has become very acute these days. To meet this situation attention will have to be paid to certain other aspects, besides the expansion of universities and their number. Among these the most important aspects that needs attention is the policy of admission in the universities. There are instances of when students of ordinary calibre getting admission while studious and deserving ones do not succeed in getting admission in colleges and to universities. The reason is not the partiality shown by university authorities but the system of different priorities in various universities. Therefore one admission policy is needed for bringing uniformity in the matter of admissions. Some people also feel that in view of the present needs and circumstances of the country, it is neither possible nor desirable to extend the facility of university education to each and every student who completes secondary education. All these are complicated problems. After all, the salvation or welfare of the country does not lie in producing huge number of graduates and post-graduates. University education should be open to only those individuals who are determined to achieve the goal of their life through the medium of higher education and who have a taste and aptitude for higher educational potential and not to every one. The statistics available after the completion of the First Five Year Plan revealed that 2.07 lakhs and 0.93 lakhs students appeared in the Art and Science subjects, respectively. In the year 1992, these numbers respectively rose to 6.3 lakhs and 3.7 lakhs in the art and science subjects, respectively. In 1955 the number of students appearing in B.A. and B.Sc. examination was 1.02 lakhs and of those appearing in vocational subjects was 0.48 lakhs. By 1992 these figures swelled upto 3 lakhs for B.A and B.Sc examinations and to 1.5 lakhs for vocational subject examinees. Some people are of the view that these statistics from the national utility point of view prove that this large number of students did not prove of much utility to the nation. Therefore, they feel that only a limited percentage of students achieving success at the secondary stage should be allowed to avail of university education.

System of Education

The falling standards of education in various universities at present is causing great anxiety. The administration, educationists and others concerned with education are making efforts to check this deterioration. Many proposals have been put forward to check this evil by Commissions and Conferences of Vice-chancellors. According to many surveys the main cause of this evil is the lack of interest shown by the teachers in teaching work. There are many reasons which have led to this situation. These days teachers have to take a large number of classes. Man's capacity of doing work has a limit and teachers can only prepare themselves for their lecture to a certain extent. So, by increasing the working hours or the number of classes the standard of teaching naturally goes down.

Another factor responsible for the fall of the standard of education relates to the emoluments of the teachers. The status and emoluments of a teacher do not compare favourable with those of other equivalent posts. So good teachers after accepting the teacher's job to start with try for a better job elsewhere and as soon as they get government or another remunerative jobs they leave the teaching professions. They, therefore, during their stay in the institutions do not show much interest in their work.

The third cause relates to training. The appointment of students coming straight after completing their studies in the university, as teachers is also responsible for the low standard of education. Although it is only at pre-university stages that demand for trained teachers is made, but trained and experienced teachers will prove of much value to universities also. It will be better if, at first, unversity teachers are appointed as research assistants and made to do research work, or such persons are selected as teachers who are working as research assistants. It will also be better if a degree or research experience of a definite period is fixed, as a pre-condition for appointment on the teaching staff of a university.

Removal of other shortcomings will also prove helpful in raising the standard of education. The teaching hours and the number of classes should reasonably be reduced, pay scales should be raised and facilities and opportunities for further studies, should be provided. Financial help during study leave or ordinary leave, maintenance of funds, and assistance for higher studies and research work should also be given to teachers.

Courses of Study in Universities

A change in national values is a natural and desirable occurence after attainment of freedom, and education is the only proper medium for bringing the people into a particular set-up. It is desirable to bring a change in the courses of study in the universities in view of the changed needs and conditions of the country. Some changes have, of course, taken place during last thirty years but much still remains to be achieved. In most universities, and particularly in affiliated colleges, the choice of subjects is limited. Students can only opt for some subjects from a particular group. The result is that the students do not get an opportunity to study subjects of their interest and as such they fail to show their full merit. It has been experienced that there is no proper scrutiny system to examine the relative efficiency of a student in a particular subject. As a result, in the absence of proper guidance, the standard of their success goes down. A system of proper scrutiny is necessary in vocational subjects so that with the help of proper guidance the students may achieve greater success in life when they pursue that vocation for earning their living.

In the higher education, the facility of opting for a particular subject must exist as a matter of principle. Another benefit that may accrue as a result of this policy is that the strength of students in different classes and subjects remains at a manageable number. Side by side, the courses of study need to be modernised. In the course of study prescribed in the institutions of such advanced countries as U.S.A. and England, efforts are being made to include some subjects of modern utility like social sciences, natural sciences, etc., as compulsory subjects. Useful portion of various subjects may be sorted out and taught as one or two separate subjects. In our universities such subjects should be included in the courses of study and taught compulsorily. Some periods in a week should be allotted for the study of such subjects. A new course of study has been introduced through the three years' degree course scheme which has now been implemented in our universities.

Examination System

Criticism have been levelled against the present-day system of examination in universities. It is a fact that as long as passing the examination remains the criterion of education, the standard of education will not go up, but the problem is how to bring reforms in the prevailing system of examination. It is not possible to effect revolutionary changes in a system of examination of such a long standing. Many educationists and Commissions on University Education after examining the various aspects of the present system have suggested a number of tests in place of a final examination after two or three years. They have also recommended that records of the progress of the student should be prepared on the basis of fortnightly or monthly tests and the percentage of marks obtained in these tests should be included in the annual examination results. It has been further suggested that records should be maintained of the class work for which a fixed number of marks should be allotted. These marks should be included in the mark-sheet of the annual examination. Besides, much care should be exercised in the selection of examiners and an examining body should be constituted for supervising the activities and programmes connected with examinations. This body should also function as a consultative committee on matters connected with examinations. These recommendations should be implemented according to needs and circumstances. Some of these recommendations have been implemented in some universities. It will be more reasonable to assess the result of external examinations along with the students success in fortnightly and monthly tests and the work done in the class and tutorial classes.

Medium of Instruction of Unversity Education

Among the various problems of university education the problem of medium of instruction is an important one. Some persons have recommended that the national language or some other Indian language should be made the medium of instruction in place of English. But keeping in view the importance and utility of the English language it was also proposed that the study of English should be made compulsory in some other form in graduate classes or it may be adopted in the three years' degree course. This proposal has, however, not met with success due to certain circumstances. However, the mother tongue as the medium of instruction has been accepted in most of the universities, because it is easier for a student to understand his mother tongue.

Duration of Degree Courses

Another problem is the fixation of duration of a degree

course. The time limit arbitrarily fixed for a particular course cannot be regarded as suitable for all. Every student will complete a definite course in different periods according to his capability, but the time-limit lowers the standard of a less brilliant student. Adequate time must be given to a student according to his capacity to complete the full course. One of the present day demands is to make suitable arrangements for those students who cannot bear the educational expenses and have to take part-time jobs to earn money for paying expenses. The duration of course in the case of such students must be comparatively longer. Such courses must also be started. Courses of study adopted beyond the fixed time limit are more convenient for part-time education.

Social Service

The development of social service and its utility is another important aspect of university education. The practice of social service is considered a part of a graduate course in some Western countries and every student has to perform social service for a definite period in a year, compulsorily. Such programmes develop in a student qualities of citizenship, and social responsibilities. For this programme the media of lectures, statements, drama, exhibition and entertainment, etc., are adopted. Such social programmes are very much needed in India. Through them the task of spreading knowledge in backward areas may easily be done.

Economy and Adult Education

Another major problem is that of financial economy and adult education. The university education is becoming expensive with every passing day. In this respect the American system is worth adopting. In America nominal tuition fee is charged from the local student in government universities and colleges. Provision of adult education exists for those who are not in a position to pay even this nominal fee. Universities in U.S.A. even help such students to get part-time jobs. Such a system is needed in India also. In our country five to fifteen per cent of the students are given government scholarship in some form or the other. Even then many students desiring higher education fail to meet educational expenses. Facilities for adult education should be provided to youths and adults engaged in some kind of profession.

Colleges Affiliated With Universities

In colleges affiliated with a university some additional provisions have to be made, besides those required in the university. It is well known that the conditions in an affiliated college are not the same which ordinarily exist in an university. In these colleges generally even those facilities do not exist which are very common in a university. All those facilities that exist and are available in universities should also be made available in affiliated colleges. The conditions in distantly located affiliated colleges are relatively different from the university. It is not necessary that the course of study suitable for the university will be equally suitable for its affiliated college. The local needs of two different places will differ. The universities should, therefore, dully consider the conditions of their affiliated colleges. It is desirable that the representatives of the affiliated college are consulted while prescribing courses of study for the university and its affiliated colleges. This will reasonably reflect the local conditions and needs of an affiliated college and give due representation and recognition to their views and requirements.

Research Work in Universities

Since Independence, facilities for research work are progressively being increased in the universities. Increase in the facilities of research work in higher educational institutions represents the rising tempo of education in general. The Radhakrishnan Commission and the Kothari Commission in their recommendations laid strong emphasis on the development of research work and as a result of increased financial help from the government, research work has made rapid progress, yet the progress made so far in this sphere cannot be claimed to be adequate. It needs to make still greater progress in order to fulfil the targets of plan on various Five

Year Plan. Some difficulties are also being experienced in this sphere. Interest in research work has not yet developed to a reasonable extent in students and teachers. The facilities for research work, laboratories, libraries and workshops are not adequate in many institutions due to want of funds. The universities are not getting enough co-operation from industries, commerce, agriculture and other departments of the government. The number of scholarships and grants is not enough. In order to create interest for research work among teachers, provisions for leave, salary, service, etc., should be made. Research experience should be made compulsory for teachers.

SUMMARY

Present Day University Education: Facilities for higher education have increased since the attainment of freedom. But the development is not sufficient. According to educational development in pilot projects nearly 1,500 universities and degree colleges should be established in the country. For acquiring vocational skill and proficiency, it is desirable to have universities in the rural areas.

University Education and Administration: According to the Indian Constitution, universities are State responsibility but the States in actual practice only frame their management rules and give financial help. Except in extraordinary situations, the universities mostly enjoy autonomy. The Central Government gives help for technical and vocational education only.

Finances: Donations and tuition fees are the only two sources of income of universities. For meeting the remaining expenditure, government gives grants which sometimes go upto 50 per cent of the total expenditure. The Central Government also gives financial help for its schemes. Even then the economic condition of many institutions is precarious and their income in proportion to the number of students is going down.

Admissions: Admission is a problem to-day and threatens to remain as such in future also. According to the national needs a reasonable system should be adopted and only deserving and a limited number of students who are keen and who desire technical and vocational education should be allowed to seek admission in institution of higher education.

Teaching System: Reforms should be introduced to check the falling standards of education. Some arrangements should be made for teachers in order to enable them to take initiative in research work and increase their professional skill.

Courses of Study: Reforms are badly needed in the courses of study prescribed in universities, but so far nothing definite has been done in this direction. It is felt that general education, natural science, and social science should be made compulsory subjects. Variety in courses of study, opportunity of reasonable choice for choosing subjects, provision of constructive and useful subjects are some of the important aspects of education for which provision must be made.

System of Examination; It needs thorough overhauling, but it is not practical to do so instantly. It is necessary to give due weightage to the results of fortnightly and monthly test, besides class work for determining the success or failure of a student in addition to only one annual examination. It will be better to set objective-type questions, besides essay type questions in an examination. The government should after proper survey and scrutiny decide about the changes.

Medium, Duration of Course, Social Service and Adult Education: In view of the utility of English language it should be made compulsory in the degree classes. Time limit for various degree courses is unpsychological and it harms students. By introducing a flexible time-limit for the causes even those young men who are engaged in other spheres will get an opportunity to educate themselves. Social service programmes should be included in higher education in order to increase its utility to the society.

Affiliation and Research: Besides providing the same facilities to the affiliated college which exist in the university, efforts should be made to prescribe courses of study according to the local needs. For providing impetus to research work, research scholarships should be increased and more facilities should be provided to teachers for doing research work.

EXERCISES

1. What ails Indian universities today? Show how you will solve any two of its problems.
2. Are the Indian universities fulfilling the responsibilities in the context of the emerging democratic values? Give your

Chapter 38

Teachers' Training

Teachers' training was not considered so important a few decades back as it is considered to-day. In the past the teachers thought that their responsibilities ended by making the students cram the prescribed course from the text-books. The art of teaching did not enjoy any reputation at that time. The teacher divided his class into small groups. Each group prepared its lessons under the supervision of a brighter student. This bright student in a way acted as a teacher. The teacher examined the work done by the groups of students. This system prevailed in India till the 19th century. The system was known as the teacher-student or monitorial system.

The teacher-student or the monitorial system was given recognition by Andrew Bell in the Madras Soldiers Orphanage in the year 1787. Gradually with the understanding of the importance of training, improvements were made in the monitorial system.

Monitorial System

The credit for giving birth to the teacher's training system also goes to individual or private institutions. First of all Dr. More opened a Normal School at Srirampur for the training of teachers for primary schools. In 1819 Calcutta a local school committee opened a teachers' training centre. Sir Thomas Munroe started a central school at Madras for teachers' training. In the same year the Bombay Deshi Shiksha Mandal trained 28 teachers for primary schools and entrusted them with the responsibility of inspecting various primary schools. The Women's Education Committee, Calcutta, started a training centre for training women teachers.

Besides the private institutions, the Government also made some efforts in this direction. In his Despatch of 1854, Wood clearly emphasised the need of teachers' training. This need was again emphasised in 1859 when it was felt that sufficient progress was not being made in this sphere. It was also decided to keep a sum apart from the school grant for trained teachers' pay. Besides, Normal Schools were opened at Bombay, Calcutta, Poona, Surat, Agra, Meerut and Banaras (now Varanasi). Three more Normal Schools were opened in the Bengal province in addition to that of Calcutta.

So far as the question of the training of secondary teachers is concerned, proper arrangements were not yet made. Training colleges were opened at Madras and Lahore in 1856 and 1881 respectively. In these colleges both graduates and under-graduates were imparted training side by side. In their training emphasis was laid on extra-curricular subjects while stress was laid on prescribed subjects in the training at Normal Schools.

Teacher's Training

The second stage of the development of teacher's training commences from 1882 and lasts till 1947. Stress was laid on the training of secondary school teachers during this period as a result of which 34 training colleges for secondary school teachers were established upto 1947 in the country. The number of Normal Schools for the training of teachers and women teachers was 339 and 189 respectively. In these institutions 2,493 graduates, 23,754 primary school teachers and 10,193 women teachers received training upto 1949.

Improvements were effected in the arrangements and curriculum of these schools as a result of the recommendations of the Indian Education Commission of 1882 and the education policy formulated in 1904. Sufficient emphasis began to be given on principles of teaching and teaching practices. The education policy laid down that the period of training in the case of graduates should be a year and two years in the case of under-graduates. A practice school (where teachers under taining could practise teaching) was to be attached with the training college for practical training. Untrained persons were debarred from entering teaching profession according to the education policy of 1913. As a result the importance of training increased tremendously. Besides, improvements were also made by the efforts of the Hartog Committee (1929) and Calcutta University Commission (1917-18).

Teachers' Training in Independent India

The aim of education in India prior to independence was to produce clerks. But with the attainment of freedom the responsibility for the development and progress of the country fell on the shoulders of the people. Hence the aim of education, too, had to undergo a revolutionary change. The aim of education in independent India is the all-round development of the individual and making him a responsible citizen. Therefore, along with basic education efforts are now being made to effect necessary changes and improvements in the educational pattern. The leaders of the country have felt that the successful implementation of all the development plans rests on able and responsible citizens and education is the only medium of making them so. Good education depends on dedicated and trained teachers. The result is that necessary improvements and changes are being made in the training arrangements. So the work of training teachers has also made strides after independance. Keeping in view the different standards of education in the country, six types of training institutions are providing training to student-teachers.

(a) *Pre-primary Training Schools*: Generally, persons having passed Upper Primary or High School examination are trained in pre-primary training schools. Considerable differences exist between the methods and courses of study in pre-primary schools in different states of the country. So, uniformity does not exist in the curricula of these training schools. The teachers trained in these schools are given training to teach in nursery, kindergarten or pre-primary schools. The Baroda University has also started a post-graduate pre-primary training diploma course for the teachers of primary schools and inspectors. The Government of India established the Indian Children Education Committee in 1953-54 for the supervision and development of pre-primary education. The Committee is still engaged in its work. On the whole, by 1992 there were about 10 Government and 90 private institutions preparing teachers for pre-primary schools.

(b) *Primary Training (Normal) Schools*: Even before independence basic education was introduced in several primary schools in accordance with the scheme of Mahatma Gandhi and at present the scheme is being actively implemented in almost all primary schools in the country. But even then there are many primary schools in every state where many non-basic primary schools still exist. So Normal Training schools and training schools run different training courses. Besides in these schools there are some teachers whose educational qualification is either High School or Upper Primary only. Therefore, two kinds of courses have been provided for these two categories of teachers and after completing two years' training one is awarded Junior Teachers, Certificate and the other Senior Teachers' Certificate. In the course for Senior Teachers Certificate more attention is comparatively paid on subjects like algebra, geometry, school and class management, etc.

There is a lot of difference between the basic and the non-basic curricula. In the basic course not only social studies, vocational training and handicrafts are included in the course, but particular stress is also given for acquiring practical knowledge. The basic course may be sub-divided into four categories, e.g., handicraft, vocational training, social education and literary knowledge. Hindustani Talimi Sangh prepared the curriculum of the basic education. Some States accepted it in toto, but some accepted it with some modifications.

Handicraft has also a place in the non-basic education. But this system is nearly extinct. Even as early as 1956-57 while there were 335 non-basic teachers' training centres, the number of basic teachers' training centres was as high as 581. By 1992, these figures have swelled upto 580 and 1,439 respectively.

(c) *Junior Training Colleges*: Mostly undergraduates work as teachers in the pre-secondary schools or middle schools. Different types of arrangements have been made by different states for their training, but generally the curriculum is almost the same; of course, there may exist some difference in standards. The curriculum is mostly divided into two parts, theoretical work and principles of teaching. For this training the Jabalpur, Sagar and some other Nagpur universities provide one years' Diploma in Training Course (Dip.T.Course) and the Baroda, Gujarat, Bombay, Karnataka, Poona Universities and some others provide one year's T.D. Course. The States' Governments in the country have also established a number of Junior Training Colleges.

(d) *Training College*: With the expansion and development of basic education the education departments of the various states had to establish institutions for the training of graduates as teachers and inspectors. Some universities have also made efforts in this direction. Besides, the Education Department of the U.P. Government and the universities and colleges at Aligarh, Allahabad, Lucknow, Gorakhpur, Bareilly, Almora, Moradabad, Kanpur, Jhans, Faizabad, Sultanpur, Delhi, Agra, Annamalai, Baroda, Varanasi, Kurukshetra, Chandigarh, Calcutta, Osmania, Jabalpur, Nagpur, Rajasthan, Vikram, Patna and many others have also made provisions for teachers' training. The teachers after training are awarded degrees and diplomas like L.T.; B.Ed; and Dip. Ed., etc. The course of this training is generally of one year's duration. There is a difference in the courses of basic colleges and other training colleges. Efforts are being made to bring a uniformity in the courses of colleges in different States. The provision for the M.Ed. degree is also made by most of the universities in the country. This is one year's advanced specialised course in education meant to produce specialists in the area of education.

(e) *Specialist Training Centres*: Provisions for specialised training in various subjects, besides teachers' training centres, are also being made. These special training centres or colleges provide specialised training and research facilities in their subjects like music, physical education, arts and crafts, domestic science and handicrafts, etc. Besides, there are some institutions in which arrangements exist for training in various subjects. The Union Government established at Gwalior in 1957, a physical training college named after Maharani Laxmi Bai.

(f) *Research Work*: A two years' Ph.D. course has been provided for post-graduate students who had passed M.A. (Education) or M.Ed. The examinations of M.A. (Education) and M.Ed. are almost equivalent in standard. The difference exists in name only. For Ph.D. a major thesis has to be submitted. It is regretted that research work in the sphere of basic education has not made any remarkable progress, despite sufficient grants given by the Government of India for this purpose.

(g) *Training of Lady Teachers:* Arrangements for the training of lady teachers exists along with male teachers in most of the training colleges, but there are some institutions which are exclusively meant for training lady teachers. The figures in 1956-57 and by the year 1996-97 have been as follows:

		No. of Lady Teachers Trainning Centres	No. of Basic Centres	No. of Students in Basic Centres	No. of non-Basic centres	No. of students in non Basic Schools
1	2	3	4	5	6	7
1956-1957	Colleges	31	1	407	30	4,154
	Schools	258	146	13, 364,	142	12, 550
1996-1997	Colleges	80	8	517	93	2317
	Schools	700	1100	50,000	993	50,000

In-service Teachers' Training

For an efficient education system in a country more emphasis has to be laid on in-service teachers training. In service teachers' training keeps the teachers knowledge up-to-date. Through this the teachers become aware of the latest educational researches, problems and information. In the absence of in-service training, it is possible that an efficient teacher of to-day may become inefficient in future, because he may be unaware of the latest educational problems and thus may lack in the up-to-date knowledge of conditions prevailing in the educational sphere. The State governments and training institutions arrange from time to time refresher courses and seminars in order to post teachers with the latest knowledge about their subjects. But this has not yet taken a regular and organised shape. In order to achieve this purpose, some training colleges have arranged expansion-centres. Their number in 1955, 1956 and 1957 was 2,441 and 53 respectively. By 1992 this number rose to 337.

The expansion centres provide for teachers in-service training through the help of long and short term courses, workshops, seminars, educational weeks, exhibitions, discussion and guidance, libraries, audio-visual aids, pamphlets and other publications. These expansion-centres receive financial help and education material and equipment from Ford Foundation and American Technical Co-operation Mission.

Some Problems Relating to Teachers' Training

After independence, efforts for the expansion and development of education were made by political parties, public and the government. Even then there exist certain problems relating to education which need to be solved to ensure all-round progress. Unless these problems are solved no progress worth the name will be made. Some of these important problems are discussed below:—

(1) *Utilitarian Education Philosophy*: The aim of our education to-day is to effect an all-round development of an

individual's personality and to make him a responsible and able citizen. In order to achieve this aim, it is necessary to introduce revolutionary changes in the present education system. The education has to be made completely practical and utilitarian. This ideology had given birth to basic education which was introduced throughout the country. Hence, efforts were made to effect changes in the courses of training schools and basic training schools. Besides, efforts have also been made to introduce changes in the courses of B.Ed. and M.Ed., examinations, etc., with the view to bring in co-ordination between life and education.

(2) *Disparity Between the Basic And Previous Curriculum*: There being two types of schools—the basic schools and the non-basic one—two kinds of training institutions in the country are imparting training in different courses. In the courses of basic training school, special emphasis is laid on practical work and social life and it has a rural bias, while in non-basic training schools emphasis is laid on principles relating to knowledge. It also lays emphasis on various teaching methods and has an urban bias.

According to the recommendations and suggestions of various Committees and Commissions it will be desirable to prepare a new curriculum incorporating the special features of both the systems which, under the previling conditions, may prove more useful. Accordingly, in the university education and in the curriculum of B.Ed., and L.T., etc. emphasis will have to be reduced on theory while more importance will have to be attached to the practical training. The course will also have to be increased. The Viswa-Bharati, the Rajasthan universities and some others are trying to pattern their curriculum to a large extent on this basis.

(3) *Narrowness of Training Courses*: The courses of B.Ed. and L.T. were prescribed at a time when basic education had not come to existence. Importance at that time was mainly attached to theory of the knowledge of principles. It is because of this reason that the curricula of these examinations needs to be amended and widened. Moreover, success will not be

achieved if, besides the amendment of curricula, the period of training is not increased in proportion to increase in the courses. Although the B.Ed. course has been enlarged and made comparatively more practical yet the period of training has not been increased. Under these circumstances the problem will not be solved by only enlarging the course. The Secondary Education Commission had this factor in view and recommended the extension of the period of B.Ed course to two years. But this had not so far become possible due to education expansion policy of the government.

Under the present circumstances some success may be achieved by implementing the three years' degree course. A three years' B.A. (Education) course may be provided. For training practical teaching experience, the schools in rural areas should be selected or the students be kept under the supervision of trained teachers of rural schools for sometime, where, besides gaining teaching experience, the students may also gain a practical knowledge of preparing the progress-report and the use of audiovisual equipments for children. They will also get an opportunity there to participate in co-curricular activities and get acquainted with the conditions of rural society. In this way the training courses may be enlarged and made more utilitarian.

It is worth mentioning here that the above problems do not relate to higher secondary schools only. The junior high-schools and primary school teachers, too, do not get enough training, because the courses at normal schools last only for about a year or so. It is necessary also for the teachers of junior high schools also that they should acquire specialised training in some sphere of education. Besides, some experts are of the opinion that training period of these teachers should also be extended to two years' duration.

(4) *Presence of Untrained Teachers in Colleges and Universities*: The teachers taking graduate and post-graduate classes in universities and colleges are mostly untrained. It is true that they are experts in their subjects yet to possess the knowledge of a subject is one thing, while having the technique

of teaching that subject is another. There may be deficiency in them in the matter of method of teaching. Therefore experts are of the opinion that the teachers in universities and colleges also should know the technique of giving lectures, explaining the subject and inspiring students towards the acquisition of new knowledge. Therefore, some sort of training is also necessary for them.

(5) *Narrowness of Post-Graduate Training Course*: The main post-graduate course in education is the M.Ed. The main aim of this examination is to provide one with specialised knowledge of education for becoming administrators or teachers in training colleges and teachers of higher standard. But it is regretted that due to narrowness of the course the desired results are not being achieved and the present needs are not being fulfilled in a satisfactory manner. Therefore, the M.Ed. course should not remain an extension of B.Ed., but instead, be divided into three parts—compulsory, optional and oral. Under each of them it is necessary to give detailed instructions in the following subjects:

- (i) *Compulsory*: Educational statistics, research, knowledge of elements of education, educational psychology, present system of education and courses in foreign countries and a comparative study of rules regarding educational administration.
- (ii) *Optional*: Specialised knowledge in a particular branch of education.
- (iii) *Oral*: Determining the success in the above subjects through written examinations alone is not enough. There should be a viva-voce test also.

(6) *Research*: The work of training institutions should not be limited to giving training only. The Secondary Education Commission has also recommended that the training institutions should also be charged with the responsibility of carrying on research work relating to education. The assistance of student-teachers and teachers of secondary schools may be taken in research work relating to the elements of education. Although research is being done on this subject in the country

but there is a need of research on social education, practical work load on teachers, vocational guidance and conditions of teachers, etc. Very little research work has been done in the sphere of education in India, but it has been found that various research centres carry on work on almost the same subject.

(7) *Lack of Uniformity in Training Institutions and Their Diplomas and Certificates*: Uniformity in the standard of the curricula of training institutions is necessary for the development and progress of training. The duration of training should be the same and the certificates awarded by them, too, should have equal value and recognition. Side by side it is also necessary to remove disparity in the standards of different institutions. In the absence of parity, the expected enthusiasm is not witnessed among the teachers. Sometimes even the institutons of education and universities of the same State show disparity in the standard of teacher's training course. To remove this inadequacy the Secondary Education Commission has recommended that post-graduate training and under-graduate training should be controlled by universities and state institutions, respectively. In order to maintain a co-ordination in both the standards, it is also desirable that a close contact is maintained between the two departments.

Teachers' Status

The status of a teacher should be very high in the society becasue he is the maker of future citizens, administrators and statesmen. But it is a matter of great regret that in India teachers do not occupy a high place in the society. The teacher who in ancient Indian culture had the same place as that of parents is unfortunately to-day considered merely as an ordinary worker. In different states the grades of salary of teachers vary. There is a considerable difference between the maximum and the minimum pay. The disparity is to such an extent that in the same state a teacher employed in a government institution enjoys better facilities than a teacher of the same standard and qualification working in a non-government institution.

The conditions of the univerity teachers may be called to be somewhat satisfactory but the teachers of affiliated degree colleges have to face many difficulties. The Union and the States governments are now paying attention to these problems and it is hoped that the condition of teachers will become better in the near future.

SUMMARY

The educational activities depend on the organisation of teachers' training. The organisation of teachers' training in India at present is not satisfactory. There is a wide disparity in the training system in the different states of India. With the coming into existence of basic education, the necessity of attaching more importance to practical aspect is being keenly felt. Efforts in this direction are being made in view of the recommendations of Radhakrishnan Commission, Secondary Education Committee, Chancellors' Conference and various seminars of educational officers.

India is very backward so far guidance and training in the sphere of technical education is concerned. Research work in the field of education, too, is not being carried on in a satisfactory manner. However, the Union and the State governments are taking steps to improve conditions in this sphere. It is also necessary to take steps to improve the conditions of teachers, but because the country is passing through an economic crisis, it is the duty of the public and teachers not to further burden the government and depend on it entirely. They should instead become self-reliant and help in improving the conditions in the country.

EXERCISES

1. Discuss the nature of training of teachers for primary schools in India.
2. Write a critical note on the current High School teacher education in India.
3. What improvements will you suggest for improving the B.Ed. and M.Ed. programmes in India and why?

Chapter 39

Problems of Technical Education

Since the attainment of freedom the progress made in the sphere of technical education in the country is not bad, but in view of the tremendous need and the present circumstances, the pace of progress is not quite satisfactory. In other words, some progress had been made but much is yet to be achieved. We have to import small and big machines and their state of affairs is some of our own peculiar problems that hinder the technical and industrial development of the country.

Unsuitable Technical Curriculum

Being predominantly an agricultural country, India's need, till some time back, was limited to the manufacture of agricultural implements only. Different sections of the society manufactured items of daily use. This section of the society in course of time, were typed different castes on the basis of the nature of their work. In due course their technical profession turned into a family profession. The son inherited the trade from his father. The shape and the make of the implements generally remained the same and simple skill was needed in their manufacture. This simple knowledge was easily acquired during the practical work; but with the development of science the nature and technique of machines is daily becoming complex. In the modern progressive society it is necessary for an efficient engineer, in order to ensure his advancement, to keep in touch with the latest developments, besides possessing good technical knowledge. This is because the engineer has to use his technical skill for the benefit of society. Hence in the curriculum, the inclusion of other subjects, besides the technical ones, is necessary. In the same way to understand the new technique, it is equally necessary for the efficient workman to have adequate knowledge of language, general science, mathematics, social science, etc. Hence general knowledge has been made compulsory in the technical courses of study in the United States of America. In India, too, the All India Technical Education Council is particularly concentrating its attention on this aspect.

Shortage of Vocational and Technical Institutions

Although during the various Five Year Plans, stress has been laid on the opening of technical institutions, but the number of such institutions is still very small. Due to lack of technical education labourers and workmen employed in various factories remain unaware of the latest technical knowledge. So they do not prove very helpful in the development of industry as per the latest technology.

Shortage of Teachers

In our country there is a big shortage of technical teachers because of lack of technical education. It is also very difficult to remove this shortage by employing foreigners as teachers because of the lack of funds. Because of the same reason, it is also a difficult problem to send a large number of students to foreign countries and get them trained. In this condition of helplessness, technical education has to be left in the charge of ordinary teachers. The main reason for not getting the services of efficient and well qualified technical teachers, is low pay scales. It is not possible to secure the services of efficient teachers by providing low -salaries. In these circumstances, it is the duty of the government to step in and take effective steps. The All India Council of Technical Education, it is heartening to note, is taking some steps in this direction. The Council has provided a five year continuous course after secondary education for higher training in technical and engineering subjects.

Lack of Good Administrators

The problem of shortage of good administrators is the result of various complex problems relating to technical education. The view that industrialisation is the main source of raising the standard of living in the present age, is now gaining ground. This view has dominated in the preparation of our various Five Year Plans. But when the administrators responsible for industrialisation themselves lack the knowledge of technical and engineering subjects, how far industrialisation will progress may well be imagined. It will not do much good if administrators specialise only in their subject, because society is also their field of activity and they have to give the benefit of their knowledge to it in a practical manner. They should, therefore, have to be fully in know of the social, economic and political developments in the society. This problem of the shortage of good administrators may be solved by establishing institutions of higher technical and engineering studies and by enlarging the scope of the curriculum. The All India Council of Technical Education is particularly alive to this situation and is making efforts in this direction.

Problem of Practical Field Work and Laboratories

The fields of practical activity of technical education are the industrial institutions and workshops outside the centres of training.. In the present state of acute financial position, it is not possible to provide large workshops in the educational institutions. Therefore, it is necessary to make arrangements for practical training in State or private factories. In this way, beside acquiring practical knowledge, the students will also get an opportunity to understand the various aspects of industrial sector side by side. As a result of such a practical training, the students will become efficient teachers, skilled workers and good administrators. This problem may further be simplified by providing part-time jobs to students in some factories. In this way, the students, besides learning, will also earn something and also acquire some experience of the industrial sector. This scheme of practical training will also help industrialisation. In addition, the problem of seeking employment, after finishing education, will also be solved to some extent.

So far as the provision of laboratories is concerned, it is necessary that each institution imparting technical education has a laboratory. But here, too, the shortage of funds creates problems.

Research Work

Although many research institutions have so far been established and research work is proceeding at a rapid pace, yet the progress in the utility and quality of the products does not compare favourable with foreign products. Even to-day, we prefer using foreign blades, pencils, pens, etc. Some articles are such that considerable expenditure involved in their production in our country and thus they become costlier than the foreign make. So, their demand is poor. Those engaged in research work should bear in mind that the aim of researches should be to produce goods of higher order and less cost in order that the articles produced may easily be consumed in the market. They should also cater to the refined taste of customers and thus attract buyers by their beauty and utility.

Provision of Education and Development of Technician's Personality

In this modern age of scientific advancement, every day new inventions, discoveries and experiments are being made. The engineers, workers and technicians, etc., have to keep themselves fully informed with these latest developments in order to keep their knowledge up to-date. If they fail to do so their knowledge will become stale. Although in India there are above 200 institutions that run diploma course, besides above 50 universities and 100 institutions providing degree courses; providing refresher course to technicians exist in the country. It is necessary to provide technical facilities to factory workers to keep them in touch with the latest developments in their fields. The technician should be given an opportunity to learn the latest developments in his spare time. Libraries should be provided for artisans and labourers. They should be afforded facilities for reading books and magazines and discuss subjects relating to their sphere of work. Arrangements should be made to impart them the desired education during their vacations or at evening centres. In this way, besides developing technical skill and knowledge, they would also develop their personality. This in turn will result in increased production, which will immensely benefit the country. The lack of knowledge of English language is the biggest handicap facing the poorly educated workmen. Unfortunately, very few standard books on technical and engineering subjects have been published in the various current languages of the country. English is still the medium of education of these subjects in our country, while countries like China and Japan have produced engineering and technical books in their national languages. However, some efforts have been started in India also since the last two or three decades and it is hoped that soon many books on these subjects will appear in the languages generally spoken by the people.

Co-operation between Government, Industry and Educational Institutions

For the development of technical and industrial education it is necessary that there exists always a balance between industries and technical man-power on the one hand, and its training and efficiency on the other. To-day we find many technicians facing unemployment. This generally happens when technical schools prescribe a curriculum without keeping in view the requirements of the industries. As a matter of fact, the technical education should be organised, keeping in view the needs of the industries. The industries should be made familiar with the latest technical developments and should be provided with efficient and well skilled hands.

Every trained man, besides getting opportunity for increasing his knowledge, should also get reasonable wages. If the government, technical institutions and industries co-operate with each other, there is no reason why the industrial development will not make rapid strides.

Summary

Modern age is the age of science. Only that country can become strong and prosperous in this age which does not lack in trained technical personnel and where provision for good technical education exists. In our country also much stress is being laid on a technical education in the Five Year Plan. But it is doubtful whether the professed aims will be achieved, as there is shortage of funds in the country. However, if we succeed in solving the problems facing technical education; the shortage of finances will not hinder our development.

Exercises

1. What are the main problems of technical education in India?
2. How should the technical education in India be organised for meeting the ever-growing needs of the nation?

Chapter 40

Problems of Adult Education

A majority of the Indian population is illiterate. The country since independence is trying to keep pace with other democratic countries of the world, but illiteracy has all along been a stumbling block in our political, economic and social progress. A nation whose people cannot understand their responsibilities towards the society, and who fail to grasp the intricacies of political problems, can hardly succeed in running the country on democratic lines. Democracy is a hoax in a country whose people swear by it, but fail to understand the principles governing it. It was on account of this factor that the leaders of the country ever since it attained freedom tried to spread social education in order to make the people politically, economically and socially strong. It may be stated here that adult education may also be called as social education, although the latter may connote many other aspects of education than merely teaching of adult only.

Aims of Adult Education

It has been universally recognised that democracy succeeds in a country where people understand its principles. This political wisdom can be attained only through education. Efforts in the sphere of adult education were started sometime back with the aim of spreading literacy, but learning the alphabets does not constitute education, although it is true that it helps in acquiring education. As long as the society lives in ignorance and people continue to be illiterate it becomes poorer and weaker because a handful of unscrupulous persons who are cunning and wealthy, wield political powers and exploit others.

For simple adult education, some time should be devoted regularly, but for technical or industrial education sufficient time has to be provided for. Such subjects should be taught to adults which interest them. The aim of adult education is not fulfilled by merely imparting bookish knowledge nor is it fulfilled by implementing a scheme constituting a programme for learning attractive words and phrases giving expression to noble sentiments. In fact, the illiterate should be taught the basic principles of education in an attractive manner. This type of adult education has no time limit. The process should continue as long as the individual lives. In this way, when knowledge develops and interest is created, people will themselves make efforts to understand the atmosphere surrounding them.

In the sphere of adult education the fact that should constantly remain before us is that adult education does not mean simply to enable some adult illiterates to put their signatures on a piece of paper, or by making some people learn the alphabets to solve some short-term problems. In India, in fact, many social evils are practised and for their eradication short-term adult education programmes will not serve the purpose. Adult education should be such as to meet the requirements of various activities in the field of social welfare. An evaluation of the efforts made in this field since the last so many decades has shown that our efforts in the past did not bear the expected fruits. The result has been that a large member of adults continued to be illiterate as before.

Adult education-drive motivated by political reasons hardly succeeds. To ensure its success, the adult education movement should aim at developing an adult mentally. It should further aim to make the adult know his responsibilities as a citizen. Emphasis should be laid on vocational education. So far, good and adequate arrangements in the field of adult education has neither been made by the government nor by the social reformers. Unless the government steps in effectively, the future of adult education will remain in dark.

For producing cultured citizens, enlightened voters, efficient craftsmen and artisans, the state should provide adult education with programmes of cultural, physical, social and vocational training. Only such education will meet the demands of a good adult or social education.

Adult Education in India upto 1937

Good work in the sphere of adult education had been done in advanced countries like Russia, Japan, Denmark, U.S.A., England, Germany, etc., while in India where the problem of adult education has been acute, adult education movement was started very late. In the countries where persons of different professions learn the three Rs, provision is also made for further education in the subjects of their likings and their professions. Training is imparted in various subjects relating to industry, commerce, literature, science, arts, etc. For persons who could not get education in their early days, centres of adult education, night schools, university extension-classes and continuation schools have been organised.

As compared to some advanced nations, the condition of adult education in our country is in a poor state. However, steps are being taken in this direction. A brief account of these steps taken in the country is given below.

Early Efforts

India did not make any noteworthy progress in the sphere of adult education during the first two decades of the 20th century. Only in the provinces of Madras, Bombay and Bengal some night schools were established, but the aims of adult education remained undefined in these institutions. Arrangements were also made in these schools to give some sort of education to boys who could not attend regular schools because their poverty drove them to work at a young age. In the year 1909 the number of such institutions in Madras,

Bengal and Bombay were 775, 1,082 and 107 respectively. The number decreased in the succeeding years. The people were given some rights by the foreign government in the year 1921 by virtue of which they entered the legislatures. The representatives of the people in the legislatures felt the necessity of adult education and they made efforts to draw the attention of the government to this important problem. Consequently, some libraries were set up.

From 1920 onwards education came in the hands of the people's representatives in the legislature. These representatives felt the need of adult education. Hence adult education made some progress in the provinces of Punjab, U.P., Bombay and Madras. In the year 1927 there were as many as 5,604 schools for adult education in Madras, 1,519 in Bengal, 193 in Bombay and 3,784 in Punjab. A statement of progress made in adult education from 1922 to 1927 as shown in the statement of the Education Ministry of the Government of India is given below:—

Year	*Number of Students*	*Number of Schools*
1922-23	17,777	630
1923-24	40,883	1,528
1924-25	61,961	2,372
1925-26	85,371	3,206
1926-27	98,414	3,784

The pace of expansion of adult education went down from 1929 onwards due to economic conditions. Many centres of adult education had to be closed down. Political upheavals and social inequalities also created obstacles. Only a few missionaries could continue their good work in this sphere.

Bombay as compared to other provinces made better progress till 1937. 'Adult Education League' of Poona and 'Sewa Sadan' 'Social League', and 'Bombay City Literacy Centre' of Bombay were some of the liberal organisations which kept on the work of adult education and through their selfless efforts nearly 143 institutions were established till the year 1923-33.

These institutions had about 5,660 student students and adult on their rolls. By 1937 the number of schools and students went up to 180 and 6,229 respectively. Libraries were also established at Baroda and Travancore but the progress slowed down by the end of the year 1937.

In the majority of provinces, with the formation of the popular ministries in accordance with the Government of India Act 1935, the people's representatives raised the voice for the expansion of adult education. The governments in provinces also felt the need of educated citizens who could understand the responsibilities of citizenship so that they might prove helpful in the implementation of various welfare plans. With Government and public co-operation the adult education programme gathered momentum and the work continued with greater vigour.

Having realised the importance of adult education the government made efforts to give it a proper shape. While laying down the curricula of adult education its sphere was extended from ordinary literacy to social education and beside making provision of books for educational purposes other equipments like magic lanterns, pamphlets and cinema-shows were also arranged.

Nature of Adult Education in Various Provinces

Before Independence

In 1930-40 the adult education programme took a new turn. A movement was launched in every province by which efforts were made that every literate person should make an illiterate literate.

Uttar Pradesh

The adult education department was established in this province in the year 1930. With the formation of the Congress Ministry in the year 1937 the programme of adult education was pursued with renewed vigour. Night schools were opened in a large number. New literacy centres, libraries and reading-rooms were established and a decision was taken to observe a 'literacy day' and a 'literacy week' every year. On the occasion of the first 'literacy day' as many as 768 libraries and 2,600 reading-rooms were opened in various villages of U.P. Forty libraries were also set up for women in 1940. In the year 1941-42, 272 more libraries were opened. In this very year 50 women welfare centres in Faizabad district were given a grant of Rs. 500 each and the government published books on such subjects as Hindi, Urdu, geography, history, arithmetic and arts for the use of adult.

Punjab

The Punjab Government sanctioned a grant of Rs. 28,800 in their first plan towards the literacy movement. With this money new schools were set up and aid was given to the existing institutions. Their number at that time was 201. The 'learn and make other learn' movement spread vigorously in the Punjab.

Bihar

In Bihar under the leadership of Dr Syed Mahmood some volunteers launched the 'make your home literate' movement with vigour as a result of which nearly 24,289 adults were made literate during 1941-42. For this every purpose the 'Provincial Public Education Committee' was appointed. The most outstanding feature of the Bihar movement was that it continued even during the war years and every year nearly two lakh men were made literate. During 1942-43, nearly 1,11,000 adults passed the post-literacy test. This work was taken up with new zeal when the Congress ministry again took over the reins of the government in 1946.

Orissa

No noteworthy progress in this sphere was made in Orissa. Only 425 adults literacy centres were opened during 1940-41 where 8,147 adults received education.

Bengal

Adult education in Bengal was under the Rural Reconstruction Department. In its curriculum subjects like animal husbandry, agriculture, hygiene, co-operation and others subjects related to village life were included and every subject was taught under the supervision of the officer-incharge connected with it. In this way adult education made rapid strides amongst the farmers in Bengal.

Assam

In the province of Assam adult education department was set up under the charge of Public Literacy Officer. Under the direction of this Officer nearly 1,200 study centres were established in Assam. During 1941 a post-adult education programme was implemented for those who had learnt the ordinary alphabets. Books and newspapers suited to their standard were published and reading-rooms catering to their taste were organised.

Bombay

The Bombay government established a Provincial Education Board in 1927. The government introduced the system of liberal grants for this work. The first Congress Ministry did praiseworthy work in the sphere of adult education. A sum of Rs. 50,000 was granted in 1942-43 for rural areas. In 1945 the government opened adult education centres at selected places and decided to spend Rs. 9,400 yearly on a centre. The target for each centre was to educate one thousand persons every year. An 'Adult Education Committee' was also established in Bombay city. Good progress was recorded in the city through this committee.

Native States

In the Mysore State the 'Mysore State Literacy Council' did commendable work. The Mysore University also did good work. Some progress was made in the sphere of adult education in Sind and some other states. Nearly, 4,050 adult education centres were opened in the Jammu and Kashmir State and about 28,000 persons passed out of these centres as literate. Literacy as compared to that in British India was higher in percentage in Baroda and Travancore States. In the hilly areas literacy efforts were greatly concentrated on the backward tribes.

After the attainment of freedom in 1947 the leaders of the country, having realised the importance of education and in the light of experience gained from the adult education movements during 1921-47, made efforts to raise resources to solve difficulties and problems that arose during these years. Sufficient literature was produced and a new system of teaching this particular literature was evolved. By then everybody had fully realised that the education of adults was necessary for the country's welfare so that the people might understand the various plans prepared for the uplift of the society and co-operate in implementing them. This aim could not be realised by simple literacy only and higher education upto some extent was necessary for adults. Adult education was, therefore, patterned on the ideal of social education.

The General Policy and Programme of Adult Education Followed During Post-Independence Era

The nation after Independence considered the illiteracy of the masses as a curse. Illiteracy is the cause of the backwardness of a country. Illiterate citizens cannot realise the importance of their vote and as such they fail to understand the significance of democracy. It was because of this fact that the Indian leaders, besides developing the entire sphere of education for children also tried to educate the adults so that they might live like worthy citizens of a free nation. In the absence of such education India was bound to lose its position in the eyes of other free nations. With this end in view the Government of India divided the programme of adult education into the following parts:

(1) To make the illiterate persons literate.
(2) To develop consciousness in adults, towards their rights as citizens.

We shall discuss onwards the general policy and programmes of adult education during the post-independence era in the country. For obvious reasons we do not intend to burden the readers with statistical data in the connection (for which any standard book on History of Indian Education may be profitably consulted). Our scope herein is very limited.

As indicated above, adults education is also termed as social education. Emphasis is given on the Education of illiterate persons and to make them aware of their rights, responsibilities and duties towards society and the country. Therefore, stress is laid on the following subjects in particular:—

(1) Knowledge of the rights and duties as a citizen and the working of a democracy.
(2) Acquiring a knowledge of the history and geography of the country as well as of the various cultures of the past and the present.
(3) A knowledge of individual and collective hygiene and basic principles of health care.
(4) Provision of such education which may help an adult to raise his financial status.
(5) Knowledge of the principles of co-existence (the entire world is a family) and world ethics besides tolerance and accommodation of other's views.
(6) Educating the higher emotions and thinking through the constructive approach towards arts, music, literature, dance.

In order to implement the above programme is 12 item-plan was chalked out and accepted on May 31st, 1948.

(1) The village school will become the centre of education, social work, sports and entertainment for the entire village.
(2) Separate time will be allotted for the education of persons of different age groups.
(3) Some days of the week will be allotted to women and girls.
(4) Film shows, magic lanterns, gramophones, projectors and loudspeakers will be provided to the centre at least once a week.
(5) Radios will be provided to schools and special

programmes will be arranged in larger numbers for school-going children and also for adults.

(6) Popular dramas with a social and public bias will be staged. Awards will be given to good performances.

(7) National and folk songs will be arranged.

(8) Handicrafts and training in other industries will be provided keeping in view the local requirements.

(9) Lectures will be organised with the help of health, agriculture and labour department on the subjects of social health and community hygiene, agriculture, cottage industries and co-operation.

(10) For developing political consciousness in the rural population, series of lectures by eminent scholars and statesmen will be arranged. Arrangements for staging film show, from time to time, will be made with the help of Information and Broadcasting Department. In order to make the programme of social education practical help will be taken of the public organisations involved in such constructive works.

(11) Sports meets will be organised from time to time.

(12) Arrangement for timely exhibitions and fairs will also be made.

In order to implement the above scheme a conference of States' Education Ministers was called in February 1949, and it was decided that 50 per cent of the adults in the age group of 12 years to 50 years should be made educated within three years. Work could not proceed according to the decisions taken at the conference. The reason being the financial difficulties faced by the States. The Central Government in order to remove the financial handicap gave the provinces help amounting to rupees one lakh during the year 1949-50. In a few States some progress was made. The Government of India constituted a committee under the chairmanship of Sri M.L. Saxena for drawing up a programme for educating in the next five years (1951-1955) people in the age group of 12 to 40 years. It was decided that the expenses incurred in implementing the decisions of this committee would be met in a ratio of 50:50 by the State Governments and the Central Government.

Whatever progress was achieved under this scheme in the sphere of social education is discussed below.

In 1951, that is, during the first year, adult education centres were opened at Delhi and nearby areas. In the villages of Delhi province 60 centres were established, and for running them in accordance with the adult education system as many as 62 teachers were trained.

In Madras State (now Tamil Nadu) the State Government established six rural colleges under the Citizen Education Scheme in 1949-50 and 100 citizenship schools were set up under the adult education expansion programme. Training centres were opened for the training of teachers in Tamil, Telegu, Kannari and Malayalam languages.

This scheme made good progress in the labour colonies of Bombay. Nearly 80 densely populated rural areas were selected for the experiment of social education. The Bombay city itself made good progress in the field of adult education. Adult education expansion officers were appointed in the rural and urban areas on area basis and every officer was charged with the responsibility of educating 1,000 adults. Labour welfare centres were opened at Ahmedabad, Sholapur, Khandesh and Hubli for the expansion of social education among the labourers.

The government hit upon a special method of popularising adult education and generating enthusiasm for it in Madhya Pradesh and Berar. 451 adult education camps were opened in 1948-49 wherein 41,274 men and 20,924 women were educated in several subjects. The government in order to create interest in adult education decided to give rupees two to every man and rupees five to every woman who helped implement adult education. The government also gave an allowance of rupees five to teachers in rural areas, besides giving them a pay of Rs. 20 per month. The government in order to further popularise this literacy programme distributed 1,000 radio-sets to rural schools.

The U.P. Government undertook the programme of adult education with great enthusiasm during the First Five Year Plan. A separate department was opened for this particular purpose. Adult education institutions were set up in large numbers in 1948-49 in which 49,392 persons received education. As many as 62 institutions were opened for women alone. The number of education schools were 2,200 in 1951-52. In July 1952, 3,600 reading-rooms for men, 435 for women, besides 1,518 adult libraries were opened. From 1948 to 1952 about 1,75,000 books were distributed and 13,50,000 persons were made literate in U.P.

The programme of adult education was implemented with great enthusiasm after 1947 in the states of Bengal, Hyderabad, Rajasthan and Jammu and Kashmir. The Government of India established an education centre for blind persons in Dehradun. The government also took steps for the education of deaf, dumb and physically handicapped persons.

The Government of India adopted the U.N.E.S.C.O. system with some modifications and started adult education centres. These adult education centres are functioning vigorously in refugee colonies. The scheme has three main objectives: (1) literacy, (2) citizenship, and (3) development of mind through the help of audio-visual shows.

The adult will be made literate according to the programme given below:—

(a) Ability to write his own name besides the name of his relations, villages, Tehsils (sub-divisions) and districts. To enable them to wirte simple letters to communicate with others.

(b) Ability to read and understand the contents of simple books and newspapers.

(c) Ability to count upto 100 and write these figures; to do simple addition, subtraction and division, to understand various types of measurements and weights; and to determine the values of coins.

For achieving the objectives of citizenship, and development of the mind, audio-visual aids, drama, sports, music, dance, radio, cinema, celebrations, fans, newspapers etc. are to be organised.

This programme was to be implemented througout the country by opening camps in every district. To implement the above programme the M.P. Government made a scheme for opening four camps in every Tehsil (sub-division of a district) where volunteers will impart education to adults. Every such volunteer was required to possess the knowledge upto class VII at least. He was also expected to be above the age of 16 years. A director was there to supervise the work of these volunteers. This camp was to work for five weeks at one place and move to another. Such camps proved to be very successful in M.P.

Having realised the utility of such camps other States in the country, too, have implemented this programme. It is contemplated to raise the duration of these camps to eight or eleven weeks as five weeks' time is not considered enough for the purpose of educating adults. The college and university students and teachers throughout the country are also being encouraged to devote some of their time in these camps as volunteer-teachers.

Community development and other expansion programmes are being implemented in every part of the country since 1952. Social education has been given priority in these development programmes. Under these schemes provision of ample facilities has been made for the all-round development of the necessities of life and arrangements have been made for the development of knowledge, political sense, citizenship, sports and entertainment, hygiene and cleanliness, etc. Experiments have been carried out in these subjects in the pilot-projects. However, it may be said on the basis of the report of the progress of the various Seven Five Year Plans* that these schemes have not so far completely succeeded in their objectives.

The outcome of the social education as included in the

*Draft of the 8th Five Year Plan, Chapter 11, p. 290-91, 1993.

First Five Year Plan was organisation of social centres, opening of Janta colleges (colleges for people) organisation of study circles in villages for the expansion of education, introduction of intensive library service, preparation of useful literature for adults and its distribution, etc.

Social Centres

To provide education and facilities for social development to rural people, public cultural-cum-welfare centres were established and these were known as social centres. Their sphere of activity was much wider as compared to that of the present education centres. The common meeting place of the village, local school or the Panchayatghar were given the shape of such centres.

Intensive Libraries

Intensive Libraries for rural people were established at various social centres but where such centres did not exist, the libraries were housed either in the local school or at the meeting room. They were opened even in the Panchayatghars or in the houses of some respectable person of the village. Books relating to civics, religion, agriculture, industries, co-operation, industrial or commercial practices, health, hygiene and domestic science were kept in the libraries.

Janata College

For producing trained workers for villages it was proposed to establish Janta Colleges. Workers trained in these colleges were to work in social centres. Public service, co-operation and co-existence were the guiding principles for these workers. These trained workers in the social centres were considered the local leaders. These Janta Colleges, unlike the other colleges, trained youths of both sexes to act as leaders of the rural workers in the sphere of cultural, social, education and other activities of public welfare.

The Government of India held a seven days' conference at Mysore in February, 1957 in order to prepare a curriculum for these colleges. The conference made the following recommendations to Government:—

1. The Janata Colleges should be patterned on old Ashram type schools where students and teachers may live together. The colleges should possess agricultural land near the premesis.
2. The supervision of these colleges should be given to well-organised and well-managed public organisations. Where such non-official bodies do not exist the government itself will take the responsibility of running these colleges.
3. Sufficient grants and help should be extended by the government to run these colleges.
4. Only those in the age group of 15 to 40 years should be admitted to these colleges and separate colleges should exist for men and women.

Literature in Hindi and regional languages were produced for adults. The Central Government has published more than 1,000 books in various languages by the year 1992. Jamia Millia, an institution in Delhi, took the responsibility of producing such literature which may suit children and adults both. In order to encourage the production of this type of literature the Central Government gives awards to deserving writers.

Similarly, awards are also given to persons contributing to people's literature. A committee consisting of experts in literature has been formed to select the literature for awards.

Summary

The percentage of literacy in India is very small. After independence the leaders' focused attention on this problem and realising the importance of education in a democracy, the people's representatives chalked out a number of schemes for eradicating illiteracy. In the first phase the illiterate adults were to be educated. Arrangements were made for their education in the subjects of their interest. Adult education centres were set up in villages and financial assistance was given to them. People inspired by the motive of selfless service

rendered valuable help. The government opened a new department to deal with this problem. Education camps on the pattern of UNESCO education camps were opened by the Government of India. Social centres, intensive libraries and Janta Colleges were established under the seven Five Year Plans.

EXERCISES

1. Describe the development of adult education in India before 1947.
2. What is to-day the aim of adult education? Describe the main lines on which efforts have been made in India to achieve this aim.
3. Explain the general policy and programme of adult education followed during the post-independence era in India.

Chapter 41

Problems of Education of the Handicapped and Disabled

In the sphere of education India is very backward in comparison to some Western countries especially so far as the education of disabled and handicapped children is concerned. Physically handicapped persons in our country are found begging. Physically, socially and mentally retarded children rebel against the society. Anti-social attitudes develop in them and impelled by undesirable impulses they indulge in anti-social activities like stealing and playing foul tricks. Their activities prove harmful for society. It is, therefore, in the interest of the nation to provide proper education facilities for them so that instead of rebelling against the society they may become a useful part of it and help in its development. It is necessary for their education to divide them first into different categories because an uniform pattern of education cannot serve the purpose of different categories of disabled, handicapped and mentally retarded children. There are certain types of disabilities that are caused by personal shortcomings. We can call these casual disabilities. Besides, if due to some internal or mental disorder changes occur in the thinking and attitudes and these are reflected in individual's behaviour, we call it symptomatic disabilities.

Casual Disabilities

This is due to either physical or mental or social factors. Physically disabled persons are those who are either dumb or deaf or blind or lame.

Mentally handicapped are those who lack average intelligence. They may be divided into two categories on the basis of intelligence test. In the first category come those who are a little below average, as far as intelligence quotient is concerned. In the second category come those persons who are known as moron, imbecile and idiot and whose intelligence quotient is less than 70, 50 and 25 respectively.

The socially handicapped are those who are orphans without home or property, have no guardians and belong to the lowest order in the society.

Symptomatic Disabilities

Man is a social being. All his needs are met by the society. His way of living is conditioned by the society he lives in. When such conditions appear that he fails to establish the necessary co-ordination between his own nature and his social environment, some changes occur in his normal behaviour. Then dissatisfaction takes root in him and he is overcome by criminal tendencies. This generally happens due to poverty, illiteracy and ignorance, lack of peace in married life and cruel treatment by family members. In these conditions children often fall prey to mental diseases. They do not take interest in their studies and they develop criminal tendencies.

Education for the Handicapped

India has made very little progress in this sphere. Even after independence disabled and handicapped persons have to take to begging in the absence of proper care and treatment. Some Christian missionaries gave attention to this problem prior to independence. For the first time, in 1883 a Protestant lady, Miss Annie Sharp opened a school for blind girls at Amritsar. Later in the year 1887 an Indian Christian, Sri Lal Bihari Shah, laid the foundation of a school for the blind persons in Calcutta. Similarly in 1890 and 1900 Miss Asquith and Anne Millard established schools for the blind at Palyam and Kottaya and Bombay respectively. Till 1955-56 no special progress could be made in this field. Grants were given by the various State Covernments to the schools of physically handicapped persons. In the year 1952 the National Child Welfare Council was set-up and a council for providing training to physically handicapped and disabled persons was established in 1955-56. In the year 1955-56 the number of institutions for mentally handicapped, physically disabled, deaf and dumb and blind persons was 3, 8, 34 and 49 and the number of students receiving training in these schools was 227, 552, 2,290 and 2,245 respectively. By 1992, the corresponding figures for such institution have swelled upto 27, 67, 103 and 337 and for students the raised figures have been 1119, 4015, 7839 and 8975 respectively.

Education for the Disabled

It is a matter of regret that so far we have not taken a census of disabled and handicapped persons in our country. Their estimated number has been based on the proportion that exists between the physically and mentally sound persons and physically and mentally handicapped persons in U.S.A. In U.S.A., their percentage is two. It is, therefore, necessary in India at first to undertake a census of such persons. Later on they could be classified in the two categories known as casual and symptomatic and arrangements for their proper treatment be provided. In this way it will be easily discovered as to what type of treatment is needed for particular handicapped individual. Mentally handicapped persons may then be sent to mental hospitals. Some children may be sent to common schools after a short period of treatment. Some will need a little change in their course of studies. Thus, there are only a smaller number of handicapped persons will be found for whom special arrangements will have to be made. The following kinds of institutions will be needed for them:

(1) Institutions for Juvenile delinquents, (2) Orphanages,

(3) Schools for the physically handicapped, (4) Schools for the blind, (5) Schools for the deaf and dumb, (6) Institutions for the mentally handicapped, and (7) Guidance and treatment centres.

Problems of Arrangements

Proper arrangements do not exist in India for the education of disabled and handicapped persons. The following are the factors responsible for this shortcoming:—

(1) *Lack of Finances*: No scheme on a large scale has so far been chalked out by the Government to solve this problem because of the shortage of funds. It is true that institutions connected with this work get grants from the Government, but this is not enough.

(2) *Shortage of Good Institutions*: Although children's centres, welfare centres and orphanages are being set up by the Government and individuals, but so far neither their number is enough nor are there proper arrangements in these institutions for educating handicapped persons.

(3) *Shortage of Teachers*: Due to lack of training facilities enough teachers are not available for the institutions of handicapped persons. Consequently, the teaching work is not proceeding satisfactorily.

(4) *More Handicapped Persons in Rural Areas*: An overwhelming majority of Indian population is rural. As such, comparatively more handicapped persons live in villages than in cities. But there are practically no institutions for their care in rural areas. The need, therefore, is to open special schools in rural areas and give the curriculum a rural bias.

(5) *Lack of Administration*: In order to make the Government efforts more useful it is necessary to have efficient administrators. Unfortunately there is a dearth of such good administrators. The success of this scheme depends on the efforts of efficient administrators.

Present Arrangements

Despite the above mentioned difficulties, whatever efforts have been made in the country, although not quite adequate, may however be regarded as somewhat satisfactory upto some extent in view of the difficult conditions. Different types of institutions have been opened in the country for different kinds of handicapped persons.

Education for the Blind

There are nearly four million blind persons in India according to a recent report of the Planning Commission in 1992, but it is a matter of pity that only a small percentage out of them are receiving some education. The Ministry of Education, Government of India, set up a unit for rehabilitation and education of blind persons under the control of Deputy Education Adviser. A blind adult training centre was opened at Deputy Education Adviser. A blind adult training centre was opened at Dehradun in 1950. In 1951 schools for the blind were opened at Ajmer and Batain (Kutch). Two years' course has been instituted in the Dehradun school. In this school blind children are taught to prepare baskets, weaving and spinning and typing besides stenography. After their training arose the problem of finding jobs for them and rehabilitation. So a department was opened for this purpose in 1955 at Madras. In 1950 a central Braille printing press was established at Dehradun to produce literature for blind persons.

Educational Arrangements of the Deaf, Dumb and Disabled

The deaf and dumb and other handicapped persons are usually educated along with blind persons. The blind persons are mostly taught music, but deaf and dumb are taught painting. They are also trained in some vocation like the blind.

Reform of Juvenile Delinquents

The problem of juvenile delinquents at present is more

complicated and is proving very harmful to the society. Acts like 'Children's Acts', 'Juvenile Delinquent Acts' and 'Reformatory Act' have been promulgated at different stages. The Central Government is giving grants to reformatory schools and such other institutions. 'Rain Baseras' (Night Shelter) are being constructed in bigger towns to provide sleeping accommodation to homeless persons. They are also being provided with vocational training to improve their lot, besides education.

Education of the Physically Handicapped

The physically handicapped persons do not need special type of alphabets as the blind require. So they are admitted to ordinary schools after necessary treatment. During their education, particular attention is paid in order to enable them to learn to make proper use of the aid-implements.

Education of the Mentally Handicapped

Mental hospitals are needed for treating the mentally handicapped. Unfortunately there is an acute shortage of mental hospitals in our country. In mental hospitals a psychological study of the nature of ailments of the patient is made and he is provided work according to his nature and liking. Treatment clinics and guidance centres are needed in these mental hospitals. Although some mental hospitals have been established in India, yet in the absence of proper arrangements full advantage is not being derived from them.

Other Institutions

There are thousands of orphanages in India run by different religious institutions for the maintenance and upbringing of orphans. These institutions receive grants from the Government. Unfortunately among these institutions there are some which do not hesitate in misusing the Government grants. They also do not hesitate in exploiting the boys and girls under their charge. However institutions like the Ram Krishna Mission, Kasturba Trust, Salvation Army, etc., are

some of the institutions that have rendered valuable service to the country. Their source of income is government grants, donations, subscriptions and help from local bodies. It is heartening to note that the Government is taking some interest in these institutions and it is hoped that by end of the 8th Five Year Plan this problem will be attended to upto an appreciable extent.

Summary

One of the reasons for growing unemployment and increase in the number of beggars is that provisions for the training of physically and mentally handicapped children are lacking. Mostly the handicapped and disabled children are found begging alms. It is a matter of regret that so far there is no census on the number of such persons. However, some efforts have been made to relieve the distress of these children since the country gained independence. Mental hospitals, deaf and dumb schools, clinics and guidance centres have been set up. The dumb are taught some craft, typewriting or stenography according to their particular inclination and ability. Though the establishment of Indian Braille Printing Press literature is being produced for the blind. Separate jails and courts have been set up for Juvenile delinquents. But satisfactory progress has not been achieved due to shortage of funds.

Exercises

1. What are the problems of education of the handicapped and disabled children in India? Suggest measures for their solution.
2. Describe the present arrangement for the education of handicapped and disabled children in India.

Chapter 42

Education of Scheduled Castes and Tribes

The economic and social development of the country will be considerably hindered. If proper attention is not paid to the education of backward classes and scheduled castes. According to the census of 1991, nearly 180,000,000 people, that is, one fifth of the total population consists of backward classes and scheduled castes. We cannot get the co-operation of these 180,000,000 citizens in our cultural, political, social and economic programmes as long as we do not carry education to their doors. These backward classes have many social evils. Removal of these social evils is our national responsibility. As long as one fifth of the population of the land remains backward in this way, we cannot become a happy and prosperous nation.

Meaning of Backward Class

The word backward class may mean differently according to a place and time. Different people may be included within the definition of backward class from the point of view of educational, social and economic backwardness. For example, only 42 percent people have been declared educated according to the census of 1991. Hence the remaining 58 percent may be called backward. Except for a few exceptions from the social point of view, people of many small communities and many upper caste Hindus may be called backward. Women may also be called backward from the social view-point. From the economic point of view, except for 5 percent of the population, the remaining 95 percent are backward. From the point of view of belief in superstitions and many such social practices, nearly 95 percent of the population may be regarded backward. But in this chapter, we are discussing backward classes according to the articles 341 and 342 of the Indian Constitution. According to these Articles, by backward classes we mean scheduled castes and scheduled tribes. These castes include all those communities which the Hindus previously considered as untouchables. Scheduled tribes include Adivasis. Nomads also come under scheduled tribes. Besides these, backward classes include some poor Muslims and people of other religions who are economically poor and are also backward culturally and socially.

Education of Scheduled Castes

Some provisions have been made in our Constitution for the improvement of the life and education of the Scheduled castes:—

1. According to the Article 17 of the Constitution untouchability has been declared as an offence.
2. According to Article 15, the so-called intouchables have been given freedom to use public places such as wells, ghats, restaurants, hotels, etc, like any other citizen.
3. According to Article 25, all religious places of Hindus have been made accessible to them.
4. According to Article 29, they have been given the right of admission in all government and recognised educational institutions.
5. According to Article 16 and 335, they have been provided reservations in all public services.

Contribution of Various Social Institutions And Leaders

Many social institutions and great leaders of the country opened several educational institutions for the welfare of scheduled castes and arranged scholarships, free education and free boarding and lodging, for them. They also provided financial help for purchasing clothes, educational equipment and books. In the First Five Year Plan, Rs. 170,000,000/-, in the second plan Rs. 410,000,000/-, Rs. 5,300,000,000/- in the third plan, in the fourth Rs. 7,000,000,000/- and in the Fourth Five Year Plan, were provided for their welfare. In the Fifth Five Year Plan, 20,000,000,000/- rupees have been provided for their welfare and education. According to the census of 1991, 17.5 percent of the total population consists of scheduled castes. Evidently, the Government has to do a lot for their welfare and education.

In the sixth and seventh Five Year Plans about Rs. 30,000,000,000/- and Rs. 45,000,000,000/- respectively were provided. In the 8th Five Year Plan it is envisaged that more than Rs. 70,000,000,000/- would have to be spent on education of scheduled castes and Tribal people.

The following table gives an estimate of the efforts made upto 1992 for the education of Scheduled castes:—

From the table, it may be concluded that the primary education of Scheduled tribes in Assam, Gujarat and Bihar is better than in others States. The education at lower primary level is deplorable in all the States. The primary and secondary education of children of Scheduled castes between the age limits of 11 and 17 years is not satisfactory, although scholarships and other financial help have been provided to them. Perhaps some improvement in their higher education is perceptible due to the scheme of scholarships extended by the Central Government. According to the table, vocational education seems to be popular almost in all the Scheduled castes. Evidently, we should try to develop vocational skill of different kinds in the people belonging to the Scheduled castes.

Dhebar Commission of 1960-61

A Commission was appointed under the chairmanship of Sri U.N. Dhebar to enquire into the conditions and problems of Scheduled castes. In its report, the commission has remarked

S. N.	State	Percentage of S/C in total population	Percentage of enrolment of Scheduled castes in the total enrolment				
			Lower Primary	Primary	Secondary	Higher Education	Vocational Education
1	2	3	4	5	6	7	8
1.	Assam	20	30	19	11	11.5	45
2.	Andhra	5	4	2	3	1	
3.	Orissa	Data not available.					
4.	U. P.	The number of Scheduled tribes is negligble.					
5.	J & K	The number of Scheduled tribes is negligible.					
6.	Kerala	3	5	3	4	—	4
7.	Gujrat	17	15	10	7	4	17
8.	Punjab	3	2.5	2	2.5	1.5	2
9.	West Bengal	8	6	5	3	2	13
10.	Bihar	12	13	9	5	39	
11.	Tamil Nadu	2	2.5	2	3	2	4
12.	Madhya Pradesh	25	16	8	4	5	9
13.	Maharashtra	9	8	3	2.5	3	5
14.	Karnataka	3	5	4	2.5	3.2	3.2
15.	Rajasthan	16	17	3	4	5	7.5

that so far no suitable provisions have been made for the education of the children of Scheduled tribes. Hence the Commission requested the Central Education Ministry to look into their problem.

The Dhebar Commission considered the residential Ashram Schools useful for the education of scheduled tribes. These Ashram schools were not only schools and hostels, but they are also cultural centres, because they encouraged the folk-ways, folk-songs and dances of the Scheduled tribes. So the Dhebar Commission suggested further development of such schools. For the development of primary education, the Commission made the following recommendations:—

1. The children of Scheduled castes and tribes should be taught some craft or industry.
2. The teachers appointed for teaching the children of scheduled castes should be given special allowance and residence facilities.
3. They should be given books, clothes, writing-materials and mid-day meal in the schools.
4. The teachers should be trained in areas where Scheduled castes live for teaching the children of Scheduled castes so that they may become familiar with the environment of scheduled castes and tribes during their training.
5. The teachers appointed for the education of Scheduled castes should have thorough knowledge of the Scheduled castes and their culture.
6. At the primary level, the mother-tongue of the scheduled castes or tribes should be made the medium of instruction. Books should also be printed in their languages.

Kothari Commission 1964-66

The Kothari Commission has given some other suggestions. Some of the main points of these recommendations are given below:—

(a) There should be some better arrangement at the

primary level. More Ashram schools should be opened in thinly populated areas.

(b) Some more schools should be opened for the secondary level and proper provision should by made for hostels and scholarships.

(c) More scholarships should be given at the higher education stage. Such persons who can devote themselves to the service of Scheduled castes, should be given a special cadre of service. In the beginning, non-Scheduled caste persons should be taken in this cadre and later on qualified persons of Scheduled castes should be included in this cadre. Needless to add that if the recommendations of Dhebar and Kothari Commissions were implemented, resulting improvement of conditions of Scheduled tribes would have been fotered to a great extent.

Criminal Professionals

Criminal professionals are those persons who before 1950 belonged to the category of criminal tribes. Their inherited profession was crimes of different kinds—such as, to break into houses, theft, highway robbery and stealing of animals. People of this class continue to wander from one place to another indulging in their old profession at times.

Before Independence

Missionaries did significant work for the education of criminal professionals before Independence. The Government has obtained the right of settling them at one place by passing Criminal Tribes Act. They have been settled in certain places and some residential schools have been opened for them. Missionaries and some other institutions have been given financial help for educating them.

After Independence

After Independence, the criminal Tribes Act was suspended, because it was not considered fair to call anyone as belonging to a tribe. Arrangements were made to provide employment to the adult of these Scheduled tribes and residential schools were opened for education of their children. The Government spent ten, twenty and forty million rupees in the first, second and third Five-Year Plans, respectively. In the forth five year plan provision was made for spending 140 million rupees on them. In the fifth Five Year Plan, more money was earmarked for them. Similarly, for the 6th & 7th plans more funds were allocated. In the 8th Five Year Plan more money has been provided.

Nomadic Tribes

Nomadic tribes have no fixed place of abode. They continue to wander throughout the country in search of a living. Their children live with them. So it is difficult for them to send their children in schools. Some measures have been suggested for improvement of their lot.

Some of the measures taken are:—

1. They should be settled in particular places. Efforts have been made to settle some nomadic tribes in Rajasthan, Orissa and Bihar. But they like to wander. They cannot stay put at one place. Hence they ran away from where they were settled.
2. Moving schools should be provided for them so that wherever their caravan moves, the school may also move with them. This experiment has been successful in Jammu and Kashmir upto some extent. The tribes there move to mountains in summer and come down to the valley in winter. Moving schools were established to educate their children. In 1992 there were about 80 such schools. In such schools, the teacher belonged to their group. This provision can only be accepted temporarily. Solution to their problem lies in settling them at one place.

Scheduled Tribes And Government

The following three types of programmes organised by the Government may be mentioned:

1. Programmes of the Central Government.

2. Programmes planned under the supervision of the Centre.
3. Programmes of different State Governments.

1. Programmes of the Central Government:

Some seats are reserved for Scheduled castes in Government services. But many vacancies are not filled since qualified persons are not available in Scheduled castes. To improve this condition, the Government have opened training centres in Madras, Jabalpur, Kanpur and Delhi for giving vocational information and education ot Scheduled caste candidtes before their enter in some Government service. These centres are known as coaching-cum guidance centres. About 50 scholarships have been provided to scheduled caste students for education abroad. In Government education centres, more then 17 (1/2) percent seats are reserved for Scheduled caste candidates. Some seats are also reserved for Scheduled caste candidates in Medical and Engineering colleges.

2. Programmes under the supervision of the Centre:

(a) Students of Scheduled Castes are given scholarships to continue education after high school. At present (i.e. during 1992-93) scholarships are given to nearly 500,000 scheduled caste students and about 80 thousand scheduled tribes students.

(b) About 25 centres are engaged in preparing scheduled caste and scheduled tribes candidates for I.A.S. and I.P.S. examinations. By 1992 about 5000 such candidates were prepared and out of them about 1000 got success.

(c) The Central Government provides sufficient finanical help to the State Governments for constructing hostels at the educational centres. Upto 1992 about 30,000,000 rupees have been provided for this purpose.

(d) Twenty institutes have been established for carrying out research regarding Scheduled castes. For contact with these institutes, a Central Research Advisory Board has been set up with about 40 members.

(e) The Central Government gives different kinds of aid for settling and education Scheduled castes. On the basis of this aid, provision is made for midday meals, hostels, residential schools, Ashrams, examination fees, scholarship tuition fees, etc.

3. Programmes of Different States:

The State Governments receive aid for Scheduled castes from the Central Government in the form of block grant or loan. On the basis of this aid, the State Governments help the Scheduled Tribes in the following ways:—

i) Running Ashram Schools.
ii) Provision of educational equipment.
iii) Establishing hostels and schools.
iv) Giving scholarships for primary and junior high school education.
v) Providing mid-day meals.
vi) Exemption of tuition fees and examination fees.

Scheduled Castes and Society

The Government help alone cannot make the Scheduled castes happy. Public co-operation is required for their welfare as Scheduled tribes problem is a social problem and it cannot be solved by any law. The problem of Scheduled castes is different in different states of the country. Evidently, an awakening should be created in the public for the welfare of Scheduled castes. Many social workers have suggested that compulsory education be implemented for their upliftment. But neither the Dhebar Commission nor the Kothari Commission made any such recommendation. The following programmes should be started for the upliftment of Scheduled castes:—

1. A survey of related places should be made for opening schools for scheduled caste children.
2. More residential schools of Ashram type should be opened for scheduled caste children.
3. Sufficient eductional facilities should be provided in all concerned places.

4. Free meals, books and clothes should be provided so that the children may be encouraged to seek education.
5. Public opinion should be mobilised for compulsory education for them through healthy propaganda.

Summary

Nearly one fifty of the population of the country consists of Scheduled and Scheduled tribes. Their upliftment is necessary for the economic and social development of the country. Several social evils are practised by them. Their removal is a national responsibility.

Provision in the Indian Constitution:

1. Untouchability declared as an offence.
2. Freedom of going to public places.
3. All religious places of Hindus opened for them.
4. Right of admission in Government education centres.
5. Reservation in public services.

Contribution of Social Institutions and Leaders: Provision of free education in different five year plans. Efforts should be made for their achieving vocational efficiency.

Dhebar Commission: Residential Ashrams, training in some craft or industry for the children of Scheduled castes. Special allowance and facilities for teaching Scheduled castes children, training college for them in the same area, their mother-tongue to be the medium of instruction.

Kothari Commission: Many primary and secondary schools should be opened. Provision of hostels. More scholarships for higher education. New cadre for persons appointed for the service of Scheduled castes.

Criminal Professionals: Criminal tribes, wander from one place to another, missionaries worked for their settlement at particular places. Residential schools, Government help to the missionaries and other institutions for their welfare.

Criminal Tribes Act suspended. Provision of money in different Five Year Plans for them.

Nomadic Tribes: They should be settled at particular places but the nomads do not stay where settled. Provision of moving schools at present. This arrangement was made in Jammu and Kashmir.

Government and Scheduled Castes: **Reservation in Government services, training centres in Madras, Jabalpur, Kanpur, Delhi and other places for them so that they may be selected for Government services. Scholarships for education abroad. Reservation for more then 17 (1/2) percent seats in educational centres, Government and for hostels for them.**

Scheduled Castes and Society: **Society responsible for their upliftment. Awakening to be created in general public for their upliftment. More Residential schools to be opened for them, free education, clothes and mean to be provided. Propaganda, for their compulsory education.**

Exercises

1. Give an account of the Scheduled tribes living in India. What should be done for the education and welfare of these tribes?
2. What is the main problem of the education of the Scheduled tribes in India? Describe the efforts made by the Government for solving these problems.

Chapter 43

National And Emotional Integration and Education

To-day there are some tendencies at work in our country which are obstructing our national integration. Different languages, states, classes and castes, political parties, tendency of ignoring national interest for personal ones, regionalism, poverty and different communities are some such elements which are challenging our national unity. We have adopted a democratic system of government. Hence, diversities prevailing in the country have to be recognised. It is not necessary that individual differences are always against national interests. In fact, individual differences often enrich our national life. But these diversities should not take such a shape as to endanger our national security and unity. To-day the diversities wide-spread in the country have threatened our national security. Some humilating incidents have happened in our country in the name of language and regionalism. Boundary disputes between two states, quarrel between two states for a particular city, communal riots and insurgency at some places, are blots on the good name of our country. This shows that we are not following the right course. Some people demand separate states on the basis of regions. To-day, the unprincipled behaviour of some political parties and their internal groupism are likely to strangulate the nation. Therefore, national integration has become one of the main problems of our education. Here we shall try to find out its solution.

Our Political Unity

Today there are some persons with confused ideas in our country, who doubt the political unity of the country. It is true that several kings ruled over this country and there have been many independent kingdoms within India from time to time. But at the same time, it is to be noted that an under current of unity has always been there throughout the country which kept the country united. Our places of pilgrimages are not centralised within a particular region. They are spread over through out the country. Rameshwaran, Dwarika, Jagannath-puri and Badrinath are notable examples. It was the wonderful wisdom of our religious leaders that they established places of pilgrimage in the four corners of the country in order that people from one corner may go to the other and may thus visit the whole country, may know each other and consider themselves an integnal part of this vast land with a feeling of oneness. Since the beginning of Indian civilization and culture, our countrymen have been visiting the different places of pilgrimage. People from north and south, east and west have been going form one part of the country to the other. Thus there have been cultural exchanges since ancient times and people have considered themselves as citizens of one country.

Different rivers of our country have been considered sacred. Krishna, Kaveri and Godavari in the south Indus in the west, Ganga, Yamuna, Sarayu and Gaumati of north India and Brahmputra in the east have been considered holy and worth-worship. Similarly, mountains in different regions in the country have been considered sacred. Different cities of the country have been recognised as places of pilgrimage and centres of culture. Thus it is clear that our sages have always tried to unite the country with a cultural thread and they have always been successful in their efforts.

This feeling of cultural unity inspired our religious leaders and social reformers to inculcate the feeling of common citizenship in our countrymen. It is because of this feeling that whenever our great leaders have raised their voice on any issue, the whole country has followed them. It was because of this that all the groups in the country struggled for feedom under the banner of Indian National Congress, forgetting their religion, caste or community and consequently won independence. The unity shown by the people during the freedom struggle was not artificial, but something natural. In fact, that was the voice of country's conscience. Gandhiji's Dandi march and 'Quit India Movement' had shaken the country so much that even the British Empire had begun to doubt its permanancy. Chinese invasion in 1962 and Indo-Pak wars of 1965 and 1971 had united the whole country and it was evinced that the same feeling of patriotism was running in the veins of the whole nation. The periods of Asoka, the Great and Akbar the Great gave us a glimpse of this kind of unity. The rebellion of 1857 is a fine example of feeling of oneness. Needless to say that we should make our political and national unity durable and should not encourage disruptive forces.

Emotional Unity

Emotional unity of our countrymen is necessary for our national integration. So long as our countrymen do not consider themselves as one and do not realise that first and foremost they are the citizens of this country and their personal, sectarian, social and religious interests are secondary, there can be no national integration. They must be made to feel that from historical and geographical point of view, India has always been one nation and will always remain so. They should be convinced that ours is a culture which every person should be proud of.

We should attract the attention of the people to this through education. By doing so all will be emotionally integrated and will rise above their personal interests for the good of the country.

Social Unity

In our country different groups based on community, religion, caste, poverty and wealth are found. These groups remain indifferent to each other and lack the feeling of national unity. They are wanted in the feeling of brotherhood. There is influence of caste in some region, strong sectarian feelings in the other and some particular religion, another. In fact, this situation is very unfortunate. For national integration it is necessary that people of different classes and communities are brought together and feeling of unity is infused in them.

For this, some collective programmes should be arranged and people of all classes, communities and different religions should be invited. Every community should be made to feel that the interest of their community lies in the interest of the country which comes first and foremost and then anything else. No class or community can make progress by ignoring the interest of the nation. Needless to say that we have to forego communalism and regionalism for social unity. This does not, however, mean that we should have no love for our community, religion or region and should forsake them. It only means that we should first think of the country and after that, of any 'ism'.

Religionism, casteism, regionism and linguism have been encouraged by some political parties in our country and these parties have acted against national unity. At the time of elections different political parties plead for religion, class, caste and region and want to secure votes on the basis of these slogans. A candidate is selected from that caste or religion which dominates a particular area. Such an action is just a misuse or religion or caste for political interest and creates conditions for national disintegration.

Inter-caste and Inter-state Marriages

Some people are of the opinion that for national integration, inter-caste and inter-state marriages should be encouraged. This means that people should marry into other castes and religions. Similarly, persons of different regions should not hesitate to inter-marry. The children born of such marriages will be above caste, religion and regionism. They will consider themselves Indians first and anything else afterwards. In support of this argument people cite the examples of U.S.A. and Japan. The Spanish, German, French and British people who settled in America after migrating from different countries of Europe, accepted inter-caste marriages. The off-spring of these people consider themselves Americans first and take pride in calling themselves as such. Similarly, in Japan also, followers of different religions are found in one family and their offsprings call themselves Japanese first and not of this or that religion or caste. Thus, national integration in America and Japan has been very much encouraged. In our country this process should be adopted voluntarily and any one who is desirous of inter-caste marriage should be encouraged and should be given special social recognition.

Economic Unity

The economic inequalities pervading the country are weakening its unity. Some have wealth beyond measure and some are dying for two square-meals a day. These inequalities will have to be removed for the sake of national integration and that no specific class or community remains backward. For this, it is necessary that minorities and backward persons are given special help. They should be given special facilities of education, houses and government services. If the backward classes are not struggling for survival they will contribute to national integration.

National Language

The question of national language has become very important for us. According to the Constitution, Hindi in the Devnagri Script has been accepted as the national language and in 1965, Hindi was to occupy the place of national language of the country. But in 1965 when this status was accorded to Hindi, riots broke out in South and in Calcutta.

If we want to encourage national integration, we should

not be in a haste to make Hindi compulsory in every region. So long as people of non-Hindi speaking areas do not agree to accept Hindi, the clause of the Constitution regarding Hindi should be kept in abeyance. We should prepare the non-Hindi people for accepting Hindi voluntarily. This does not mean that knowledge of English is not useful for us. In fact, our education cannot be considered complete so long as we do not acquire good knowledge of English. In order to benefit from international culture and knowledge, the knowledge of English is very necessary. So, the subject of English should not only be available in our schools, colleges and universities but it should be made compulsory upto the intermediate or degree stage. Inspite of all this, we have to adopt our own language and so far that language is Hindi and so long as the related clause of the Constitution is not changed, we should strive for the acceptance of Hindi as a national language in such a way that one day the whole country may be prepared to accept it gladly. But as long as non-Hindi people do not show their willingness to accept it, Hindi should not be imposed on them as it will only hinder national integration. Therefore, we should try to see that our national language Hindi (or any other Indian language) is helpful in national integration rather than an obstruction. Evidently, we have to work in this direction cautiously, affectionately, sympathetically and with consideration for the feelings of others.

Education

Education is a powerful means for national integration. Through education we can inspire the future citizens. So the aim of national integration is to be kept supreme in organising the different components of education, framing the curriculum, in the class-room teaching, in educational centres, cultural activities, in the organisation of co-curricular activities, in the management of schools, in the various stages of education — schools, colleges or universities. In the appointment of teachers, in the distribution of education facilities, in the composition of text-books, we should follow such policies as will encourage national integration rather than helping the divisive tendencies of class, community, religion or region, etc.

In the present situation of the country and in the international context the need for unity should be emphasised more vigorously. We have to be careful that no disruptive forces work against national integration. If we follow the suggestions given, we shall be successful in maintaining national unity.

SUMMARY

Disruptive forces threaten national and emotional integration.

Our Political Unity: India has always been considered as one nation. Our places of pilgrimage exist through out the whole country. Cultural exchanges between people of different regions. Recognition of the sacredness of rivers and mountains of the entire country; feeling of a common citizenship in the countrymen. The whole country was one during struggle for freedom, unity of the country during Chinese invasion in 1962 and Indo-Pak Wars of 1965 and 1971.

Emotional Integration: Necessary to forsake personal, sectarian, social and religious interests for the welfare of the country. Devotedness towards the country. Creation of suitable literature by poets and authors for emotional integration.

Social Unity: To inculcate feelings of unity amongst different communities, classes and religions, collective programmes necessary. Casteism, communalism linguism and regionism to be forsaken.

Inter-caste and Inter-state Marriages: To be encouraged and recognised but no social movement to be undertaken for them.

Economic Unity: Removal of prevailing economic inequalities.

National Languages: No imposition of Hindi on non-Hindi regions, to prepare non-Hindi people by intelligent persuasion.

Education: Education a powerful means of national integration. To encourage national integration by intelligent organisation of curriculum teaching, cultural activities, schools organisation, appointment of teachers, distribution of educational facilities and composition of text books.

Exercises

1. Discuss the role of education for the national and emotional integration of India.
2. Enumerate the various tendencies working against the national and emotional integration in India and explain how they can be controlled.

Chapter 44

The Problem of Student Unrest

To-day in the different educational institutions of our country whether they are high schools, intermediate colleges, universities, vocational or general degree colleges, movements by students in one form or the other have become the common feature of the day. So far no satisfactory steps have been taken by our educationists, administrators, experts and specialists on educational policy to overcome this menace. In this chapter we shall discuss the problem of student unrest.

Universal Student Unrest

In fact, student unrest is pervading throughout the whole world. The young generation, in the various contexts of life, thinks it desirable to humiliate their elders by their unrestrained, immoral and unworthy behaviour. Not only the general public but the governments of many states in our country have been appeasing the students through some rules and regulations. The situation had deteriorated so much that the use of unfair means in the examinations, intimidating the invigilators by show of force in the examination hall, looting of shop-keepers on the road, destruction of shops, houses and cinema houses in resentment or acts of arson, disrespect to their teachers, forcing the Vice-Chancellors, teachers or authorities to accept their demand through gheraos, etc. have become common occurrences. The problem before us is to understand the reasons for such a state of affairs and find ways of improving this unfortunate situation.

Efforts by the Government to Assess the Problem

The unruly behaviour of the students has agitated the Government and the concerned authorities. In fact, the Government is more concerned about their habit of destruction. The policy of violence will not bring any reforms. So the Government has set up various committees to look into the problems of the students.

Suggestions of Kothari Commission

In the opinion of the Kothari Commission of 1966, the responsibility of students indiscipline is not one-sided but multi-sided. Evidently, we cannot achieve any solution to this problem unless parents, guardians, teachers, political parties, State Governments and students, all try to understand their responsibilities and perform their duties accordingly. In fact, we should try to remove all those shortcomings and defects in our educational programme which give rise to student unrest. The standard of student-services should be improved. In the various education institutions, the teachers, students and administrators should move towards harmonious co-existance. Kothari Commission has held our educational system, too, responsible for student-unrest because so far it lacks adequate provisions for student-welfare. We should give priority to remove this short-coming. In the opinion of the commission, student-services should be recognised as integral part of education. Some important services which are neccessary from the point of view of student welfare are metnioned below:—

1. *Health Service*: Health services for students should be established in all educational centres.

2. *Guidance and Counselling*: The students need guidance and counselling regarding various courses. Hence there should be counselling bureaus at every educational centre.

3. *Orientation of New Students*: In the beginning of the session, new students are admitted in every university or college. Some programmes should be organised for the adjustment of these new students. Every effort should be made to seek the co-operation of senior students in such programmes. Full information regarding their boarding and lodging, place and timings of their classes, amount of fees to be deposited by them and various rules and regulations of the university or college should be given to the new students.

4. *Student-Union*: The student-union has become an important organisation for the students. It is necessary, therefore, that qualities of restraint, discipline and creativity are developed in students through it.

5. *Hostel*: Proper arrangement of hostels should be made in every college and university. Fulfilment of minimum requirements of their lodging and boarding is necessary.

Trigun Sen Committee

In 1965-67, the Indian Government organised a committee under the chairmanship of Dr. Trigun Sen to suggest some measures for student-welfare. The committee gave the following suggestions:—

1. Students should be included in various programmes of universities and colleges.
2. Small hostels instead of big hostels should be established and 50 to 60 students should be kept in each hostel.
3. Teachers of good ability and character should be appointed in universities. For this, special method of selection should be evolved.
4. A consulting-centre should be established at each university in order to help the students.
5. Political parties should not interfere in any way in the affairs of the universities or colleges.
6. Education should be vocationalised, that is, a student should find himself capable of joining some specific vocation after his education .

Meeting of Student Representatives in 1969

Education Ministry of India and University Grants Commission jointly organised a meeting of student representatives from 23 to 25 May, 1969. The deliberations of this meeting made it clear that the students want the following things for their welfare:—

1. Their inclusion in the various programmes of the University.
2. Reforms in courses and examinations.
3. Correlation of education with employment.
4. The membership of N.C.C. should be optional.
5. There should be a student-union in each university.

Gajendra Gadkar Committee 1971

In June 1969, the University Grants Commission appointed a committee under the chairmanship of Dr. P.B. Gajendra Gadkar, Vice Chancellor of Bombay University. The Committee submitted a report in 1971, the main recommendations of which are as follows:—

1. Students should be given representation on the various committees of a university.
2. Admission policy should have the recognition of the public.
3. It will not be proper to include students in the academic council of the Univeristy as they are not mature enough for consultation on academic matters.
4. There should be a student-union in each university.
5. There should be proper arrangement for cultural and social activities in each hostel.
6. There should not be more than 30 colleges affiliated to a universtiy.
7. Some autonomous colleges should be established in different regions in order to relieve the university from the pressure of affiliated colleges.

Causes of Student Unrest

We are indicating below some main causes of student unrest:—

1. Defective Education System

The present education system does not fulfil its proposed aims and nor does it give the students any practical skill which can make them capable of taking up any job after their education. As a result, the students do not find themselves capable of fending for themselves. Passing of examination has become the sole aim of present education.

2. Aimless Life and Uncertain Future

The present education does not give the student any such qualifications which may assure to them a certain future. Now-a-days, there is great unemployment in our country. The report of the Employment Directorate tells us that during 1965 and 1970, the number of unemployed persons has doubled. During 1970 and 1972 it was one and a half times. In 1965, the number of educated unemployed was about 850,000[1]. According to the Director of Employment and Training, in 1972, the number of unemployed had risen upto 2,500,000[2]. This situation makes it clear that unemployment in the country is on the increase. The young generation is the victim of this unemployment. Consequently, student unrest and indiscipline has touched it peak.

3. Economic Difficulties

Our economic difficulties have become so complex that we do not know as to what will be the economic situation in the future. Most of our students come from families that are economically poor. Such families cannot easily give higher education to their children. Sixty per cent of our students generally do not get education after high school. Out of the remaining, 20 per cent students who go to colleges or university, come from middle class families and 20 per cent

---

1. Dr. Sushila Mehta—"Student violence", Oxford and Y.B.H. Publishing Co. 1972 pp. 133.
2. Directorate of Employment and Training, Govt. of India, August 1972.

from upper class families. The present higher education has become so expensive that the students find it difficult to bear this burden. So it is natural for students to agitate.

4. Excessive Number of Students in the Class

Generally, the number of students in every class is so high that the students and teachers are unable to establish contact with each other, that is, the teachers are unable to understand the difficulties of individual students. Likewise, the personality of the teacher has no impact on the students. There are several colleges and universities where class-rooms, laboratories, libraries and teachers are not available for several departments. In such a situation, unrest and indiscipline amongst students is not surprising.

5. Defective Teaching Methods

The teaching methods in our schools, colleges and universities have become defective. They do not arouse curiosity in the students for new knowledge nor do they increase knowledge. The result is that the students do not find the classes interesting nor are feeling of respect generated towards most of the teachers who have an indifferent attitude. Consequently, students pass the examination by hook or by crook, such as, craming or on the basis of guess papers sold freely in the market or on the basis of copying in the examination-hall by terrorising the invigilators.

6. Indifference of the Family-Members

The influence of the family members on the students is negligible to-day. Parents, elder brothers or sisters pretend to be so busy that they do not hesitate to say that they have no time to attend to the studies of their wards. The results is that the students wander about unbridled and they ruin the conduct and character of others also and thus bring dishonour and anguish to themselves and their family by their indisciplined behaviour. Needless to say that so long as the responsible members of the family do not fulfil their responsibility towards their wards, the indiscipline prevailing amongst students will not end and nor will the unrest and discontent calm down.

7. Unsuitable Teachers

To-day in our schools, colleges and universities, we find many such teachers who have no interest in their teaching work. All concerned persons know it well that in every department of colleges and universities, there are some teachers who do not go to teach in the classes even for a day. They are either engaged in petty politics or in manipulations. Such teachers present a wrong example by their behaviour and conduct. As such, the students coming in contact with such teachers learn nothing but roguery. Besides, many teachers suffer from different types of inferiority complexes. Due to this, some undesirable elements remain inherent in their behaviour and many students who come under their influence are inclined to follow suit.

8. Student-Union

In our various educational centres, the students naturally are eager to organise unions and generally they are provided adequate facilities to do so. But in the process of organisation and elections of these unions, various political parties and teacher-politicians try to serve their vested interests. The interference of the political elements vitiates the nature of the student unions in various ways and generate a sense of indiscipline in the students.

9. Lack of Co-curricular and Creative Activities

The function of an educational centre is not simply to prepare the students for examinations. In fact, the aim of education is to develop the entire personality of the individual harmoniously. This development is not possible only through the curricular teaching. For this, various co-curricular activities such as games, sports, contests, competitions, dramas, music, magazines, collective social service, etc., are necessary because through them the different aspects of the personality of a person manifest themselves and attain the high state of development.

10. Defective Examination System

The examination system is such that the teaching process has become dependent on it. The passing of examination has become the sole aim of education. Due to this examination system, the students have begun to think that there is no need of studying throughout the year and only a little study near the examination time will be sufficient. So rest of the time may be spent recklessly. As a result of this tendency, the students are left with a lot of unoccupied time which they spend in indisciplined activities of various types.

11. Elements of Indiscipline and Anarchy Prevailing in the Society

The elements of indiscipline and anarchy prevailing in the society, in fact are reflected in the indisciplined behaviour of students. Generally, the students may be divided in three categories. The first category consists of those students who are interested in studies and after finishing the studies they become engineers, doctors, administrators and other Civil Servants. The second category is of those students who take admission in colleges and universities simply as a matter of fashion. Such students mostly come from traders, contractors and other business class families. Their aim is not to imbibe the cultural or real nature of learning. They consider the classes as picnic spots. The third category is of the student politicians. They are connected with different political parties and at their instance they indulge in various kinds of indisciplined activities.

The Eighth Five Year Plan is to begin in our country shortly. But targets fixed regarding education in the first seven Five Year Plans could not be achieved. Hence our schools, colleges and universities have not become constructive, cultural and social centres in the real sense. Under such a situation there is little wonder that our younger generation is standing on a cross-road, little knowing in which direction to move. As a result, it is aimless, dissatisfied and misguided. So long as we are not successful in giving it a right direction, it will continue to remain discontented and indisciplined.

Remedy for Student Unrest

Amongst many educational problems, the problem of removing students-unrest is one of the main ones. Experts are deliberating about the measures that should be adopted for effecting necessary improvements in the system of education and for enabling the students to become capable of joining some useful vocation after their education is complete and thus to save them from falling victims to different political propaganda and misguided persons. We should take some such steps which may discourage the youth from taking only higher education. This does not mean that we do not want to educate our young men and women worthy of higher education. In fact, we want to develop intellegent and worthy young men and women who will provide leadership in different walks of life. Along with it, some such vocational programmes have also to be organised in which some willing but less brilliant students during their education or after their education, may takc admission and earn their living after learning useful skills in them.

It will be a matter of great concern if the society does not fulfil the above mentioned responsibilities. It is a matter of regret that many of our youngmen want to go abroad after their higher education for the sake of higher emoluments and higher standard of living. Who is responsible for this state of affairs? We have mentioned in the preceeding pages that the different wings of society are dissatisfied with the behaviour of students. Who is to be blamed for this? We can unhesitatingly say that our social structure, educational system and politics all put together are responsible for this. Hence all concerned will have to make necessary efforts to solve the problems of students.

Summary

Student-unrest ordinary feature in educational centres. Student-unrest universal. Painful behaviour and activities demonstrated by our students.

Effort of the Government to Assess the Situation: **Suggestions of Kothari Commission:— Responsibility of student unrest on several persons. Hence, the co-operation of teachers, authorities, government, general public and students, desirable.**

Health services, guidance and counselling, orientation of new students, student-unions, hostels.

Trigun Sen Committee: **Participation of students in various activities, small hostels to be established, appointment of able teachers, advisory centres, no interference by political parties, education vocation based.**

Meeting of Student Respresentatives in 1969: **Students want to be included in various programmes, improvement in curriculum. Education to be related to employment, membership of N.C.C. to be optional, student union in every university.**

Gajendra Gadkar Committee: **Representation to students, change in admission policy, more than 30 colleges to be affiliated to one university; establishment of autonomous colleges.**

Cause of Student-Unrest: **Defective education system, aimless life and uncertain future, economic difficulties, excessive number of students in the classes, defective methods of teaching, indifference of family members, indifferent teachers, students' union, lack of constructive co-curricular activities, defective examination system, indiscipline prevailing in society.**

Remedy for Student-Unrest: **Only a few students to be given higher education, small vocational programmes to be started so that willing students may take advantage of the same. For this the co-operation of government education centres and different units of society necessary.**

Exercises

1. Describe the nature and causes of students unrest in the country and give suggestions for its remedy.
2. What are the factors mainly responsible for the student unrest in India? Describe the evil effects of this unrest. What remedies will you suggest for removing these evil effects?

Chapter 45

The Problem of Text Books

The instinct of acquisition is innate in man. We find that even small children accumulate some such things which they like to regard as their own. Man has sublimated this instinct. Consequently, we have treasures in the form of many symbols of civilization and culture. Books are also a part of these treasures. Man wants to express his experience and knowledge in writing for the benefit of others. So he has produced books. Text-books are prepared by selecting some materials from books having original and permanent value. Various text-books are prepared for different subjects for various levels of education. To-day text-books have special importance.

Utility of Text-Books

Some persons do not believe in the utility of text-books. However, we shall have to accept their importance. Neither the teacher can take the place of the text-book nor can the text-book replace the teacher. Both have their own importance. Text-books prescribe the limit of knowledge to be given to the students. There is always the fear of a teacher going astray while imparting knowledge in the absence of a text-book. Through text-books it is possible to place facts and informations before the students in a systematic manner. The students revise the taught subject matter with the help of text-books.

History of Text-Books

The history of text-books in our country is not very old. In the ancient and middle ages some text-books were prepared on leaves of palm trees or copper-plates. After the invention of paper, manuscripts were prepared on paper. The number of such manuscripts was so limited that an ordinary student could hardly have any approach to them. Therefore, oral education was very much in vogue. After the establishment of the rule of the East India Company in India, Calcutta Education Press was started in Calcutta in 1824. Thus printing of books was begun in this country. In 1854, the recommendation for the publication of books was made in the Wood's Despatch. As a result, many books in English, Persian and Sanskrit were published. But no Education Commission or education committee ever gave any concrete suggestion for improvement of text-books. We do not find any concrete suggestion for improvement in text-books in the reports of Indian Education Commission, 1882, Calcutta University Commission of 1917-1918, Hartog Committee of 1929 and Wood Abbot Report of 1936-37. After 1910, the Indian leaders paid some attention to education. But except for the formation of education policy, they could not pay any attention to other details regarding education.

In 1937, when the Congress Ministries were formed in some States under the Government of Indian Act, 1935, our national leaders turned their attention to text-books. In 1937-38, the first Acharya Narendra Dev Committee, U.P., gave suggestions for the improvement of books. It recommended that text books should be rewritten according to new needs and should be edited by a board constituted by the provincial government and further that books should be prepared by different authors.

In January, 1943, a meeting of Cultural Advisory Board was held and it was suggested that once selected they should be retained at least for three years. The Board also suggested that the books should be made available at reasonable prices and the publishers should not try to exploit the students Books should be published by good publishers alone and good authors should be encouraged to write books.

In 1953, the second Acharya Narendra Dev Committee, U.P., again considered the issue of text-book and gave the following suggestions for its improvement:—

1. The headmaster and the teachers alone should have a right to select text-books.
2. Any selected text-book should be retained at least for three years.
3. The government should make arrangement of good books.
4. Sufficient time should be given to authors for writing books.
5. Provision should be made to give reward to authors of good books.
6. The responsibility of publishing books should not be taken by the government.

In 1952-53 the Mudaliar Commission condemned the prevailing low standard of text-books and emphasised the need for their improvement.

In 1954, an international group under the Ford Foundation studied the standard of some text-books current in India. This group suggested that the Indian Government should prescribe some rules for composition of books and the publishers and writers should prepare books according to those rules. But the government should not take the responsibility of their publication upon itself.

In 1964-66 the Kothari Commission considered the issue of text-books. The Commission had been of the opinion that subject experts do not take interest in writing text-books. The concerned authorities behave dishonestly in the selection and approval of books. The Commission said that there was a need of research in the field of text-books. The Commission has suggested that text-books should be published by the education department of the Government.

The General Defects of Modern Text-Books

1. The books are not prepared according to the standard of students at different level. The authorised publishers are mainly guided by the aim of earning money.
2. The printing and get-up of the books is not according to the desired standard. Often rough paper is used for books. They are not properly bound.
3. The prevailing text-books present the knowledge not in the context of utility of the subject in life but in an unconnected form which makes the subject uninteresting.
4. Most of the authors do not care for the needs of the students while preparing the text-books. So the text-books are not related to the needs of the students.
5. The prevailing text-books do not encourage the feeling of national integration and international understanding.
6. In the composition of text-books, attention is not paid to the methods of teaching. Hence the teachers fail to take any advantage from them.
7. Text-books lack in necessary pictures, diagrams and suitable illustrations. So they are generally below the mark.
8. Generally, there are serious mistakes of printing and language in the text books, because they are prepared in a hurry.

Some Suggestions for Improvement of Text-Books

1. Some text-books should certainly be prepared by the education department of the government. Their standard should be high in all respects so that other publishers may prepare suitable text-books of the standard of the text-books published by the government.
2. The text-books should have suitable pictures, diagrams and illustrations in order that they may seem interesting to the students.

3. The text-books on different subjects should not be limited. Six or seven text-books of each subject should be prepared so that headmasters and teachers may have full freedom of selecting the best book.
4. Pressure should not be exerted on schools authorities and teachers in the selection of books.
5. The text-books should not cast any reflection on any society, class, community or religion. They should help in developing the feeling of national integration and international understanding.
6. Text-books should be prepared by subject experts. The authors should be given rewards for good books.
7. At the national level, good authors should be invited to write text-books for different levels of education.
8. The Central and State governments should work together for preparation of suitable text-books.
9. Some standard foreign text-books should be translated into Indian languages. It will facilitate availability of suitable text-books. This policy should be particularly followed for scientific and technical subjects.
10. The correction of text-books should be a continuous process and for this a committee should be permanently appointed.
11. There should be a government agency for the composition and publication of text-books in every State. This agency should publish some standard text-books of all subjects, but other publishers should also be free to publish good text-books on all subjects.

Experts have emphasised the necessity of nationalization of text-books.

The Necessity of Nationalization of Text-Books

1. We have declared education free and compulsory for children upto 14 years of age according to our Constitution. Although so far we are far behind in achieving this goal, yet efforts have started in this direction. As a result, the number of students at

different levels in every State has increased enormously. So the need of different text-books for different levels of education and for different classes has arisen. Taking advantage of this situation, many publishers and writers are engaged in preparing low-standard books for quick profits. It is the responsibility of the government to put a stop to this trend. So the government should take full liability of publishing suitable text-books for different classes.

2. Basic education has been recognised as the general national policy for primary education for the entire country. But this aim is not being achieved mainly for want of suitable text-books, although there are some other reasons also for its failure. Of course, some books related to basic education have been published by the government. But more efforts are needed in this direction. This is possible only through the policy of nationalization of books.
3. In order to raise the standard of text-books, the Indian Government is encouraging research in the field of text-books. But publishers cannot be compelled to accept the good results of this research. It is necessary, therefore that the Central Government or State Government should undertake the responsibility of composition of good text-books. So the nationalisation of text-books is necessary.
4. It is more convenient for the government to prepare ideal text-books because it has got all the necessary resources. On the basis of these ideals books, other publishers and writers will try to prepare good text-books. Evidently, nationalization of text-books will be useful.
5. Text-books are a good means for developing feelings of national integration and international understanding in the future citizens. This source can be suitably utilised only under the control of government, otherwise people of different classes, communities, castes and

religions may use this source for serving their vested interest. So nationalization of text-books appears to be necessary for our healthy national development.

6. Nationalization will make good books available to students at more reasonable prices. It will give some relief to the guardians, because they can ill-afford to pay high prices for books prepared by private publishers.
7. Nationalization of text-books will enable the government to give books free to poor students more easily. This will help poor students.
8. The publishers do not like to publish books on some optional subjects because the number of students in those subjects is limited and there are low profits in their publication. So if some publisher brings out such books, he produces them in a careless manner. Through nationalization good books will be made available even in optional subjects, as the aim of the government will be to render service in the field rather than to earn money.
9. Nationalization will bring uniformity in publication whereas the publications by different publishers lack this. The nationalization of books will help the teachers in understanding the prescribed courses soon. The books of other publishers some times make it difficult for the teachers to understand the prescribed courses.
10. The nationalization of text-books will give some income also to the government. This additional income may be utilised by the government for educational development. It is evident now that the nationalization of text-books has several advantages.

Nationalization of Text-Books in some States of India

Different States have adopted different policies regarding nationalization of text-books. There is in some States complete opposition against nationalization of text-books, and in some there is partial nationalization and some have nationalized text-books completely.

1. *Andhra Pradesh*: All the books upto primary stage have been nationalized.
2. *Tamilnadu*: Books were nationalized here but the distribution of books was placed in the hands of book-sellers.
3. *Kerala*: Books were nationalized in this State also. But in 1958-59 a committee was organised to enquire if the nationalisation has not been used for propagating communistic ideas. The committee in the report revealed that such an effort was made through nationalization of text-books. So the nationalization of books was stopped there.
4. *Orissa, Maharashtra and Gujarat*: No significant efforts have been made for nationalization of text-books in these States.
5. *Bihar*: In this State, school books have been completely nationalized. The profit earned through sale of books is used for the welfare of poor students.
6. *Punjab*: School books have been completely nationalized in this State.
7. *Uttar Pradesh*: All the books upto junior high school have been nationalised.
8. *Rajasthan*: A Board has been established for nationalization of school books. Deputy Secretary of Education Department, a member of Revenue Board, Secretary of Finance, Director of Education, an officer of Civil services or an officer of the rank of Director of Education are the members of this Board. The return from the nationalization of books is very good and for this a Reviewer Board and High Power Committee have been established. Their establishment has facilitated the work of nationalization. The Reviewer Board consists of renowned educationists as members. The members of High Power Committee are a judge of High Court, a member of Rajasthan Service Commission and the Chairman of Nationalization Board. The decision of Reviewer Board is sent to the High Power Committee for approval.

Problem Arising from the Nationalization of Text-Books

The aims with which text-books have been nationalized in the whole country, are not being achieved. Some problems have arisen due to nationalization. Some of them are:—

1. *Propagation of Political Views*: There are several political parties in our country. The party which will be in power in the state is likely to start propagating its political ideology through the nationalization of books. This is exactly what happened in Kerala. When communists came into power there, they began to propagate their views through text-books. Similarly, the B.J.P. Government in U.P. during 1991 and 1992, began to emphasize the inclusion of some basic elements of ancient Indian culture in the preparation of school text-books. This action of the B.J.P. Govt. has been criticised by many other political parties in the country which stand for appeasement of certain groups of people for ensuring their votes during election days. Thus it is clear that any political party can try to propagate its political ideology through nationalization. This will hamper free thinking and democracy will be jeopardised.

2. *Disappearance of Teacher's Freedom*: Nationalization forces the teacher to teach approved text-books only. Before nationalization, the teacher was free to select one book out of three or four published text-books. But due to nationalization he does not have any such freedom. Thus he faces absence of inspiration for idependent thinking. To meet this requirement Kothari Commission has suggested that even under nationalization, three or four books should be published on one subject and the teacher should be free to select one out of them.

3. *Absence of Different Social View-points*: Through text-books we can carry the culture of the society to the students. In fact, they are the best source to fulfil this aim. But under nationalization, books are written only by a few selected persons and, therefore, different social view points are not included in them and our culture is presented to students only partially.

4. *Publishing of Books Not in Time*: It has found many times that under nationalization, the text-books are published long after the beginning of the session because in the process of publication the book has to pass through some kind of red-tapism. This creates a serious hinderance in the study of students.

5. *Lack of Competition among Authors*: Good books are prepared through competitions. Before nationalization, many writers engaged themselves in writing books. They tried to surpass each other in excellence. But this competition is not possible now, because only a few selected persons are required to prepare books. Consequently, standard of books is not forthcoming. Several kinds of defects are noticed in them.

6. *Mistakes of Printing and Language*: The Government nationalised the text-books to get rid of mistakes of printing and language in them, because books prepared by different publishers were full of such mistakes. But books prepared under nationalization are not free from such defects.

7. *No Proper Distribution of Text-books*. Under nationalization, too, the government depends on book-sellers for distribution of books. Due to this reason books do not reach the students in time. For this it will be better if co-operative societies for books are organised in schools and books are sent directly to them by the government. The government could also distribute the books through its various offices in the beginning of the session.

8. *No Proper Reduction in Prices of Books*: The private publishers fixed arbitrary prices of books. After nationalization it was hoped that books will be available on reduced prices. But hopes were belied because the government has to depend on private presses for printing of books.

Suggestions for Making Nationalization a Success

1. **At least two years time should be given to the authors for preparing books. The time of six months or one year given till now has been inefficient.**

2. The government should adopt the policy of 'no profit no loss'. Thus, low price books may be made available.
3. The government should obtain paper for books from the mills directly. For pictures and blocks it should organise its own museums. By adopting these measures books may be given to students on a fair price.
4. The government should invite new authors for writing of books. This will bring novelty in the style of books and chances of their becoming more interesting will increase. Emphasis should be laid on the inclusion of pictures, diagrams and suitable illustrations for making the books interesting.
5. The government should establish research-centres for improving the art of composition of books. The findings of these research centres should form the basis for writing books.
6. The government should have its own press for publication of books so that books may be printed at reasonable cost.
7. Good authors should be invited for writing books. Proper remuneration and rewards should be given to encourage them.
8. The teacher should be given some freedom in the selection of books. For this at least three books should be published on one subject.
9. Approved text-books should not be changed soon. They should be allowed to continue at least for five years.

Summary

Books a part of our culture. Special importance of text-books.

Utility of Text-Books: Indicator to teachers regarding prescribed course, facts and informations in a methodical form, help students in their studies.

History of Text-Books: Handwritten books on copper-plates in ancient and middle ages, some hand-written books on paper after the invention of paper. Printing of books in India since 1824. After the Wood's Despatch of 1854, books in English, Persian and Sanskrit were published. Emphasis of the publication of suitable text-books of Acharya Narendra Dev Committees, 1937 and 1953. Mudaliar Commission in 1952-53 and Kothari Commission in 1966.

General Defects of Text-Books To-day: Not according to the needs of students, earning money main aim in their publication, rough paper used, get-up of books not attractive, knowledge is presented in a unconnected form, no stress on national integration and international understanding. No proper attention to methods of teaching, absence of necessary pictures and suitable illustrations. Mistakes of printing and language.

Suggestion For Improvement in Text Books: The government should prepare some books as ideal, contain suitable pictures and illustrations, 5 or 6 books on every subjects, teachers should be free to select one out of them, should foster national integration and international understanding, writing by able persons, good authors to be rewarded, the Central and State Governments should work together to improve quality of books. Translation of standard foreign books into Indian languages. Committee for suggesting improvements, publication of books by government, but freedom to other publishers also for publication.

Necessity of Nationalization of Text-Books: To discourage worthless publishers and authors, nationalization necessary, good books at low price possible, help to poor students possible, good books even in optional subjects may be published, uniformity in books.

Nationalization in some Indian States: In Andhra Pradesh, Tamilnadu, Kerala, Bihar, Punjab, Uttar Pradesh and Rajasthan, nationalization to great extent. Success in some and failure in other States.

Problems Arising out of Nationalization of Text-Books: Propagation of political ideology, disappearance of teachers' freedom, absence of different social viewpoints, publication not in time, lack of competition between authors, mistakes of printing and language, no proper distribution of books, no reduction in the price of books.

Some Suggestions for Making Nationalization a Success: Atleast two years time for writing a text-book, policy of 'no profit no loss' to be auopted, reduction in prices of books, encouragement to new authors, suitable pictures and diagrams, establishment of research centres, Government should have its own press, freedom to teachers in the selection of books, at least three or four books on one subject.

Exercises

1. Analysing the utility of text-books, point out the defects in prevailing text-books in India.
2. Give some suggestions for improvement in the current text-books in India.
3. Why is nationalization of text-books necessary? Point out the problems arising from nationalization of text-books in India.

Chapter 46

Public Schools in India

The General Nature

Some people may think that the Public Schools are those educational institutions which have been established with public help in different regions and which provide educational facilities for all children without any distinction of caste, class, colour, community or belief. The name of these schools gives also the impression that they are run on democratic principles and they will be providing better facilities of education to common and poor children in comparison to other schools and colleges. But in reality, these schools are just the opposite to these pre-suppositions.

These schools have been established according to the whims of the founders at selected places without any consideration of the suitability of the place. Generally, these schools have been established by big industrialists and wealthy people and now they are run by charging high tution fees and help by the founders from time to time. Rich people donate some money to such schools every year to lessen their burden of income-tax. There is no connection of local or regional public in their organisation. These schools are run contrary to democratic principles. Generally children of rich people only can take admission in these schools. The fees and other expenses charged in these schools are so high that children of average

or poor families cannot even imagine being able to afford admission in these schools. Sometimes, gifted children of average families are able to get admission in these schools after receiving help from the Government or scholarships from big industrialists. But they become victims of inferiority complex and ill-will among children of wealthy families. Consequently, the development of their personality becomes stunted.

Public Schools of U.K.

Public schools in India have been established on the pattern of the public schools of U.K. In U.K. this tradition may be said to have started with the establishment of the oldest public schools in the later part of the fourteenth century. Other schools of the type were established in the fifteenth/sixteenth centuries. In the beginning, the form of these schools was almost like other schools. The only difference was that these schools were run without any Government help. Their main aim was to prepare Christian gentlemen of desirable behaviour for socal, religious and political leadership in future life. The following are some oldest public schools in U.K:-

Winchester	—	1382 A.D.
Eaton	—	1441 "
St. Paul	—	1510 "
Shewsberry	—	1552 "
Westminster	—	1560 "
Merchant Taylors	—	1561 "
Rugby	—	1567 "
Harrow	—	1571 "
Charter House	—	1611 "

Although the earlier form of public schools of U.K was like that of other average schools, but at that time also, they had their own peculiarities. Firstly, the place of teachers and headmasters of these schools in some sense was very much like the veteran teachers of the ancient Indian Ashrams and Gurukuls. They had sufficient freedom in formulating their educational programmes and other allied provisions. They were responsible for all arrangements concerning education. They enjoyed special respect in society.

Another characteristic of these schools was that special emphasis was laid on the formation of character. Almost all the students were residential students and efforts were made to make them disciplined and develop qualities like tolerance, co-operation, dutifulness, partiotism and religious faith etc.

Tradition of Public Schools of U.K.

New traditions of public schools originated in the beginning of the nineth century. By that time many other schools on the pattern of nine big schools described earlier had been established. The tradition upto that time was that the schools which had satisfactory provisions of education, resident students, good results and those schools whose graduates could get admission in Oxford and Cambridge Universities for further studies, were called Public Schools. Later on, the tendency developed that those schools, the headmasters of which were nominated as members of Headmasters' Conference were called Public Schools.

These schools have their own characteristics of arrangement and educational standard. Firstly, the tuition-fee and other expenses in the schools have been raised so high that children of average and low-income families find it difficult to bear the expenses. Secondly, for admission, preference is given to those students whose parents have been the students of these schools. Thirdly, the standard of education has been raised and students are kept in preparatory schools attached to them before admission. Thus, three or four years and money of students are wasted.

The present number of such public schools in U.K. is about 80 or so. These schools have been praised in books written from time to time. These schools have been admired even outside Europe and the famous leaders in the foreign countries have been connected with these schools in one way or the other. Shri Jawahar Lal Nehru of India was student of Harrow

School. The boys in these schools are developed in a particular pattern by keeping them in hostels so that they become accustomed to behave according to the ideals of the school. The controlled and regulated life of hostels affects the health and mode of behaviour of the students. Special emphasis is laid on food, study, rest, games at a fixed time. During hostel life, the students develop their talents in different activities, to move ahead of others, winning positions and getting respect from their class-fellows and affection and praise from teachers. This method helps them in future life. Being away from the family, they compensate feelings by getting sentimental satisfaction from their specific-achievements.

Criticism of Public Schools

With the evolution of progressive educational thought in U.K the tradition of public schools has been criticised. Although some changes have been made in the programmes of new public schools but their traditions have been far behind the progressive thought in the field of education. A supporter of progressive thought, L.B.Pekin has remarked that "there is nothing praisworthy in the organisation of public schools. Whatever has been written in the appreciation of these schools, has been written only because it has been considered honourable."

Some unsocial features have come to light regarding the public schools. Some persons brought honour to these schools by getting great success, honour and high posts and by their contribution in the expansion of British empire; but in the background there was their failure in the social field due to emotional frustrations. The inhuman behaviour and cruelty demonstrated by those people for the expansion of imperialsim, gives the idea that slavery, unsociability, corporal punishments and mental complexes experienced during the hostel life in these schools have created in them great hatred for man. The atmosphere in several public schools has been found to be undeveloped, unsocial narrow and vicious in many respects.

Due to the country-wide criticism of public schools, the

need to bring improvement in them was felt. The education Act (Butler Act) of 1944 laid stress on bringing improvement in public schools and the Flemming Report published in the same year also criticised public schools and suggested some measures for their improvement. For improvement it was suggested that admission in these schools should be open also to middle class children who cannot study in them due to paucity of funds. It was further suggested that at least 25 per cent of the total strength of students should be of such students who lack material resources. The organisers of public schools themselves have tried to bring improvements in them after ascertaining their shortcomings. But even now they lack the desired improvements.

When the British empire established itself firmly in India, the wealthy in India began to send their children to England for study. These children were generally sent to public schools. But they had to face great difficulty due to the different educational standard and a totally different life style. The children of some Rajas, Maharajas and Taluqdars and other rich people did not even get admission there. So some princes and rich people thought of establishing public schools in India on the pattern of British public schools. For this purpose, they donated money generously. For the organisation of these public schools, headmasters from England on high salaries were appointed. Thus, the beginning of establishing public schools in India was made. As in England, the public schools here, too, are expensive and for rich people only. In the beginning, public schools started in India were called Chiefs' College.

The famous advocate of Calcutta, S.R.Das, was the first to think of establishing a public school in India. He wanted that children of all classes of society should be admitted in this public school. For this purpose, in 1929, he established Indian Public School Society and collected 14 lakh rupees. But due to his death, the plan could not be implemented. However, it was due to his influence that Doon Public School was established in 1935.

In India, Chiefs' Colleges on the pattern of Public schools of England were giving education to the children of princes,

Rajas, Maharajas, Taluqdars and wealthy people at several places. These colleges were also given government grants. In 1930, in the wake of freedom struggle, a protest was voiced as to why the public schools, i.e., Chiefs' Colleges, be given any grant from the public-exchequer when those schools did not admit the children of common people. Consequently the government was forced to stop the grant. As a result, the Chiefs' Colleges had to face financial difficulties. In 1939, they called a conference in Simla. It was decided there that the Chiefs' Colleges be called public schools in future. It was also decided to incorporate Indian culture in the educational system and to establish a body called Indian Public School Association. In 1939, a meeting of the Headmasters of Public Schools was held in Gwalior. Indian Public School Conference was organised in this meeting and the headmasters of public schools became the members of this conference. The Education Commissioner of the Indian Government, Sir John Sargeant was present in both the meetings held in Simla and Gwalior. He considered the establishment and development of public schools in India important. He stressed the need of developing public schools in India for the development of qualities of leadership in Indian children because he thought that India had to run her own administration some day.

It may be remembered here that even after the establishment of Indian Public School Conference many Chiefs' Colleges did not like to become its members. Daily College, Indore; Admission College, Lahore; Bhonsla Military School, Poona; Rajkumar College, Rajkot declared themselves as public schools. These schools wanted to gain the support of the leaders of Indian National Congress. The headmaster, Mr. Smith of Rajkumar College Raipur invited Gandhiji to his school. But Gandhiji did not agree with the policy of maintaining public schools. So he did not accept the invitation. Even Mr. Smith continued to have faith in the utility of public schools and he continued to remain active to get the support of other leaders. He believed that many leaders did not agree with the Basic Education of Mahatma Gandhi. So he thought that he would get the support of such leaders.

It has been stated earlier that most of the Chiefs' Colleges did not accept the membership of Indian Public Schools Conference. The Principal of Mayo College, Ajmer, Mr. Sto expressed the opinion that his college belonged to a special category and hence he would not bring his college within the orbit of other public schools. Other colleges too, had the same notion. In 1940, a meeting of headmaster of Public Schools was held in Raipur. In that meeting the conditions for membership of the Indian Public Conference were determined and it was also decided that the study of Indian languages should be made compulsory for public school students. Shortly after this, the public schools of Delhi, Ajmer and Bikaner became the members of the Conference. After the recognition of Public School Conference in this way, more public schools were opened. Among them, the Yadevendra Public School of Patiala (1948), Pilani Birla School (1944), Maharani Gayatri Devi School of Jaipur (1943), and Birla Vidya Mandir of Nainital (1947) are worth-mentioning. The Education Ministry of the Government of India took over the administration of Lawrance School of Sanavar and Lawrance School of Lovedale from the Defence Ministry, but handed it over to Committees formed in 1953.

Thus, public schools continued to develop in India. But after the attainment of freedom in 1947 it looked as if the future of public schools in India was dark because they began to be considered as an obstacle in the development of the growth of democratic system in the country. They were considered as symbols of British Empire and foreign culture. The continuance of English as medium of instruction and neglect of Indian culture in these schools became a matter of concern for everyone. But some influential supporters of English mode of living and culture lent support to public schools. As a result, public schools continue to exist even to-day.

In 1952-53, the Mudaliar Commission studied the working of public schools and recommended to continue them although it gave several suggestions for improvement. In the opinion of the Commission, the public schools develop qualities of leadership. So it is better to improve them rather than to close them. This recommendation of the Mudaliar Commission has given them much support. Moreover several Indian leaders demanded special place for English in the educational system for the sake of International understanding. Such developments gave great encouragement to public schools. Many public schools were opened at various places and they are favoured even today by the rich and ambitions persons who take pride in sending their children to these schools.

The Kothari Commission of 1964-66 has recommended the abolition of public schools. In the opinion of the commission, it is not fair to maintain public schools in the democratic system of India. Public schools point out to a special class-system. But those who rule the country want to maintain them. So long as the President, the Prime-Minister, Ministers, Governors and other administrators do not send their children to average schools no improvement is possible in the condition of the average schools. Therefore, the Kothari Commission has recommended that this undemocratic tradition of public schools be abolished.

Some Famous Public Schools of India

At present there are more than sixty public schools in India. Some military schools established in India may be counted as public schools. It is to be remembered that only fifty percent of public schools have accepted the membership of Indian Public School Conference. Some missionary schools in the different parts of the country also work on the pattern of public schools. Some notable public schools are as under:-

(1) Sindia School, Gwalior, (2) Daily School, Indore, (3) Rajkumar College, Rajkot, (4) Raj Kumar College, Raipur, (5) Doon School, Dehradun, (6) Birla Vidya Mandir, Nainital, (7) Modern School, Delhi, (8) Yadevendra Public School, Patiala, (9) Birla Public School, Pilani, (10) Mayo College, Ajmer, (11) Sardul Public School, Bikaner, (12) Maharani Gayatri Devi Girls Public School, Jaipur, (13) Hyderabad Public School,

Hyderabad, (14) Sivaji Preparatory Military School, Poona, (15) Lawrance School, Lovedale, (16) Vikas Vidyalaya, Ranchi. (17) Lawrance School, Sanavar.

The General Nature of Public Schools

In accordance with the rules of the public school, every student has to live compulsorily in the school hostel. During the six working days of the week, there is teaching work for six hours daily and the rest of the time is to be spent by the students in the hostel or in co-curricular activities. Whether the student is in the school or hostel or engaged in co-curricular activities, he remains under the supervision of school authorities all the time. The school determines the daily programme of 24 hours for the student. Generally, the student has to get up early in the morning and he has to take part in one activity or the other till eight or nine o'clock at night. The time for bath, food, sleep, and study, etc., is fixed.

Mathematics, languages, literature, history, geography and science are the main subjects of study. Commerce and agricultural subjects are not encouraged. Besides study, facilities are provided in sports like swimming, horse-riding, wrestling, gymnastics, and for hobbies like photography, crafts and art, etc. The supervision and control of teachers can be seen in all the activities. The students of higher classes work as monitors or prefects for junior classes. Like the teacher, the students of higher classes keep control on co-curricular activities of junior classes. But this control is exercised according to a systematic plan under the supervision of a teacher. The feeling of co-operation, responsibility and competition is developed in the students. For this, activities like excursions, scouting and volunteer-corps are organised. It is expected of the students that they will follow their teachers. Thus, the responsibility of the teacher is very much increased. The students are divided into several groups. These groups are called 'houses'. The leadership of the 'house' is entrusted to students. Thus qualities of leadership are inculcated in them. The atmosphere of the house is like that of a family.

The warden of the hostel behaves like a father. Thus the atmosphere of the house is cordial.

The public schools, generally possess all necessary resources and equipments. A big school building which includes different class-rooms for different subjects, big hall, library, laboratory, hostel, play-ground and necessary material for cultural activities are all available there. In order to maintain their autonomy, the public schools do not take any government help. The headmasters and teachers are paid high salary. The arrangement for their boarding and lodging is generally made by the public school. Thus, the standard of the teachers is generally high. The headmaster has got full authority to admit or to remove any student from the school. He is also authorised to appoint or promote teachers. Thus, the atmosphere of a public school is quite different from that of an average school. The public schools charge very high fees from the students in order to meet their expenditure. The average annual expenditure of a student in public school is nearly fifteen to twenty thousand rupees. Evidently, the children of common people cannot study there.

Merits of Public Schools

Some people have praised the public schools very much. According to them qualities of co-operation, leadership and shouldering responsibility are developed in the student studying in these schools. In the free atmosphere of public schools, the students get opportunities for the development of personality, because the students are not prepared for the examinations alone. The aim of education there is the development of personality. All kinds of necessary resources are available there. The teachers and students do not face any difficulty in their work. The condition of ordinary secondary schools in our country is not good. They face scarcities in many ways. So, in a way, public schools are ideal for them. Because of this, any school showing better performance compares itself to a public schools.

Demerits of Public Schools

The public school has also been much criticised. Some people are of the opinion that the public school is against democratic view-point. Children of ordinary people do not get admission in these schools because they are so expensive that children of only the wealthy businessman or high officials of government, ministers and other administrators can study in them. These people consider it against their dignity to send their children to ordinary schools. Thus, the children of a special class study in public schools whether they are capable or incapable. They lead their life in an atmosphere of luxury and affluence. This school life leaves a peculiar impression on their personality. They become accustomed to a luxurious and affluent life even after leaving the school. Consequently, tendency of exploitation develops in them. They will not hesitate to exploit anyone for the satisfaction of their wants in their future life. The children who have studied in public schools consider themselves superior to the children of ordinary people although they may be inferior to them in ability. Thus, undersirable complexes may develop in their personality. The students of public school try to maintain distinction in society because they think that their status is higher than those of others. In the democratic India of to-day where people find it difficult even to get two-square meals a day, the continuation of pubic schools is a mockery of democracy. If during the period of education the children of the present day India are not able to understand the magnitude of poverty in the country and if they are not able to understand the fundamental problems of the country, it will be waste of educational efforts. In that case, through education, we will be making them hypocrites, deceitful, un-Indian and of diffused personality. Needless to say that the public schools are moving in this direction. So in the present Indian society, public schools should not be encouraged and the sooner they are closed the better it is.

Complex Problems Arising from Public Schools

Due to the above demerits, the public schools have created

some complex problems. Some of these are being indicated below:—

1. *Creation of a Special Class*:

We have mentioned earlier that in a public school, the atmosphere is that of luxury and affluence. The students get all sorts of facilities and comforts. Children brought up in such an atmosphere try to get such facilities in future life also and in their efforts they do not care for fair and foul means. In a poor country like India such people will surely exploit others. Whether they are capable or not, they consider themselves superior to others. Thus, the atmosphere of public schools gives rise to such a special class with cannot be reconciled with our democratic system and the social and economic conditions prevailing in the country.

2. *Neglect of the Principle of Equal Opportunity for Development*:

In a democratic system, the principle of equal opportunity for development is recognised. Public schools clearly neglect this principle. Only children of rich people can study there, whereas many able children are deprived of such facilities. Sometimes some children of poor families are sent to study in them by providing scholarships but the percentage of such children is negligible. So to allow public schools, to continue is an insult to democracy.

3. *Public Schools a Cause for the Poor Condition of Schools Meant for the General Public*:

Children of rich people, minister and other influential persons and high officials study in public schools. When their children are able to get educational facilities in well-equipped public schools why should they bother for the education of general public? This is one of the reasons that the condition of the general schools is so miserable. They have neither good buildings nor furniture and other necessary equipments. For these reasons, senior officials and the influential people do not like to send their children to study in general schools. If they are forced to send their children to general schools, they will pay attention towards improving the condition of general schools. It is evident then that so long public schools exist, the condition of general schools will not improve.

4. *Complexity of Language Problem due to the English Medium of Public Schools*:

English is the medium of instruction in the public schools. So the people who have studied in these schools have good command over English. They do not have good command over the mother-tongue. Such people support English for use in future life. Since English is the language of the Government, such people are able to get government services easily. Thus, a special class of the supporters of English is being created due to the public schools. This class in not in favour of giving due place to the mother-tongue in educational and administrative fields. Hence the complexity of the language problem is maintained, due to these public schools.

5. *Public School—Another System of Secondary Education*:

The secondary schools of our country suffer from scarcities in several ways. Secondary schools are very important for any country because the future citizens of the country receive education in them. But our secondary schools are incapable of providing useful education to future citizens. In contrast, the public schools are such secondary schools that are providing education to the children of a select band of well-to-do persons. Thus, in our democratic country the citizens are getting two types of secondary education. In a democracy two types of educational systems at the secondary level will be harmful because they encourage groupism.

Suggestions for Reforms of Public Schools

1. **The admission in public schools should be open** to the **children of general public also. Such steps** should be **taken that brilliant students are not denied** admission **in them due to their poverty.**

2. Public Schools should be run on the basis of Indian background and culture. So far they have been copying the public school of England. The medium of instruction there should be mother-tongue instead of English. Thus, public schools should either be Indianised or they should be closed.
3. To enhance dignity of labour, ordinary crafts should find a place in the education of public schools in order that after learning such crafts, the students realize that administrative services alone are not the only good profession as is usually the tendency of students studying in public schools.
4. The expenditure of public schools should be reduced. The fees charged in these schools should be reduced so that the children of general public may take admission in them. In such a situation, the Central and State Government both should provide financial help to public schools.
5. The name of the public schools should be changed to Janta schools. They should be considered Janta schools rather than private schools. Indian educational system, Indian culture and Indian problems should receive special attention there. Efforts should be made to adopt ancient Indian Gurukul system as far as possible.
6. The students for admission in these schools should be selected on the basis of merit. For this, emphasis should not be laid on the knowledge of English. This selection should be open to the children of all classes of society. If some child is poor, the government should undertake the responsibility of his entire expenditure of education. In selection, the consideration of his being rural or urban, rich or poor or of a particular region should not interfere in any way.
7. It is good that provision for good education is made in public schools, but their pomp and show, luxury and wastage should be stopped. They should not have more

than the needed resources. Simple standard of living should be encouraged there. All the students should lead a simple life.

8. The salary of Public School teachers should not be more than the salary of general secondary school teachers otherwise, they will consider themselves superior to other teachers. They can be provided lodging and boarding facilities within the school premises so that they may perform their duties carefully.
9. Public schools should be provided all the facilities by the government, but in order to maintain their usefulness, it is necessary that they are kept away from the red-tapism and pressure of educational authorities, otherwise there will be no difference between them and the general scnools. The headmaster of these schools should be free in every respect so that he may arrange all necessary facilities for the development of the personality of children and at the same time work according to democratic traditions.

Summary

General Nature: Established by wealthy people. Against democratic principles. Only children of wealthy people can be admitted.

Public Schools of U.K.: Beginning in the fourteenth century in England. Aim to produce gentlemen and Christians. Headmasters there free to organise educational programmes. Special emphasis on character formation. Hostels compulsory. Efforts to develop qualities of patriotism, co-operation, dutifulness and religious faith. Abundance of sources of income. Hence do not depend on government aid.

Traditon of Public Shools in U.K.: Admission of their students in Cambridge and Oxford Universities. Public schools recognised as members of 'Headmasters Conference'. Crowds of Students for admission. Preparation in 'Preparatory Schools' for admission to public schools. Tuition fees and other expenses exhorbitant. Hence children of poor persons cannot come for admission. Preference in admission to those students whose parents have studied in these schools. Efforts to bring reforms in public schools due to country-wide criticism. Recommendations by Education Act of 1944, and Flemmings Report for reforms.

Beginning of Public Schools in India: Some wealthy persons invited headmasters from U.K. to start public schools on the pattern of the public schools there. In the beginning public schools in India were called Chiefs' colleges, meant to give education to the children of princes and wealthy persons. Opposition by Indian leaders. Organisation of Indian Public School Conference. Only a few Chiefs' colleges accepted its membership, gradually the Chiefs' colleges began to accept the membership. Opposition of undemocratic system of public schools after attainment of freedom in 1947. Supporters of English mode of living still support them. Suggestion by Mudaliar Commission for reforms. Kothari Commission (1964-66) recommended their abolition.

General Form of Public Schools: Every student a resident of a hostel. Control of teacher or his representative monitor the students in all their activities throughout the day. Encouragement to the student for participating in sports and hobbies like swimming, wrestling, horse riding, photography, crafts, etc. Development of the feeling of co-operation, responsibility and competition. Division of students into houses. All resources available. No government aid. High salaries to teachers. Headmasters have full authority.

Merits of Public Schools: Development of co-operation and responsibility in students. All facilities available. Ideals for other schools in some ways.

Demerits of Public Schools: Against democratic traditions. Very expensive. Only children of rich persons can study in them. Students consider themselves superior to the students of other schools whether they are capable or not.

Problems Arising out of Public Schools:

1. Creation of a special class.
2. Neglect of the principle of equality.
3. Public schools responsible for the deteriorating general schools.
4. Complexity of language problem as English is medium of instruction.

Suggestion for Improvement in Public Schools:

1. Admission should be open to poor students also.

2. **Their Indianisation necessary.**
3. **Sense of dignity of labour to be developed.**
4. **Expenditure should be reduced. Central and state financial help should be provided.**
5. **Their name should be changed to 'Janta Schools'.**
6. **No compulsion of the knowledge of English, for admission.**
7. **Their pomp and show and luxurious ways should be stopped. Simple life should be encouraged.**

EXERCISES

1. Give a description of Public Schools of U.K. and explain how the Indian Public Schools are similar to them.
2. How did the tradition of Public Schools develop in India?
3. Analyse the merits and demerits of Public Schools in India and give suggestions for their reforms.
4. 'Maintaining of Public Schools is a mockery of democratic system.' Comment on this in the light of Indian Public Schools.

Chapter 47

Moral Education

The development of morality is an important aspect of formation of good character. To-day, there is deterioration of morality in society. The moral aspect has been neglected not only at the social level but at the national level also. In the educational programmes only mental development has been emphasised.

Aims of Moral Education

In the modern age, the aim of education is all-round development of personality. In the present educational system, provision has been made for only intellectual education. For a successful life, such important human qualities as sympathy, co-operation, mercy, compassion, love, truth, sincerity, etc. have been ignored. The development of such human qualities along with intellectual development should be the aim of moral education.

Character Formation

Character is very important in life. Nothing is lost when wealth is lost, something is lost when health is lost but everything is lost when character is lost. Thus character development is the important aspect of personality.

Character is related to morality. The definition of a man of character is very wide. A man of character feelings which are human and are directed towards the good and happiness of others. Such a personality can be developed by moral education. For the formation of character of future citizens moral education should be given from their very childhood. The method of imparting moral education has to be different from that of intellectual education. It cannot be given only through lectures. Children by nature like to imitate. So for moral education, it is necessary that the teachers are men of good character, in order that the students may imbibe their good qualities.

Moral Education and Religions

The idea of character formation is kept in the background of all religions. Religion is specially important in moral education from this point of view. All the religions teach the importance of adopting truth, non-violence, compassion, pity and benevolence. But to-day, religion has taken the form of groupism and communalism which is harmful for character development. In the present circumstances moral education can only be related to human religion. So in the absence of suitable conditions, the teachers should adopt a religion which is based on the principles of humanity and this alone should be made the basis and medium of moral education.

Moral Education and Good Behaviour

Good behaviour is a significant part and powerful medium of moral education. The practical aspect of the teaching of good manners is very gradual. It begins with the first stage of the development of life. Being imitative by nature, children can learn good manners from their family. The parents can make their children cultured by paying attention to their behaviours and by correcting them when required. Good manners may form a background of moral education and for this the teacher should be well-mannered in order that they may be ideals and worth-imitating for children.

Moral Education at the Various Levels of Education

Attention is paid to the students' age, intelligence, capacity and mental level while determining educational programmes. Similarly for moral education also, programmes should be designed to suit the students of different levels.

Primary Stage of Education

At the primary stage, due attention should be paid to the interest of students. The educational programmes should be sufficiently interesting. Poems, stories and songs, etc., are able to hold the child's attention.

Considering the understanding level at the primary level, the curriculum should be brief and teaching methods should be easy. Education regarding obedience to parents, keeping of promise, love and sympathy amongst brothers may be given through quotations from Mahabharat, Ramayan, the Holy Quran, the Bible and Guru Granth Sahib. Moral education may easily be given by selecting stories from ancient Indian books like Vedas, Purans and Panchtantra, Shravan, Prahlad, Dhruv and Harish Chandra and Aesoph's Fables.

The children may be made familiar with the different religions and societies of to-day in order to develop an international understanding.

Secondary Stage of Education

At the secondary stage, the mental level of students becomes quite mature that more concrete programmes for character formation may be started. In order to make the youth successful in future life, the programme at this stage should be of various kinds.

At the secondary stage students should be given opportunities of work for the welfare of man and society and efforts should be made to inculcate in them ethical virtues. For the formation of character, illustrations and stories may be cited according to need. But care should be taken to safeguard the personal feelings of the students.

College and Higher Stage of Education

At the college and higher stage, the students prepare themselves for future life. So at this stage, the programme of moral education should be wide. A man of character, rising above the considerations of nation, community, class, religion and group, full of human sentiments. He considers the entire world as his home and others as members of his family. At this stage, the teacher occupies an important position for moral education and he may place the character of a really great man as a mirror from which the students may imbibe many good qualities.

SUMMARY

Aim of Moral Education: To give education in sympathy, co-operation, mercy, compassion, love and truth. Moral education is necessary for character formation. Teacher to be a man of character.

Moral Education and Religion: Religion necessary for moral education. The teachers and parents should be cultured in the behaviour.

Moral Education at the Primary Stage: Co-curricular activities should be interesting. Obedience to parents, devotedness to teachers, keeping of promise, love and affection amongst brothers and sisters to be a part of moral education. Concrete examples are to be given for this.

Moral Education at the Secondary Stage: Various programme for formation of character. Creative programmes for human religion. Safeguard of personal feelings necessary.

College and Higher Education: Preparation for life. Faith in human religion. To consider the whole world as home.

EXERCISE

Discuss the need and nature of moral education at the various levels of education in India.

Chapter 48

Religious Education

The Need for Religion

In the beginning, the idea of religion might have been a divine inspiration, the basis of which might have been logic or personal belief. How the modern, advanced religious belief developed in men, is a subject for research. To-day one may wonder as to how the modern religious concepts came to being? In the beginning the nature of religion was quite liberal, but to-day it has become narrow. Superstitions have crept into it. Some people hold different views regarding the same religion. Science has helped in removing many superstitions, fears, doubts and orthodox view from religion. But science never says that man does not need religion.

To-day if Dharm (religion) is taken in a wider perspective, man can create conditions of peace, hope, love, sympathy and contentment all round us by bringing an end to frustations, mental-tensions, quarrels, jealousy, discontentment and discomfort. Faith in religion can lead the world to brotherhood and peace. Religion establishes human-values, cultural-traditions, ideals and moral understanding in human society. Religion, in India, pervades through out the whole life of an individual. We have many religions. People in our land develop their culture freely under the purview of these religions.

Relation of Religion to Human life

The most developed period from the viewpoint of religion

in India has been the Vedic period when religion was considered as a basis for human life and source of inspiration for virtuous conduct. Since then religion has been inspiring people to follow the right path, improve their conduct and inbibe human virtues. It is possible that certain superstitions, conservatism, frustrations, fears and doubts might have crept into religion due to ignorance. Self-confidence has always been with man in the form of religion. Religion by adding to the human qualities, has made man capable of self-confidence, self-reform, self-realization, self-discipline, self-reliance and self-development.

Relation of Religion to Education

In the olden days, religion was the main basis of human life and was the chief source of human education. Dharm, Arth, Karm and Moksh, (Religion Wealth, Pleasure and Liberation) were the chief aims of life and these were attained through education. Religion was the basis of education during the Vedic, Brahman and Buddha periods. The meaning of religion (Dharm) was so wide in these periods that a man devoid of religion was considered as dead. Religion was an important source of virtuous conduct, morality, sociality and humanity. During these periods an effort was made to study religious books, to engage in meditation and thought and to lead life according to the religious knowledge gained. Religion was completely related to education. In fact, the religious bodies were educational institutions also. In the medieval period, educational institutions (Pathashalas and Maktabs) were related to religious places (temples and mosques). Buddha Vihars and Mathas (monasteries) were closely related to education. An attempt was made to inculcate morality through religious education. This was one of the aims of education also.

Religion was an important aspect not only in Indian traditions, but also in the European traditions. Education of children in Europe was related to the church and was given under their protection. Monks and priests were the organisers and teachers. Different religious institutions have made outstanding contribution in the field of education. In India the efforts of Arya Samaj Sanatan Dharm, Jain Dharm and Christian missionaries etc., are praiseworthy. Churches in Europe and U.S.A. hold a key position in the organisation of education even to-day.

True Meaning of Religion

Vedas are the oldest books and are the repository of all knowledge. Herein religion has been described in its wider perspective. According to the Vedas, the efforts which inspire man for virtuous conduct and develop human qualities, fall in the category of religion. The modern word 'Religion' cannot be a synonym for 'Dharm', because 'Dharm' has been considered as all-pervading in Indian scriptures. In fact, whatever qualities a person acquires are his Dharm. Here qualities mean human qualities which are universal.

In Islam 'mazhab' is a way of imparting education for virtuous conduct. According to Islamic philosophy 'Namaz' 'Roja' and 'Haj' are considered as method for creating universal love and feeling of neighbourhood. Social service is considered as a part of Islamic religion. According to Christianty feeling of pity, sympathy and love for humanity and devotion to duty are included in religion.

Religion and Sects (Belief)

Some narrow-minded people show unnecessary opposition by comparing religion with sects. We should clearly understand the meaning of religion and sects. Religion is taken in the wider sense which means spiritual development of human society through the welfare of mankind. In other words, religion means human religion which every society is prepared to accept. A sect (belief) is a specific religious viewpoint of a group of persons. That is the individual belief of the persons of that group, based on the wider values of religion. It is not necessary for other sects to accept that belief. Hindu religion accepts the opinion of Vedas, Islam that of the Quran and Christians of Bible.

Islam Dharm has its origin from the word 'Salm'. 'Salm'

means peace which has been interpreted as knowing God peacefully and surrendering the self before Him. This is the true nature of Islam. Whenever some one seeks the shelter of God, forgetting his vanity and pride, he attains all-round development and divinity radiates from his personality. In Christian religion Christianity was formed from the word 'christos' which means 'bathed in Divine wisdom'. Thus Christianity extends that divine wisdom which creates brotherhood, love, sympathy and tolerance in the human society.

Vedic religion is based on Vedas. 'Ved' means 'knowledge'. Hence Vedic Dharm means the scientific knowledge, which by recognising the existance of 'Inner Self' and 'Supreme Self', i.e., 'Antaratma' and 'Parmatma', develops human qualities like non-violence, truth, humanism, love and compassion, etc.

Thus religion is a source of morality. Science can be of great help in this direction, but science devoid of religion is meaningless. Religion is all-pervading and universal. So it should be included in education.

Mis-use of Religion and Violence

Due to ignorance and superstitions some unwise followers of religions have strangulated humanity and have committed great atrocities. The reason for such violent attitude has been mis-interpretation of religion. Religious reformers born from time to time led the people to the right path and presented the true nature of religion. Buddha, Mahavir, Shankeracharya, Guru Nanak, Dayanand, etc., were such great personalities. In the Western countries Rousseau and Locke helped to save education from wrongly interpreted religion.

The aim of education is all-round development of men. The same is the aim of religion. So because of this common aim the correlation of education and religion is quite natural. Since earliest times in India, education and religion have been related to each other. With the break of this relationship, indiscipline, violence and immorality have increased. According to Dr. Sarvapalli Radhakrishnan the reason for all vices and troubles pervading the world is want of morality which has been created due to education being not correlated to religion. In Western countries also movements were started for educational organisation by correlating religion and education. Sunday School Movement, Religious Education Movement were some such movements in which the demand for integration of education and religion was asserted. The world has witnessed the evil effects of materialism. Now, the need for education integrated with religion is being felt throughout the world. In fact, if religion is treated as 'human religion', a revolution may be brought out in the improvement of education. Peace can be established in the world through a religion-integrated education based on thinking of universal peace, universal-brotherhood and universal good.

On the basis of the viewpoint expressed above, it seems useful to impart religious education by integrating education and religion. But it is necessary to consider points both in its favour and against.

Arguments Against Religious Education

Those who want to separate religion from education, argue:—

1. To give a place to religion in education is not practicable, because children of all religions come to receive education in schools. In such a situation which religion is to be taught in a school? If one particular religion is taught in the school, the followers of other religions will not accept this position. This will lead to mutual ill-will, quarrels and disturbances.
2. Religious education is generally based on preaching. So long as desired changes are not brought about in the environment and ideal examples are not presented, till then good conduct cannot be spread through religious education. Hence mere teaching of religious doctrines in schools will not achieve the goal of education.
3. Doubts and mental conflicts are created in children as they cannot understand the abstract meanings of sin, virtue, reward and punishment as explained in religious education in school.

4. It is not possible for some teachers to analyse religious knowledge dispassionately because they may be faithful only to one particular religion. Consequently, the students will be incapable of understanding the true and obscure meaning of religion. It will be better to analyse religion with the help of science, but the teachers will not accept it because science may injure their personal beliefs. It is a difficult task to correlate education and true human-religion. Every teacher may not be capable of this.
5. We have already observed that religion means human religion through which human qualities should be developed. But history bears a testimony to the fact that humanity has been oppressed in the name of religion and in place of love, compassion, sympathy and co-operation, the feelings of enmity, hatred, jealousy and opposition have grown. Such examples in the history of religion may create irreligious feelings in children.
6. Man imbibes 'religion' through self-realization. Self-realization is individualistic. Hence inclusion of personal elements in religious conduct is natural. In the school environment, collective and social tendencies are found. So personal viewpoint of religion cannot be given importance. This viewpoint may be acceptable to some children, but not to others who follow other viewpoints.

Arguments in Favour of Religious Education

There may be some strength in the above arguments. But this strength holds good only if education is imparted on the basis one particular relgion without understanding the true meaning of religion. Religion is universal, omni-present and eternal. It is necessary to present its universal form. The following arguments may be presented in favour of religious education:—

1. All-round development of man is not possible only through physical, mental and intellecutal development,

as this requires spiritual development also. Physical comforts alone do not provide real pleasure and peace. The more a man is absorbed in worldly pleasures, the more he is attracted towards them. He tries to get the physical comforts of this material world through all possible means (even through inhuman action). This disturbs world peace. Various subjects such as geography, science, etc., lead to physical, mental and intellectual development, but they do not develop one's spiritual side of life. For spiritual development religion-oriented education is needed. Only then the goal of an all-round development in the individual may be achieved.

2. Lack of religious faith in man is the cause of his troubles. All the vices of the world such as enemity, jealousy and intolerance are due to irreligiousness and materialistic tendencies. Hence, religious education is necessary in order to get rid of inhuman tendencies.
3. We have said earlier that religious education becomes defective only when religion is treated in its narrow form. Religion is not to be identified with any sect or opinion. The essence of all sects is the true religion. True religion alone can be called human religion. If it is taught through education, the follower of any religion will not be ignored. It will be worthwhile to provide education in high human ideals which are adored by people of every religion instead of giving place to the rituals of different sects.
4. The aim of education is all-round development of the individual in which development of character is the main aim. Religious education is the best sources for character development. To-day education being devoid of religion, the character of many of our youths is not what it should be.
5. In countries where people are basically religious, religious education will be useful from educational point of view. Education based on religion will be easily understandable and interesting in such country. India

is one such country. But religion should not be taken in its narrow form. By adopting essence of all the sects, religious education should be given in its wider perspective.

6. In the modern world scientific experimentalism, scientific inventions, scientific thinking, intellectual and materialistic developments have been continuously going on. Consequently, the progressive countries have achieved material affluence. But have these countries become happy and peaceful inspite their affluence? The two World Wars are the consequences of the materialistic selfishness. Inspite of all efforts world peace has not been achieved so far. The sole reason for it is the neglect of spiritualism. The truth is that materialism and spiritualism should be integrated through religious education. So it will be necessary to impart universal religious education in schools. In India, Shri Syed Ahmad Khan, Radhakrishnan, Madan Mohan Malviya, Mahatma Gandhi, Dayanand Saraswati, Ravindranath Tagore, Aurobindo and many other great men have advocated religious education. Smt. Annie Besant and Mira Behn and Mataji considered it necessary to integrated education and religious education. While integrating education and religious education we shall have to keep it in mind that the religion to be integrate should be human-religion and not based on the beliefs of one particular sect.

To be Cautious in the Teaching of Religion

An evaluation of advantages and limitations of religious education leads us to be conclusion that religion should be given a place in education. One of the objectives of religious education is self-realisation and to inspire virtuous conduct. Sermons and instructions alone will not achieve religious aims. Moral development and virtuous conduct through religion is possible only when opportunities are provided for such behaviours. A religious atmosphere in schools may make it possible. The students are greatly influenced by the ideal behaviour of teachers. So the teachers themselves should present examples of ideal behaviour by leading a religious, moral and virtuous life. The teaching of religion alone cannot create a religious atmosphere in schools.

Religious education should be kept away from narrow mindedness. It will be better to give religious education based on logic, analysis and criticism, otherwise it may lead to supersititions, jealousy and narrow-mentality.

In schools, religion should not be taken as an end in itself. It is simply a means for all-round development of the individual. The schools are not to be made into temples, mosques, or churches by tilting religious education to ward a particular sect. Schools are not to fulfil the function of religious institutions, rather the religious institutions should work as schools. If religious institutions make an attempt for the all round development of children through spiritual development, they will certainly lessen the burden of schools. It is, therefore, necessary for the religious bodies to take the form of education obligations to the extent possible.

Educational Functions of Religion

A man is attracted towards religion only when he is mentally healthy and a sound mind resides in a sound body. So it is the function of religion to co-operate in the physical development of children.

Religion should always mean performing of duties. The first field of performing duties is this world (Ih-Lok). Karma-Kshetra (the field of action) is another name for Dharm-Kshetra (field of religions). The man who succeeds in the Karma-Kshetra of this world is entitled to reach the other world (Parlok). Therefore, religion should prepare man for the Karma-Kshetra (field of action). The field of action of the individual is determined on the basis of his aptitudes. So religion should inculcate in the child the ability to choose his field of action according to his interest and aptitude and to get success by engaging himself in it.

The basis of religion is knowledge. An ignorant person

cannot be religious. The bases of religions are logic, analysis, observation, contemplation and freedom of thought. So the child should be provided opportunities for independent thinking, logic, meditation, analysis and observation with an open mind. To have faith in religion without independent thinking, logic and analysis will be blind-faith and fanaticism.

Some people consider aesthetic sense and artistic sense as hindrance to religion. But this is not true. Satyam, Shivam and Sundarm (Truth, Bliss and Beautiful) are the bases for artistic and aesthetic senses. Satyam and Shivam are the bases of religion. A thing which is not true or for happiness cannot be beautiful. The spread of sculpture and architecture and poetry, etc. Throughout, history was based on true religious feelings. The carving of Jain idols in Allora Caves and Jatak stories connected with the life of Lord Buddha and their carving in Ajanta, the poetry of Sur, Tulsi and Mira are all considered unique for propagation of religious feelings. So religion should develop our aesthetic sense also.

Although the real function of schools is to develop the moral character of the child, but religious institutions can bring about better moral character development, if they pay attention in this direction. The very meaning of religion is to inspire virtuous conduct, which develops moral and ethical qualities. To-day, the country needs able and noble citizens.

Thus after studying the merits and demerits and functions of religious education we come to the conclusion that religion should be included in schools as a means of all-round development of children.

SUMMARY

Need of Religion: Man thought of religion on the basis of logic, faith and personal beliefs. The original basis of religion was dutifulness and virtuous conduct. Material comforts alone do not give peace. Spiritual development is necessary for lasting peace. This development is possible only through religion.

Relation of Religion to Human Life and Education: The development of man is due to his imbibing human qualities. These human qualities are developed by religion and education. In ancient times education was dominated by religion. Vedic and Brahman and Buddhist periods illustrate this.

Meaning of Religion and its Mis-use: The meaning of religion to develop spirituality by inspiring virtuous conduct. Vedic religion, Islam and Christianity believe in this. Religion is wider and sectarianism is narrow. It is wrong to consider religion and sect as the same. People have committed atrocities in the name of religion. There has been human massacre. This is irreligious.

Relation of Education to Religion: Religion and Education have remained correlated from the Vedic period to the Buddhist period. In the modern times the relation of education and religion has broken down due to growth of science and technology. In fact, true meaning is not understood.

Religious Education and its Analysis: The impracticability in religious education, its sermonising bias and lack of virtuous behaviour accordingly, non-exposition of true religion, absence of human religion and its non-availability in schools, are some of the defects. Religious education is necessary for all-round development, materialistic and spiritualistic thinking and its co-ordination, for moral development and virtuous conduct.

Hindrances in Religious Education: Fanaticism and considering religion as an end in itself are great hindrances.

Educational Duties of Religion: Physical development, enjoyment of wordly pleasures, development of artistic and aesthetic senses. Development of character and morality are to be achieved by religious institutions.

Exercises

1. What is the true meaning of religion? Discuss its relationship with education?
2. What is the need of religion in life? Should religious education be given in schools? If yes, why?
3. What should be the form of religious education? What are the the possible difficulties in imparting religious education in India?
4. How can religious institutions fulfil educational functions? Explain.

Chapter 49

Indianisation of Education

The spirit of a country is inherent in its culture. The main function of education has always been to transmit the culture of the country to its future generations. After the British rule became well established in our country in the nineteenth century, the education system was shaped to serve the British purposes. As a result, the education system always remained aloof towards the Indian culture. But after the achievement of freedom in 1947, the need to free the education system from this serious defect has become very important. Now we want to Indianise our education. In this chapter we will discuss this problem.

Meaning of Indianisation

Different persons have given different views regarding the meaning of Indianisation. The meaning of Indianisation was considered to be the following of Indian methods in place of British methods in the Indian national life. This was a narrow meaning of Indianisation. According to the wider meaning of Indianisation, it is to so include the foreign elements in the Indian public life that it is made richer while maintaining its national and cultural characteristics. This meaning also includes the inculcation of the feeling of social and national responsibility in the public life of the country. It is to be remembered that we have to overcome the tendency of

Hinduisation, as proposed by some narrow minded persons, in our-effort for Indianisation. In fact, we have to keep Muslims, Christians, Sikhs, Sindhis and other countrymen with us in the sequence of Indianisation, otherwise Indianisation will be meaningless.

Indianisation does not mean making it governmental. Its aim is the development of the feeling of proper social and national responsibility in the people. National feeling should not be interpreted in the political context alone. The national feeling goes further by including political sincerity in it. Attachment to the country, feeling of pride for our cultural heritage, respect for national language, national-flag, national leaders, national anthem and national beliefs are all included in it. Those foreigners who have come upto our expectations in these various contexts, may also be considered worthy of this national feeling. For example, Smt. Annie Besant and Mr. Stocks, though they were not born in India, will always remain a part of our national life since they proved true to our expectations. Contrary to this, many persons who were born in Indian can never come in the purview of our definition of Indianisation. if they have proved disloyal to our country. The national feeling of a person is his inner inclination. His religion, caste, language or political party have very little influence on it. By Indianisation we mean this favourable inner inclination of an Indian though he may have any religion, language or political faith.

The Meaning of Indianisation of Education

The Indianisation of education means that education has got to be geared to the needs and aspirations of the country. For this adjustment we have to continue to move with the ever-changing nature of Indian culture. To make education capable of fulfilling the demand of the country and to mould it according to the needs of the time, will be called Indianisation of Indian education.

After Independence in 1947, new needs and aspirations have arisen in the Indian public life. Consequently, the unsuitablity of education as implemented by the British disturbed our minds. So, the rulers of the country made several efforts to bring the much needed changes in the educational system of the country. In these efforts generally the following three main characteristics may be noticed:

1. *Effort of Re-inclusion of the Basic Elements of Ancient Indian Education in the Education-system*:

The establishment of D.A.V. Colleges and some Gurukuls on the basis of the views of Swami Dayanand Saraswati is an example of such an effort. Some educational centres established by Ram Krishna Mission, Shantiniketan established by Ravindra Nath Tagore and starting of various Vidyapeeths and Jamia Millia are other examples of such an effort.

2. *Effort of Making the Education of the Country Modern in all Possible Ways*:

Educational policy framers and the government have realised it well that education may be capable of preparing worthy citizens according to the present day needs only when modern western knowledge and science are adequately included in our education.

3. *Basic Education*:

The educational system initiated by Mahatma Gandhi was a praiseworthy effort of inculcating self-reliance, constructive skill and practical knowledge in our students. Being dissatisfied with the prevailing education, Mahatma Gandhi advised the implementation of the Basic Education scheme. It was a revolutionary step for a change in the very base of our education system, i.e., at the stage of primary education. This revolutionary step had the following main points.

1. The child will be the centre of education.
2. He will learn while working.
3. The work by the child during the process of learning will be productive.
4. Some craft will be the pivot of education.
5. Children will imbibe the feeling of dignity of manual labour.

6. The medium of education shall be the mother-tongue.
7. The various subjects will be taught by correlating them with a selected craft.
8. The teachers and students will do their work based on the ideals of truth and non-violence.
9. The teachers and students both will work for social upliftment.

Evidently, these ideals were placed before us to provide a starting base for education and to prepare worthy citizens. However, it is true that basic education has not been able to achieve its proposed objectives so far, but it must be admitted that basic education has been a revolutionary effort in the direction of Indianisation of education.

4. *University Commission of 1948-49, Secondary Education Commission of 1952-53 and Acharya Narendra Deo Committees of 1939 and 1952-53*:

The University and Secondary Education Commissions appointed by the Indian Government and Acharya Narendra Deo Committee appointed by the Government of U.P. have been efforts of Indianisation and modernisation of University and Secondary education in their specific contexts.

5. *Kothari Commission 1966*:

This Commission appointed by the Indian Government is yet another revolutionary effort for the Indianisation of education. The essence of the recommendations of the Commission is briefly given below as it fits in with the need of Indianisation of our education.

1. The development of the social, moral and spiritual beliefs of India should be made possible through education.
2. The development of democratic ideals should be done through education.
3. Increase in production is possible only through education.
4. Modernisation of the country can be done through education alone.

5. Education should help in the development of social and national integration.

In July 1968, our Government announced a new National Education Policy on the basis of the recommendations of Kothari Commission. This declaration is a example of our effort towards Indianisation. The following are some of the main elements of this declaration:—

To bring education close to public life. The following programme should be adopted to do so:—

(a) To make efforts for the qualitative improvement at all the stages of education.
(b) To develop new moral and social beliefs.
(c) To make continuous efforts for the extension of educational opportunities.
(d) To pay special attention to science and industry at every stage of education as far as possible.

In order to achieve the above objectives, the Indian Government has decided to work according to the following principles in the field of education:

1. *To make education free and compulsory for the first 14 years.*

2. *Increase in the salary and allowances of teachers and provide them a high status in society.*

3. *Encouragement to all Indian languages and the National language:* In order to improve the culture, literature and philosophy and public life, the government has decided to develop all Indian language, the national language and culture. Along with it, for expansion of knowledge, it has stressed the need of encouraging the study of English and some other international languages.

4. *National Service and Work Experience*: The aim of national service and work-experience is to be achieved according to the capacity of the students at every stage of education.

5. *Equality of Educational Opportunity*: Equal opportunities of education are to be provided to the children of

various regions, such as, remote hill areas, and desert lands and to backward and disabled children, children of tribal area, and gifted children.

6. *Science Education and Research*: In order to make the country prosperous, science education should be emphasised and new research should be conducted in this field.

7. *Development of Talent*: Talent (meritorious persons) in the country should be discovered and developed.

8. *Education in Agriculture and Industry*: Speical attention should be paid to the development of agriculture and different industries in order to make the country self-sufficient.

9. *Preparation of Books*: Various original books on science and knowledge should be prepared and the gifted authors should be rewarded for their works.

10. *Reforms in the Defective Examination System*: For the proper evalution of students' achievements, the examination system should be reformed.

11. *Necessary Changes in Secondary Education*: Secondary education should be extended to those areas where it has not been provided so far. Facilities for technical and vocational education should be available at the secondary stage.

12. *Regarding University Education*:

(i) Technical and vocational education should be extended to the University stage.

(ii) Laboratories, libraries and other necessary material-aids should be made available at this stage.

(iii) New universities should be established after careful deliberation.

(iv) Improvements in research, training and post-graduate curriculum should be brought about.

(v) Some model research centres should be established. But these centres should work under a university.

(vi) Short-term education and correspondence education plans should be started.

(vii) Literacy and adult education should be extended.

(viii) Necessary resources should be developed for encouraging games and sports among students.

(xi) Proper attention should be paid to the education of minorities.

(x) Reorganisation of educational structure of the whole country is necessary.

(xi) Secondary education upto 10 years, higher secondary education for two years and graduate education for three years, that is, the pattern of 10+2+3 should be implemented throughout the country.

Although educationists hold diverse views regarding how to better Indianise education, all agree that that Indianisation of education is imperative.

SUMMARY

Meaning of Indianisation: During the struggle for freedom, its meaning was to adopt Indian methods in place of British methods. But this meaning was narrow. In fact, in its wider meaning it connotes conservation of our culture by enriching it on the basis of good qualities of others.

Meaning of Indianisation of Education: Education to be geared to the needs and aspiration of the country.

1. Inclusion of the basic elements of ancient Indian education.
2. To modernise education by all possible means.
3. Basic education, an example of Indianisation.
4. University Education Commission of 1948-49, Secondary Education Commission of 1952-53 and Acharya Narendra Deo Committee.
5. Kothari Commission 1966.
6. Our National Policy of 1968.

According to this policy to bring education close to public life, qualitative improvement of education, development or moral and social beliefs, development of educational opportunities, attention on science and technology, free and compulsory education upto first 14 years, improvement in the status of teachers, encouragement to all Indian languages, social service and work-experience, science education and research, development of talent, education in subjects concerning agriculture and industry, preparation of books, improvement in the examination system, necessary changes in secondary and university education, expansion of adult-education, attention on the education of minorities, change in educational pattern.

Exercises

1. What is the meaning of Indianisation of education?
2. How can our Indian education be Indianised? Give your constructive suggestions in this regard.

PART V

Russian Education

50. Introduction
51. Democratic Philosophy of Education in Russia.
52. Control of Education in Russia
53. Pre-primary Education.
54. Primary Education.
55. Secondary Education.
56. Teacher Education.
57. Higher Education.
58. Adult Education.

Chapter 50

Introduction

The major portion of Russia falls in Asia, but it is considered as a powerful European nation. With the break-up of U.S.S.R, Russia has now adopted a democratic system of administration under its new government established in 1992.

The Geographical Position of Russia

In size and area Russia is the biggest country in Europe. In the east it touches the Pacific ocean and extend to the border of many European countries in the west. In length from east to west it is about 1000 kilometres and its breadth is about 500 kilometres at many places. Its population is about 8,00,00,000 after the breaking of the previous Soviet regime.

It has many types of climate, such as cold, temperate and polar. In the east and centre of the country there are summer rains. The land abounds in natural resources. Agricultural and industrial life is the common pattern of living. The country has two principal parts, Asian and European. The Asian part is full of minerals. The rivers have strong currents. Hence they are utilised for producing electricity. Forests full of various types of trees are extensively found in Russia. The country has some oil-wells also. Moscow is its capital.

Before the Revolution of 1917

Before the revolution of 1917 Russia was a backward

country. Feudal lords and poor farmers formed the principal portion of the population. The feudal lords ruthlessly exploited the farmers. The Church held the general public in blind religious superstitions. The industrialists of Europe exploited the raw materials of this country. Russia depended on these industrialists. The farmers were laborious but poor because of lack of latest agricultural implements. Agricultural output was unsatisfactory. The feudal lords and the Church men wanted to keep the general public illiterate and poor in order to maintain their own dominance. They were leading luxurious life. Inspite of large reserves of coal, oil and iron available, the industrial development of the country was negligible.

Educational History of Russia

Upto the nineteenth century about 90% of the people were illiterate in Russia. Poverty and unemployment was the cause of the hopeless condition of the people. The public was under the complete dominance of Czar and the Church. In this vast country there were various languages, races and religious sects. The country was backward. The minorities were neglected. There were some centres of scientific research, education, music and culture, but they were not open to all.

Education was mainly religious in nature and was organised by the clergy. Many minority groups had no scripts for their languages. Education was meant for the people of the upper classes. The Czar commanded strict control over education. Students who revolted were jailed for life. Many of them left the country due to fear. Universities also were under the control of the Czar. From 1682 to 1725, under the rule of Peter the Great, there was some educational development. Hence, he is truely regarded as the father of Russian education. He has inscribed on his private seal - "I am one of those men who are in search of knowledge and are always eager to learn." Peter the Great in 1633 had established a board of education at Kiev and he had also established fifty such schools in which 3,000 children of churchmen were receiving education. Some other primary, secondary and navel training schools were also established. In 1726, the Russian Academy of Sciences was founded and the university and preparatory schools affiliated to it were reorganised.

Catherine II (1729-1796) started a state educational policy. In a district, schools with two year curriculum and in a provincial town schools with five year curriculum, were established. In 1764 some special boarding schools were also opened for girls from the upper strata of society. Thus, in all, about 40 big and 255 small schools were established.

Form 1801-1825, during the rule of Alexander I, education registered good progress. He established an education ministry in1802 and declared education free and universal. Around 1804 he established 6 universities, many provincial schools with four year curriculum and some district schools with two year curriculum and many one year rural schools. At many places education was made free, and students were given special allowances and scholarships. About 70,000 students were receiving education in 1,400 schools. Even then the public was generally indifferent to education.

Nicholas I (1825-1855), like his predecessors, was interested in the development of education. He established special schools for children of upper classes and tried to spread women's education also. Strict disciplinary measures were introduced in the schools and the system of charging fees was also started. The king promulgated an order barring admission to children of farmers to universities and Gymnasia. It was also ordered that logic should not be taught in schools as it was against the interest of the kingdom. The purpose of education was declared to make students loyal to the State, Church and King. Some schools were established for providing technical education. Nationality, orthodoxy and autocracy were accepted as the chief basis of education. Secondary schools were declared for upper classes only. By imposing a strict discipline on universities, their academic freedom was badly curtailed.

The period of Alexander II (1855-1881) in the history of Russian education is considered as a period of educational reforms. The restrictions imposed on the universities were removed. Secondary education was reorganised. Primary schools were opened in many States. Women education was encouraged by opening of a womens' training school in 1863. Through the 'Primary Schools' Law of 1864, position, race and religion were not given any importance for admission in primary schools. The teaching of science was encouraged and attempts were made to expand education in rural areas also. New teaching methods were introduced. A medical college was established for women. Girls' schools were established at Petersberg and in many other prominent cities. But due to the death of Alexander II in 1881 there was a break in the development of education. Consequently, strict controls were again imposed on universities. This resulted in students' strikes. Students were jailed. Many schools were closed due to students' movements. A feeling of opposition sprang up in the public against the Church, Parochial schools and Alphabet schools. At this time Zestov established some Zestov schools but the government encouraged its old alphabet schools. By 1902 religious education reached the peak of its development. Afterwards due to public opposition its influence began to fade.

In 1905 a revolution brokeout in Russia. Some groups organised themselves against the Czar. Between 1906 and 1907 some changes became necessary in education and the economic policy. As a result of the First World War dictatorship gained ground in Russia, Germany, France and Italy. Consequently, democratic traditions declined. In 1917, Alexandor Derenshky established a revolutionary government by removing the imperial government. Under the leadership of Lenin and Trotsky a government of Bolshevists was established and a federal government was instituted having representatives from all the races and languages in the country. The control of the Church on education was totally abolished.

The communist government was determined to remove illiteracy. It published grammers books, dictionaries and text-books of various languages. It tried to unite the country. In order to bring the various dialects closer to each other, development of education was considered necessary. An attempt was made to spread primary education throughout the whole land. Scripts were given to those languages which had none. Vocabularies of various languages were developed. Russian language was used as a medium for propagating the views of Marx and Lenin. Minority groups were made literate. Their vocabularies were developed. They were acquainted with the nature of industrial development. The backward races were also taught the Russian language in order that they might also read and understand books which contained matters pertaining to vocational, industrial and agricultural skills.

For the Russification of the country, the Soviet government opened Russian schools which imparted education on the basis of communist ideology. Restrictions were placed on the Holy Syuod, Bishop of the Diocese and Church Councils. Studying in Russian schools were made compulsory for all. The Zestov schools, municipal schools and people of Poland and Lithuania were compelled to send their children to these schools.

Four years of elementary education was arranged through a compulsory education scheme in Soviet Union. The communist movement of the government won the heart of the people and the students were also greatly influenced by the same. The Provisional Government between 1917-1921 could not do much for education, but whatever it did was complete in itself. In 1918 religious education was banned and the whole education system of the country was placed under the Department of Public Instruction. The authorities of the local organisations were given more powers. Universities were granted more autonomy. Under the new system of Education, Curators, Directors, Inspectors and Council of Primary Education was abolished.

According to the Act of 1918, four year curriculum schools were established for children between the age group of 13 and 17. Schools were also established for children between 8 and 13 years of age. Secondary education was made compulsory for children between the age group of 8 and 17. Chidren's Homes and schools were established in opposition to family life and in support of communistic ideologies. Educational institutions were given powers to determine the curriculum and to prescribe the text books. A collective body was established giving representation to students, teachers and school councils. Thus a system was given to school administration. But Children's Homes and schools and collective body system were never successful. At this time many multi-occupational schools and polytechnic schools were also established.

The period between 1921 and 1927 may be regarded as revolutionary from the point of view of education. During this period secondary schools and centres of vocational training were reorganised. Primary schools and centres of vocational training were reorganised. Primary schools were no longer to be regarded as independent units. Higher education was also reorganised. The State Scientific Council took upon itself to organise the educational programmes. Primary education was made a four year course and secondary education into a seven or nine year course. Teaching of communist doctrines and study of Soviet revolution was made compulsory. Educational programmes were to be organised on the basis of social tendencies, nature and labour. The Union and the provincial governments were to shoulder the entire expenditure on education. The children of labourers were encouraged to take admission in schools. All these educational upheavals created some confusion among the students.

Consequently, Stalin started his first five year plan (1928-1932). The Central Executive Committee, on August 14,1930 took the momentous decision that the rural children over eight year of age would have to study four year curriculum and the children of the same age group in industrial town were required to study a seven year programme. Arrangement was made for adequate higher, professional and technical education and research. The poor children were to be provided clothes, refreshments and boarding facilities. Competitive examinations were introduced for admission to centres of higher education. Restrictions placed on the study of various subjects were removed. Thus the standard of education was raised. Teachers' training institutions were also established. During 1929-33 the strength of students increased every year. New school buildings were constructed and old ones were repaired. Thus Stalin's first five year plan has been of great significance.

The Soviet government reorganised the secondary schools' curricula of general and cultural education. The government established a university of culture for higher technical schools. Maintenance grants were given for national industrial reconstruction. Rules for attendance and other allied matters were determined for higher schools. Communist principles were incorporated in the entire educational set-up. Education of backward people was encouraged.

During the Second World War, because of the German invasion, teachers and students were deputed to the military services. Consequently, many schools were closed. However, some schools continued to function for promoting essential educational services. The Moscow University at this time published 15 hundred scientific papers. Rules for compulsory education were redetermined. The system of awarding gold and silver medals and certificates was started for encouraging bright students. Separate schools were started for boys and girls. A plan was formulated in 1944 for the development of the Leningrad and Rostov universities. In the same year five hundred teachers were awarded medals for their special trainings in the field of national economy. Sufficient money was spent for reconstruction of old buiildings of educational institutions and other buildings for universities and laboratories. After the end of the Second World War, new centres of higher learning were opened and a five year plan (1946-1950) was started for rehabilitation of citizens in certain areas of the country. In this plan special attention was paid to scientific research and technology. Under these plans about 120 higher educational institutions were established and 13 lakh persons having obtained secondary education and seven lakhs having achieved higher education, were deputed for doing developmental work in the various parts of the country. In

1952, 3,75,000 students were admitted in correspondence courses and other higher institutions. The government arranged for educational expenditure to the tune of 8 thousand rubles. This amount was 12.6% of the total budget. In the fifth five year plan (1951-1955) the Nineteenth Congress of Communist Party gave directions for higher education.

Plans were made for the expansion of universal secondary education in various cities. Arrangements were made for technical, adult, general, correspondence and evening part-time education.

SUMMARY

Russia had been a backward country during the rules of Czars. Then education was available only to the people of the higher classes.

The Geographical Position of Russia: Full of natural resources. The climate is temperate and cold. Rivers serve as transport passage. Coal and wood are in abundance.

Educational History of Soviet Russia: At first education was under the State and Church. First of all Peter the Great recognised the state responsibility over education. In 1633, 50 school boards were established. Primary and secondary schools were reorganised. Catherine II extended state control and administration over education. Women education was started in 1764.

In 1825, two year course in district schools, four year course in provincial schools and six universities were established. Nicholas I introduced military discipline in schools.

The study of logic was stopped. Nationality, despotism and religion were emphasised.

Alexander II introduced reforms between 1855-1881. He opened women's training schools in 1863 and ordered for universal education in 1864. Rural education was developed.

Restrictions were imposed on universities. Zestov schools were established. Religious educations was at its peak in 1902. Students who protested were jailed.

In 1905 revolution began and the public was reorganised against the Czar. In 1917, Alexander Kerensky was deposed. Union government was established under Lenin and Trotsky. Education felt the political and economic impact.

The communist government enriched various languages and gave

scripts to certain languages which had none. An attempt was made to spread literacy. A plan was made to educate farmers and labourers as a result of industrial revolution. Russian language was made a medium for propogating communist doctrines.

The whole country was distributed under 15 educational regions. Each region was placed under a curator who was appointed by the minister. The curator appointed inspectors of schools and teachers.

Study of communist doctrines was made compulsory. Four year primary education was made compulsory. Secondary education was made free. Children's Homes were established. Polytechnics were established.

On August 14, 1930, the union government made four year curriculum for rural children and seven year curriculum for industrial towns compulsory. Arrangement was made for technical education and research work. Admission-examinations wese introduced for higher education. School buildings were repaired. Stalin's first five year plan succeeded. General and cultural education was also emphasised. A separate culture university was established. School attendance rules were framed.

In 1941, due to the German invasion during the Second World War many teachers and students were enlisted into the army. A system was started to award gold and silver medals and certificates to the meritorius students. Teachers were awarded medals for contribution to cultural education and national economy.

Exercises

1. **Give a brief account of education in Russia before the twentieth century. Was the system of education satisfactory during the period? If not, why?**
2. **Discuss the place of Peter the Great and Alexander II in the development of Russian education.**
3. **Discuss the impact of the communist government on education in Russia before the Second World War.**

Chapter 51

Democratic Philosophy of Education in Russia

Before we come to discuss the democratic philosophy of education in modern Russia, it is necessary to have a look on its previous communistic philosophy of education.

The Communistic Philosophy of Education

Social traditions have their inevitable impact on the educational system of a country. Under the Communist regime, U.S.S.R. was no exception to it. The various races, communities and languages of this great country posed a big educational problem so the communist leaders evolved an educational philosophy in order to meet the social aspirations of the people inspite of their varying differences which had to be ultimately reshaped in order to form a unified pattern.

The communist ideology before the breaking up of U.S.S.R., in 1992 influenced the educational goals and the educational system of the country. The communistic pattern of society in U.S.S.R. believed that all the citizens must imbibe the communistic ideology. It was thought that it could be possible only through education.

The U.S.S.R. philosophy stood for the establishment of a classless society in order to bring together the majority of the proletariats. This was aimed at so as to do away with the existing social classes. All the means of mass communication of the country were directed towards the achievement of this goal. Consequently, the individual did not have much say in any matter pertaining to the state affairs. No body could dare oppose the communist ideology. The news-papers, radio, television and cinemas, etc. were all propagators of the government creed. The farmers and labourers were given special importance because they were considered as the backbone of the society.

Some of the Main Aspects of the Communistic Educational Philosophy

One of the characteristics of communist ideologies has been that it accepts the process of evolution. Hence, the current pattern must not be identically the same as it was a few years ago. Accordingly, necessary changes have to be introduced in any educational pattern. In the communistic philosophy traditions do not play any important role. Therefore, unlike other countries, in the U.S.S.R. educational system had no hereditary features. It was believed that all the necessary equipments of education for an individual were already present in the society. It was the individual who through his innate capacity could derive the necessary elements for his all-sided growth. If one did not do so, the fault was his, and not that of the society. This further meanst that the individual had not exercised himself fully towards his own growth. Therefore, everyone must imbibe a capacity to adjust oneself in his environment. It was expected of every individual in U.S.S.R. that he would be self-disciplined and dutiful for drawing out the best of the instructional processes present in his environment.

Purposes of Education in U.S.S.R.

Upto the 19th century the Russian despots could give only primary education to children of farmers and labourers. Secondary education was given to the children of only high class people and elites. Thus, the then rulers wanted to keep the farmers' and labourers' children illiterate. They feared that they would resist their slavery after being well educated. Hence, they were not admitted to Grammer Schools of the day.

But after the revolution of 1917 changes of far-reaching consequences were introduced in the educational system. The first effort of the USSR government was to remove illiteracy.

At this time the aim of the government was to expand communism and to prepare citizens who had faith in the same. Towards the realisation of this aim changes in the educational system were gradually introduced as the policy of the communist party desired from time to time. To make education available equally to all was considered as a constitutional necessity.

The Principal Tenets of Democratic Philosophy of Education in Modern Russia

But since the breaking up of U.S.S.R. in 1992 into a number of independent states, the educational philosophy of Russia has been repatterned on democratic lines in place of the pervious communist ideology. Now the major emphasis in education is to educate the individual regarding his rights and duties as a citizen of a democratic state. This revolutionary change has made a great impact on the attitudes and life pattern of the Russian people. Now the people in Russia are to be educated about democratic traditions which guarantee freedom of speech and expressions to all individuals as long as they do not interfere with others' rights. In this new outlook of life, the individual has to be respected and has not to be coerced to follow any pariticular mode of life. At this stage it is too early to specify the exact philosophy of education that Russia will follow. But since now the country has rejected the communist ideology in preference to a democratic philosophy of life we may easily imagine which educational philosophy will be ultimately followed in this country. As the various relevant publications in the field of education in Russia indicate, we may safely speak about the educational philosophy to be followed there. Some specific basic ideas with regard to educational philosophy to be adhered to in Russia may be mentioned as below:—

1. To develop a sense of world citizenship in the minds of the people in general, because this is an age of internationalism and no country can afford to keep itself aloof. So the commonness of humanity has to be emphasized in any scheme of education.
2. To develop a sense of co-operativeness which will foster the feelings of love, sympathy and co-operation which are very necessary for one's own growth and also for the country at large.
3. To introduce a vocational point of view in education in order that all the human and natural resources may be ultimately explored for the benefit of every citizen and also for the nation. Needless to remark that without the necessary vocational training the various capacities of the individual will not be developed and this will be against the growth of the individual and also of the nation as a whole.
4. To develop the qualities of citizenship in order that each may learn about his rights and duties in a democratic set-up.
5. Education has to be developed in such a manner as to ensure the growth of all the citizens to the maximum limit possible. In order to attain this objective there should be various types of schools, colleges, universities and technical and vocational training centres spread all over the country. Upto a certain stage education has to be made free and compulsory. There should be both part-time schools and night-schools in order to enable some persons to earn while receiving education.
6. Introduction of necessary changes from time to time in education has to be accepted as a need in the modern world which is ever-changing in respect of various human aspirations.

7. Special provisions in education must be made for the dull as well as brilliant children. No one should be deprived of educational facilities because of poverty or social status.
8. In the field of education particular attention has also to be paid to establishment of well-equipped laboratories of all types in order that the vocational and technological advancements may not be impeded.

Summary

The Communistic Educational Philosophy of U.S.S.R.: To bring in change in education according to the changing communistic views. To spread communistic ideas and to produce citizens having faith in communism. Education to develop love for labour and communism. If any one fails in his life, it is his own fault, because he has not utilised his innate capacity well, as the necessary environment was already available to him.

The Principal Tenents of Democratic Educational Philosophy in Russia:

1. To develop a sense of world citizenship.
2. To develop a sense of co-operation.
3. To introduce a vocational point of view in education.
4. To develop qualities of citizenship.
5. Education to ensure the growth of all citizens.

Exercises

1. Discuss the basic nature of communistic philosophy of educatior in U.S.S.R. as existed upto 1991.
2. Explain the meaning of principal tenets of democratic philosophy of education as obtained in modern Russia after the breaking up of U.S.S.R.

Chapter 52

Control of Education in Russia

The Control Pattern as Existed in U.S.S.R

Before the revolution of 1917 the imperialist government exercised complete control over education. But afterwards the government established educational institutions according to communistic doctrines. Education was centralised and put under strict state control.

A national unit was formed for supervision and administration of all educational centres in U.S.S.R. The Education Ministry exercised complete control over organisation and administration of education. Education Ministry had its sections of Ministry of Culture and Ministry of Higher Education. For industrial and vocational education the co-operation of All Union Ministry of Labour was obtained. The responsibilities for universities and teachers' training institutions rested on the Ministry of Higher Education, but technical and industrial education was looked after by the Joint-Education Ministry.

The educational policies were determined by the communist party. The communist party introduced a uniform educational policy in the country. The Joint Educational Ministry determined the educational policy by convening a congress from time to time. The congress was the first and the only unit for determining the educational policy. All the states had to implement this policy. Other local, regional, and divisional units had no say in the planning of educational policy. The Joint Ministry of Education had more than 16 administrative units. Each unit was called a department of education which looked after the development of education under its sphere. It had nothing to say about the educational policy. It had just to implement it. According to the constitution of 1936, the Union Government laid down the following education goals for the country:—

1. To spread universal, free and compulsory education in all the states.
2. For children between 7 and 15 years of age education to be made compulsory.
3. Secular education based on State Instructions will be free from church influence.
4. Boys and girls will be given equal facilities for secondary and higher education.
5. Everyone will be given primary education through his mother tongue.
6. From the fourth class Russian language will have to be accepted as a second language.
7. Private schools will not be recognised.
8. Education will be fully under the state control.

The Joint Education Ministry in determination of its educational policy had to consult the General Committee of Communisty party, Council of People Commission of Soviet Union and Central Executive Committee. The Planning Commission approved the expenditure on education.

Education Through Regional Units

As we have already said earlier, there were 16 educational regions in the country and these were called education departments. These various education departments functioned like subordinate authorities under the Joint Education Minister.

The regional education department had many subdepartments under it, such as, social and politechnic, etc. The department of literature and publication arranged for books, newspapers and magazines and cultural performances and films. It also looked after educational administration, expenditure and school buildings. Teachers training was controlled by it. Department of Adult Education and Department of Vocational Education were looked after by it. Department of Scientific and Art Institute organised teaching in science, fine arts and music.

The Education Minister was a member of the council of ministers of the Soviet Union Republic. The Education Minister was responsible for all the planning in education for the country. At times, he participated in the Meetings of Local Education, Research Institute and Local Education Conference.

Communist Party Decided Educational Policy

All the citizens were not the members of the communist party. Less than 10% of the people were enrolled as the members of the communist party. General Secretary of the party was very often the real ruler of the country. Education was used as a chief means for creating faith in the public for communism. Therefore, communist policies were incorporated in the educational system. The Youth Communist Organisation arranged for education in communist ideologies for all the communists at centres of education after the general teaching classes got over. This organisation prepared future administrators and leaders of the communist government.

A Central Committee determined the chief communist policies which were to be carried out without any question. The educational policies, too, were determined by the Central Committee.

Control of Education in Democratic Russia To-day

Districts, cities and towns are considered as independent units in the Russian educational system of to-day. The district is the largest unit which is sub-divided into cities and towns which have their own departments of education. Many rural regions have combined to form a rural educational district which is given legislative, administrative and executive powers.

Each city, town and village chooses its own representative who is known as a member or deputy. Such members or deputies form an administrative committee which appoints a Director of Education who is the chief executive officer of the education department. The public expects from its elected representatives that they will arrange for education according to their need.

School buildings and educational equipment upto the secondary stage of education are under the direct control of Director of Education, i.e., the chief execuitve officer.

The principal of the school occupies an important place in the system of local educational control. He is selected by the department of education of the Local Executive Committee. For internal school arrangements the principal is wholly responsible. He appoints other teachers and workers after consultation with Local Executive Committee. There is a Local School Council for the advice of the principal. The council consists of the principal himself, teachers and school workers.

The government of Russia has arranged for uniform, universal and compulsory education in order that the local public may co-operate in its own educational affairs. This arrangement is well accepted by all concerned as the guardians co-operate fully in the education of their wards by giving all kinds of financial help and full co-operation.

In Russia there is a School Parent Association in each locality for fostering co-operation in various types of developmental enterprises in the area of education. This association participates in leisure-time activities organised by students. It also helps needy children and orphans.

There are local school inspectors who are selected from the local teachers having at least three years' teaching experience. In garde, these inspectors are lower to inspectors appointed by the Education Ministry. They help teachers in their day to day teaching work.

Financial Help Granted

Various educational centres in Russia are given necessary financial grants. Guardians and members of local committee also share a part of the financial responsibility pertaining to Nursery and Kindergarten schools. The industrial organisations of the country forego a part of their wages for pre-primary education. The provincial government also helps in erecting buildings of Nursery and Kindergarten schools.

In addition to guardians' help, the state government also gives adequate help to primary and secondary schools. Ricl guardians have to bear the total expenditure of the education of their wards, whereas those with low income get free education for their children.

The Russian government gives adequate help for higher education. Many scholarships have been instituted. The state is fully responsible for teachers' education. According to the data available in 1992 for social and technological education about 79% of the expenditure was shouldered by the government and 25% by the local organisations.

SUMMARY

The Pattern Control of Education as Executed in U.S.S.R. upto 1991: The Joint Educational Ministry was the central administrative unit. It had many other such subsidiary ministries. The Communist Party chalked out the educational policies. The Community Party had directed the union government to make education compulsory, free and universal for children between 7 and 15 years of age.

Control of Education in Russia To-day: District, city and town are local units. Each unit has its own education department and executive committee. Its members are elected by the public. This committee chooses the director of education. School-parents association. The principal occupies an important place.

Financial Help to Educational Institutions: State governments, local organisation and school parents association give financial help. The state government has the whole responsibility of teachers' education.

Exercises

1. Describe the nature of control over education as existed in U.S.S.R. upto 1991.
2. What is the nature of control over education in modern Russia today?

Chapter 53

Pre-Primary Education

The Scheme of Pre-Primary Education

The modern pre-primary education in Russia is meant for children between 3 to 7 years of age. The purpose of pre-primary education is to prepare children for primary education. Pre-primary education in Russia may also be regarded as an attempt to provide a necessary psychological environment, according to democratic philosophy of life. At the pre-primary stage an attempt is made to promote healthy growth of children.

The Ministry of Health is responsible for pre-primary education. The Ministry of Education encourages the opening of nursery schools and kindergartens. Many organisations such as, factories and mills run their own pre-primary schools. The guardians give some fees for lunch and breakfast only.

Nursery Education

In the Russian education special attention is paid to the educational environment because the same will mould the character of children. The educational processes affect the physical development of the child. Hence, health visitors or school physicians pay special attention to the health of children before they are admitted to nursery schools. When the children attain the age of about a year and a half health visitors or school physicians carry out periodic checks to monitor the childrens' habits and natural propensities. Through physical activities based on improvised equipments, children are led towards healthy growth. Adequate attention is paid on social development by providing such activities which entail the co-operation of a number of children. Suitable toys and play-devices have been arranged for children in nursery schools.

Nursery schools, through health visitors and school physicians, maintain direct relationships with parents so as to educate them regarding health habits of children and ingredients of balanced diet. Milk-distribution centres also provide necessary information in this regard. The kindergarten school teachers visit homes and prepare children in advance for kindergarten education. There is a close co-operation between nursery and kindergarten schools. The nursery schools prepare children for kindergarten schools. The government encourages people to open nursery schools in their respective areas. The government provides some financial grants for this purpose. Housing Committees in various areas provide full financial assistance to nursery schools in their areas.

The Kindergarten System

The kindergarten system is little different from the nursery system. The kindergarten schools are very helpful to working mothers who admit their children to these schools. For rural areas there are summer kindergartens for working mothers. Industrial institutes and the business centres finance kindergarten schools in their areas. The guardians share the expenditure of their wards. But the pension-holders, war casualty families and unmarried mothers have to shoulder only a partial expenditure on their wards. This partial share is determined according to the number of children and the income of the guardians.

The kindergarten schools' teachers visit nursery schools and homes for preparing children for kindergarten education. In kindergarten schools dance, music, physical exercises, sports and recreational activities are arranged. For these, suitable curriculum have been so prepared as to inculcate the spirit of team co-operation in children. They are also given opportunities for acquiring knowledge by visiting social centres and other places worth seeing. After their visits to these centres, children are encouraged to write down their experiences. Thus some practice in writing is given. Relevant and suitable pieces from the writings of poets and writers are used for entertaining and also to impart necessary knowledge. The children are helped to develop a democratic out-look. The lady-teachers teach reading, writing and arithematic and behave like mothers. The school time is generally of 6 hours duration.

Summary

The Pre-primary Education Scheme: This scheme in Russia is generally meant for the young children of the working mothers. The pre-primary schools are directly controlled by the Ministry of Education. Special attention is paid to health and cultivating good habits.

Nursery Education: This is meant for working mothers' children less than 3 years of age. Health visitors look after the physical activities of the children. Through various types of plays co-operative spirit is developed in the children.

Kindergarten Schools: These are meant for working mothers' children between 3 and 7 years of age. Before admission to these schools children are prepared for the same in nursery schools and in homes. Reading, writing and arithematic are taught here. Healthy habits are developed. Guardians give fees but war-sufferers, unmarried mothers and pension-holders are not to pay any fees.

Exercises

1. Describe the system of pre-primary education in Russia to-day.
2. What can India learn from the pre-primary education as obtained in Russia to-day?

Chapter 54

Primary Education

Primary Education Scheme

Adequate attention has been paid to primary education in Russia. Education for the children between 8 to 12 years of age has been made free, universal and compulsory. Four graded primary schools have been established. Some of these schools are one-room schools as well. The Ministry of Education is responsible for primary education.

Time and Classes

Class teaching method is usually emphasised. Individual teaching is also given. However, there is little scope to children for self-activity. They have generally to do assigned work. For older children the period is for 40 minutes and for the younger ones it is shorter. The students respect their teachers. The school time is generally from 9 a.m. to 2.30 p.m. Due to environmental factors this timing may be changed. Younger children are given leave at 1.00 p.m. Teachers work for 4 to 6 hours. For extra-work the teachers are paid extra-allowances.

Schools are held in buildings of bricks and mortar and also in tents at places. One-teacher-schools, one-class schools and four-graded-primary schools are found in Russia. In some backward areas schools are held in tents because of the mobile nature of the inhabitants.

Discipline in Primary Schools

Earlier strict disciplinary rules were not imposed but now each school has to follow some disciplinary rules. It is so because of the impact of the Second World War. It was thought that adults had the experience and capacity to determine the nature of future of the children. Therefore, a disciplinary environment is necessarily created for children. However, the personality of the child is developed in a democratic environment.

In 1943, 20 rules of discipline were promulgated regarding personal and social behaviour considered good for all citizens including the teachers. These rules were introduced into the schools through the language text books. The students were encouraged to memorise these rules. These rules pertain to home and social life of children. For example, children under 16 years of age were not permitted to see any drama or cinema picture after 10 p.m. In the night they were not allowed to roam about on the street. If any child goes against these rules he was regarded as a psychological case and was given the necessary treatment. All these rules have been now relaxed and the parents are now free to look after the growth of their children in their own way.

Curriculum and Examination System

Curriculum:

The Ministry of Education prescribes the curriculum for primary education. Teaching of vocabularies and use of words are specially emphasised. All the subjects are compulsory. For the first three classes, under the supplementary programme, are included experiments, demonstration, field-trips, dramatizations and fine arts. At times, the children are taken to the professional theatres also.

Language, mathematics, geography, history, music, nature study and physical education are taught. Reading, writing and use of grammar are well practised. In the teaching of geography, local geography is also taught along with geography of the country. In the teaching of various subjects, different types of material aids and devices are used. Charts, films, maps and models are also employed. Some text-books are published with a view to encourage experimental work in the schools. These text-books are translated into regional languages also. Childrens' interests, aptitudes and needs are emphasised in the preparation of text-books. The teachers are allowed to make minor adjustments in these text-books according to their local needs. In the revision of text-books, the points of view of teachers according to the local requirements are duly considered.

For the six days in a week lessons are prescribed in the text-books. In the classes I and II, 24 lessons, in the class III, 25 lessons and in the class IV, 27 lessons are taught in a week. Generally, a teacher teaches all the subjects to a class. At some places a teacher continues to teach the same group of children in the four successive years of primary education. The period is of 45 minutes followed by 10 minutes leisure. There is a 15 minutes interval. The parents pay for the lunch of their wards.

The Examination System:

There is an examination committee consisting of the principal and two other teachers. The inspector of schools of the region is also present at the time of examination. The examination is generally oral. At the end of the fourth year there is a transfer examination, after passing which the child enters the junior high school.

The Ministry of Education prints examination cards for guidance of the primary schools. This card contains various types of examination questions, some of which are to be used in the examination. In the oral examination correct pronunciation and the method and style of giving the answers are considered of great importance. The examination system at the primary stage is so well developed that there is a cordial relationship between the students and examiners. No partiality is shown.

SUMMARY

The Primary Education Scheme: For the children between 8 to 12 years of age. Afterwards it was made compulsory for children between 7 and 15. Strict disciplinary rules are followed with a democratic out look. All the subjects are compulsory.

An examination committee consists of the principal and two teachers. The Inspector of schools is also present. The Ministry of Education prepares an examination card.

EXERCISES

1. Describe briefly the primary education in Russia to-day.
2. Give your own evaluation of primary education as prevailing in Russia to-day.

Chapter 55

Secondary Education

The Secondary Education Scheme

During the third decade of the current century, a 10 year school plan for children between 7 and 17 years of age was started. This pattern combined both primary and secondary education and it aimed at centralisation of schools. But after the Second World War this 10 year plan was divided into three groups. The first four years of this plan were given to the primary stage and the remaining six years to secondary education. The secondary education was further divided into two parts—junior high and high schools stages. Thus, classes I to IV made primary education, V to VII junior high school education and VIII to X high school classes. The junior high school for children between 12 to 14 years of age and high schools group for children between 15 to 17 or 18 years of age were arranged.

In Russia both 7 year and 6 year patterns exist. In the 7 year pattern 4 year primary education and 3 year high school education is arranged in the same building or another place nearby. In the 6 year pattern 3 year junior high school and 3 year high school education are combined. Ordinarily, 7 year pattern schools are more in favour.

Co-Education

Upto 1943 co-education was prevalent. But after 1943 some

instances of indiscipline were marked and schools for boys and girls were separately established. Gradually, this change reached the junior high school stage as well. Only in rural areas and in vocational education both boys and girls were taught together in junior high and high school classes. But now most of the high schools are co-educational. Needless to say that the primary schools are also meant both for boys and girls.

Curriculum, Time-Table and Classes

Curriculum for Junior High School Classes:

In classes V, VI and VII, general science, mathematics (arithmatic, algebra, geometry and trignometry), history, geography, art, mechanical drawing, Russian or a local language are taught. If the school is in the Russian region, Russian is taught from the class III otherwise its teaching begins from class V. Students have to learn physical education and social studies compulsorily. In classes VI and VII the teaching of physics and chemistry also begins.

The High School Curriculum:

In class VIII, IX and X the importance to high academic education is realised. Hence, mathematics and science are specially emphasised. Since 1947 logic is also introduced. Russian literature and technology are also included in the curriculum.

The Time-Table and the Classes:

The last day of the week is generally a holiday. In cities the schools run for 6 days, whereas in rural areas they run for all the 7 days. The academic year is from September 1 to June 30. Each class begins from September 1, but various classes end on various dates in June. There is a winter vacation from December 30 to January 10 and spring holidays from March 26 to 31. At some places the spring holiday is for full one month, i.e., from March 26, to April 26. This distinction is due to the climate of the region concerned. In cities, for class V, there are 26 periods per week and for other classes 27. In rural areas, for class V, there are 31 periods per week and for other classes 32. Each period is of 45 minutes duration. The school starts from 8 or 9 in the morning. The system of subject teacher is practised. For backward students individual attention is specially paid. Grading is also done according to the age of the students. At the age 11, 14 and 17, there is generally a transfer examination.

Fees and Teaching of Various Subjects

Fees: Upto class VII there is no fees. In the classes IX and X and in vocational and technical schools, some fees are charged. The fee is generally 3% of the total expenditure per student. Orphans, children of invalid parents and soldiers are not charged any fees. Meritorious students are exempted from paying any fees; instead, they are given scholarship.

Religion and Foreign Language Teaching: Teachers cannot give any religious instruction in the school. Under foreign languages, French, German and English are preferred.

Social Studies: It is intended to acquaint the students with social, economic and political organisation of the country and also of other countries in the world. For this a definite curriculum is prescribed.

Physical Eduation: Physical education has been compulsory since 1944. In the last three classes of secondary education it becomes like a formal military training. The drill sergeant takes attendence and gives instructions in physical education to a class of fifteen students. Girls have to learn nursing art and the mechanism of telephone and radio operation.

Examination System

In the examination system are included a test on the entire work of the session and also the conduct, behaviour and regularity of the students. Excepting class VII and X examinations of other classes are conducted in June. The medium of examination for class VII and X is Russian language. Except mathematics, other subjects are examined orally. There is an examination board consisting of the education officer, principal, subject teacher and two other teachers. On the basis of the examination results, bright students are awarded silver or gold medals. Exceptionally bright students are admitted to universities without having passed the high school examination.

Vocational Selection

According to the law of compulsory education in Russia, children upto 15 years of age, i.e., upto class VII have to be present in schools. No child below fourteen years of age can be employed in any industry. Thus, class VII is the turning point in education. That is why, only after passing class VII the vocation of the student may be decided. Under this system students having obtained very high marks in class VII are sent for higher education or high technical training, the second class students are sent for ordinary professional or mechanical training and average students are sent to some industrial centres, if they are willing to go.

In vocational selection, students are given due guidance keeping in mind their interests and capacities. Through newspapers, magazines and in public places necessary vocational informations and guidance are given to students. In fact, students of class VII, IX and X are prepared for higher education. The representatives from higher education institutes occasionally meet students of classes X and try to attract them towards higher education.

Technical Education Technicums

In Russia there are about six thousand technicums for training of middle grade specialists for various technical fields. These technicums offer three to five year curriculum for children who have passed class VII and provide training in various industries, agriculture, health services, economic law, teaching and transport, etc. The Education Ministry prescribes the curriculum for each of the areas. There are separate centres for training in various areas.

For students of class VII who score average marks, practice schools are run. By taking admission to practice schools, students become good workers in certain areas. These schools are of three types. The first type prepares half-skilled workers after giving six months training for working in mines, small industries and other constructive schemes. The second type gives two years course for preparing mechanics in transport, machine making factories. The third type provides training in rail, telegraphy and telephone fields. In all these arrangements, the desire, interest and aptitude of the student are adequately honoured according to the demands of democracy.

The technicums provide free education. The trainees are given the necessary training. No one can leave without completing the training and even after completing the training, one has to observe certain prescribed rules and discipline. The graduates of the technicums may choose to serve for 4 to 5 years in related areas.

Summary

High School Scheme: Ten year scheme divided into primary, junior high and high schools. Classes V, VI and VII are added to the primary school to make a seven year scheme. Co-education is prevalent.

Curriculum, Time-Table and Classes: Separate curriculum for junior and high school classes. From Class V Russian language along with regional language. All subjects are taught. In cities six days and in villages seven days a week. Twenty seven periods in cities and thirty periods in rural schools. Both individual and class-teaching.

Fees and Subjects Teaching: No religious teaching. French, German and English are taught. Social, economic and physical education compulsory. Wards of soldiers and invalid guardians and orphans obtain free education. Scholarships for better students.

Examination System: Oral examination. The whole session work, conduct and discipline taken into consideration. Vocational selection after class VII.

Technicums: Three types of factory-schools. Various types of training schools for various fields.

EXERCISES

1. Give a brief account of the high school education in Russia as obtained to-day.
2. What aspects of secondary education of Russia have appealed to you most and why?
3. Describe the nature of technical education in Russia.

Chapter 56

Teacher Education

The development of education depends upon the ability of the teacher. After the Revolution of 1917, there has been a tremendous expansion of education in Russia and the number of students increased hundred times. Hence, necessity of able teachers was acutely felt. In order to get efficient teachers short-term training courses were introduced and untrained teachers were also given teaching assignments. Shifts were introduced in the schools. Soon arrangements were made for the training of untrained teachers. But the Second World War impeded the training of teachers. After the War, for the development of vocational and industrial education, the necessity of teachers was again felt. The system of compulsory and free education also directed the attention of the government on teacher education.

Pre-Primary Teacher Education

For this stage generally, there is a three year curriculum. This training system is divided into sixteen parts. These parts are completed in 175 hours in one year. There are independent training centres for nursery and kindergarten teachers. In this training the subjects taught are history, hygiene, physical education, psychology, history of education, reading method, speech-style, story-telling, nature-study, music and painting The researches done at this stage are also brought to the notice of the teacher.

Primary School Teacher Education

There are teacher institutes for elementary teachers providing three year course. The graduates of class VII may be admitted to this course. Municipal boards in towns and cities and certain bodies in rural areas arrange for this education. The regional departments of education exercise full control over these.

Teachers do practice teaching in training schools. Lecture method is the basic system of teaching. Each trainee has to acquire proficiency in some musical instrument. In addition, he has to learn history, geography, arithmetic, Russian and regional language, nature-study, psychology, art of teaching, physical education, music and painting.

Junior High School Teacher Education

The Institute provides training to junior high school teachers. Graduates of class X may be admitted to this course. The trainees have to learn physical education, health education, psychology and pedagogy. The trainee has to specialise in the teaching method of the subject also. The entire curriculum is divided into three parts. In the first part one has to learn mathematics and physics, in the second part Russian language and history and in the third part chemistry, biology and geography. Each Institute of Teacher Training has a model school where practice teaching is done.

The Secondary School Teacher Education

There is a Secondary Education Institute for preparing high school teachers. It has a four year curriculum. It is of graduation standard. The minimum qualification for admission is high school certificate or admission certificate examination for higher education. In the first year of the course there is theoretical teaching. In the second and third years, practical work is also included along with the theoretical ones. Regional language is the medium of instruction. The study of Russian language is compulsory.

The curriculum is divided into three parts. The first and

second part include teaching of professional subjects and the third part generally consists of practice teaching.

Under the professional subjects are included pedagogy, educational development, teaching method and psychology. In another group known as the socio-philosophical group, there are history, Russian language and literature, and political economy. This group, too, is compulsory. In the third part the student teacher has to specialise in the teaching of some subjects.

For semi-trained teachers there is a short-time teaching course. After passing this course the teacher is given a teaching diploma. The duration of this short time course is one year, and students having passed high-school are admitted to it. For training lady-teachers, class XI is attached to the high school. In this class, teaching method is taught to the teachers. Women, after having passed this class are appointed as teachers in primary schools.

In-Service Training

For the teachers already teaching in some schools, there is a training programme. This programme is of two kinds. The first is called refresher training. Under this programme the teacher is acquainted with the latest researches in the field of education. The second programme is for semi-trained or untrained teachers. Such persons after passing the second programme are given teaching certificates.

For various districts a particular place is selected for in-service training. In each district there is a bureau of education which provides educational informations and counselling. The teachers in the rural areas are greatly benefited by this arrangement. Debates, lectures, exhibitions and teaching models are also organised for the benefit of such teachers.

The High School training institution in cities provide in-service training. Some of them offer a two years evening course and organise seminars, conferences, exhibitions and debates for the benefit of teachers.

There is a system of correspondence training for in-service teachers. The Education Ministry and some teachers' training departments organise the correspondence course. This course also serves trained women teachers.

The Service Conditions of Teachers

Salary and Facilities: The monthly salary of teachers generally ranges between 1200 to 2500 rubles. The salary of a teacher is based on four hours of work per day. So, many teachers earn more by putting in more hours as extra labour. The qualifications, teaching experience and individual efficiency actually determine the salary of a teacher in Russia. In order to develop the efficiency of a teacher a more efficient teacher is given a higher salary. A teacher acquiring a special qualification or degree is immediately given 100 or more rubles as increment. Teachers are given in-service facilities. Boarding and medical facilities are also provided. Lady teachers are given maternity leave.

Teachers' Association: There are teachers' associations of teachers for various levels, such as pre-primary, primary, secondary and higher. Each teacher has to be a member of the association meant for his level. The teachers' associations are organised not for compelling the government to concede to their demands but, for solving academic problems. Every teacher pays about 3% of his salary as the association-fee. There are organisations after the name of subjects as well. These are meant only to solve the related educational problems.

Summary

Pre-primary Teacher Education: Three years' course. Separate arrangement. Professional subjects, history, Russian language and literature, science, social science and fine arts are taught. Independent arrangement for nursery and kindergarten schools.

Primary School Teacher Education: Students having passed seventh class are admitted. In addition to professional subjects some of the subjects of the high school curriculum are also taught. Primary schools are attached for practice teaching. Ladies receive training by teaching in attached class XI.

Junior-High School Teacher Education: Graduates of class X or higher education are admitted. Specialisation in subjects.

High School Teacher Education: Four years course. Curriculum divided into three parts.

In-service Training: This is arranged for giving adequate information about relevant research to in-service teachers. One year course. Regions distributed into districts.

Conditions of Teachers: Salary between 1200 to 2500 rubles. Extra pay for extra work. Boarding and medical facilities. Teachers' associations for each level.

Exercises

1. Describe the nature for teacher education at the pre-primary and primary levels in Russia.
2. How is the teacher education at the junior, high and secondary stages organised in Russia?
3. What aspects of teacher education in Russia have appealed to you most and why?

Chapter 57

Higher Education

Administration of Higher Education during the Soviet Regime

Universities, higher schools or institutes impart higher education in Russia. The State Training schools meant for specialists are controlled by Commissariate of Education and all technical schools are controlled by the Committee for Higher Technical Education. Before 1946, higher schools were controlled by that ministry in relation to which workers were to be prepared and trained. But this system presented an administrative difficulty. Therefore, the general methodological guidance was given under the control of the Committee on High Education. This committee was later changed into Ministry of Higher Education which was connected with the Ministry of Culture. For local administrative facility, an academic council consisting of professors is appointed. This committtee looks after the appointment of teachers, teaching work and research.

The Current Prevailing System

Method of Admission:

After passing secondary education all the citizens between 17 and 35 year of age may sit for an entrance examination if they want admission to some school or institute of higher education. The student of literary group give the entrance examination in Russian language, history, English and either German or French and geography. For admission to higher technical schools mathematics, physics, chemistry, Russian language and literature and a foreign language are subjects for which canditates must take test. Examination is both written and oral. Students awarded silver and gold medals are exempted from this examination.

University System

Department:

According to various subjects there are various departments, such as agriculture, military science, technology, fine arts and education. Special attention is paid to the teaching, social economic training and industrial practice. For these subjects, there are special universities.

Arrangement for Vocational Selection:

Before admission to a university the student has to choose a vocation and prepare himself for the same.

Rector:

The rector is the chief administrative officer of a university. He has two assistants, one for educational programmes and another for financial and administrative affairs. For the various subjects there are deans of various faculties. There is a learned council and a senate. A dean has four to nine faculties under him. Each professor has to teach and guide researches.

Curriculum and Duration of Higher Education

Curriculum:

The teachers and students have to work according to the prescribed curriculum and programme schedule. Laboratory work, general lectures, workshop practice, and seminars are the essential parts of the curriculum. Each teacher and the student is given a copy of the curriculum in the beginning of the session.

The Academic Session and Duration:

An academic session consists of two terms. The first term extends from September 1 to January 23. This is followed by a winter vacation of 2 weeks. The second term is from February 7 to July 1 followed by a summer vacation of two months. There is an examination at the end of each term. After passing the examination the student may be admitted to the new course. If one is regular in the practical work, he is declared passed and is allowed to continue his education.

The duration of higher education is generally of four to six years. According to the nature of education, duration is determined. Generally, pedagogical and vocational institutions have four year course, higher technical schools have five year course and medical institutes have six year course.

Practical Work:

Each student has to do practice work and has to acquaint himself with the nature of the job which he will be called upon to do later. Engineers, foremen and others have to do practical work in their respective areas.

Scholarships, Library and Correspondence Course

Scholarships:

The state provides scholarships to progressive students. Directors of Education decide about these scholarships. Students with an excellent academic record get regular stipends in addition to 25% additional grant for their other expenses. Thus, a student is able to pursue his studies with single-minded devotion. A stipend may be between 500 rubles to 800 rubles. It is awarded on the basis of type of higher education and year of study. Students with special abilities in studies and research works are awarded scholarships instituted after the names of great writers and scientists. The wards of invalid war-soldiers are given free education. Higher education fee is from 40 to 60 rubles per month. Physical education is a compulsory part of general education. Each student is given boarding and medical facilities.

Library:

Libraries are free in Russia. They are full of books and study-materials. There are reference-books of all types. The library of Moscow University is of world fame.

Correspondence Course:

Correspondence course are prevelant in Russia for about the last 40 years. In 1992 there were about 100 correspondence courses institutions. Their admission rules, curriculum and examination systems are the same as for regular students. After examination, students taking correspondence course are awarded degrees like regular students. The government has accorded equal status to this educational system.

SUMMARY

Administration and Admission Rules: Medal holders have not to appear for any entrance examination.

University System: There are departments of agriculture, military science, education, fine arts, industry, technology and sociology. The rector is the administrative officer with two assistants. Each faculty has a Dean, Professor and student representatives.

Curriculum, Academic Session and Duration: Studies and Laboratories. An academic session of two terms—one from September 1 to January 23 and the other from February 7 to July 1. Examination at the end of each term. Duration is of 4 to 6 years.

Scholarships, Library and Correspondence Course: Scholarships after the name of great writers and scientists. Library fee. Correspondence course degree the same as of the regular course.

EXERCISES

1. Describe briefly the nature of higher education in Russia.
2. What aspects of higher education in Russia have appealed to you most and why?

Chapter 58

Adult Education

Before 1991

Illiteracy in Russia before the Revolution of 1917 was the highest in the world. But, after the Revolution the communist government tried to spread literacy and bring knowledge to people as far as possible. Due to enforcement of free, compulsory and universal education, the communist government succeeded in spreading literacy. However, in some distant rural areas many illiterate persons were found.

Democratic Set Up

Under the adult education plan now the present Russian government wants that everybody should acquire education at least upto class X. After passing class VII a large number of students enter vocational, professional and technical training centres. About twenty percent of students go for higher education. Evidently, the adult education upto class X poses a difficult problem. The Russian government through evening and part-time classes has arranged for adult education for the workers. Various industrial, vocational and business centres have to arrange for adult education for workers in their own areas. This adult education is generally of two years continuous education. In this course 4 to 5 hours teaching is arranged per week. Some organisations provide general education along with training in their specific or technical or vocational areas.

In rural areas educational opportunities are not so rich as in urban places. In many cities, departments of education and local organisations offer five year educational programmes for adults. Many local councils, too, try to remove illiteracy by providing adult education. In the system of university education as well, some lectures are organised for adults. Now a system of Sunday universities has been started for education for in-service persons. Many educational centres, therefore, lecture-organisations and music-clubs provide recreation and cultural education to adults. Many public clubs, libraries, theatres and cinema-halls impart social, political, educational and economic informations to adults. Many museums and exhibitions are organised in the areas of agriculture, industry and business for acquainting adults with latest scientific developments in various fields. Many radio-centres broadcast professional, political, industrial and educational programmes for educating adults. Many trained guides are appointed in various museums for imparting necessary informations to adult visitors.

The Russian government has arranged for many mobile museums, libraries and cinemas for educating adults in various aspects of active life. Many universities give correspondence courses for the benefit of adults.

Summary

After the Revolution of 1917 literacy spread. Now departments of education, industrial centres and professional centres provide adult education. Providing knowledge upto class X to adults. Sunday universities, evening universities, museums, clubs, exhibitions, theatres, cultural centres, radios, cinemas and libraries spread adult education. Mobile libraries, museums, theatres and cinemas also help in spreading education in adults.

Exercises

1. Describe the nature of adult education in Russia.
2. What aspects of adult education programmes as current in Russia will you like to adopt for adults in India and why?

PART VI

General Trends in Comparative Education

Chapter 59

General Trends in Comparative Education

Some general trends are quite evident in the educational systems of various countries under review. Variations found in them are due to the differences in the gradual development of their various stages of education. In fact, they also appear to be under an impact of identical public demands. In this part of the book it is proposed to understand such demands.

Ever-increasing Importance of Pre-primary Education

Importance of pre-primary education was not very much socially recognised before the advent of the nineteenth century. Upto the 18th century it was thought that during early years of life the parents were best suited to look after the education of their young ones. But due to the impact of industrial revolution this idea was discarded and the parents began to feel the necessity of sending their children to schools. This urge was also there because of the pressure that both the mother and father should earn in order to make their life more comfortable as demands of life were ever-increasing. Hence women also began to take up outside jobs along with men. This situation created the necessity of developing some such institutions which might take care of young children while the mothers were away at work. These institutions gradually sprang up at various places according to the pressing social demands. These places were entrusted with the responsibility of teaching young ones the elementary Reading, Writing and artithmatic. Thus a wave of social demands gave rise to the idea of the pre-primary education. The women while going to work in office or factories used to leave their young ones at these places and pick them back while coming back home after offices or factory hours. In the beginning no time-table was fixed up for teaching such young children. The main job of such places was to look after the natural necessities of admitted children and to arrange for their food and minimum comforts. Gradually, these places were transformed into certain formalities and they began to take the shape or infant classes or small schools. Pestalozzi, Froebel and Maria Montessori did pioneer work in organising infant education in nursery or pre-primary schools. Thanks to their efforts that today all over the world, running of infant classes, nursery and pre-primary schools has become a fashion of the day and now most of the parents try to get relief from the burden of looking after their young ones and teaching them the preliminary reading, writing and arithmetic. By and by the conviction gained ground that the period between early three years to six years of age is very important in the development of a child. Hence importance of nursery or pre-primary education has been recognised. To-day most of the parents prefer to send their children to pre-primary schools whether both the mother and father have to be out for their jobs or only one of them has to go out for this purpose. It has now become a status symbol for many parents to be able to send their young children for pre-primary education. As a result, there is a mushroom growth of pre-primary or nursery schools at several places in various countries. So it has become now difficult to believe whether such pre-primary institutions were started only for the infants of working mothers. In the beginning the charge of pre-primary education has been under private hands, but now in some countries the governments have also accepted some formal responsibility for running pre-primary and nursery schools directly or giving adequate financial assistance to private bodies for running them smoothly.

Primary Education

Even uptill now, it has not yet been possible for many countries to provide the required facilities for free and universal primary education to children within six to ten or eleven years of age. It will be futile to repeat what we have already stated about the various problems of primary education in the various countries under review in the foregoing parts of this book. However, it may be reiterated that they are still grappling with the problems of acute shortage of trained teachers, suitable school buildings, transport facilities for school-going children especially of distant areas full of difficulties due to dense forests, hill-tops and small rivers which place great impediments for young children in crossing over. Above all, the paucity of funds is blocking all proposals for reforms and expansion of primary education all over the world. Thus these are some of the major trends in primary education which are still defying smooth solutions because of the implied difficulties.

A student of comparative education has to understand the national circumstances of a country and general trends of the age separately. The knowledge of the general trends will help one to find out solutions of common problems from examples of other countries and to save oneself from adopting wrong methods for facing the implied difficulties.

Secondary Education

The position of secondary education is not good, because its conception and structure are undergoing changes. As a result, practical difficulties have surfaced up. For a student of comparative education, secondary education provides so much scope of study that it surpasses the limits of other stages of education which are apparently clearer in their perspectives and approaches.

The educational system of each country has its own unique feature because social, economic, cultural and historical circumstances of each one have been different. Nevertheless, it is quite natural to perceive some common trends in the educational system of each country, because human beings, ultimately, have to strive after some identical mundane and spiritual goals.

Three Major Trends in Modern Secondary Education

There appear to be three major trends in modern secondary education all over the world:

1. Unprecedented expansion of secondary education in each country.
2. A trend towards comprehensive co-ordination between primary and secondary education, and
3. Integration of cultural and vocational elements in the curriculum.

Onwards we shall understand the nature of these basic trends:-

1. Unprecedented expansion of secondary education: It is true that population explosion is a cause of expansion of secondary education, but this phenomenon alone should not be attributed to this explosion. Another cause of this expansion has been the wide expansion of primary education after the Second World War. A chain of primary schools spreading all over in each country has necessitated the expansion of secondary education. Hence almost in all the countries enrollment of students in secondary schools has increased beyond control and parents are hard hit to get their wards admitted to secondary schools of their choice.

2. Towards Comprehensive Co-ordination between Primary and Secondary Education: This trend is a result of huge expansion of secondary education. Upto the nineteenth century it was generally thought that primary education was complete in itself as it was meant for those children under tender age who had compulsionarily to take up some job after completing it. Secondary education, too, was considered to be complete in itself and it was principally meant for those who wanted to continue these studies in universities or other centres of higher education. Then seeking admission to a secondary school after graduating from a primary school was beset with many difficulties. From the advent of twentieth century the belief in people gradually developed that education is a continuous process and it is wrong to divide it into primary and secondary education. It is just possible that some children, due to their social and mental limitations, differ from each other. But this feature does not warrent to prescribe different levels of education. Therefore now primary and secondary education are considered as steps of one continuous process of education.

In most of the countries, to-day, the period of compulsory universal education is being increased in order that all the children may go upto the first phase of secondary education and see for themselves whether they can benefit from onward education. Besides, in several countries, secondary education has been made free. Children from poor sections of society are provided with books and free boarding and lodging. In many areas, transport facilities are also made available for school children. A tendency is also found for increasing the age-limit for choosing some vocation. Due to this tendency vocational courses have been instituted in secondary school curriculum in many countries.

Simultaneously, a trend is also seen to accept common courses of studies even at the junior secondary school stage. In some countries, efforts are also on to develop schools with comprehensive curricular varieties in order to enable children of all sections of society to get admission. In such comprehensive schools, guidance and counselling services have been organised for helping children to choose suitable courses of studies.

3. Integration of Cultural and Vocational Elements in the Curriculum: Alongwith the previously mentioned trends in secondary education, the traditional literary curriculum has been expanded by incorporating in it modern literary studies, modern sciences, commerce and some other technical subjects. Needess to add that introduction of such subjects in the curriculum has been done because of the unavoidable pressure of industrialisation. However, reformers of education have realised that at the secondary level, the major emphasis should also be on providing sufficient general education in order that the youths may develop in themselves the requisite capabilities for acquiring technical efficiencies through later training.

The Need of a Flexible Curriculum

In many countries efforts have been made for making the curriculum flexible in order to accommodate the capabilities and aptitudes of various types of students. Hence the curriculum is now being modified in terms of the need of students, and local and national requirements. Now an attempt is also seen to make the curriculum for promoting the physical, mental, emotional and moral development. The individual and social points of view are now kept in view in prepairing a curriculum. The curriculum is now being diversified for meeting the varying interests of students. The ideal of correlation and integration of various subjects is being adhered to for doing away with the idea of separate subjects which are now accepted as the integral branches of the same "knowledge —tree". Learning by doing at the primary stage and learning by production at the secondry level have been accepted as the ideal to be followed. It is believed that this approach to education will minimise the problem of unemployment and qualitative improvement, too, will be effected at the same time. Mexico has accepted this principle in developing its educational system. Russia and many African countries are trying to correlate their educational systems according to rural requirements. In Hungary, the curriculum is so made as to save the student from physical and mental fatique by encouraging him to do some personal practice. In France ample scope has been allowed in the curriculum for co-curricular activities which include "physical training" and "games and sports". For this purpose in Belgium some secondry school classes are organised near sea-shores, forests and hill-tops which are sometimes covered with snow.

The Problem of Over-Loaded Curriculum

This problem is being faced by several countries since the middle of the 20th century, An overloaded curriculum makes a student over-burdened with school work and home-tasks given by respective teachers of the school. This problem is particularly related to those secondary schools which prepare student for further university studies of academic nature. In U.S.A., the problem of over-loaded curriculum is not very acute, because the curriculum is very much diversified there. In other countries the curriculum is generally over-loaded because of the belief that the intellectual subjects should be studied for a longer period in order to derive adequate benefit from the same. Such a situation increases the load on a student's mind and his total development is adversely affected. Due to enormous expansion of secondary education, the problem of over-loaded curriculum is being experienced by most of the parents. In is felt that for solving this problem, great care should be taken particulary in understanding the aims of education at the time of developing the curriculum and preparing the textbook for the same. Reformers of education should also emphasise the kind of expectations from efforts in various areas of education and accordingly introduce suitable methods of teaching.

Variations are there in the causes of over-loaded curriculum in different countries. In some countries the number of subjects to be taught at the secondary level has led to over-loaded curriculum. In some countries the compulsion of studying a foreign language at the secondary stage has partly resulted into an over-loaded shape of the curriculum. In some countries due to the pressure of international relations the study of two modern foreign languages has created a difficulty in forging out a lighter curriculum. This situation is applicable in India and in some other Asian and African countries. In some countries, the study of regional languages has been made compulsory along with the mother tongue. There are some such regional languages in which suitable books in science, mathematics are not available. In such a situation, the students have to study English, French and other well-developed languages in which standard books in various subjects are found. In India in non-Hindi areas, the student has to study Hindi as the national language.

The problem of over-loaded curriculum is associated with social conditions also. So its satisfactory solution may be found by making some social changes as well. However, this problem has its educational aspect also and its solution may be sought by educationists through selection of only objective areas of knowledge and give them alone a place in the curriculum. During the Second World War such selections were made in the areas of science and mathematics in many European countries with great success. Accordingly, such selections were made in other countries also during the post-war era. These selections have proved to be practicable for classroom purposes through introducing changes in the teaching methods with the help of audio-visual aids and other new technologies of teaching. The experiment made in relation to forging out a core-curriculum is also another attempt for easing the problem of over-loaded curriculum. The concept of core-curriculum refers to the idea of "general science" which may include physics, chemistry, botany, zoology and other like subjects under the core-curriculum idea. The term "social studies" has also been forged out for incorporating history, civics, geography, economics and sociology into one group, so grouping of subjects under broad areas of "general science" and "social studies" has reduced the number of subjects to be taught at the secondry level and accordingly the problem of over-loaded curriculum has been partially solved. But for a successful solution of the issue it has also been recommended that good advanced books and teaching material aids are necessary along with modification of teacher education programme accordingly.

The problem of over-loaded curriculum is also related to the dominance of external examinations at the secondary stage of education. These examinations force teachers to teach such aspects of prescribed and other books which have no utility from educational viewpoint. So now in many countries greater emphasis is laid on internal evaluations by teachers. Thus the importance of external examination has been minimised. In some countries both internal and external evaluation systems have been accepted by allowing 60 per cent weightage to the external and 40 per cent to the internal evaluation. These are some of devices thought of for solving the problem of over-loaded curriculum.

Now in many countries experiments are being made in the area of teaching methods. Scientific and technological advancements have led to inventions of teaching aids of various kinds. Teachniques of programmed learning or instruction, teaching machines and teaching technology are being continually developed all over the world. Audio-visual aids are being emphasised in view of their utility. In European countries, India and in many other lands Open Universities have been established. Such universities benefit those persons who have not been able to derive advantages of university education because of their earlier adverse circumstances. Open Universities mainly depend upon correspondence courses allied with periodical contact programmes. T.V. and radio channels are also utilized in telecasting and broadcasting lessons to aspirants. Now some languages are taught through structural methods or through the medium of cultural development. The tendency to impart education through the mother tongue is gaining ground in various countries.

The Teacher and the Student

The teacher plays a very important role in the entire educational process. The student has to be given the necessary knowledge and practical training in various aspects of life as far as possible. Because of the ever-developing techniques in the area of teaching methods it has become now very necessary to introduce some changes in the teacher education programmes in order to facilitate the learning process. In-service teacher and pre-trained teacher programmes teacher's training techniques are being reorganised in view of the newly devised teaching machines and other mechanical aids. Efforts are on to mould teacher-training programmes for preparing teachers for rural areas according to the local requirements. In order to meet the shortage of trained teachers, short-term training programmes are being devised. For this purpose part-time and correspondence curriculum system are also being preferred in some countries. An attempt is also made to develop the quality of leadership in teachers.

The child has been accepted as the focal point in the entire educational process. Hence in all the countries education is being made child-centered. Giving proper attention on the individual differences of students is being particularly emphasised in various countries.

Administration and Discipline

The adequacy of educational administration and discipline has an effective impact on the entire educational system. To-day educational centres are beset with problems of indiscipline and bad administration. These days there is a colossal lack of such administrative authorities, who are able to establish a good workable relation between the public and government workers. At some places UNESCO is trying to train persons for producing reliable government workers. The educational administration is being decentralized for making it more relevant, practical, meaningful and flexible. Now a need for dynamic administration is felt in place of the old traditional one.

For improving the tone of educational administration it is felt all over the world that students, teachers and guardians should be made responsible for improving educational administration. In many European countries by enlisting the co-operation of children, teachers, guardians and public representatives, an attempt is also seen to make the educational administration related to life of the people. This approach has proved to be helpful particularly at the secondary and higher education stages. Yugoslavia is a good example of this feature, because therein the school administration and discipline, the principal, students and teachers are considered equally responsible for creating a good tone.

Without introducing the necessary reforms in the inspection system the administration and discipline cannot be improved. Therefore the term 'supervision' is now being used in place of inspection, become the word 'inspection' connotes a sense of bitter criticism and a feeling of ago. The term 'supervision' envelopes within itself a feeling of co-operation and advice between teachers, students and guardians. With this point of view some persons are now given training for becoming good supervisors.

School Building and Expenditure

Buildings are necessary for opening schools. In many countries scarcity of suitable school buildings is felt. At some places temporary sheds or improvised structures are used for running some schools. Many old buildings so far used for running schools are not suitable. Hence there is a pressing necessity for raising new buildings for schools. This will entail huge extra-expenditure. So expenditure on education is ever-rising beyond the available resources. Besides, enough funds are required for purchase of some reference books, organising laboratories and other teaching material aids. In India, Argentina, Russia and many European countries shift system has been adopted for accommodating more classes and students. At some places the system of 5 or 4 days a week has also bee introduced.

The problem of expenditure on education has necessitated the introduction of "economics of education" as a subject of study for teacher-trainers. Now education is being accepted as an investment. In all educational planning an attempt is made to minimise the expenditure as much as possible and also to check the possible wastage involved therein.

Research

Now in the field of education in all the countries, the system of traditional research is being replaced by applied and experimental research. The research is no more now an intellectual exercise alone. It is now brought to the functional level more. The main purpose of research in education is now to bring out reforms in educational procedures. Instructional, problematic and reformation—oriented research now are being more emphasized. Such a trend is seen in various countries of more the world.

Functional Literacy

Each country is now striving to wipe off illiteracy from its border. But so far no country has fully succeeded in doing so. One of the reasons for its failure is that literacy programme has not been quite functional and the programmes have never been continual for a sufficient duration. If the literacy programmes are related with production, then the illiterate adults will be utilizing their literacy in various practical phases of life and they will never forget it. It is better if the literacy programmes are related with the professions of illiterates adults. Then they will become more keenly interested in acquiring literacy.

In the foregoing pages we have hinted at some world-wide trends in educational systems. These trends have given rise to some other worldwide problems in education. Now we shall hint at some these problems.

The Problem of Change in the Conception of Education

Due to changes in social values principally arising from scientific and technological developments, the very conception of education has been modified. The head of humanity has been down in shame because of inhuman atrocities committed by the so-called civilized nations during the Second World War. In fact, the education prevailing in such nations has been defective and incomplete. The given education at the time failed to develop human virtues in the people. Then, education was concentrated towards the material and the related intellectual advancements. That education failed to develop moral and spiritual qualities in the people. This position bespeaks of backwardness of education. This shortcoming may be removed when the very conception of education is revolutionalised towards making it more human and progressive.

Those who regard education as an investment have looked at it purely from a materialistic viewpoint. In this concept, education becomes only a means of economic development. It is not regarded as a medium for spiritual advancement. To-day the most urgent need is that of world peace. The education which is regarded as a means for economic development can fulfil only some selfish ends and it can never develop human virtues. The education that develops moral and spiritual values may prepare a reliable background for establishing world peace by way of preparing such persons who will strive for the same. To-day money is being spent for physical and mental health, but nothing is being done for advancement of the 'self'. Only one nation cannot do much towards establishing world peace. In fact, all the nations should strive for it.

The nations that are regarded as developed are, in fact, undeveloped from the moral and human point of view. It is they who have posed a danger to world peace. Therefore the very conception of education should be so revolutionized that a society full of moral and human virtues is developed. Only then the various problems of the world may be solved within one frame of universal brotherhood.

Undoubtedly, the entire world, to-day, is enjoying the unprecedented benefits of scientific and technological advancements. There has been a great impact of the same on education as well. There has come a change in the social structure also. In view of the need of the changed social structure, we shall have to relate our educational efforts to the same. Unemployement and social unrest have been developed due to lack of close relationship between education and the changing society. For economic development we shall have to make our people self-dependent, and the national production will have to be increased. For this, more expenditure will be necessary for technological and industrial development.

Education is a life-long process. It must not be limited only to the boundaries of schools, colleges and universities. To-day we are not able to utilize those informal means of education which are in abundance alongwith educational institutions. Family, neighbourhood, society and social, religions and cultural institutions and media of communications contribute a lot towards education of people. Due to our multifarious engagements we find no time to come into their close contact. So by revising the concept of education we shall have to accept the informal means also as a source of education. This revising will also bridge the gulf between society and educational institutions.

Now education is not meant only for higher classes of society. In fact, it has become a right of the common man. So each country has to see that no one is deprived of this opportunity. We have to incorporate this kind of thinking in our new conception of education. Education should be such as to provide employment to all according to their interests. It should increase national production and incomes. Only general education cannot achieve this goal. Hence vocational education will have to be developed along with general or liberal education.

Democratization of Education

Foreign powers ruling over certain countries denied the opportunity of education to the common man. For example, an ordinary citizen did not enjoy the required educational facilities for his all round development during the British rule in India. The countries which have won freedom from the bondage of foreign rule should expand education in such a manner that it reaches all. Attempts should also be made to educate illiterate persons. Thus both qualitative and quantitative improvement should be effected in our educational endeavour.

The rise in population has made education very expensive. Now to provide education to all has become an acute economic problem. There is a shortage of school buildings, trained teachers and necessary material aids for use in educational procedures. Enrollment of students is increasing and it has become difficult to provide the needful to students and teachers. In such a situation we have to revise our conception of education and make it less expensive and more useful for the common people. U.N.E.S.C.O. records indicate that there have about 15 crore persons receiving education in the world in 1961. This figure has now in 2001 risen to more that 200 crore. The enrollment of students has increased at each stage of education—primary, secondary and university. The enrollment figures have been highest in Asian countries, the second in order comes Europe and the third is Russia.

The Problem or Bringing in Efficiency in the Educational System

We have said before that the expansion of education has increased the expenditure on education everywhere in the world. In the process of providing education to the common people, there has been quantitative improvement, but this position has adversely affected the qualitative side. The main reason for this feature may be attributed to lack of efficiency in the educational system. It has so happened, because alongwith procuring quantitative improvement, the national income did not increase. Therefore the expenditure could, be increased only in a very inadequate manner. This has resulted into placing pressure on the national treasury. In 1960 in U.S.S.R. the expenditure on education per student was 82 rubels and in 1969 this expenditure become 155 rubles per student. In India this expenditure in 1960 per student was 71.8 rupees and in 1969 it become 98.7 rupees. After 32 years i.e. in 2001 this expenditure in India per student has reached upto 350 rupees only. In view of the soaring prices, this increment cannot be regarded as satisfactory. Under this situation we cannot think of efficiency in education. Lack of efficiency in education has led to wastage and stagnation in education. Money spent on education cannot be meaningful unless we succeed in putting a check on wastage and stagnation. This needs efficient educational planning.

Problem of Education not Being Related to Life

The aim of education is to effect an all-round development of an individual. At present we are not able to achieve this goal because education is not related to life. This is a problem for all the countries of the world. At present, education is neither fulfilling the needs of the individual, nor is it able to meet the requirements of society. There is a gulf between society and education. The individual, to-day, is not self-dependent. He is not able to derive full benefit of education that he is getting. The main reason for this situation is lack of relationship between education and society. To-day throughout the world education is being made a means for vocationalization. But the vocational twist should not be only job-oriented. It is necessary to make education production oriented. The individual should be able to utilize the fruits of his education if it is moulded towards production. This will ease the problem of unemployment and the individual will be able to contribute his share in national production. This will be possible only when education is related with life. In fact, the utility of education consists in one's ability in solving his life problems himself, of course, with the help others at times.

Many countries have planned their education to-day keeping the above things in view. Some countries have changed the shape and organization of their higher education for solving their problems. Through the consent of its people, Albama has changed the aim, curriculum and administration of education. Rumania has enacted laws for bringing changes in its educational system. Ghana, Spain, Brazil and Yugoslavia have made surveys in their lands with a view to effect changes in their educational systems according to the needs of their people. France, India and some other countries have also tried to relate education with social and economic development. Japan, Thailand and Turkey have made central committees for reforms of their educational systems. Sweden and Spain have organised researches in education for finding out measures for reforms in education.

Women Education

In modern times, happily, it is seen that women are gaining singular partenership along with menfolk in the various social, political and economic pursuits. Alongwith this partnership they have also acquired equal rights for receiving education and entering into all types of services. Very recently, from the close of February, 1997 the Indian Parliament has been seriously considering for passing a law in favour of women's partnerships in various areas of life. Almost in all the countries of the world, to-day, the boys and girls have been granted equal rights for receiving free universal education upto the secondary stage. However, it will have to be admitted that in some countries boys outnumber girls in secondary schools and in some girls do so. For example, in U.S.A., industrial countries of Europe, Canada and New Zealand girls lag behind boys in schools and in many countries of South America, Africa and Middle East Asia the number of boys in secondary schools is larger than that of girls. In countries where there are separate vocational secondary schools, the number of girl students is higher that of boys. Thus keeping in view the entire global picture at the secondary level, the boys are outnumbering girls. At the university stage also the number of boys is still higher.

The poorer position of girl students in schools may be attributed to some social and economic causes. Still in many countries some resentment exists regarding equal partnership extended towards women, particularly in acquiring leadership in business, industries and higher government services. Simultaneously, the position of women with regard to marriage and domestic work remains inferior to that of men and this situation works as a great hinderance for women to forge their path ahead along with men. As a result, girls have to abandon their schools and colleges earlier that boys. This condition is persisting even in those countries where secondary education has been made almost free both for boys and girls, as the parents do not allow their daughters to receive education at least as long as soon are permitted. But now due to modern changes in technological and economic areas, the need of trained hands is being felt so acutely that both the men and women are being employed in industrial pursuits. It may be noted that now women have also succeeded in acquiring almost equal efficiencies in various fields of work along with men.

University Education

In many countries adequate arrangements have not yet been made for university education. Universities all over the world are facing acute economic shortage. The problem of students, indiscipline, relationship with the government, duration of degree courses the problem of university curriculum and teaching, examination system, expensiveness of higher education, the problem of hostels, libraries and affiliated colleges are some of the burning issues facing educationists all over the world.

Summary

Ever-increasing Importance of Pre-primary Education: All over the world there is now a chain of nursery schools, Kindergarten and Montessori schools which impart pre-primary education. A status symbol for parents in sending their children for pre-primary education. Hence mushroom growth of institutions imparting pre-primary education.

Primary Education: In many countries inadequate provision for universal education, India is a country in this position.

Secondary Education: The position is not good. The conception and structure under dispute.

Three Main Trends in Modern Secondary Education

1. Unpreceedented expanses of secondary education.
2. A trend towards comprehensive co-ordination between primary and secondary education.
3. Integration of cultural and vocational elements in the curriculum.

Unprecedented Expansion: Population rise and expansion of primary education are principal causes.

1. Towards Comprehensive Co-ordination between Primary and Secondary Education : Primary and secondary education are parts of one continuous educational process. In serveral countries secondary education has been made free. Vocational courses have been instituted in the curriculum. Schools with comprehensive curricular varieties. Guidance and counselling services have been organised.

2. Integration of Cultural and Vocational Elements: Place to modern literary studies, modern sciences, commerce and some technical subjects.

The Need of a Flexible Curriculum: Curriculum to be modified and diversified for accommodating students of varying capabilities and for catering to the various local and rational requirement. Learning by doing at the primary stage and learning by production at the secondary level has been accepted as the ideal of education.

The Problem of Over-loaded Curriculum: This problem is more acute for those students who have to proceed for university-education. The number of subjects to be taught necessarily has led to an over-loaded curriculum. Selection of openly objective areas of various subjects may make the curriculum lighter. Core-curriculum is another device for making the over-loaded curriculum lighter. Dominance of external examination has been minimised by introducing the system of internal evaluations.

Teaching Methods: Due to scientific and technological advancements new teaching methods have been devised. Programmed learning and teaching machines and audio-visual aids. Open Universities, correspondence courses. Use of T.V. and Radio. Structural methods in teaching languages. Mother tongue as the medium of instruction.

Teacher and the Student: Teacher education programme to be modified. In-services and pre-training teachers programmes to be reorganised, short-term teacher education programme, preparing teachers for rural areas, Education to be child-centred. Proper attention to be given on individual differences.

Administration and Discipline: Problem of indiscipline and bad administration. Educational administration to be decentralized. Co-operation between students and teachers is necessary for making the administration more dynamic for rooting out the problem of indiscipline. The term supervision to be used in place of 'inspection'.

School Building and Expenditure: The need for new building involves huge extra expenditure.

Research: The fashion of applied and experimental research has been introduced in place of traditional research method.

Functional Literacy: Literacy programmes is related to the actual life and profession of the illiterate adults.

Chance in the Conception of Education: Changes in social values and technological developments have changed the old conception of education. Education to be made more human, moral, spiritual and progressive.

Democratization or Education: Education must reach all.

Bringing in Efficiency in the Educational System: No qualitative improvement in face of quantitative improvement. Wastage and stagnation in education must be checked for the sake of efficiency.

Education should be Related to Life: A gulf between education and life. Education not only a mean of vocationalization.

Women Education: Women, to-day, are getting greater share in various walks of life than ever before. Boys and girls are enjoing equal rights to education.

University Education: Economic shortage, indiscipline, problems of admission and examination, curriculum and affiliated colleges are some of the burning issues.

Exercises

1. Discuss the general trends in pre-primary and primary education that we find to day all over the world.
2. Explain the major trends with regard to secondary education to-day.
3. Discuss the problem of curriculum for secondary education from various angles with regard to its general trend.
4. What is the problem of change in the very conception of education to-day in the world and why ?
5. Explain some general trends in various fields of education in the modern age.

Bibliography

Education in U.S.A.

1. Briggs, T.H., Secondary Education, Macmillan, 1950.
2. Conant, J.B., Education and Library, The New American Library, New York, 1952.
3. Carmer and Browne, Contemporary Education, Harcourt Brace & Co., New York, 1956.
4. De Young, C.A., Introduction to American Public Education, 3rd Edn., McGraw Hill Book Co., Inc., New York, 1955.
5. Henry J. Otto, Elementary School Organisation and Administration, 3rd Edn., Appleton-Century Crafts, New York, 1954.
6. Hutchins, R.M., The Higher Learning in America, Yale University Press, Haven, 1952.
7. Kandel, I.L., The New Era in Education, Houghton Mifflin Co., 1955.
8. Kempfer, H., Selected Approaches to Adult Education Bulletin No. 16, 1950. Federal Security Agency, Office of Education, U.S.A.
9. Kenneth, R.K., Education in U.S.A., Alven Redman Ltd., London, 1956.
10. Lee, Gordon C., An Introduction to Education in Modern America, Henry Holt & Co., New York, 1953.
11. Meyer, A.E., The Development of Education in the Twentieth Century, 2nd Edn., Prentice Hall, 1956, Printing.
12. National Education Association, Fiscal Authority of City School Boards (Research Bulletin No. 28) N.E.A., Washington D.C., 1950.

13. Pascow, A. Garry, Education of the Disadvantaged. A Book of Readings, Edn., Holt Rinehart and Winston, 1967.
14 Pines, Maya, Revolution in Learning, Harper & Row, 1967.
15. Rogers, F.M., Higher Education, The United States , 3rd Edn. Pub., The U.S.I.S., 1960.
16. Ulich, Robert, The Education of Nations, Harvard University Press, Cambridge, Mass, 1961.

Education in Great Britain

1. Adaval, S., Teacher Education in U.K., Garg Bros., Allahabad.
2. Alexander, W.P., Education in England, Newness Educational Publishing Company Ltd., London 1954.
3. Barker Sir Earnest, British Universities, Longmans, Green & Co., 1949.
4. Cramer, J.F. & Browne, G.S., Contemporary Education, Harcourt, Brace & Co., New York, 1956.
5. Curtis, S.J., History of Education in Great Britain, University Tutorial Press Ltd., London, 1957.
6. Dent, H.C., Education in Transition, Routledge and Kegan Paul, London, 1945.
7. Dent, H.C., Secondary Education for All, Routlege and Kegan Paul, London, 1949.
8. Dent, H.C., Growth in English Education, Routledge and Kegan Paul, London, 1954.
9. H.M.S.O., London, Education Act, 1944.
10. H.M.S.P., London, Educational Reconstruction (White Paper), 1943.
11. H.M.S.O., London, Primary Education, Suggestions for Teachers, 1959.
12. London Country School, The Organisation of Comprehensive Secondary Schools, London, 1953.
13. Lowndes, G.A.N., The English Educational System, Hutchinson University Library, London, 1960.
14. Lester Smith, W.P., Compulsroy Education in English, UNESCO, Paris, 1951.

15. Richardson, C.A., Education of Teachers in England, France and U.S.A., UNESCO, 1963.
16. Robins Committee Report, 1963.
17. University Grant Commission, University Development Report in the Years 1947 to 1952, H.M.S.O., London, 1953.

Education in India

1. Chaube, S.P., A Survey of Educational Problems and Experiments in India, Kitab Mahal, Allahabad, 1965.
2. Chaube, S.P., Secondary Education for India, Atma Ram & Sons, Delhi, 1956.
3. Chaube, S.P., A History of Education in India, Ram Narain Lal Beni Madho, Allahabad, 1965.
4. Chaube, S.P., Bharat Me Shiksha Aur Uski Samasyen, Vinod Pustak Mandir, Agra, 1976.
5. Chaube, S.P., Bhartiya Shiksha Ka Ithas, Ram Narain Lal Beni Madho, Allahabad, 1959.
6. Nurullah & Naik., A Students' History of Education in India, Macmilian & Co., Lyd., Bombay, 1962.
7. Safaya, Dr. Raghunath, Current Problems of Indian Education, Dhanpat Rai & Sons, Delhi, 1966.
8. Zellnner, A.A., Education in India, Bookmann Associates, New York, 1951.

Education in Russia

1. Bernstein, Mikhail, Higher Education in the U.S.S.R during and after the War, The Educational Forum, Vol. XII, No. 2, Jan, 1948.
2. Counts, G.S., The Challenge of Soviet Education, McGraw Hill Book Co., Inc., New York, 1957.
3. Hans, N., History of Russian Educational Policy, London, P.S. King & Son Ltd., 1931.
4. King Beatrice, Russia Goes to School, The New Education Book Club, William Heinemann Ltd., London, 1948.
5. King, Beatrice, Changing Man, The Education System of the U.S.S.R., John Day, New York, 1957.

6. Korol, A.G., Soviet Education for Science and Technology, Chapmann and Hall Ltd., London, 1957.
7. Pinkevitch, A.P., The New Education in the Soviet Republic, New York, The John Day Company, 1929.
8. Singh, Raja Roy, Education in the Soviet Union, Ministry of Education, Government of India, Delhi, 1962.
9. Ulich Robert, The Education of Nations, Harvard University Press, Cambridge, Mass, 1961.

Index